Frontiers in American Philosophy
VOLUME II

Frontiers in American Philosophy

VOLUME II

Edited by Robert W. Burch
and Herman J. Saatkamp, Jr.

Texas A&M University Press
College Station

Copyright © 1996 by Robert W. Burch and Herman J. Saatkamp, Jr.
Manufactured in the United States of America
All rights reserved
First Paperback Edition

The paper used in this book meets the minimum requirements
of the American National Standard for Permanence
of Paper for Printed Library Materials, Z39.48-1984.
Binding materials have been chosen for durability.

Library of Congress Cataloging-in-Publication Data

Frontiers in American philosophy / edited by Robert W. Burch and
Herman J. Saatkamp, Jr. — 1st ed.
    p. cm.
  ISBN 0-89096-588-9 (v. 2 : alk. paper) ; ISBN 1-58544-002-7 (pbk.)
  1. Philosophy — United States. I. Burch, Robert W. II. Saatkamp.
Herman J.. Jr.

91-19447
CIP

Contents

Foreword
Herman J. Saatkamp, Jr.   page ix
Preface
Robert W. Burch   xi

PHILOSOPHY, SEMIOTICS, AND INTERPRETATION

Pragmatic Philosophy of Language Based on
  Transcendental Semiotic
  Karl-Otto Apel   3
Modernity, Interpretation Theory, and American Philosophy
  Thelma Z. Lavine   26

EDITING AMERICAN PHILOSOPHERS

Editing the Classical American Philosophers:
  Dewey, James, Peirce, Santayana
  Jo Ann Boydston   43
Editing Peirce
  Christian J. W. Kloesel   53
Final Intentions, Social Context, and Santayana's Autobiography
  Herman J. Saatkamp, Jr.   63

THE NATURE OF PHILOSOPHY

The Modern Relevance of the Mathematical Philosophy
  of Charles S. Peirce
  Carolyn Eisele   79

Can Philosophy Have a Nationality?
Gerard Deledalle 86

EXISTENTIALISM AND PHENOMENOLOGY

Pragmatism and Heidegger:
A Common World
Sandra B. Rosenthal 95
Pragmaticism Is an Existentialism?
Kenneth L. Ketner 105
To Create the Absolute Edge
David G. Leahy 112

SANTAYANA

Santayana: Spirited Spirituality
Morris Grossman 125
Animal Faith:
Santayana and Strawson
Edward S. Shirley 133
Pragmatism and Irony in Santayana
Henny Wenkart 143
Santayana:
Objective Overreach?
Angus Kerr-Lawson 158
Santayana and the Many Faces of Realism
Henry Samuel Levinson 165

DEWEY

Dewey, Virtue, and Moral Pluralism
James Gouinlock 175
John Dewey's Limited Humanism:
The Sectarian Stance of America's Philosopher of Holism
Michael Eldridge 182

AMERICAN PHILOSOPHY AND ORIENTAL THOUGHT

Internal and External Frontiers of Classical American Philosophy:
Santayana's Differences from James and Dewey in World-Perspective
David A. Dilworth 195

Democracy and Feudalism
  Zhu Xinmin — 206

PHILOSOPHY AND LITERATURE

Josiah Royce:
  Literature and Humanism
  John Clendenning — 215
Reconstructing American Philosophy:
  Emerson and Dewey
  Russell B. Goodman — 223

COMMUNITY AND CULTURE

The Search for Commonality in a Diverse World
  Patrick J. Hill — 233
Community and the Cultural Frontier
  John J. Stuhr — 243
Spatial and Temporal Ethics
  Peter A. French — 256

APPLIED PHILOSOPHY

A Roycean Pragmatic:
  Insights for Applied Ethics
  Mary B. Mahowald — 267
Process-Relational Philosophy:
  The Raw, Unabashed Cash Value of a Mere
  Metaphysical Speculation
  Pete A. Y. Gunter — 277
Of Algorithms and Apple Pie:
  A Pragmatist Critique of AI
  Peter Limper — 283

PEIRCE AND BUCHLER

Peirce on Evolution by Revolution
  H. William Davenport — 293
Buchler's Poetic Theory:
  Questions of Meaning and Interpretation
  Richard E. Hart — 302

The Subject as Index and Icon:
A Critique of Kaja Silverman's Reading
of C. S. Peirce on the Human Subject
Lenore Langsdorf — *311*

AESTHETICS

Through the Beautiful to the Human (The Aesthetic
and the Ethical in the Experiencing of Landscape)
Nikita E. Pokrovsky — *323*
Community and Creativity:
Toward a Deweyan Aesthetic of Human Existence
Thomas M. Alexander — *328*
Meaning in the Arts:
Considerations for a General Theory
Armen T. Marsoobian — *338*

WILLIAM JAMES

James, Putnam, and Metaphysical Materialism
Gerald E. Myers — *349*
James's Pragmatic Personalism
Eugene Fontinell — *356*
Jamesian Reflections on Will, Freedom, and Values
Robert Kane — *365*

Contributors — *375*

Preface

ROBERT W. BURCH

This second volume of proceedings of Texas A&M University's international conference *Frontiers in American Philosophy* took an unexpectedly long time in editorial preparation. It is hoped that the volume's contents will be found to justify, at least in part, any undue waiting for its appearance.

The essays in volume 2 are, if anything, even more varied and adventurous than those in volume 1. Whether it be a Ketner amalgamating Peirce with existentialism and with the contemporary American novel, an Apel demonstrating the power of American philosophy to incorporate within itself insights in transcendental philosophy and contemporary philosophy of language, a Dilworth probing traditional Japanese thinking with traditional American philosophical instruments, or any of a host of others—each author has set herself or himself the task of reaching out from the core of familiar themes in American philosophy to new frontiers. The results show an astonishingly variegated fecundity in the native soil of our American homeland.

It is impossible to thank all those who have contributed in one way or another to this volume. But I should like to single out from the multitude two helpers whose work was not only invaluable but all the more remarkable because they were students. It would have been immeasurably more difficult even than it was to produce a translation of Professor Apel's German text without the initial work of Karen Antell. And without the Herculean labors of Gordon Pettit, who alone contributed over three hundred intensive hours to details, the second volume would have taken still another half-year to appear.

Because in the strange world of contemporary academic life, the class of those who perform the real labor and the class of those who receive the credit for it are all too often disjoint, it has seemed meet to thank Mr. Pettit by including in these prefatory remarks a comment by him.

> The conference *Frontiers in American Philosophy* took place before my involvement in formal philosophical studies, and I was unable to attend the conference. It has been my pleasure, however, to be able to participate vicariously in it through my responsibilities as editorial assistant for the preparation of this sec-

ond volume of proceedings of the conference. This volume should allow the reader to also participate vicariously by enjoying the written works of those who contributed papers. As I become more familiar with contemporary American philosophy, I am increasingly inclined to describe the climate of American philosophy in much the same way that John Dewey described our universe in *Experience and Nature* [in *The Works of John Dewey: The Later Works, 1925–1953*, ed. Jo Ann Boydston (Carbondale and Edwardsville: Southern Illinois University Press, 1981–88), vol. 1, p. 67]. It is a "world which is not finished and which has not consistently made up its mind where it is going and what it is going to do." I eagerly anticipate seeing what is to unfold before us in American philosophy as we approach the twenty-first century.

So, Mr. Pettit, should we all.

Foreword

This is the second volume based on papers presented at the Frontiers in American Philosophy Conference, Texas A&M University. The history, development, influence, and current edge of American philosophy are the subjects.

This volume is launched during a period when globalization is paramount and when the traditional roles and capabilities of the United States are in question. Emerson once said that a friend is Janus faced, looking to one's past and one's future. As we turn toward the twenty-first century, these articles are written by thoughtful allies, looking forward through the developments presently shaping philosophical inquiry in the United States and backward to the origins and plurality of the American intellectual heritage. Not a parochial or narrow perspective, the focus on American philosophy sharpens the dialogue that clarifies and explicates American thought in the context of a world community. Acknowledging the pluralism of American intellectual life, there is no effort to define an American ethos. Instead, the volume is festive, celebrating the diversity of thought and influences in American philosophy.

I am grateful to the many persons who made the volume possible and to the support of Texas A&M University. In particular, I am grateful to my colleague Bob Burch, who has undertaken the larger and more difficult tasks in editing this book.

This work is guided by the aurora of the twenty-first century and the seriousness of Santayana's oft-quoted remark: "Those who cannot remember the past are condemned to repeat it." With these as our cicerones, we offer this second set of readings for your pleasure and knowledge.

Herman J. Saatkamp, Jr.

PHILOSOPHY, SEMIOTICS, AND INTERPRETATION

Pragmatic Philosophy of Language Based on Transcendental Semiotic

KARL-OTTO APEL

1. Introduction to the Problem[1]

1.1. EXPLANATION OF THE TITLE

In the following I want to attempt to sketch in the most meager way the program indicated in the title by seeking to fix its place in the foundational discussion of contemporary philosophy. This can be characterized, as the title suggests, by its relation to three concepts of positions in contemporary philosophy:

    a. to the "pragmatic turn," which is discussed above all in language-analytic philosophy and the theory of science that is associated with it;

    b. to semiotic—here above all in the sense of the triadicity of the sign relation emphasized by Charles Peirce, as well as the three dimensions of the scientific thematization of sign functions distinguished by Charles Morris: syntactics, semiotics, and pragmatics;

    c. to transcendental philosophy—understood here in the sense of a critical reconstruction and transformation of the form of the *prima philosophia* established by Kant, which above all is supposed to answer the question of the conditions of the possibility of valid argumentation.

This just-mentioned question can be considered a key to understanding the envisioned starting point. Here, argumentation is being claimed to be philosophically ulterior—argumentation that, according to the pragmatic and the linguistic turns of contemporary philosophy, is to form the starting point for transcendental questions and, in doing so, is also to form a final justification of validity through transcendental-reflective arguments.

1.2. The Methodologically Ulterior in Philosophy: The A Priori of the I-Consciousness, the A Priori of the Prereflective Life-Practice, or the A Priori of Language?

The appeal to the (methodologically) foundational character of a standpoint, in the sense of the indubitability of an intuitive certainty, is characteristic of modern philosophy, for which methodological reflection is a distinguishing mark. The *cogito, ergo sum* of Descartes can be considered the first paradigm of this argumentative strategy, even if here the transcendental character of the thinking in general that is foundational for thought was still not worked out in its distinctness from every possible empirical-introspective or metaphysical self-knowledge. That occurred first through Kant, for whom thinking in general "must be able to accompany all my representations" and for whom the "transcendental synthesis of apperception" forms the "highest point" of the "transcendental deduction." In this sense, the ulteriority of the transcendental I-consciousness remains determinative for German idealism, for neo-Kantianism, and even for the transcendental phenomenology of Husserl.

Now, the methodological ulteriority of the statement "I think" and of transcendental consciousness has not remained undisputed. Starting even in the late Husserl, it has been opposed by the "deeper," because prereflective, ulteriority of the "life-world" or by "Being-in-the-world" (Heidegger), and even before that by the ulteriority of "living" (Dilthey) or by material, social "Praxis" (Marx). In fact, it can be shown that the givenness of a life-world that is comprehensible and thus meaningful to us cannot be apprehended as an intentional achievement of a reflective, pure consciousness: not only in the popular sense of the *primum vivere, deinde philosophar* but also in the sense of the quasi-transcendental problem of object-constitution or sense-constitution. Just this conscious reflection can have insight that the "meaningfulness" (Dilthey) of the life-world presupposes a prereflective sense-constitution on the basis of a bodily-a-priori, a Praxis-a-priori of interests that lead to knowledge, and an a priori of facticity and historicity of Being-in-the-world.[2]

But placing into question the methodological ulteriority of the transcendental consciousness of the I-think by arguing along this line—that is, by recurring to the prereflective ulteriority of life-Praxis—is manifestly ambiguous. Precisely the circumstance, that this question can summon up a reflective insight into the priority of the prereflective presupposition of life-Praxis for the understanding of the constitution of both world and sense, shows that the question has not gone beyond the fundamental idea of the transcendental ulteriority of the reflective a priori of consciousness, but that it itself still presupposes that the ulteriority of the *ego cogito* from the beginning was essentially related to reflection in the sense of possible doubt and investigation of claims to worth. In this respect it has by no means been refuted by anything brought forth so far. Indeed, simply stunning became the revolutionary idea, inaugurated by Kant and renewed by Husserl, that the question concerning the conditions of the possibil-

Pragmatic Philosophy of Language

ity of valid knowledge could be sufficiently answered by recurring to the object-constituting achievements of the consciousness that is presupposed in reflection upon validity—and that is therefore, so to speak, immanent in reflection. The consciousness-a-priori of reflection upon validity found itself, as it were, confronted with a prereflective—and thus far a life-Praxical a priori of the constitution of sense, which is necessarily prior to it as "forestructure" of the understanding of the world (Heidegger), but which insofar as possible admits of a rational reconstruction according to the a priori of reflection upon validity. (But more upon this later!)

So far, the most important rival of the a priori of consciousness in connection with ulteriority has not yet been introduced: the transcendental-semiotic a priori of sign-mediation and of language-mediation in intersubjectively valid thought. In short: the a priori of language. Its distinctness lies, as is to be shown, in the fact that it is coordinated with the prereflective life-Praxical primacy of the a priori of sense-constitution as well as the reflective primacy of the a priori of reflection upon value. For not only does it correspond, as the chief condition of the preunderstanding of the world, to the hermeneutic prestructure of the life-world, it also proves itself to be a presupposition of the most radical reflection on and inquiry into life-worldly presuppositions of world understanding, insofar as it makes possible the intersubjective validity of reflective thought within the framework of argumentative discourse. In short: the a priori of language conditions the ulteriority of the argumentation that was asserted above (as ulterior).

The primacy of the a priori of language asserted here, in contrast to all other viewpoints claimed to be ulterior, still requires a more precise explication. Let us now insert a historical consideration, in order to make more exactly comprehensible the discussion of the a priori of language in its relation to the programmatic discussion of the transcendental-semiotic transformation of transcendental philosophy.

1.3. The "Hermeneutic-Linguistic-Pragmatic-Semiotic Turn" of Contemporary Philosophy:
An Overview and Description of the Problem

In regard to the transcendental-semiotic standpoint indicated just above, the possibility of a convergence (which is, of course, dependent upon our ability to honor the "insofar . . ." clauses) of the following, originally distinct, starting points of thought has, in my opinion, only recently been shown:

> a. of the post-Heideggerian hermeneutics qua language hermeneutics (Gadamer)—insofar as the temporal sense- and truth-event of "tradition mediation" can be placed under the regulative principles of a transcendental hermeneutics;
>
> b. of the language-game theory of the late Wittgenstein—insofar as the functional necessity of the presupposition of a transcendental language game can be shown, in light of the multiplicity of incommensurable language games;

c. of the theory of "speech-acts" resulting from Austin and Searle—insofar as the performative-propositional "dual structure of discourse" and of its "relations to the world" (Habermas) can be interpreted transcendental-pragmatically;

d. of the constructivist pragmatics of language initiated by P. Lorenzen—insofar as it can be shown, via transcendental-pragmatic reflection, that its methodological reconstruction of the activities of discourse as the pragmatic "basis of semantics and syntax"[3] already presupposes the prepropositional double structure of discourse and of its relations to the world as an a priori of argumentation and also, insofar as that goes, as an a priori of teaching and learning in exemplary introductory situations;

e. of the pragmatistic semiotic deriving from Charles Peirce—insofar as the naturalistic-empirical understanding of this starting point (for example, the behaviorist semiotics of Charles Morris), deriving from Peirce's normative, quasi-transcendental, semiotic logic of investigation can be interpreted as only inappropriately rejected, and insofar as this naturalistic-empirical understanding can be interpreted in the sense of a transcendental semiotics, pragmatics, or hermeneutics, respectively.

Common to the preceding starting points for thought is that they all agree—because of their recourse to the a priori of language and to the dependence of thought and knowledge on intersubjective agreement that this a priori implies—on the more or less radical overcoming of a presupposition that has been obligatory for Western thought at least since Augustine: namely, the presupposition of methodological solipsism acclaimed most recently by Husserl for fertile and radical thinkers.[4] I understand this to include the insinuation, which still prevails today (if not empirically, in the sense of the superfluousness of the socialization process, then at least in principle) that one must be able to arrive alone and for oneself at valid results of thinking and knowledge.

This standpoint, in my opinion, is not only put forth when one begins from the notion, as did Locke, that thought is primarily allotted to private ideas, but also if one starts out from the belief, as did Kant, that a prelinguistic faculty of rules, based on consciousness in general, is able to assure the intersubjective validity of our knowledge, without the requirement in principle for an intersubjective division of linguistic meaning and thus communicative understanding. (I do not believe that Kant steps beyond the point of view of methodological solipsism in the *Critique of Judgment*—at least not through an adoption of "common sense" [*Gemeinsinn*] and of the "agreement" of others, for the "agreement" of others is for Kant, as in the Aristotelian-stoical consensual theory of truth, merely a subjective criterion of truth that is useful in practice for the avoidance of errors. Only the "formal" criterion of "agreement of knowledge with itself, or with the general laws of the understanding and of reason"—which are the same thing—is considered to be the "objective criterion of truth" by Kant.[5] Thus, it is not insinuated, as at first by Charles Peirce and Josiah Royce,[6] that reaching objective truth is in principle dependent on a process of communicative sign interpretation in the in-principle-unlimited "community of interpretation" of scientists [*Wissenschaftler*].)

The alternative, which lies at the foundation of the thesis that "methodological solipsism" has been overcome, is, in my opinion, even more radical than the distinction between "monological" and "dialogical" thinking proposed by Habermas, for even this "monological" thinking in the sense of Habermas—for example, the working out of mathematical operations and of logical conclusions—is to be thought of as "following rules" in Wittgenstein's sense and as dependent upon comprehensibility in principle, and controllability, by others. Of course, I would not go so far as simply to deny an autonomous evidence of consciousness for the correct following of rules and to make the possible "correctness" of the following of rules completely dependent on the factual existence of a social "custom" or "form of life." This consequence of a radical Wittgensteinianism seems to me to lead instead to a relativistic dead end. This consequence would not, in my opinion, be compatible with the concept of competence (in following rules) and would have dubious results: for example, for the understanding of moral knowledge. And naturally it would not be consistent with a transcendental-philosophical interpretation.

Now at this point we come across the principal problem of our intended transcendental-semiotic interpretation of the "linguistic-pragmatic-hermeneutic turn" of contemporary philosophy. If thinking and knowing—in the sense of overcoming the "methodological solipsism" of the classical transcendental philosophy of consciousness—are made dependent on communicative agreement in the medium of historical language (and that means any cultural language that is ever criterial for a form of life), then a contingent a priori of the life-world—in perhaps the sense of "facticity" and "thrownness," as well as the "belonging-to-Being" of the human "Being-in-the-world" (Heidegger)—seems to have to take the place of the universal "logos of classical transcendental philosophy." It is not surprising that a convergence of the tendencies of the "hermeneutic-linguistic-pragmatic turn" originating with Heidegger, Gadamer, and the later Wittgenstein seems to be accomplished along the lines of a "detranscendentalization" and a dismissal of all universal claims to validity.[7] The "neopragmatism" of Rorty meets here with Heidegger's (and Derrida's) historical relativizing of the "logos" of Western philosophy and science, in the sense of its possible superannuation through the "revealing-concealing event of Being," which has engendered this relativizing as an epoch.

Can an effective argument be brought against the necessity of the "detranscendentalization" asserted by Rorty and the postmodernists and which is associated with the "linguistic-pragmatic-hermeneutic turn"? Doesn't this follow with necessity from the character of contingence of the a priori of language?

A first indication of the short-sightedness of this conclusion can be gotten, in my opinion, simply out of our confrontation up to this point of the a priori of language with the a priori of consciousness of the traditional transcendental philosophy. Understood in the sense of the "detranscendentalization," the valorization of the a priori of language manifestly leads to the same contradiction as the valorization of the ulteriority of life-Praxis and life-world already did earlier: as a summons to the insight into the contingency of the a priori of language, it also seems only to confirm the value-theoretical primacy of the ulteriority of reflective consciousness. So far, this interpretation of the a priori of language is not able to show that, as we asserted earlier, even the reflective insight of consciousness as such, with intersubjective claims to validity, presupposes the a priori of language as the a priori of argumentation. If the latter is to be shown to be ulterior for philosophizing, then it must be taken as a claim to be a condition of the possibility of the universal validity of philosophical insights. In that case, therefore, the a priori of language of thinking and knowing—insofar as it is ulterior for philosophical argumentation—cannot be sufficiently determined by its character of contingence.

Now, in fact, neither the late Wittgenstein nor Rorty nor any post-Heideggerian representative of the "linguistic-hermeneutic-pragmatic turn" has up to now been able to forgo the presentation of their theses against the possibility and necessity of universal claims to value and principles in the usual form of the appeal to philosophical insight into the universal validity of argumentation (for example, about the incommensurability of language games and the forms of life associated with them). Otherwise they would have had to stop philosophizing. (Rorty's and several postmodernists' proclamations promoting the literarization of philosophical discourse are traitorous here; for this flight from argumentative discourse, in order not to remain unnoticed, must be brought to expression as proclaimed in theses with claims to universal validity.)

In short: performative self-contradiction has become the trademark of *this* interpretation of the "linguistic-pragmatic-hermeneutic turn" of contemporary philosophy.[8] From this I draw the conclusion that it has been indicated that provisionally one is not to interpret the sketched-out turn of contemporary philosophy in the sense of the "detranscendentalization," but instead in the sense of a critical transformation of classical transcendental philosophy.

Now, this must actually lead—in connection with the five starting points for thought of the "hermeneutic-linguistic-pragmatic-semiotic turn" introduced earlier—to the attempt to show the possibility of a sometimes specific transcendental-philosophical interpretation (or reinterpretation). And, indeed, this must thus lead because the meaning of the programmatic "insofar" clauses (see above) is explicated in the sense of whatever is a type of transformed transcendental philosophy, thus in the sense (a) of a transcendental hermeneutic, (b) of a theory of the transcendental language game, (c) of a transcendental-pragmatic interpretation of the theory of speech acts, (d) of the constructive pragmatics of language, and (e) of a transcendental semiotic that contains from the start transcendental hermeneutics and pragmatics.

Because such an undertaking would exceed the "pragmatically" possible scope (though of course not the framework) of the inquiry at hand, I consider myself forced to refer to studies that are already available with regard to points (a), (b), and (c).[9] With regard to (d), I must leave it as a programmatic thesis. But I would like to try to show in an example that (e), the conception of a transcendental semiotic, represents not only a definitely specified transcendental interpretation of the semiotic originated by Peirce but that it also, as was shown above, is able to form the basis for the convergence of the remaining starting points for thought from the perspective of a new paradigm of the *prima philosophia*.

2. The Transcendental-Semiotic Paradigm of the *Prima Philosophia* as the Foundational Perspective for a Reinterpretation and Integration of the "Hermeneutic-Linguistic-Pragmatic Turn" of Contemporary Philosophy

In the following I begin with two schemata of thought, which—so to speak—elucidate the iconically-diagrammatically (in the sense of Peirce) representable relational core of the conceptions of semiosis—as well as semiotic—which conceptions set the standard in contemporary philosophy.

The first schema concerns the most fundamental, in my opinion, thesis of the semiotic founded by Peirce as a semiotic logic of investigation: the thesis of the triadicity of the sign relation or, as the case may be, of sign-mediated knowledge of the real. It can be represented thus:

Schema 1

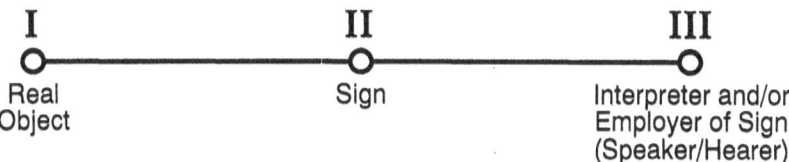

I	II	III
Real Object	Sign	Interpreter and/or Employer of Sign (Speaker/Hearer)

In Peirce's words, "A sign, or representamen, is something which stands to somebody for something in some respect or capacity."[10] Or, "A sign is a conjoint relation to the thing denoted and to the mind."[11]

The second schema, which can be developed from Peirce's schema, forms the basis of the 1938 "Foundation of the Theory of Signs" of Charles Morris. This schema, mediated by Carnap, has determined up until the present not only the basic problem of language-analytic philosophy but also that of the analytic theory of science—above all, its development in the sense of the "pragmatic turn." It could best be represented somewhat thusly:

Schema 2

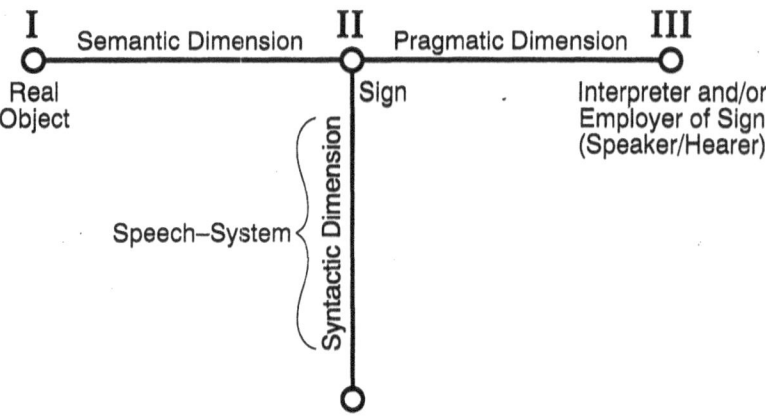

Before I go more closely into the interpretation of the two schemata, I must point out that, in the context of the foregoing discussion, I am not primarily interested in an interpretation of Peirce or Morris,[12] nor in founding semiotic as a strong empirical theory—whether it be in the sense of a basic discipline of linguistics or beyond that of the cultural sciences or even of a hypothetical metaphysics of evolution in the sense of Peirce. Instead, I am much more concerned about the possibility—and the methodological necessity—of a transcendental semiotic and, within its compass, of a transcendental pragmatics of language. The methodologically comprehensible necessity of a transformation of the idea of the *prima philosophia* in the sense of the above-named disciplines should, of course, be founded on a thesis that derives from a Peirceian inspiration. In my opinion, only a transcendental interpretation of semiotic is in the position to explain and to redeem the sense claims and truth claims of the Peirceian insight into the triadicity in principle of the sign relation, for it can be shown that any nontranscendental semiotic interpretation of the two basic schemata, at least on the level of philosophy, must lead to abstract conclusions that are false—for example, with regard to the foundations of the theory of science and of ethics.

2.1. The Transcendental-Semiotic Interpretation of Peirceian Semiotic

2.1.1. Transcendental-Logical Versus (Metaphysical-)Empirical Perspectives of Peirceian Interpretation

It is first to be pointed out that the circumstance that Peirce understands the sign relation as one of sign-mediated knowledge refers to the necessity of a transcendental-semiotic interpretation, for only from this perspective can the priority of the cognitive sign function over other sign functions be vindicated, as is yet to be shown.

This also signifies that the often-troubling dispute over the priority of semiotic or philosophy of language (or of language-analytical philosophy) cannot be decided from the Peirceian view simply by saying that philosophy of language represents merely a special discipline of semiotic—perhaps as a thematization of a subset of signs or of the last phase of the cosmic evolution of sign processes on the stage of cultural evolution. Such a thematization is, to be sure, possible within the framework of the Peirceian "metaphysics of evolution," but this inevitably presupposes the methodology of sign-mediated human knowledge,[13] in the sense of the Peirceian "classification of the sciences."[14] And thus far, for Peirce too, the a priority of language exists within the framework of the normative semiotic logic of knowledge, for only this makes possible the symbolic interpretation that is constitutive of intersubjectively valid (capable of consent) knowledge. Interesting as well as by all means important for epistemology is the fact that Peirceian semiotic, in contrast to the language-analytic philosophy developed so far, can show that and why language as a medium of knowledge cannot consist solely of purely symbolic signs; and that, instead, in order to mediate "intuition" (*Anschauung*] and "concept" (*Begriff*) in Kant's sense and get correct the "causal component of sense" in perception, language requires such signs as those that mediate the linguistic symbol-function with the extralinguistic (natural) sign functions of "indices" and "icons" (or, in other words, the "thirdness" of the conceptual interpretation with the "secondness" of the causal reciprocity between "I" and "not-I" and with the "firstness" of the relationless evidence of the "Being-thus" [*des Soseins*] of the phenomena of pure intuition). Precisely the last-mentioned advantages show themselves, in my opinion, only within the framework of a resultant transcendental-semiotic interpretation (that is to say, one understood as a transformation of Kant).

In this context there arises also, I believe, the possible solution to a wider, irritating basic problem of Peirceian semiotic. The specifically semiotic texts of Peirce often suggest, instead of the triadicity of sign relations, a replacement of the two nonsemiotic relata of the sign by other signs, in such a manner that on both sides an infinite regress arises.[15] In place of the real object of sign reference there seems to step a sort of "immediate object" that merely in the light of being signified appears as something, which "immediate object" then refers to a still further immediate object, and so on *ad infinitum*. To this regress there corresponds the following one: that in place of the real interpreter steps the so-called-by-Peirce "interpretant"—that is, an interpreting *sign*—that for its part again refers to an(other) "interpretant," and so on indefinitely.

In this way the impression arises of a philosophical semioticism, for the sake of which the world resolves itself into signs because of positions in which the interpreting person appears merely as a sign in the infinite process of sign interpretation, which continues natural evolution and constitutes the phases of cultural evolution.[16] These positions have very recently stirred up great fascination among representatives of the "semiotic turn," and they find corresponding positions in French poststructuralism, for which the person as well as reality—the "signifié"—seem to resolve themselves into the web of reference of the "signifiants."[17]

Indeed, a reconstruction of Peirceian philosophy, in the sense of the normative, semiotic logic of research—which for Peirce took the place of Kant's transcendental logic in 1867–68 and in the lectures on pragmaticism of 1903 is even presented as the "normative science" of all empirical-hypothetical metaphysics and special sciences—can show that the possibility of infinite semiotization of real sign-relata possesses, indeed, only empirical relevance but nonetheless may not encroach upon the presupposed triadic system of relations of (transcendental-)semiotic philosophy.

If it were correct that the nonsemiotic relata of sign relations—the real object and the real interpreter—were in principle nothing but signs, then—and this is shown by the Peirceian analysis of the triadic sign function—the meaning of "signs" would have to resolve itself away in the same way that the meaning of "dream" or "consciousness" resolves itself if someone, following the Cartesian "problematic idealism," should draw into doubt the reality of the external world by arguing, "Perhaps the so-called 'real' is only a dream (or, alternatively, is only in my consciousness)." (Correspondingly, the following is also valid: if the world is literally to be understood as a text; that is, as a web of "signifiants" without "signifié," then one would not be able to say precisely this point. In that case, one would have to be able to speak about the "signifiant" as "signifié.")

On the other hand, it can also be shown that the empirical semiotization of real processes of knowledge—of the object possible for them and of the possible subject—does not stand in contradiction to the transcendental-semiotic primacy of the triadicity of sign relations. If, in particular, knowledge of the real is in principle not intuitive but instead "sign-mediated," then it can be seen that the stable a priori triadic basic structure of sign-mediated knowledge demands, on the side of the real relata of sign relations, an in-principle infinite process of mediation, if the goal of knowledge of the real is to be reached in an empirically realizable process of research (= a process of drawing conclusions and of interpretation). At this point it is possible and also necessary to explicate more exactly the transcendental-semiotic transformation of the Kantian type of transcendental philosophy—which was made possible, in my opinion, by Peirce—and furthermore of the idea of the *prima philosophia* in general.

2.1.2. Transcendental-Semiotic Derivation of the Three Main Paradigms of the *Prima Philosophia*

If one starts, as Peirce does, from the idea that the structure of sign relations is equally well the structure of sign-mediated knowledge of the real (and one is justified in doing that, at least on the level of epistemology—and also on the level of the methodology of semiotic as knowledge of the functions of signs), then the following consequences may easily be drawn from Schema 1 (see above) with regard to the possible paradigms of the *prima philosophia*.[18] Three paradigms can be distinguished, according to whether the foundation of the *prima philosophia* takes into consideration only the first, or else the first and the third, or else all three positions in the triadic sign relation. The thematizing of objectivized "Being," in the sense of the first position of the triad, is characteristic for metaphysics qua ontology; the thematizing of the first and third positions in the sense of the subject-object relation of the consciousness of objects is characteristic for classical transcendental philosophy; and the thematizing of all three positions in the sense of the sign-mediated interpretation of the world is characteristic for transcendental semiotic. Let us consider this distinction more exactly.

Paradigm 1: Ontological metaphysics in the pre-Kantian sense is characterized by the circumstance that it thematizes neither the triadic sign relation nor the diadic subject-object relation of knowledge as the methodologically relevant condition of the possibility and validity of knowledge of "Being." That does not mean that it cannot give a theory of knowledge or a theory of language or signs for this paradigm; it only means that knowledge relations and the sign relations that mediate them are not thematized in a reflective perspective as conditions of the "objecthood" (objectivity) of the world, but rather merely—immediately in the *intentio recta*—as objective relations between entities in the world.

The reflective deficiency of this paradigm of *prima philosophia* shows itself above all, in my opinion, in its setting two problems: first, in the aporetic of the classical correspondence theory of truth and second, in the aporetic of the problem of the ultimate foundation of principles.

The aporetic mentioned first rests on the circumstance that the correspondence, or adequation, between mind (or expression) and the things or situations themselves must—no matter from which side it is considered—be presented as a relation between objectifiable things in the world and correspondingly must be examined. Kant, however, already showed that this is not possible, because knowledge of objects can never be compared with anything but knowledge of objects.[19] The leading basic aporie nowadays of ontological metaphysics manifestly lies in the fact that the subject-object relation of knowledge, which is a presupposition of all knowledge of objects as a condition of their possibility, in principle cannot be reduced to an inner-worldly object-object relation. With this insight, the fundamental starting point indicated above of the second paradigm of the *prima philosophia* is clearly brought near.

The aporetic of ultimate justification connected to the ontological-metaphysical paradigm also points in the same direction. In my opinion, it rests upon the fact that on the level that is suited to ontology of the objectifiable relations of predicate logic, an ultimate principle that is not itself grounded by being derived from something else can never be given. Upon this fact rests the peculiarly dogmatic character of all metaphysics, insofar as it starts from axioms that are no longer put into question.

Paradigm 2: As a way out of this dilemma in the sense of the second paradigm, one could look at transcendental reflection on the ulterior subjective conditions of thinking about and knowing an objectively given world, which reflection was prepared for by Augustine and Descartes. The paradigm of the *prima philosophia* that is now standard is defined by the fact that the objectivity of Being as such reflects—that is, in principle gets understood as a correlate of—the transcendental subjectivity of consciousness in general. Corresponding to this, the self-reflection of transcendental subjectivity in Kant, and even more radically in post-Kantian idealism, can take over the function of ultimate justification.

Beyond all that, Husserl, the last classical thinker of the second paradigm of the *prima philosophia*, provided a solution for the problem of truth as well as for the problem of ultimate justification, in the sense of a transcendental phenomenology of the subject-object relation; that is, of the strict correlation of intentional acts of consciousness and given phenomena. The ultimate justification results here from recurring to the function of the "I think" as well as of intentional consciousness, which function is not to be thought away in the attempt to bracket belief in the existence of the world. The explication of the meaning of truth as correspondence results from the reflection of the intentional consciousness upon the evidence of the fulfillment of its intentions concerning affairs by virtue of the self-givenness of phenomena.

In this way, Husserl in fact avoids the aporie of the first paradigm of the *prima philosophia*, which appears in the form of a *regressus ad infinitum* starting from the inadmissible objectivization of the subject-object relation of knowledge. The statement "I think," properly understood, is in fact ulterior for thinking, and the ascertainment of the fulfillment of the sense-intention of the statement "The cat is on the mat" through a corresponding perception of the given phenomenon can, in fact, be valid as the procurement of evidence for the agreement of the statement with reality. This agreement is what is meant by the predicate "is true" insofar as an intersubjectively shared understanding of the meaning of the statement—and correspondingly of the phenomenon to be identified—can, as a rule, be presupposed in the life-world.

With this "insofar" clause the characteristic aporie of the second paradigm of the *prima philosophia* is nevertheless also already indicated. Phenomenal evidence—be it perceptual evidence mediated by the senses or evidence in the sense of "categorial intuition" (Husserl)—is inevitably evidence that is interpreted linguistically. That means it is (at least at the level of science) to be equated with *truth* only insofar as the intersubjective validity of linguistic interpretation—which is straightforwardly presupposed in the life-world—can be discursively grounded. This, however, as distinct from the ascertainment of phenomenal evidence, can never be a matter only of my consciousness; the corresponding claim to validity must instead, in the community of interpretation of sign-interpreters, be redeemed as capable of consensus. To it, however, belongs—in addition to the experimental or observational procurement of evidence—the steady work on the language of interpretation, and in connection with the interpretation itself (which, according to Peirce, is bound up with "synthetic conclusions"), also the consideration of criteria of truth that are not related to empirical evidence, above all such as coherence, which in the discursive formation of a consensus in the community of research must be mediated with the interpretation of the empirical evidence.[20] With the foregoing, the decisive key words for an introduction to the third paradigm of the *prima philosophia* are expounded.

Paradigm 3: The third—the transcendental-semiotic—paradigm of the *prima philosophia* is, in my opinion, completely constituted in an instant by the fact that instead of the dyadic subject-object relation, the triadic relation of sign-mediated and/or language-mediated knowledge is reflectively thematized as the transcendental condition of the possibility and validity of knowledge. From this substitution all consequences in the sense of a transformation of classical transcendental philosophy can be derived.

On the one hand, this is not guaranteed merely by the "linguistic turn" of contemporary philosophy but by the fact that the linguistic turn is supplemented by the "pragmatic turn" in the sense of the triadicity of the sign relation. This again cannot—as is still to be shown in the Morris-Carnap schema—be redeemed by an empirical or metalinguistically semanticized formal pragmatics, but instead only by a reflective-transcendental pragmatics of language. On the other hand, the semiotic transformation of transcendental philosophy may not be exhausted in the fact that "symbolic form" is considered as a semiotic condition of mediation of the "transcendental synthesis of apperception" (as with Cassirer) or because Kant's "representations" or "appearances" are interpreted as signs.[21] For with this incipient semiotic transformation, merely the positions of Paradigm 1 and/or Paradigm 2 of sign relations are considered, while the position of Paradigm 3, that of sign interpretation, either is occupied by Kant's "consciousness in general" qua faculty of precommunicative synthesis of representations (as, for example, with Schoenrich),[22] or else is not considered at all (as, for example, in Wittgenstein's *Tractatus*, if one interprets it as a "Critique of Pure Language";[23] that is, as transcendental onto-semantics in which the synthesizing function of the transcendental "I" is, in a certain sense, replaced by the "logical form" of language itself).[24]

What is required instead is a transcendental-pragmatic transformation that integrates a priori the transcendental-semantic transformation of the subject function of sign-mediated knowledge, in the sense of the function of sign interpreters. This, however, implies overcoming the methodological solipsism (Husserl) of classical transcendental philosophy, which overlooked the division of linguistic sign meanings as a condition of the possibility of the intersubjective validity of sense and thus far also of valid knowledge.

This step toward transformation leads, of course, at once to the fact that one must realize the dependence of thinking and knowledge on the conventions of meaning of the concrete, "natural" languages, as well as on the rules of distinct, and completely incommensurable, language games: a starting point for modern linguistic hermeneutics lies here.[25] Indeed, any interlingual discourse (above all, any philosophical discourse that is directed toward translation and that indeed thematizes, insofar as possible, even the language-dependency of meanings) shows that we inevitably count upon the openness of all natural languages in the direction of an anticipation, even if counterfactual, of purely intersubjective (that is, interlinguistically valid) meanings. Thus far, the equation of meaning with actual "use in the language," suggested by the later Wittgenstein, is unsatisfactory. It must at least, in the sense of Peirce, be supplemented by a normative-pragmatic doctrine of the "logical interpretants" of correctly understood signs; that is, in the sense of the regulative principles of interpretation in the sense of the universal validity of sense, which is implied in the meanings of words in all natural languages. A splendid example of the possible translingual elucidation of prescientific word meaning in the sense of Peirce's pragmatic maxim was the new determination of the meaning of "simultaneity" through the—pragmatic-semantic—thought experiments of Einstein's special theory of relativity. A corresponding progressive new determination of the meaning of "justice," for example (or *justitia* or *Gerechtigkeit* and so forth), represents, in my opinion, a standing problem of philosophy, which of course is just as much directed to word meanings as natural science is and which also does well in the first place and thereafter to ascertain "use in the language."

The circumstance that not only the listener as interpreter but also the speaker as user of the language presuppose the "use in the language," and also transcend it, in the sense of accepting the claim of the purely intersubjective validity of sense, is shown most significantly in assertive speech acts. For these, as expressions of linguistic sentences with a universal claim to truth, must implicitly presuppose both the regularly, conventionally limited sense of the sign meanings of individual languages and the potentially universal sense of linguistic signs. (Habermas asserted a universal claim to validity that is in general normally connected to the "illocutionary force" of speech acts, in an extrapolative generalization of the universal claim to validity of assertive speech acts,[26] which I believe can also be applied to claims to truthfulness of expressive speech acts and to normative claims of correctness of regulative speech acts.[27]

In the sense of the transcendental-pragmatic transformation of the subject-function of sign-mediated knowledge postulated by us, one can summarize the points of the indicated dialectic of language-dependency and of the universal claim to validity as follows.

As a sign interpreter, the subject of knowledge must understand himself or herself a priori as a member of a real and a counterfactually-anticipatorily insinuated ideal "community of communication and interpretation" (Charles Peirce and Josiah Royce). This is not only in reference to the linguistically mediated interpretation of the world but also in reference to the subject's self-understanding, hence to the linguistically interpreted evidence of the *je pense* as well as the "I think" and the *ego cogito* that are interpreted linguistically by Descartes and even by Kant and Husserl.

If the just-postulated transformations of transcendental philosophy are executed in the sense of the triadic basis of a transcendental semiotic, then, in my opinion, the results are the following solutions to the problem of the explication of truth and to the problem of ultimate justification, which solutions are typical for the third paradigm of the *prima philosophia*.

Peirce clarified the possible solution of the first problem by the regulative idea of a final—that is, by implication, one no longer questionable through critique—consensus of an unlimited community of investigation about the acceptability of fallible hypotheses.[28] The main point of this solution lies, I believe, in the fact that on the one hand it transcends a priori every conceivable factual consensus; and on the other hand, as critique displays, it nevertheless, on the basis of the available, possibly conflicting criteria of truth (see above), makes into an exercise the constantly renewed production of a discursive-argumentative consensus of the community of investigation.

The possible solution of the second problem appears to lie in the fact that immediately the "I think," in the sense of the subject-function of sign-interpretation that is ulterior in discourse, is understood as "I argue." Then, the pragmatic presuppositions (as regards rules and existence) of arguing must be ascertained, for their conflict leads to a pragmatic (performative) self-contradiction on the part of those arguing. In this way, an "evident" premise of logical derivation is not dogmaticized, as in the metaphysical paradigm. Also, the alleged prelinguistic and precommunicative givenness of the "I think" is not understood as evidence independent of interpretation, as it is in the paradigm of classical transcendental philosophy; instead, to speak in the sense of the late Wittgenstein,[29] the "paradigmatic certainties" of the language game of philosophical argumentation are reflectively ascertained. This language game cannot, of course, be thought of adequately as a historically contingent language game among innumerable other ones; instead, it must be reflected upon as that language game in which one inevitably claims that one, above all various language games—no matter how distinguished—can make assertions with an a priori universal claim to validity (for example, with Wittgenstein, that language games stand in the relation of "family resemblance" to each other). And insofar as philosophical discourses are supposed to make sense at all, the participants must also always in principle maintain that, in this language game, the universal claims to validity (see above) that in other language games are exposed as debatable can be founded in a not merely conventional sense. In short: philosophers must, on penalty of performative self-contradiction, distinguish the language game of argumentative discourse as the ulterior transcendental language game.[30]

2.1.3. Diagrammatic Representation of the Result of the Transcendental-Semiotic Transformation of the *Prima Philosophia*, and Its Consequences for a Corresponding Interpretation of the Morris Schema of Semiotics

I would like to represent the considerations that have been sketched so far of the transcendental-semiotic transformation of the starting point of the *prima philosophia* in a schema, which consists of a transcendental-pragmatically accentuated expansion of the schema of the triadic sign relation in the sense of Peirce:

Schema 3

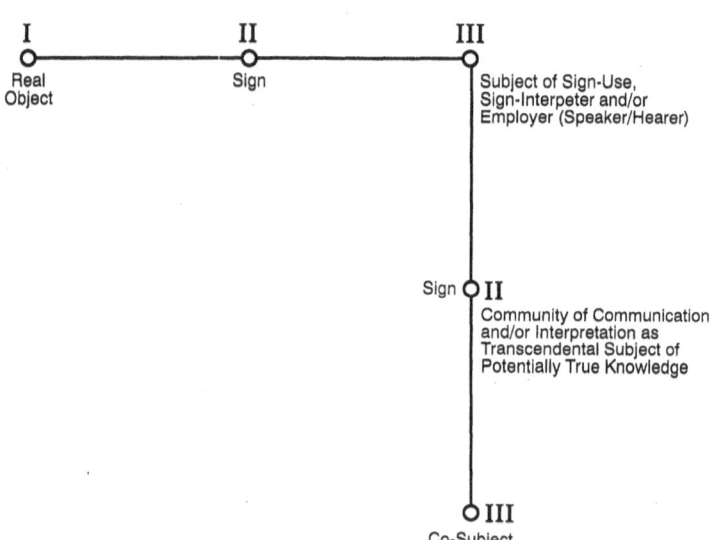

In the sense of the *speech act theory*—that is, in the sense of the performative-propositional double structure of illocutionary acts and the sentences that explicitly express them, which was worked out by Austin and Searle and expanded by Habermas—one could explicate Schema 3 by means of the following schema:[31]

Schema 4

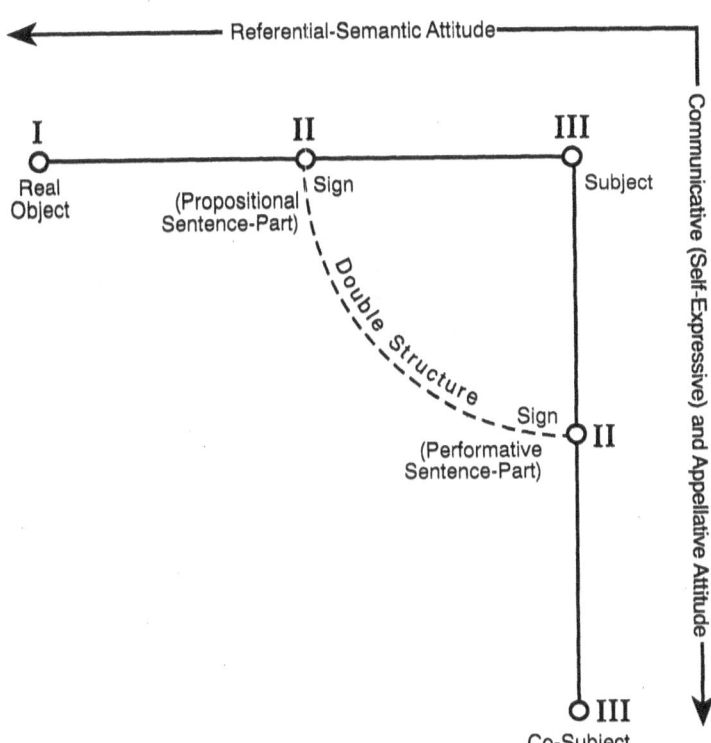

Finally, one could include in the representation the Morris schema (Schema 2), which, going beyond Peirce, considers the relations of signs to one another, relations that are conditioned by the current language system. In doing so, one must consider that the signs—which act only as an instrumental medium in knowledge of objects and not as an object, much like the actual human body as opposed to the objectified human corpse—become a theme of understanding in the context of communicative agreement, just as in the hermeneutic sciences correlated with this agreement. (Morris's insinuation that the relations between the signs in a language system are only of a syntactic nature is quickly and silently corrected here. In this regard, see below.)

From this, then, we get something like the following schema, which, in the sense of Royce,[32] brings to expression the in-principal *complimentarity* of the cognitive exchange with nature (ascertainment of the "cash-value" of signs) and of the communicative exchange in the "community of interpretation" of human beings (ascertainment of the "nominal value" of signs):

Schema 5

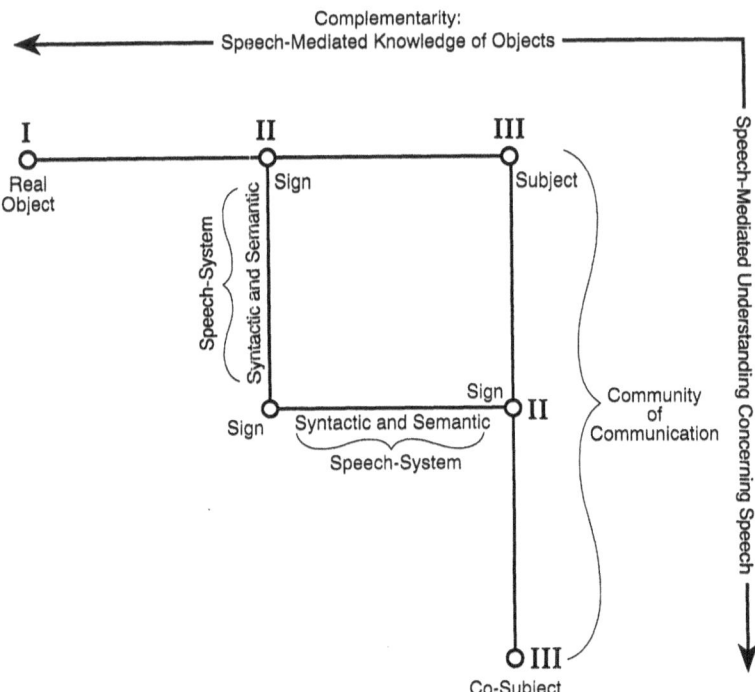

However, the interpretation suggested here of the Morris schema—as a transcendental-semiotic (and this also means transcendental-pragmatic and transcendental-hermeneutic) interpretation—does not thoroughly correspond to the actual agreement on the Morris schema of semiosis by its founders or to its reception—particularly as mediated by Carnap—in the analytic philosophy of the present. Because of considerations of space, in the following I can only intimate by means of a brief exposition of a further schema the distinction between the transcendental-semiotic interpretation and the usual interpretation of the Morris schema in analytic philosophy and at the notable (from a transcendental-semiotic point of view) "abstractive fallacies" of the usual interpretation.[33]

Pragmatic Philosophy of Language

2.2. Transcendental-Semiotic versus Empiricist Interpretation of Semiotic

In the exposition of the following schema, we begin by referring to some relatively easily corrected "abstractive fallacies" that were suggested by the original Morris schema. They fit together well with the fact that Morris, in his conception of semiotics of 1938, introduced *pragmatics* as a discipline purely supplementary to the (logical) *syntax* and *semantics* already founded by Carnap.

Schema 6

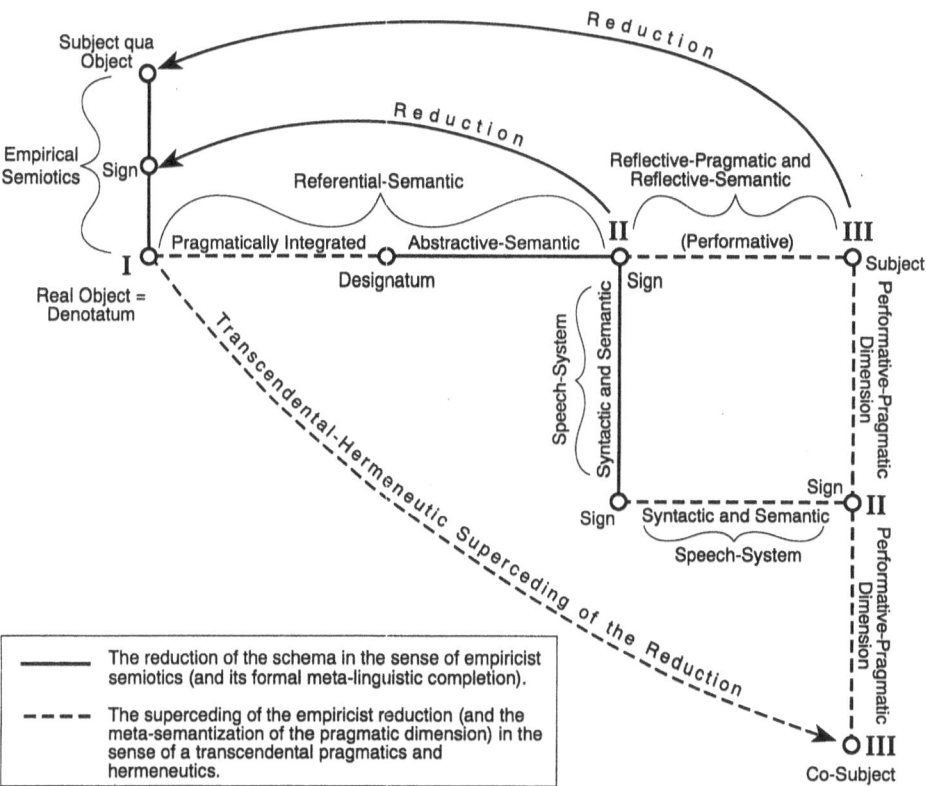

a. Morris manifestly insinuated, on the ground of his acquaintance with a construct-language in the sense of Carnap, that the system-conditioned relations of linguistic signs to one another needed only to be of a syntactical kind. This claim, however, cannot be upheld with regard to natural languages; for here, not only are the syntactical relations themselves already semantically predetermined (as especially the discussion about "generative linguistics" has shown), but also one must take into account "paradigmatic" relations (for example, "field" structures) between the meanings of the signs of a system of language.

b. A further erroneous suggestion of the original schema of Morris is that it gives the impression that the abstractive-semantic dimension of signs reaches out, so to speak, to the real objects of sign reference—as if semantics in abstraction from pragmatics could thematize not only the designatum of the sign (for example, unicorn), which is provided for in the language system, but also the real denotatum of the sign, which possibly is capable of being identified by a real sign interpreter in the world. This "abstractive fallacy" (which, taken strictly, also appears wherever one characterizes any philosophical position that thematizes truth-conditions as verification-conditions as does "formal semantics") was corrected by Morris himself, after it was addressed by Dewey in 1946[34] and Carnap in 1942,[35] for the benefit of an integrative pragmatic conception of semiotics, which thematizes not only the empirical fact of semiosis but even the constructive activities of a "pure, formative" syntactics, semantics, and pragmatics as "sign-mediated behavior."

Are all "abstractive fallacies" of the Morris schema corrected now? Or, put differently, does the schema now consider the triadicity in principle of sign relations in the sense of Peirce?

Such a conception, which might still be said to be predominant among semioticians today,[36] overlooks, in my opinion, the following: the current performative-self-reflective knowledge of illocutionary—and possibly also prelocutionary—intentions, which binds the speaker to his or her acts of speech, can in principle not be thematized in the empirically-behaviorally conceived semiotics, not even with the help of a metalinguistic semanticization of the pragmatic dimension,[37] which forbids itself pragmatically self-referential discourse, probably out of fear of semantic antinomies. Without reflective-pragmatic knowledge of the speaker's intention, however, it can give neither a knowledge of the claims to validity of the speaker's speech acts nor a hermeneutic understanding of the sign-mediated behavior of the listener in the sense of illocutionary speech acts with their respective claims to validity. (Naturally, because of [its reliance upon] mere observation of behavior, there is also no understanding of the "institutional facts" of rule-guided speech behavior.)

Nevertheless, even if, as it often happens tacitly today, methodological behaviorism is given up for the sake of a behavior-theoretical conception, a merely empirical conception of semiotics is not suited to do justice to the normative-hermeneutic, or to the philosophical-normative, concerns of sign-understanding. This, too, can be explicated by an example of the clarification of meaning in the sense of the "pragmatic maxim" of Peirce. If this means, "Consider whatever effects, having any conceivable practical relevance, that we ascribe to the object of our conceptions in our representation,"[38] then we are primarily thinking of a situation in which a scientist would like to clarify the meaning of an unclear concept (for example, Einstein's situation with regard to the meaning of the "simultaneity of two events"). But this means that the position of the scientist here is not that of the empirical linguist or the social scientist, who is interested in ascertaining the actual effects of sign interpretation—which are normally conditioned by the use of language and by the surrounding circumstances—but instead is the position of the participant in communication, who is interested in such effects as possibly have never been reached—representable in thought experiments (for instance, sense perceptions brought about by operations of measurement)—that *would* correspond to the normatively correct interpretation of sign meaning (the "logical interpretant" in the sense of Peirce). The interpreter of a text, who is interested in correct judgment concerning the claim to validity that is bound up with text-signs, manifestly is in principle in the same situation.

In all these paradigmatic cases of a normative hermeneutics, the sign interpreter obviously cannot remain in the position of observation and description of the facts of sign-mediated behavior. Instead, he or she must manufacture a communicative relationship with regard to the signs to be interpreted—actual utterances or texts—which relation is determined by the heuristic anticipation of the possible intersubjective consensus of all conceivable sign interpreters about the claims to validity (sense, truth, truthfulness, normative correctness) that are connected with speech behavior. This means, however, that one can no longer abstract from the transcendental-hermeneutic and transcendental-pragmatic dimension of ongoing, self-reflective sign interpretation, which, as subject-cosubject relation, is constitutive of the (unlimited) community of communication as transcendental subject of sign interpretation. In short, the empiricist reduction (see Schema 6) of the transcendental dimension of semiosis must be superseded. And it should be clear that not until it is superseded do we redeem the claim to validity of the thesis of the triadicity of sign relations as the actual condition of the possibility of sign-mediated knowledge in the sense of the third paradigm of first philosophy.

Notes

1. The English version of this paper is a translation by Robert W. Burch with Karen Antell from the original manuscript in German.
2. See also Karl-Otto Apel, *Transformation der Philosophie*, 2 vols. (Frankfurt am

Main: Suhrkamp, 1973), vol. 1, "Introduction," and vol. 2; Karl-Otto Apel, *Die Idee der Sprache in der Tradition des Humanismus von Dante bis Vico* (Bonn: Bouvier, 1963); Karl-Otto Apel, "Das Leibapriori der Erkenntnis," *Archiv fuer Philosophie* 12 (1963): 152–72, reprinted in H. G. Gadamer, *Neue Anthropologie*, vol. 7 (Stuttgart: G. Thieme, 1974), pp. 264–88; Karl-Otto Apel, "Zur Idee einer transzendentalen Sprachpragmatik," in J. Simon, ed., *Aspekte und Probleme der Sprachphilosophie* (Freiburg: Alber, 1974); and Karl-Otto Apel, *Der Denkweg von Charles Peirce* (Frankfurt am Main: Suhrkamp, 1975).

3. See H. J. Schneider, *Pragmatik als Basis von Semantik und Syntax* (Frankfurt am Main: Suhrkamp, 1975).

4. See also Apel, 1973, vol. 2; and D. Boehler, 1985, *Rekonstruktive Pragmatik* (Frankfurt am Main: Suhrkamp, 1985).

5. Compare also Immanuel Kant, *Gesammelte Werke* (Academic Edition: Berlin, 1923), vol. 9, p. 51.

6. Compare Charles Peirce, *Schriften I*, mit Einfuehrung von K.-O. Apel (Frankfurt am Main: Suhrkamp, 1967); and Charles Peirce, *Schriften II*, mit Einfuehrung von K.-O. Apel (Frankfurt am Main: Suhrkamp, 1970). See also Apel, 1975, and Apel, 1973, vol. 2, pp. 157–220.

7. Richard Rorty, *Consequences of Pragmatism* (Brighton: The Harvester Press, 1982).

8. See Karl-Otto Apel, "Fallibilismus, Konsenstheorie der Wahrheit, und Letztbegrundung," in W. Kuhlmann, ed., *Philosophie und Begrundung* (Frankfurt am Main: Suhrkamp, 1987).

9. See Apel, 1973; also Karl-Otto Apel, ed., *Sprachpragmatik und Philosophie* (Frankfurt am Main: Suhrkamp, 1976); and Karl-Otto Apel, "Die Logos-Auszeichnung der Menschlichen Sprache: Die philosophische Relevanz der Sprechakttheorie," in H.-G. Bosshardt, ed., *Sprache interdisziplinaer* (Berlin and New York: W. de Gruyter, 1986), pp. 45–87.

10. Charles S. Peirce, *Collected Papers*, ed. Charles Hartshorne, Paul Wiess, and Arthur Burks (Cambridge, Mass.: Harvard University Press, 1931–1958), vol. 2, para. 228, hereafter cited as CP 2.228.

11. CP 3.360.

12. See Apel, 1975; also Karl-Otto Apel, "Charles W. Morris und das Program einer pragmatisch integrierten Semiotik," in *C. W. Morris: Zeichen, Sprache, und Verhalten* (Duesseldorf: Schwann, 1973), pp. 9–66, reprinted in A. Eschbach, ed., *Zeichen ueber Zeichen ueber Zeichen, 15 Studien ueber C. W. Morris* (Tuebingen: G. Narr, 1981), pp. 25–82.

13. Compare Apel, 1975, p. 159.

14. Compare, for example, CP 1.185–1.186.

15. Compare especially C. S. Peirce, *Semiotische Schriften*, vol. 1, ed. Helmut Pape (Frankfurt am Main: Suhrkamp, 1986).

16. See CP 5.313-5.315.

17. Compare, for example, Jacques Derrida, *Grammatologie* (Frankfurt am Main: Suhrkamp, 1984), p. 83.

18. Compare also Apel, 1974; also Karl-Otto Apel, "Transzendentale Semiotik und die Paradigmen der *prima philosophia*," in E. von Buelow and P. Schmitter, *Sprache und Verhalten* (Amsterdam: John Benjamins B. V., 1979), pp. 101–38.

19. Immanuel Kant, *Gesammelte Werke* (Berlin: Academy, 1923), vol. 9, p. 53.

20. Compare Apel, 1983; also Karl-Otto Apel, "Das Problem der phaenomenologischen Evidenz im Lichte einer transzendentalen Semiotik," in M. Benedikt and R. Burger, ed., *Die Krise der Phaenomenologie und die Pragmatik der Wissenschaften* (Vienna, Austria: State Press, 1986), pp. 18–99; and Apel, "Fallibilismus."

21. Compare G. Schoenrich, *Kategorien und transzdendentale Argumentation: Kant und die Idee einer transzendentalen Semiotik* (Frankfurt am Main: Suhrkamp, 1981).
22. Ibid.
23. As does Eric Stenius, *Wittgenstein's Tractatus* (Oxford: Basil Blackwell, 1960).
24. Compare Apel, 1973, vol. 2, p. 28.
25. Compare Apel, 1963 and Apel, 1973.
26. Juergen Habermas, "Vorbereitende Bemerkungen zu einer Theorie der kommunikativen Kompetenz," in Juergen Habermas and N. Luhmann, ed., *Theorie der Gesellschaft oder Sozialtechnologie* (Frankfurt am Main: Suhrkamp, 1971). See also Juergen Habermas, "Was heisst Universalpragmatik?" in Karl-Otto Apel, ed., *Sprachpragmatik und Philosophie* (Frankfurt am Main: Suhrkamp, 1976), pp. 174–272; Juergen Habermas, *Theorie des kommunikativen Handelns*, 2 vols. (Frankfurt am Main: Suhrkamp, 1981), vols. 1, 3; and Juergen Habermas, *Vorstudien und Ergaenzungen zur Theorie des kommunikativen Handelns* (Frankfurt am Main: Suhrkamp, 1984), vol. 1, p. 2.
27. Compare also Apel, "Die Logos-Auszeichnung."
28. Compare Apel, 1973, vol. 2, p. 2.; also Apel, 1975; Karl-Otto Apel, "C. S. Peirce and the Post-Tarskian Problem of an Adequate Explication of the Meaning of Truth: Towards a Transcendental-Pragmatic Theory of Truth," in Eugene Freeman, ed., *The Relevance of Charles Peirce* (La Salle, Ill.: The Hegeler Institute, 1983), pp. 189–223; and Apel, "Fallibilismus."
29. See Ludwig Wittgenstein, *Ueber Gewissheit* (Frankfurt am Main: Suhrkamp, 1970). Accordingly, see also Karl-Otto Apel, "Das Problem der philosophischen Letztbegruendung im Lichte einer transzendentalen Sprachpragmatik," in B. Kanitscheider, ed., *Sprache und Erkenntnis* (Innsbruck: Institut fuer Sprachwissenschaft der Universitaet, 1976), pp. 55–82.
30. Compare Apel, 1973, vol. 2, p. 220; also Apel, "Das Problem der philosophischen Letztbegruendung"; Apel, "Fallibilismus"; D. Boehler, *Rekonstruktive Pragmatik* (Frankfurt am Main: Suhrkamp, 1985); and W. Kuhlmann, *Reflexive Letztbegruendung: Untersuchungen zur Transzendentalpragmatik* (Freiburg: Alber, 1985).
31. See Apel, "Die Logos-Auszeichnung."
32. Josiah Royce, *The Problem of Christianity* (New York: Macmillan, 1913), vol. 2, pp. 146ff.; see also Apel, 1973, vol. 2, pp. 199ff.
33. Compare in this regard Apel, "Charles W. Morris"; also Apel, "C. S. Peirce"; and Apel, "Die Logos-Auszeichnung."
34. John Dewey, "Peirce's Theory of Linguistic Signs, Thought, and Meaning," in *Journal of Philosophy* 43 (1946): 85–95.
35. Rudolf Carnap, *Introduction to Semantics* (Cambridge, Mass.: Harvard University Press, 1942).
36. See R. Posner, "Charles Morris und die verhaltenstheoretische Grundlegung der Semiotik," in A. Eschbach, ed., *Zeichen ueber Zeichen ueber Zeichen, 15 Studien ueber C. W. Morris* (Tuebingen: G. Narr, 1981).
37. See Rudolf Carnap, "On Some Concepts of Pragmatics," *Philosophical Studies* 6 (1955): 89–91; also R. M. Martin, *Toward a Systematic Pragmatics*, ed. L. E. J. Brouwer, E. W. Beth, and A. Heyting (Amsterdam: North-Holland Pub. Co., 1959); and Richard Montague, *Formal Philosophy: Selected Papers of Richard Montague*, ed. Richmond H. Thomason (New Haven: Yale University Press, 1970).
38. CP 5.402.

Modernity, Interpretation Theory, and American Philosophy

THELMA Z. LAVINE

I. Modernity and the Interpretive Turn

This is a story about Modernity and its relationship to the interpretive turn in modern philosophy, intellectual culture, and American philosophy. The interpretive cultural anthropologist Clifford Geertz would perceive this as an I-story, hopelessly relativized by my personal and professional perspectives, and thus only a half-story, fashioning a reality by the power of rhetoric. But as a philosopher examining Modernity I present myself as truthful and as affirmatively telling a true story about the structure of modern philosophies—in the language of philosophy, a metaphilosophy in historical form.

The interpretive turn in philosophy[1] was ushered in by Kant's critical philosophy, which attempted to reconcile the epistemological conflict between rationalism and empiricism and to overcome the self-criticism of philosophy stemming from Humeian empiricism. Kant's resolution of these problems was by means of a formal interpretation theory, which identifies within knowledge, in addition to our sensory receptivity, an interpretive element drawn from the rational power of the mind: the pure concepts of the understanding, which are a priori, universal, and necessary conditions of the possibility of experience and knowledge. After Kant, the problems of interpretation and the clarification of a theory of interpretation became central to Hegel and Marx and to various nineteenth-century social philosophies and philosophies of history; to late nineteenth- and twentieth-century American pragmatism and to sociology of knowledge; and to later twentieth-century transcendental phenomenology, ontological hermeneutics, critical theory, and deconstruction.

The distinctive feature of interpretation theory from Kant and the German Enlightenment to contemporary French poststructuralist deconstruction is the thematization of subjective or group mind, or the phenomenology or ontology of understanding, or linguistic structure, or the transcendentality of rational rules as a constitutive element in what is experienced or known. Common to all these philosophic movements, although they are unequally self-reflective, is the epistemological, interpretational principle that what is known is not apprehended as given in completed form, but that through being interpreted by the conferring of meaning or the imposing of conceptual or linguistic structure, what is known is in some measure constituted or "created." With the interpretive turn consciousness has become self-consciousness, in Hegelian terms; knowledge has become reflexive, in contemporary human science terms, seeking the theoretical structures with which its ideas are laden.

Trespassing the boundaries of conventional fields, the interpretational principle, with its constitutive self-consciousness and reflexivity, may be seen as the hallmark, the distinctive intellectual criterion, of Modernity: from Kant to Kuhn and Hawking and the quantum theory debates; from Hegel, Marx, Durkheim, Weber, Schutz, and Mannheim, Royce, Dewey, and Parsons to Berger and Luckmann's social construction of reality and Garfinckel's ethnomethodology; from Husserl to Heidegger, Gadamer, Habermas, Apel, and the Gadamer-Habermas debates; from Saussure and Levi-Strauss to the deconstructions of Barthes and Derrida; from Freud to Sartre, Lacan, Ricoeur, Thomas Mann, Lionel Trilling, and Saul Bellow.

But the pervasiveness of the interpretive turn in Modernity is marked by the rise and development of conflicting forms of interpretation theory, and these reflect the rise and development of the conflicting structures of Modernity. Modernity can be viewed both with respect to its historicality and its conceptuality. Historically, Modernity as a socio-cultural phenomenon has been evolving until the present time since the late seventeenth century, the beginning years of the historical periodization conventionally identified as the Enlightenment. By the end of the eighteenth century and the early nineteenth century, Modernity has undergone a disruption, manifesting itself at the beginning years of the conventional periodization that identifies the Romantic movement. Corresponding to the historical disruption of Modernity into its Enlightenment and Romantic phases is the conceptual diremption of Modernity into the conflicting cognitive-cultural frames of Enlightenment and Romantic Modernity.

Modernism begins historically as Enlightenment Modernity, and from it come the powerfully emergent historical forces of modernization and the features of what we mean by modernity: science and technology, the continuous technological improvement in agriculture, mining, transportation, communication, engineering, and medicine; industrialization; urbanization; democratic capitalism; and classical political liberalism. As a cognitive-cultural framework, Enlightenment Modernity is a cluster of cognitive, methodological, and normative claims concerning the self, knowledge, morals, politics, and history. Enlightenment Modernity claims the primacy of reason in all significant domains: substantive reason yields self-evident truths concerning human nature, including the universality of rationality, the inalienability of natural rights, and equality under the law; scientific reason yields an epistemology and a methodology for attaining objective and valid knowledge. Together, substantive and scientific reason yield a natural law of progress for the universal benefit of humanity, according to which expanding scientific knowledge is put into practice as technology and natural rights truths are put into practice to democratize social institutions. Through the power of substantive and scientific reason Enlightenment Modernity carries the hope of emancipation—from factual falsity, superstition, and prejudice; from the irrational myths and dogmas of authoritarian institutions; from exploitative beliefs and traditions. Enlightenment-style liberation proceeds by demystifying and delegitimating; its goal is a world of truth in which reason is the ground of science, morality, and politics.

Romantic Modernity arose historically in Rousseauian and Blakeian cultural revolt against the increasingly mechanized and disenchanted world of Enlightenment scientific reason, followed later by the political revolt of the Wars of Liberation against the Enlightenment symbolism of the military conquests of Napoleon. Romantic Modernity as a cognitive framework is dialectically linked to Enlightenment Modernity as its antithesis. The aim of Romanticism, as proclaimed by the Catholic royalist Josef de Maistre, "is absolutely to kill the whole spirit of the Eighteenth Century [Enlightenment]." The views of Romantic Modernity crystallized into oppositional categories as a counter-style of thought: the primacy of spirit in opposition to that of reason; opposing the focus on fact and externality, and the claims of scientific, instrumental reason in defense of the objectivity and validity of knowledge. Romanticism offers the truths of history, culture, tradition, art, the "inward path," and the dialectic of personal and collective will. Romantic Modernity rejects the autonomous rational individual of Enlightenment democracy, with his inalienable rights and independence, and it rejects Enlightenment Modernity's bourgeois public world administered by communication technologies, industry, and governmental bureaucracies. Romantic Modernity builds politically not upon the individual but upon the group and moves in the direction of a politics of organic unity, a collectivism of the left or the right. Finally, Romantic Modernity has its own counter-style of emancipation. For Romantic Modernity, struggling against the hegemony of the Enlightenment mentality, emancipation is felt to be freedom from the oppressive Enlightenment world of bureaucratized government, dehumanizing and exploitative corporate industries, mass education, and mass politics. True freedom for the person or the group lies in the power to be authentically self-expressive. Romantic Modernity's style of demystification is antinomian, consisting in the denial that any authority is binding upon the individual spirit and its untrammeled will.

The structure of Modernity has now been seen to be a framework that exists in the form of counter-frameworks that are constitutive of it. Modernity is the confluence of two dialectically opposed cultural-intellectual styles, each subverting, demystifying, and delegitimating the other's conception of the human being, truth, morality, and politics and the appropriate methodology for knowing them. Thus the heritage of Modernity is the mutual destruction of its component mentalities. In response to this diremption, the great intellectual figures of Modernity have attempted to design integrating paradigms: such integrating constructions provide a key to the work of Hegel, Marx, Weber, Freud, and Habermas. I shall argue that paradigms attempting an integration of Enlightenment and Romantic Modernity provide the key to the very rise of classical American philosophy.

II. Modernity and the Types of Interpretation Theory

In the course of the diremptive development of Modernity, three principal types of interpretation have evolved: formal, contextual, and hermeneutical-textual. Enlightenment interpretation theory, as first formulated by Kant, is formal and rational, claiming against authoritarian dogma and empiricist skepticism that the validity of scientific knowledge is grounded upon the transcendental, rational, pure, universal, a priori certainty of the categories of the understanding by which mind conducts the interpretive activities of experience and knowledge. The most important single criterion of the Enlightenment type of interpretation theory is the attempt, modeled upon Kant, to establish an absolute, rational, or transcendental formal foundation for knowledge. As in the case of Kant's battle against Humeian skepticism, the search for a formal ground for knowledge is undertaken in opposition to some perceived state of theoretical relativism or skepticism in the intellectual culture or in the self-criticism of philosophy. Beyond Kant, formal interpretation theory appears notably in the work of Husserl, Dilthey, Peirce, Lewis, and Habermas.

By contrast with Enlightenment formal/rational interpretation theory, contextual interpretation theory claims that all interpretive structures conferred by mind are themselves empirically conditioned. Arising with the post-Enlightenment increasing self-differentiation of European or American social groups and with the post-Enlightenment emergence of the historical, biological, and social sciences, contextual interpretation accounts for the differences in group interpretive structures by the variety of empirical circumstances that give rise to them. Contextual interpretation reflects in part the characteristic anti-Enlightenment, counter-style mentality of Romantic modernity. Although deriving from the Hegelian and Romantic tradition, contextual interpretation theory is linked also to the empirical conceptualizations and modes of explanation of the scientific tradition of the Enlightenment in its inquiry into the empirical conditions of divergent interpretive structures and their changes. Contextual interpretation appears notably in its first phases in Hegel and Marx, and it is characteristic of important aspects of American pragmatism, interpretive sociology, sociology of knowledge, and psychoanalytic theory.

Formal interpretation reappears with the distinctive responses of Dilthey and Husserl to the problems of relativism in late nineteenth- and early twentieth-century Continental intellectual and political culture, with Dilthey, although under Romantic influences, attempting to provide a Kantian-type foundation for the human sciences. Husserl's phenomenology, on the other hand, sought an absolute foundation for knowledge by means of the object-constructing operations of a Kantian transcendental ego. The failure of Husserl's project of phenomenology as a priori transcendental subjectivity led him instead to a descriptive phenomenology as the science of the *Lebenswelt,* a study of the underlying structures that hold for any life-world. Husserl's phenomenology of the life-world proved to be acceptable to Heidegger, Gadamer, and subsequent hermeneutical phenomenologists; they saw Husserl's life-world as preparing the way for Heidegger's antiepistemological phenomenology of *Dasein.* However, the hermeneutical interpretation theories of Heidegger and Gadamer defined themselves precisely in opposition to the Kantian heritage of both Dilthey and Husserl and especially to Husserl's formal interpretation theory, attacking Husserl's transcendental phenomenology for its rationalism, foundationalism, a priorism, and intuition of essences.

Hermeneutics as a type of interpretation theory rejects as "objectivism" any methodology, replacing it with the old hermeneutics model of religious or legal textual interpretation. For hermeneutics the interpreter of human meaning is not a neutral scientific observer, but "always already" has a preunderstanding, a preinterpretation, of his object.

With Heidegger, hermeneutics begins to signify an antirationalistic, antimethodological mode of interpretation theory: exclusively discursive, characterized by linguisticality and historicality and by the absence of formal grounding or of reference to nonlinguistic realities. Thus although hermeneutics derives from Romanticism, as does contextual interpretation theory, hermeneutics may be seen to be a radical form of interpretation theory from which concrete empirical content has been eliminated. The concrete historical genesis of interpretive structures, as these were insightfully discerned by Hegel, Marx, Mannheim, Dewey, and Mead, is not to be found in hermeneutics, for which "historicality" signifies a mode of being of interpreter and text instead of a mode of empirically knowable reality.

Heidegger's crucial significance in the evolving of interpretation theory and the rise of hermeneutics is his instituting "a revolution in thought" by breaking with the epistemological question, "What can a knowing subject understand?" and asking instead, "What kind of being is it whose being consists in understanding?" With Heidegger understanding is no longer regarded as a mode of knowledge but as a mode of being. By inaugurating this revolution in thought, Heidegger is able to undercut, as misconstrued, the longstanding problem areas with which, since Kant, interpretation theory, epistemology, and methodology of the natural and social sciences have been concerned. But on the other hand, the avoidance of these problems by the ontological turn makes it impossible for him to contribute to their solution. Heidegger's hermeneutics of *Dasein*, the human mode of being whose being consists in the understanding of Being, explicates *Dasein's* always already existent preunderstanding of Being; interpretation as a mode of *Dasein* can only make explicit what is thus already presupposed, with the result that all knowledge is subject to the hermeneutic circle and the loss of objectivity. Nor can *Dasein,* trapped in the hermeneutic circle, lead Heidegger to an ontological ground in Being.

For Gadamerian hermeneutics, historicality and linguisticality are the ontological frames of human experience and the conditions of the possibility of understanding; interpretation is thus relativized to the ontological absolutism of history and language. In opposition to the Enlightenment view that autonomous reason, free from prejudice, tradition, and authority, is operative in the natural and human sciences, Gadamer argues that historicality always characterizes reason; that the interpreter's rational capacity is always already within his own historical horizon; and that understanding is possible only within a framework of tradition. In a deliberate assault on the Enlightenment's celebrated delegitimation of prejudice and the traditions and authority with which prejudice is sustained, Gadamer argues that prejudice is the very condition of understanding for the historical consciousness.

Gadamer's specific contributions to ontological hermeneutics—"rehabilitated" tradition, effective-history, horizon-fusion, and a substantive hermeneutic circle—are interpretive features that exhibit the inescapable relativity of interpretation to his ontological frames. But because Gadamer offers no reliable criteria for distinguishing legitimate from illegitimate prejudices, nor for identifying commonality between interpreter and text, nor for identifying and criticizing horizon-fusion, nor for a cognitive and moral critique of tradition and language, one can only invoke Hegel's famous comment on Schelling's Absolute, as the night in which all cows are black. In the night of Gadamer's ontological hermeneutics, all traditions (including the German tradition) are indiscriminately black—historical and linguistic.

Gadamer's hermeneutics present an explicitly Romantic attack upon Enlightenment epistemology and philosophy of science. His ontological interpretation theory subverts the subject-object relationship, the critical autonomy of consciousness, the significance of objectivity and truth in knowledge, normativity in human affairs, and nonlinguistic realities as they relate to the various sciences, to technologies, and to historical understanding itself.

The ontological hermeneutics of Heidegger and Gadamer, constructed in the shadow of Germany's defeat in two world wars and of nazism and the Holocaust, reflects the heritage of Romantic cultural despair. This heritage turned interpretation theory away from the Enlightenment rationalism of formal interpretation theory with its implicit optimism and universalism and away from the concrete empiricism of post-Hegelian contextual interpretation, with its implicit critical potential drawn from psychoanalysis, sociology of knowledge, and the critique of ideology.

With Derrida, the role of hermeneutics, which begins in modernity with Heidegger's Dasein and the Call of Being and is developed by Gadamer's ontologizing of language and tradition, takes a Nietzschian turn. Derrida reflects the anti-Enlightenment thematics of post-World War II France, which rejects rationalism, the natural sciences as paradigmatic of truth, the epistemological and moral autonomy of the individual, the concepts of humanism, and social progress. Derrida is in accord with hermeneutics with respect to overcoming epistemology and any Kantian-type formal foundation for knowledge or any contextual mode of interpretation, displacing these by a hermeneutics exclusively of texts, which are "always already" interpretive and linguistic. As Derrida is influenced by hermeneutics and proceeds to deconstruct it as a hidden "logocentrism," he is also influenced by structuralist linguistics and proceeds to its "poststructuralist" deconstruction. From structural linguistics, Derrida appropriates the conception that meaning rests exclusively on differentiation and binary opposition within the self-referential sign-system of language.

As an interpretation theory characterized by negativity, deconstruction engenders no theory and few theoretical structures: the interrelated concepts of logocentrism, the metaphysics of presence, and the prioritization of binary opposition are relied upon to carry the theoretical burden. Logocentrism loosely defines the principal characteristic of Western thought, its misguided search for an unmediated, indubitable center or ground that guarantees the certainty of knowledge. Logocentrism is explicated by the metaphysics of presence, which signifies an immediate, intuitive, self-certifying meaning conveyed by the human (or divine) voice, and thus by the prioritization of speech over writing. The practice of deconstruction is served by a battery of deconstructive strategies that work "in the margins" of texts, deconstructing by identifying difference, supplementarity, dissemination, undecidability, and metaphoricity. By these means Derrida's project of deconstructing logocentrism purports to dismantle Western philosophy and the ensemble of Enlightenment conceptualizations, the stronghold of the Western quest for certainty. The dismantling fails to take place. The deconstruction is restricted to certain selected metaphysical systems and rests primarily on an argument from the absolute exclusivity of alternatives: either metaphysics is free of imprecision of meaning, metaphoricity, and contradiction, or metaphysics, like literature, is merely figurative and indeterminate in its meanings, and the governance of philosophy over the intellectual culture should come to an end. Long before Richard Rorty, but not in the name of American pragmatism, Derrida announced that the binary opposition between philosophy and literature that has traditionally prioritized philosophy can now be reversed.

But Derrida acknowledges the aporia that lies within deconstructionist interpretation itself: its unsurpassable contradiction between the gratifications of deconstruction and the inescapability of the logocentric structures that it seeks to destroy. Derrida identifies with the Nietzschian "joyous affirmation" of deconstructing, contrasting this with the Rousseauian affirmation of origins, structure, truth, and ethics, and he is led by this to propose a theory of "two interpretations of interpretation." Here, in this departure into metaphilosophy, Derrida the joyful Romantic (unlike the Romantics of cultural despair) concurs with Habermas, the sober, complex defender of Enlightenment rationality, in the perception of Modernity as the conflict of Enlightenment and Romantic mentalities and their interpretive modes.

III. Critical Theory, American Philosophy, and the Dialectic of Modernity

The two preceding sections of this article have examined the fate of the interpretive turn in relation to the conflict within Modernity between its Enlightenment and Romantic components, in the course of which we have witnessed the greater philosophic energy of the Romantic hermeneutic interpretation theories, an energy that spirals downward, from Heidegger's "lordly" dismissal of all of Western philosophy (excluding the pre-Socratics) to Derrida's deconstruction of Western philosophy in its entirety, with no exceptions. The flawed monologic course of hermeneutic-textual interpretation theories appears indeed to reflect the present situation of philosophy, which is marked by the decline of analytic philosophy and also of the various Continental philosophic traditions. Most of the practitioners of these philosophies appear now to be engaged in the activity that Thomas Kuhn labeled "mopping up," after the dominating paradigms have lost their intellectual power.

By contrast with such mopping-up activities on both sides of the Atlantic, the intellectual vitality of critical theory, represented by Juergen Habermas, Karl-Otto Apel, and others, calls for analysis and appraisal. It is my purpose in this section of my discussion to present the impressive strengths of critical theory and to show that the course of American philosophy already exhibits these and other strengths and that their reappropriation opens a new frontier for American philosophy.

The philosophic productions of Juergen Habermas stand in sharpest deliberate contrast to the ontological and linguistic hermeneutics of Heidegger and Gadamer and their antirationalistic subversion of knowledge, truth, and normativity and also to Derrida's deconstructive hermeneutics *in extremis*. Habermas is a Western Marxist and a second-generation representative of the critical theory of the Frankfurt School, whose original members had fled from the threat of Nazi persecution. Despite the postwar pessimism of the older generation, Habermas became committed to the goal of finding an adequate ground in social theory for a social practice that would escape a recurrence of the pathologies of the Nazi past. The entire intellectual effort of Habermas, in its comprehensive productivity, may be seen as a moral-political pursuit of an "Archimedean" point for social theory upon which to construct a theory of a liberated and just society.

Knowledge and Human Interests is Habermas's first major work in the pursuit of his theoretical goals. Habermas draws here upon the three modes of interpretation theory: formal, contextual, and hermeneutic-textual, in identifying the cognitive interests that serve the imperatives of human life—maintenance of the material base of life; dependable networks of communication in a natural language; and critical reflection. These three imperatives are the roots of knowledge and are naturalistic; they lie within "the natural history of the species." The cognitive interests of three categories of knowledge serve these imperatives. (1) Empirical-analytical sciences, natural and social, which produce nomological propositions, serve the technical interest in control of nature and social organization; these sciences correspond to the dimension of work in human life. (2) Historical-hermeneutical sciences and the humanities make possible intersubjective communication, symbolic interaction, and interpretive understanding; they serve the practical interest of communication and intersubjectivity and correspond to the dimension of interaction in human life. (3) Critically oriented sciences, specifically psychoanalysis and critique of ideology, serve the emancipatory interest, which identifies, and liberates from, hidden forms of distortion, whether psychological or the distortions of false consciousness; these sciences correspond to the dimension of power in human life.

In the language of Kant, Habermas argues that the three cognitive interests—technical, practical, and emancipatory—are "the necessary conditions of the possibility of experience that can claim to be objective." His point is that as invariant conditions for the possibility of objective experience, cognitive interests have a "quasi-transcendental" cognitive status: they are transcendental in their epistemological function and naturalistic in their source. Habermas's theory of cognitive interests is the first in a series of his attempts to provide a formal, transcendental set of conditions for knowledge, which are tied to empirical aspects of human life.

But the logic of Habermas's project remains unchanged from his early *Knowledge and Human Interests* to the recent *The Theory of Communicative Action*: it is to combine a modified form of the transcendentalism of Kantian formal interpretation theory with the social content of empirical interpretation theory and with a hermeneutics of communication. This project, which gives a coherent Hegelian account of the totality of the interpretive spheres of human knowledge yet provides a formal Kantian transcendental status as well as empirical content, is Habermas's first and most challenging theoretical innovation. It is also the object of critical attack. The same boldly innovative logic and similar problems appear in Habermas's more complex pursuit of an Archimedean point for social theory in the rationality inherent in human communication.

The moral force of Habermas's search for an Archimedean point for social theory that would preclude the repetition of the social pathologies of the recent past emerges with the famous Gadamer-Habermas debates, which erupted with Habermas's publication in 1967 of "A Review of Gadamer's *Truth and Method*." Habermas agrees with Gadamer that the approach to social reality is necessarily through interpretive understanding, mediated by language that is carried in cultural traditions. But Habermas opposes Gadamer's absolutizing of language and cultural traditions, which implies "that we are delivered up to happenings (tradition) in which the conditions of rationality change irrationally, according to time and place, epoch and culture." Habermas argues that for *Truth and Method* the cultural and linguistic relativization of all possible understanding yields a hermeneutic limited exclusively to dialogue and an interpretation of social reality that is uncritical, language-bound, and tradition-bound. Habermas makes the trenchant claim that "Gadamer's prejudice for the rights of prejudices certified by tradition denies the power of reflection,"—the power of ideological and psychoanalytic critique.

The debate appears to have intensified Habermas's goal to break out of the contextual and situational relativism of Gadamerian hermeneutics, to break out of Heideggerian pessimistic *Gelassenheit* and Gadamerian traditionalism in order to construct a rationally supported ground for social inquiry.

In these goals Habermas may be seen to be a "foundationalist" in the Kantian, rational transcendentalist variant of foundationalism. He falls, then, into the category of Enlightenment formal interpretation theory; yet his transcendental structures are characteristically tied to empirical-scientific conditions of Romantic contextual interpretation.

The developmental line of Habermas's extraordinary command of the intellectual culture of modernity appears to have proceeded from an early orientation in Kant and German idealism, to the critical theory of the Frankfurt School, to post-Heideggerian hermeneutics, to twentieth-century positivism, to American pragmatism, to Anglo-American language philosophies. Against the closed monologic frame of Gadamer's hermeneutic of tradition, Habermas emerges as a synthesizer in command of the vast sweep of the intellectual culture of modernity, attempting to "bring under one roof" the natural sciences and the human sciences, hermeneutics and critically oriented sciences—contemporary Enlightenment and Romantic structures. In deliberate opposition to Gadamer's rehabilitation of tradition, Habermas announces his commitment to the rehabilitation of the theoretical and practical universal reason of the Enlightenment, which he sees as part of the "uncompleted project of modernity."

The task of any social philosophy may be said to be to reappropriate, interpret, and evaluate the intellectual structures of its time. But Modernity has been presented in this article as incorporating two opposing cognitive-cultural frames that are constitutive of it. Thus contrary to the search for a single criterion, or legitimation for our beliefs about the world and ourselves, the significance of Modernity is that our beliefs cannot be so legitimated. As the carriers of Modernity, we are the producers of two meaningful worlds, Enlightenment and Romantic, each of which says, "Goodbye to all that" in relation to the other.

America was born into Modernity with the sailing of the Great Migration under the dissenting religious banner of the Protestant Era, in quest of religious freedom. By the third quarter of the eighteenth century, American intellectuals such as Jefferson, Madison, and Hamilton inevitably shared the perspective on human nature and politics of the English Enlightenment. The same cluster of beliefs concerning human nature, knowledge, politics, and history that defined the intellectual style of seventeenth- and eighteenth-century England provided the form and content of the meaningful universe of the American Founders. But the British Enlightenment principles had been transferred by the Errand into the Wilderness to the New World of America, to the early experiment of the Puritan theocratic communities, to new experiences in American local self-government, and to physical and then political separation from British centers of commerce and culture as well as to new exceptional economic conditions. Doubts with regard to the functionality of certain of the Enlightenment views to solve problems within the situation of the American reality led the Founders to reconstruct those doctrines, and so began the Americanization of the Enlightenment that came to a climax in the Constitutional Convention of 1787.

The American nation, having been born into a reinterpreted and Americanized Enlightenment Modernity, is an instance of the activity of the interpretational principle as the hallmark of Modernity. And under the necessity of problem-solving in situations in which Old World conceptions came into ineffectual conflict with new American conditions, there arose in practice what was to become, for Peirce and Dewey, the theory of inquiry as the resolution of a problematic situation. And by the 1890s, the critical problematic situation produced by Enlightenment Modernist forces of modernization, linked with the rapid post-Civil War industrialization, urbanization, immigration, and governmental bureaucratization, led to a response in the form of the rise of classical American philosophy.

Classical American philosophy came into being as an intellectual and moral response to a crisis brought on by the effects of Enlightenment modernization upon American life. The response of American philosophy was to assimilate the newly available philosophic views of European Romantic Modernity as an antithetical way of perceiving the problems of Modernity and to integrate the two cultural styles, Enlightenment and Romantic Modernity, into a philosophy for an America whose national, legal, and cultural identity was in Enlightenment truth. Each of the classical American philosophers worked through the conflict and the integration in his own way. Insofar as it is possible to speak of American philosophy, it is to perceive its characteristic form in the attempt to integrate the Enlightenment and Romantic modes of thought. What is characteristic of American philosophy, especially of pragmatism, is its incorporativeness, its attempt to hold together the Enlightenment instrumentalism of science and technology and the Romantic expressiveness of personal and group life. Each of the classical American philosophers was attempting to provide an enriching reconciliation of these cognitive structures of the modern world, which would constitute a unifying public philosophy for America.

After the long monologic linguistic hegemony of logical positivism, analytic philosophy, and hermeneutics, the classical philosophic project of explaining, understanding, and working through the richly complex conflicts of Modernity is now emerging as the reopened frontier of American philosophy.

Is such a project an achievable task for an American philosophy that is concerned with its future course and the challenge of renewal and growth? Reference has been made to the flourishing of Critical Theory by contrast with the current waning of other contemporary philosophic movements. Can Habermas's theory of the relation of knowledge to human interests be of use as a model?

The power of Habermas's *Knowledge and Human Interests* is that it provides a meaningful map of the intellectual world that is integrative (through the theory of interests) and also includes a critical dimension. Most importantly, it attempts to establish a transcendental ground for knowledge, to escape from historicism, traditionalism, and from cultural and linguistic relativisms deriving from the Romantic modes of interpretation theory.[2]

It is noteworthy that Habermas, following the lead of the Frankfurt School,[3] identifies the Enlightenment, but not the Romantic, component of Modernity. Yet the distinction is implicit in his threefold "quasi-transcendental" cognitive interests and the three types of disciplines that incorporate them:

- technical cognitive interest: incorporated in empirical-analytical sciences
- practical cognitive interest: incorporated in historical-hermeneutical sciences
- emancipatory cognitive interest: incorporated in critically oriented sciences

Implicit in the threefold distinction is a dichotomy between the technical interest and the practical and emancipatory. In Habermas's later *Theory of Communicative Action* it is presented as the distinction between purposive-rational action (identifiable as Enlightenment) and communicative-symbolic action (identifiable as Romantic). The Enlightenment and Romantic frames could in principle claim, then, quasi-transcendental cognitive status, because they connote the purposive-rational action of controlling nature and the communicative-symbol action of understanding and criticizing meaning.

It is also noteworthy that Habermas does not identify the distinctive types of interpretation theory: formal, contextual, and textual. Because his focus is upon formal, transcendental interpretation, he underemphasizes both the contextual and textual modes of interpretation as inextricably relativistic. However, contextual interpretation, which is the characteristic mode of American interpretation, embraces text and context. It perceives thought structures in relation to explanatory schema within the context; it thus incorporates explanation and understanding; it provides the critical interpretive mode of psychoanalysis and ideology-critique; it reaches upward to the hermeneutical analysis of texts and downward to the a priority of concepts in experience, which are absolute in their logic yet pragmatic in their origin, which constitute a kind of transcendental ground that is retrievable from the epistemological analyses of Peirce, Lewis, and also Dewey.[4] Contextual interpretation is potentially incorporative of both formal and textual interpretive modes; it is in principle the most expansive and comprehensive of the modes of interpretation.

The structure of the paradigm of contextual interpretation as it pervades American philosophy includes an identifiable subject, self, or community, surviving in its environment by means of reliable, grounded knowledge; the presence of an immediate or long-range "problem" that is productive of stress, conflict, or indecision; the explanatory analysis of the problem, causal and circumstantial; and the experimental and creative engendering of an interpretive structure that yields an understanding of the situation and attempts a successful resolution-reconstruction in practice. It is this mode of philosophizing that is distinctively American and sets it apart from current monologic discourse; it is what is meant by "American" philosophy: the interaction within the paradigm, of self or community, the problem, explanation, understanding. It is in this sense that one can speak of classical American philosophy's incorporativeness, its inclusiveness, its attempt to hold together the Enlightenment instrumentalism of science and technology and the Romantic expressiveness of personal and group life.

Thus the American philosophers whom we regard as classical, in their efforts to integrate Enlightenment nomological explanation with Romantic modes of interpretation, engendered a variety of middle-level and major contextual interpretations: Peirce's community of scientists, Royce's community of interpretation, James's psychological perspectivism, Dewey's problematic situation, Mead's generalized other, and Lewis's conceptualistic pragmatism. All of these interpretive constructs have linkages to knowledge; they are engaged in bringing to bear the existing stock of knowledge and specific developments within the disciplines—the natural and human sciences and the humanities—upon problems of human life.

The following outline of a map of the intellectual world of modernity serves the American mode of philosophy, whose intellectual constructs are linked to funded knowledge. Most specifically, it seeks to serve the linkage of American philosophy with the typology of disciplines and thus indirectly with the realities to which they refer. The map identifies what Alfred Schutz has named the "stock of knowledge," the general features of the available knowledge upon which common sense and research can draw. It identifies the two general types of disciplines deriving from the two modes of Modernity; it includes the levels of theoretical sophistication, from theory-formation to the construction of universalizing disciplinary paradigms; and it identifies the formation of social philosophies as the primary theoretical integrating agency, with the task of appropriating, interpreting, evaluating, and creatively unifying into a constructive theory the cognitive-cultural structures of its time. At the present time of renewed intellectual primacy of theoretical physics and the biological sciences and of the continuing concern for the future of the humanities, the map serves to identify areas for philosophical exploration in the American mode: the nomological-explanatory, the hermeneutical-historical, the critical-normative.

The situating of the problems of contemporary philosophy in the historical frame of Modernity in its Enlightenment and Romantic, its Kantian and Hegelian polarities has a special significance for American philosophy. It is in part a consequence of the archaeology of American thought, in Puritanism and the Enlightenment, which is to say in two great rule-derived and rule-generating, absolutizing traditions, that the Romantic modes of thought have assumed for America the aspects of an intellectual and cultural confrontation. The working through of this conflict, and its social, economic, political, and personal determinations, has been going on since the origin of American philosophy, as has been argued in this writing. It takes on of necessity the form of a global mission for America in relation to the various Romantic politics of the Second and Third World nations.

Perhaps of greater immediate significance for American philosophy is the recognition that the working through of conflicts is finally done by individual human beings. "How is it possible to live as a mechanism of biological drives and still be true to myself?" asks the dissenting psychoanalytical psychiatrist. The Kantian-type answer is that it must be possible because it actually happens: we do live as biological mechanisms seeking to be true to ourselves, but we do so at a cost—intellectual, social, and psychological. This situation of the self in Modernity raises the question of endeavoring to construct again a public philosophy for America as was attempted by the American Founders and the classical American philosophers. From the common stock of knowledge, from the disciplines, the disciplinary and critical theories, and the universalizing paradigms there exists the potentiality of the emergence of a public philosophy in the sense of a shared and ongoing interpretation of the meaning and direction of the common culture. Elements of a public philosophy would include a philosophical anthropology, incorporating conflictual aspects of the self; reflection upon the multiple realities of the Life-World; the pluralism of ethnic and interest groups and the demands of national unity; the Romantic syndrome of domination, alienation, and liberation in American culture and personality; the new horizons of theoretical physics; the competing paradigms of economics and sociology; and the renewal of the religious and aesthetic consciousness. Here is the possibility of a philosophy of reappropriation and creativity. Such a public philosophy would serve deep spiritual needs and would make possible the transformation of America into a Royceian community of memory and of hope. The idea of such a public philosophy would provide a personal redemptive truth for American life and a contribution to the reopened new frontier for American philosophy.

Notes

1. Parts of the present discussion of interpretation theory appear in T. Z. Lavine, "The Interpretive Turn from Kant to Derrida: A Critique," in *History and Anti-History in Philosophy*, ed. V. Tejera and T. Z. Lavine (The Hague: Martinus Nijhoff, 1988).

2. Juergen Habermas, *Knowledge and Human Interests* (Boston: Beacon Press, 1971).

3. Max Horkheimer and Theodore W. Adorno, *Dialectic of Enlightenment* (New York: Seabury Press, 1972; orig. 1944). Horkheimer and Adorno view the Enlightenment as dominating all aspects of society in the form of purposive-instrumental rationality, to the point of betraying the Enlightenment ideals of truth and freedom. Hence the dialectic of Enlightenment, which obscures the dialectic of Modernity.

4. This transcendental ground of knowledge that is implicit in Peirce, Dewey, and Lewis challenges Habermas's two efforts at a transcendental-pragmatic ground of knowledge, that of cognitive interests and of validity claims in the ideal speech situation.

EDITING AMERICAN PHILOSOPHERS

Editing the Classical American Philosophers: Dewey, James, Peirce, Santayana

JO ANN BOYDSTON

We are now, in the last half of the twentieth century, in the midst of a major development in American philosophy: the effort to collect, organize, and publish the collected works of the classical American philosophers. Four such editions are now in progress: the works of John Dewey, William James, Charles Sanders Peirce, and George Santayana. Because these editions are well under way, we will some time early in the next century have access to the full range of American philosophical thought presented in an organized fashion.

A number of institutions, presses, and editors have made long-term commitments to the editorial projects: each undertaking reflects the contributions of these persons and institutions in a slightly different way. Starting in 1961, *The Collected Works of John Dewey* was supported (including publishing costs) by Southern Illinois University at Carbondale with only $20,000 of nonuniversity support, through the ten years necessary to plan the complete edition and to publish the first five-volume series—*The Early Works, 1882–1898*. Along with Southern Illinois University, the University of Virginia, Indiana University at Indianapolis, the University of Tampa, Texas A&M University, the American Council of Learned Societies, various foundations, and private donors have given money, facilities, staff time, outright gifts, and in-kind contributions to make the first stages of these editions more than just a worthy goal. All four are now solid reality.

Above all, the philosophical community and the entire scholarly world owe a tremendous debt to the National Endowment for the Humanities. Since 1972, grants from this federal agency have contributed substantially to the planning of the philosophical editions and to the editorial work on the volumes. Volumes planned and published by the four projects are: first, *The Collected Works of John Dewey*, in thirty-seven volumes plus a thirty-eighth cumulative short-title and subject-index volume; next, *The Works of William James*, soon to be completed in eighteen volumes, with an edition of letters in the planning stage and already funded; next, *The Writings of Charles Sanders Peirce*, with three volumes published, a fourth almost ready, and others in various stages of preparation; and, finally, the *Works of George Santayana*, planned in nineteen volumes, of which the first has been published and the second, approved by the Committee on Scholarly Editions, is now in the proof stage.

The existence and progress of these four editions clearly constitute a frontier in American philosophy that has been conquered in the last twenty-five years. It is a frontier so unparalleled that it almost obscures an even more momentous development that the editions embody. That development is a sweeping transformation in the editing of philosophical texts. Major changes in editing works in the English language began to take definite shape in the 1960s; it is now clear that the philosophical editions have not only participated in and benefitted from what can be labeled a revolution in editing but have also played a major role in that revolution. Fredson Bowers said in 1980, "When the history of scholarship in the twentieth century comes to be written, a case can be made that it will be known as the age of editing."[1] Bowers's own 1963 essay entitled "Textual Criticism" had a direct and powerful impact on the editing revolution. What he wrote there twenty-five years ago seems obvious to us today. He said that "any critic or historian or linguist would prefer to discuss a literary work on the basis of a sound text. It is all too easy to erect an interpretation on the false evidence of a typographical error, as some distinguished critics have demonstrated. For example, F. O. Matthiessen identified 'soiled fish of the sea' as a *discordia concors* that 'could only have sprung from an imagination that had apprehended the terrors . . . of the immaterial deep as well as the physical.'. . . Unfortunately, credit for this metaphysical shock should properly go to the unknown compositor of the reprint consulted, whose memory or fingers slipped while trying to set 'coiled fish of the sea.' Spectacular examples can be multiplied of like unhappy results when critics have relied in vain on corrupt editions for an accurate transmission of an author's words."[2]

But at the time Bowers made those statements, scholarly editing as we know it had not become an identifiable and coherent discipline. In 1963, we at the Dewey Project had been gathering the writings of John Dewey for more than two years to prepare a collected edition of his works; we had not been aware of the kinds of problems that Bowers described. Our biggest task in the beginning was simply determining how much material Dewey's writings involved; as you now know, it is considerable. We had to locate, copy, collect, and give some useful order to that material without a bibliography to guide us. We had to decide whether to arrange Dewey's writings logically or chronologically, a matter greatly influenced by copyright permissions. As the collecting and planning proceeded, difficulties began to surface connected with the numerous reprintings of both articles and books, as well as revisions and variant versions of

Dewey's writings. Our awareness of those problems, however, was still on the level of *selecting* texts to reprint instead of on the level of problems *in* the texts themselves.

Even though Bowers did not mention "philosophers" among those who would prefer to erect interpretations on the basis of a sound text, it was immediately clear to me that his comments applied not just to the Dewey texts but to all philosophical texts. The whole notion of using textual criticism as the basis for editing *any* nineteenth- or twentieth-century works in English was still very much in its infancy: only one collected edition had actually formulated textual principles and procedures and published a volume. That was *The Scarlet Letter* in *The Centenary Edition of the Works of Nathaniel Hawthorne*.[3] Literary scholars had earlier, in the 1950s, started a movement to support collected editions of the major American literary figures: Cooper, Crane, Emerson, Hawthorne, Howells, Irving, Melville, Simms, Thoreau, Mark Twain, and Walt Whitman. In 1963, the Modern Language Association established the Center for Editions of American Authors (now the Committee on Scholarly Editions) to find funding for those editions and to set editorial standards and principles to guide their development. The CEAA guidelines were first published in 1967; since then, more than 265 volumes have been published with the "Approved Edition" emblem, signifying that the volumes have met the committee's standards.

Publication of the CEAA guidelines and standards marked the beginning of the editing revolution. In this revolution, Fredson Bowers has played the pivotal role: first, his writings laid both the theoretical and practical groundwork for modern editorial practice; second, he has been directly involved in editing not only a number of literary editions but also the editions of the classical American philosophers. Starting in 1965, he served as consultant to me on the Dewey edition; he is the textual editor of *The Works of William James* and will continue in that role for the James letters; and I, in turn, have worked from the outset with both the Peirce and Santayana editions.

All volumes published in the Dewey, James, Peirce, and Santayana editions carry the CSE emblem. These include, so far, thirty-four volumes in *The Collected Works of John Dewey* and a volume of Dewey's poems; seventeen volumes in the James edition; three in the Peirce; and one in the Santayana.

The CSE guidelines that the philosophical editions follow are, in effect, a distilled reflection of the major developments in twentieth-century editing.[4] Therefore, the simplest and most productive way to describe what has happened in editing American philosophy is to examine the way those standards are put into practice in volumes of philosophical writings.

Physically, volumes of philosophical works with the CSE emblem look different from volumes edited in the traditional way. In addition to the philosophical texts, the volumes always include a substantial amount of back matter, or apparatus, where the results of the painstaking editorial work behind each volume are recorded. Customarily, the historical and textual records are discreetly tucked away in apparatus sections at the back of the book, instead of in intrusive footnotes or annotations or on divided text pages. Although the apparatus is the most indispensable and enduring part of each CSE volume, it probably constitutes the least understood aspect of modern editorial practice.

The kinds of information that appear in the apparatus and the way that information is organized and presented have now become recognizably standardized.[5] The Committee on Scholarly Editions requires that the editor "describe the history of the text or texts, describe or report the various authoritative forms of the text, demonstrate why the particular copy text has been chosen, and defend the rationale for any emendation of that copy text." Therefore, in a prose section (not a table), every CSE volume explains the history of the text and its variant forms, shows which versions are authoritative, and describes, in general terms, what changes have been made in the course of editing the text. In the Dewey edition, we discuss the genesis, transmission, and publishing history of the text in a textual commentary; in other editions, some of this information appears in the introduction as well as in a textual commentary or note on the texts. CSE-approved texts are "purified" by expunging errors that may have occurred in publishing or in reprinting. The texts are also made to conform as nearly as possible to the author's own intention for that text, not only by correcting errors but by restoring censored or omitted parts and by incorporating the author's later revisions. Editors of literary works correct errors, of course, as in Bowers's example of the "coiled/soiled fish of the sea." But a single letter variant in a philosophical text is more critical and clearly of a different order of importance than it is in a so-called literary text. In the Dewey texts, a variant of only one letter—wrong, omitted, or transposed—often makes a different word, an easily overlooked word, that completely changes Dewey's intended philosophical meaning. Think for a moment about the implications of substituting in Dewey's texts the word "causal" for "casual," and the reverse, "casual" for "causal." Ponder if you will the difference between "idea" and "ideal," or between "word" and "world," or, in a discussion of James's *Psychology*, between "psychical blindness" and "physical blindness."

At the next level of textual complexity, emendations must be made to correct outright errors—once again, errors with real philosophical significance—that may have been made by a printer. A highly selective list of major corrections from *The Collected Works of John Dewey* can serve to illustrate this point.

    1. From "Knowledge as Idealization," *Mind* 12 (1887): "We have complaints that the Empirical School has neglected the native relating capacity of the mind." *Corrected from*: "The Empirical School has neglected the native reading capacity of the mind."[6]

    2. From "Ethics and Politics," *University Record* 3 (1894): "An equal emphasis upon securing such conditions of action as will bring personal insight and choice." *Corrected from*: "personal and choice insight."[7]

3. From "The Relation of Philosophy to Theology," *Monthly Bulletin of the Students' Christian Association* (University of Michigan) 16 (1893): "Atonement is the coming to consciousness of what has always been here,—man's true relation with God. It is nothing but a change in consciousness." *Corrected from*: "It is nothing but a change in conscientiousness."[8]

4. From "Reconstruction," *Monthly Bulletin of the Students' Christian Association* (University of Michigan) 15 (1894): "Now we see the universe as one all-comprehensive, interrelated scene of limitless life and motion." *Corrected from*: "one all-comprehensive unrelated scene of limitless life and motion."[9]

5. From "Evolution and Ethics," *Monist* 8 (1898): "What are courage, persistence, patience, enterprise, initiative, but forms of the self-assertion of those impulses which make up the life process?" *Corrected from*: "persistence, patience, enterprise, initiation."[10]

6. From *Art as Experience* (New York: Minton, Balch, 1934), "In short, the reciprocal interpenetration of parts and whole." *Corrected from*: "the reciprocal interpretation of parts and whole."[11]

7. From *Quest for Certainty* (New York: Minton, Balch, 1929), "What *is*, in the full and pregnant sense of the word, is always, eternally." *Corrected from*: "the full and pregnant sense of the world."[12]

8. From "Nature and Reason in Law," *International Journal of Ethics* 25 (1914), "Nature also means . . . the present state of things so far as that is connected with the antecedent condition by causal laws." *Corrected from*: "connected . . . by casual laws."[13]

9. From *Democracy and Education*, "But these 'minds' are the organized habits of intelligent response which they have previously acquired." *Corrected from*: "which they have previously required."[14]

10. From the 1932 *Ethics* (New York: Henry Holt and Co., 1932), "It is absurd to object to a national plan for mitigating suffering and injustice on the ground that it was first tried in Europe." *Corrected from*: "a rational plan."[15]

Not only does the Committee on Scholarly Editions insist that every *word* in a text be examined, that errors be corrected, and that an attempt be made to recover the author's intentions for that text, it also requires that variants in punctuation, capitalization, spelling, and italics be accorded equally careful treatment. Unfortunately, many editors continue to believe that these features of a text are unimportant and that they can safely be ignored or, in the course of editing, altered with impunity. As space does not permit detailed discussion of this aspect of editing, here are only four examples from *The Collected Works of John Dewey* to emphasize that punctuation often makes a substantive difference.

11. From Dewey's article "Moral Philosophy," in *Johnson's Universal Cyclopedia*, "Instead. . . . of continuing the parallelism between the inner and the outer (that is, the moral motive and political structure). . ." *Corrected from*: "the

moral, motive, and political structure."[16]

12. In Dewey's 1889 article on George Sylvester Morris, " . . . led Professor Morris to write in the following words, of Plato." *Corrected from*: ". . . led Professor Morris to write in the following words of Plato."[17]

13. In Dewey's first book, *Psychology* (all twenty-six printings), "Sounds vary (1) in intensity; (2) in pitch; (3) in tone-color, or quality." *Corrected from*: "(3) in tone, color, or quality."[18]

14. From *Quest for Certainty*, "There is a divisive pride of the learned, as well as of family, wealth and power." *Corrected from*: "family wealth and power."[19]

As a companion exercise to correcting and purifying texts, the CSE stipulates that the editor must *record* all emendations, *discuss* problematical readings, and *report* variant readings from all texts that have authority. This information is ordinarily arranged in two tables: the list of emendations and the historical collation. The emendations that the editor has made and the source of those changes are important for several reasons: careful users of the text may want to see whether they agree with the editorial choices, and their agreement or disagreement may be based on the source of the change; notes explain reasons for making changes that might seem problematical or for not making changes that might have been expected.

The list of variants in all printings of the work—called a historical collation—is equally important because it constitutes an invaluable historical record of the development of the text. Here the story of the developing text is told through the author's revisions and printer's intervention in all different versions of the text. Here are listed all the ways the author polished and changed the text throughout its history. The timing of revisions is particularly significant in studying the philosopher's thought; the historical collation is the record of *how* Dewey revised his own text as well as *when*—either continuously over a period of time or in a swoop after an intervening period of years.

These records are also an invaluable resource for the study of works that have an underlying typescript or manuscript. For instance, in the John Dewey Papers are the complete typescripts for two of Dewey's major works, *Logic: The Theory of Inquiry* (New York: Henry Holt and Co., 1938)[20] and *Theory of Valuation, International Encyclopedia of Unified Science*, vol. 2 (Chicago: University of Chicago Press, 1939).[21] Many of Dewey's own typescripts also exist and have been studied and recorded; in these two cases, however, we have only the version prepared by a professional typist and corrected by Dewey. The special significance of these typescripts is that both came to the Center for Dewey Studies from Sidney Hook, whose corrections and revisions are identifiable. The apparatus of volumes 12 and 13 of the *Later Works* makes clear which readings in the final printed version were Dewey's and which were Hook's, accepted by Dewey. The table of author's alterations for each typescript records the details of Dewey's creative process right up through correction of final proofs.

Another section of the apparatus identifies the sources of all of Dewey's quotations and shows where he varied from the original. In the text, some of Dewey's misquotations must be allowed to stand because he bases an argument on his version of the quotation. But if it is clear that the printer has made a mistake in the quotation, that error is corrected in the text. A few representative examples of such corrections follow.

> 15. In *Quest for Certainty*, quoting Cardinal Newman: "The Church holds that it were better for sun and moon to drop from heaven, for the earth to fail, . . ." *Corrected from*: "for the earth to fall."[22]
>
> 16. A striking example of Dewey's own misquotation (from Alexander Bain) that makes in print exactly the opposite point from the one he intended is this: "The child's susceptibility to pleasure and pain is made use of to bring about . . . obedience, and a mental association is rapidly formed between disobedience and apprehended pain." *Corrected from*: "a mental association . . . between his obedience and apprehended pain." This problem occurred twice in Dewey's writings: first in the 1894 *Study of Ethics* (Ann Arbor: Register Publishing Co., 1894)[23] and again in the 1908 *Ethics* (New York: Henry Holt and Co., 1908).[24]
>
> 17. Quoting Frederick Barry in *Quest for Certainty*: " . . . by the art of designing, guided by an aesthetic appreciation of symmetrical figures." *Corrected from*: "guided by an aesthetic application of symmetrical figures."[25]
>
> 18. In *Art as Experience*, quoting Robert Browning: ". . . discrepancies between the attributes of the poet's soul, occasioning a want of correspondency between his work and the verities of nature—" *Corrected from*: "the varieties of nature."[26]
>
> 19. From Dewey's "Review of George Santayana, *The Life of Reason*," *Educational Review* 34 (1907), "We exist through form, and the love of form is our whole real inspiration." *Corrected from*: "our whole real aspiration."[27]
>
> 20. In his essay entitled "The Applicability of Logic to Existence," *Journal of Philosophy* 27 (27 March 1930): 174–79, in which he quotes from Ernest Nagel's article "Can Logic Be Divorced from Ontology?" Dewey says, " 'Fix one context.' " On the same page, not quoting from Nagel, "this work of reflection in fixing context." *Corrected from*: "content," in both cases.[28]

Thorough searching to locate, compare, and verify quotations is not a requirement of the Committee on Scholarly Editions; it is, however, demanded by conscientious editing, as is the identification of the exact printing and edition of the references an author used. Variants between Dewey's direct quotations and their sources are listed in each volume and keyed to the complete listing of all his references, even quotations that are next to impossible to locate, such as "I read recently in the *New York Times* that . . ."

Another section of the apparatus that appears in the Dewey volumes—starting with *Democracy and Education*—is the pagination key to the original printings of books. This makes it easy for scholars to refer to the secondary literature that has page citations to original printings of Dewey's works.

The final CSE requirement—that the editor must meticulously proofread every state of the physical production of a text and its apparatus—might seem gratuitous. Anybody who has published knows that this stage of the publishing process is fraught with peril, but in these editions, especially in the production of the textual records, it is even more frightening. To prevent endangering all the previous editorial work, CSE editors schedule at least three *oral* readings of proof: against copy-text, against printer's copy, and against every stage of corrected proof. All apparatus must be page-keyed to the final printed version at the time of proofreading, so that just mechanically the proofreading is enormously time-consuming. But it can also be rewarding and reassuring. Two examples follow: one we caught in proof and one the University of Chicago Press did not.

21. "James, William (1842–1910), was JR's closet friend."[29]
22. "Pubic School 45 of the Indianapolis school system is trying . . ."[30]

When we committed ourselves to the use of the techniques of modern textual criticism in editing the works of John Dewey, we were concerned about philosophers' reception of this innovative approach. It turned out that the philosophical community was ready, as James Collins said in his 1968 *The Modern Schoolman*, "for at last achieving scholarly control over the text and the developing thought of Dewey," and for the "responsible approach . . . which will finally release us from the tyranny of house style, printers' flourish, and the many other variations which have made the study of this period so uncertain."[31]

The value and importance of the editions of the classical American philosophers are now widely recognized; as the Dewey edition and the James edition near completion, the texts are increasingly used and appreciated. It is clear that publication of *The Collected Works of John Dewey*, of *The Works of William James*, and, in time, of *The Writings of Charles Sanders Peirce* and *The Works of George Santayana* represents an American philosophical frontier of great magnitude. Now that we have in effect conquered that frontier, we must look ahead to the next goal. That goal should be a more intensive, critical, and sophisticated study of our own American philosophers, putting to best use the almost unlimited resources being created in the volumes of Dewey, James, Peirce, and Santayana. The apparatus sections of these volumes are the most expensive parts to prepare and publish. Such a rich research lode is worth the investment for present and future generations of scholars only if it is fully used and fully exploited in philosophical analysis and interpretation. This is the *next* frontier to be explored in American philosophy.

Notes

1. Fredson Bowers, "Editing a Philosopher: The Works of William James," *Analytical and Enumerative Bibliography* 4 (1980): 3.
2. Fredson Bowers, "Textual Criticism," *The Aims and Methods of Scholarship in Modern Languages and Literatures*, ed. James Thorpe (New York: Modern Language Association, 1963; rev. ed. 1970), p. 23.
3. Nathaniel Hawthorne, *The Centenary Edition of the Works of Nathaniel Hawthorne*, 1962.
4. Committee on Scholarly Editions, "Introductory Statement," *Publications of the Modern Language Association* 92 (1977): 583–97 (periodically republished with minor changes). The committee's most recent statement is "The Committee on Scholarly Editions: Aims and Policies," *Publications of the Modern Language Association* 100 (1985):444–47. It appeared again, slightly altered, in September 1988.
5. See G. Thomas Tanselle, "Some Principles for Editorial Apparatus," *Studies in Bibliography* 25 (1972): 41–88.
6. John Dewey, *The Collected Works of John Dewey: The Early Works, 1882–1898*, 5 vols., ed. Jo Ann Boydston (Carbondale and Edwardsville: Southern Illinois University Press, 1967–72), vol. 1, p. 190. Hereinafter this work will be cited as *EW* followed by a volume and page number.
7. *EW* 4:372–73.
8. *EW* 4:367.
9. *EW* 4:102.
10. *EW* 5:43.
11. John Dewey, *The Collected Works of John Dewey: The Later Works, 1925–1953*, 17 vols., ed. Jo Ann Boydston (Carbondale and Edwardsville: Southern Illinois University Press, 1981–88), vol. 10, p. 321. Hereinafter this work will be cited as *LW* followed by a volume and page number.
12. *LW* 4:116.
13. John Dewey, *The Collected Works of John Dewey: The Middle Works, 1899–1924*, 15 vols., ed. Jo Ann Boydston (Carbondale and Edwardsville: Southern Illinois University Press, 1976–83), vol. 7, p. 57. Hereinafter this work will be cited as *MW* followed by a volume and page number.
14. *MW* 9:38.
15. *LW* 7:433.
16. *EW* 4:146.
17. *EW* 3:8.
18. *EW* 2:60.
19. *LW* 4:245.
20. *LW* 12.
21. *LW* 13: 189–252.
22. *LW* 4:42.
23. *EW* 4:330.
24. *MW* 5:322.
25. *LW* 4:122.
26. *LW* 10:327.
27. *MW* 4:234.
28. *LW* 5:205. See also Ernest Nagel, "Can Logic Be Divorced from Ontology?" *Journal of Philosophy* 26 (19 December 1929):705–12.

29. *The Letters of Josiah Royce*, ed. John Clendenning (Chicago: University of Chicago Press, 1970), addressees' biographical information, p. 657.

30. John and Evelyn Dewey, *Schools of To-Morrow* (New York: E. P. Dutton & Co., 1915); *MW* 8:205–8.404. The error appeared in a proof for *MW* 8:255.

31. James Collins, *The Modern Schoolman* 46 (1968): 60.

Editing Peirce

CHRISTIAN J. W. KLOESEL

"It is very true that this great man, whose utterances still have their lessons for the world, with wholesome influences for all plastic minds, should be studied in a complete, correct, and critical edition."

If I told you what I have spent much of my time doing during the last several weeks, you might get a skewed view of what editing Peirce means. I have been writing and editing (not Peirce, but) our next renewal application to the National Endowment for the Humanities (and have tried to persuade the National Science Foundation once again to share the burden), for editing Peirce is—like editing James, Dewey, and Santayana—an expensive enterprise. Though the NEH contributes but 20 to 25 percent of our total project costs, it could fairly be said that, without the NEH, editing Peirce (in Indianapolis) might be different from what it has been and is, and what it is likely to be during the next few years.

I should have spoken 5½ years ago at the eighteenth annual conference on editorial problems at the University of Toronto entitled "Editing Polymaths": that "awkward class of great writers," according to the conference proceedings, "whose works are not restricted to one field."[1] But as it turned out, Peirce was not on the program. I am pleased to make up for the omission here in College Station, though I will not say much about how editing Peirce means—and is made difficult by the fact that we are—"editing a polymath."

I will also say little about Peirce the man and thinker. Though few of us have read the one book Peirce published during his lifetime, *Photometric Researches*,[2] we are all familiar with the *Collected Papers*,[3] Peirce's *Contributions to "The Nation*,"[4] *The New Elements of Mathematics*,[5] his *Complete Published Works*,[6] *Historical Perspectives on Peirce's Logic of Science*,[7] and the two volumes of his letters to Lady Welby.[8] Because the editor, or one of the editors, of each of these editions of Peircean writings is amongst us, I wonder if this should be a session on "Editing Peirce through the Ages." What I am trying to say, of course, is that the topic is nothing new, even if in Indianapolis we do things somewhat differently from the way they have been done elsewhere.

A word about Peirce's writings and about what he published and did not succeed in publishing or perhaps never intended to publish. The irritation of their doubt relieved by the title of the eight-volume *Collected Papers*, many people believe that Peirce did not produce much during his lifetime. They also believe that, after his more than thirty years in the United States Coast and Geodetic Survey, he lived by giving occasional lectures, by writing book reviews, by pursuing wild-eyed schemes for inventions, and by pure charity. There is some truth in all but the first belief. Peirce produced an enormous amount of material, though he never became the gentleman-writer-philosopher that might have been. He did everything I just mentioned—and became, according to Charles Hartshorne, the American Leibniz,[9] and, according to Ernest Nagel, "the most original, versatile, and comprehensive philosophical mind this country has yet produced."[10]

Peirce published some ten thousand pages (or twenty volumes of five hundred pages each) during his lifetime, consisting of his one book, several hundred book reviews, hundreds of dictionary definitions, numerous technical and scientific reports, reports on meetings and conferences, and the scores of epistemological and metaphysical as well as logical and pragmatic articles we all know. What is less well known is that he left behind at his death enough unpublished manuscripts to fill another eighty or ninety volumes (excluding his correspondence). Obviously, not all of these deserve publication, and many are merely of historical or biographical interest, but a truly representative edition of Peirce's writings—including his work in logic and philosophy, in mathematics, history, and psychology, and in the various hard or special sciences (I might mention that Carolyn Eisele has recently reminded us again that "in the analysis of any component of the thought of C. S. Peirce, it is well to keep constantly in mind the fact of his close association with living and developing science,"[11] and she has admonished us not to forget the importance of his mathematics.)—should consist of at least sixty volumes. Unfortunately, none of us will live long enough, nor is there money enough, to prepare such an edition. We in Indianapolis are trying to meet the demand half way, in thirty volumes.

Another word, now, about Peirce the editor and author familiar with the world of editing and publishing. Peirce knew of copyists, compositors, editors, and publishers, and he either complained about them or simply saw them as parts of the whole process. There are instructions to copyists, editors, and printers in a number of manuscripts, as in MS. 1043, a five-page untitled note on chemical valency, at the beginning of which we read, "The five pages separately numbered in red to be printed in small type at the end of the article." (Although Richard Robin indicates that the note belongs with MSS. 1041–42,[12] it instead completes a now reassembled [as MS. 282a] excellent twenty-five-page version of the 1905 essay on "The Basis of Pragmaticism," consisting of one loose [title] page from MS. 280, nineteen pages from MS. 908, and the note from MS. 1043.) In a letter dated 7 November 1883 to Superintendent Hilgard of the Coast Survey, Peirce explains missing brackets in a galley proof: "The square brackets could not be made on the type-writer, and I had intended to insert them in the copy for the press";[13] apparently, he forgot to do so. Alas, we generally know little about Peirce's attention to and care with the correcting and editing of page or galley proofs, for few are extant. There is not very much in the correspondence, either.

In at least one place, in an earlier letter to the Coast Survey Office dated 23 October 1873, Peirce leads us to believe that he paid little attention to such matters. Commenting upon an advance printed copy of "On the Theory of Errors of Observation,"[14] he writes, "The punctuation has had no attention in the proof reading. Had I supposed it would not have, I would have taken pains to have it right in the MS. But it has never been my habit to do that as proof-readers attend to it."[15] But Peirce is not telling the truth. Given usual Coast Survey procedures—reports were edited by the superintendent and assistants, copied by a copyist, and then sent to the printing office—we can only assume that Peirce was less careful with those reports than he was with manuscripts sent elsewhere.

He was always careful with his published articles. He usually labeled at least one offprint "Working Copy" and made frequent annotations and corrections. So seriously did Peirce take his published work that, when he distributed offprints of his 1880 memoir "On the Algebra of Logic,"[16] he sent along a printed letter. Dated 15 September 1880 and addressed to "Dear Sir" (though he certainly gave one to Christine Ladd-Franklin as well), the letter contains notes and corrections to twelve pages of the published article, which should "be inserted before reading the article."[17]

Peirce shows his understanding of the editing-publishing process very clearly in "An Apology for Modern English," a manuscript written in 1899.

> A compositor is paid so much for the thousand ems,—a meagre sum for which he is not only obliged to set up the type, but also to correct what is set up, until the proof-reader declares that it "conforms to the copy." Further corrections are time-work, and a compositor would be disgraced who should not take it very leisurely; so that these corrections become mighty expensive. They are commonly paid for by the publisher; but if, as not seldom happens, they triple and quadruple the cost of composition, it is the author who has to pay. I have said that the compositor has to make his matter "conform to the copy." But he could not, at the rate he is paid, take note of just how the author has spelled each word. Nor is this desirable; for the author, as like as not, is but a so-so speller. The compositor reads a clause, and then proceeds to set it up, spelling each word correctly, ac-

cording to the standard adopted by that printing office. The author, if he is wise, will quietly submit; for otherwise he would have a fight on his hands, with a bill for time-work in case he were to carry his point.[18]

"The Editor's Manual," a ninety-two-page manuscript written in 1900, is of little use, unfortunately, in editing Peirce, for it deals primarily with spelling, whose sole object, Peirce says, "is to render words recognizable."[19] The subject matter is similar in "Jottings on Punctuation," written a year earlier. After discussing the psychological principles underlying such punctuation as comma, period, colon, and semicolon, Peirce suggests that "we ought to make it a rule that the burden shall lie upon every mark of punctuation of proving its possible utility."[20] And in an untitled manuscript written in 1906, he says (with little conviction): "Let every man make his own selection for the very purpose of disproving the popular prejudice that all educated people spell one way."[21]

Peirce shows greater conviction, both positively and negatively, in his reviews of the work of other authors and editors. He repeats A. C. Fraser's plea for a new edition of Locke's works, and says, as I do in the opening epigraph, "It is very true that this great man [Locke], whose utterances still have their lessons for the world, with wholesome influences for all plastic minds, should be studied in a complete, correct, and critical edition."[22] In a review of William Beckford's gothic novel *Vathek*, Peirce gives a recipe for an immortal book: "Write it at one sitting in 3 days and 2 nights; devote 3½ years to improving it, and then publish it as near as possible as it originally was."[23] "Unhappily," he says of Kamensky's translation of Mendeleev's *Principles of Chemistry*, "it is impossible to praise the work of the editor. Errors of every description abound."[24] We catch a touch of sardonic humor in yet another review: "Just one year after the appearance of Dr. Frank Hall Thorp's *Outlines of Industrial Chemistry* comes a new and revised edition. If the determination is to revise this publication yearly, it will undoubtedly gain vastly in importance."[25] Of Titchener's translation of Wundt's *Principles of Physiological Psychology*, Peirce claims that "unerring judgment has been exercised in the editing. . . . The author's slips," he goes on to say, "if not too numerous, have to be corrected, with or without mention, according to circumstances."[26] In the most interesting review of all, especially for those who have learned their substantives and accidentals, a review of Fraser's 1901 edition of *The Works of Berkeley*, we read: "Whether for an ordinary reader of philosophy, this edition or that in Bohn's 'Philosophical Library' is to be preferred is a delicate question. The text of either [that is, the substantives] is excellent, although neither, we are sorry to say, respects Berkeley's punctuation [that is, the accidentals], which is a part of his style."[27]

But to get back to editing Peirce. In the second lecture on pragmatism given at Harvard in April 1903, Peirce remarked: "But I must tell you that all that you can find in print of my work on logic are simply scattered outcroppings here and there of a rich vein which remains unpublished. Most of it I suppose has been written down; but no human being could ever put together the fragments. I could not myself do so."[28] I suppose that the statement applies to Peirce's extralogical writings as well, though he probably would not therefore have called the Peirce Edition Project staff superhuman. But this is what editing Peirce means: collect the scattered outcroppings, discover the rich vein, put together the fragments, and publish what there is time and space to publish—and edit and publish it according to the textual standards of the MLA's Committee on Scholarly Editions, for, without them, there will be no support from the NEH. Without them, there will be no critical, that is authentic and reliable, edition.

Our kind of editing Peirce began with Manley Thompson's *Pragmatic Philosophy of C. S. Peirce* in 1953[29] and Murray Murphey's *Development of Peirce's Philosophy* in 1961.[30] These works showed that the topical arrangement of the *Collected Papers* might not be the best way to approach Peirce; that a chronological study, a study of the development of Peirce's thought, might also be of value; that to understand Peirce, it might be important to know not only *what* he said but *when* he said it. Discussions of a new edition began not long after.

But chronology was not all. Murphey had hinted at the importance of Peirce's mathematical writings, and others began to insist upon the importance of his work in the natural and social sciences, in experimental psychology, and in philology. Although the (too ambitiously named) *Collected Papers* omits nearly all of Peirce's mathematical and scientific writings and many of his philosophical, philological, logical, and historical papers, it has rightly set our scholarly standard. The other editions I have mentioned are similarly valuable. Yet none conveys a true sense of the breadth of Peirce's wide-ranging activities or his contributions to a great variety of disciplines, and only one or two is guided by the belief that his writings are, as he said of Plato's, "worthy of being viewed as the record of the entire development of thought of a great thinker."[31]

Discussions of a new edition began in earnest in October, 1973, at a conference in Milford, Pennsylvania, where Max Fisch presented "A Plan for a New Edition."[32] He proposed three principal editorial policies: (1) the new edition should be chronological (instead of topical); (2) it should distinguish among four kinds of writings (those published in Peirce's name, those published anonymously or pseudonymously, those not published but intended to be or close to publication, and those not published or intended to be published in anything like the form in which we have them); and (3) it should keep series of papers or lectures intact, uninterrupted by other papers written or published between the first and last of the series. (As examples of such interruption, we may consider the six "Illustrations of the Logic of Science" as these appear in the *Collected Papers*.)[33] Fisch's plan also had three prerequisites: (1) the editor of the new edition should have an electroprint copy of all unpublished papers worthy to be considered for publication; (2) the Harvard Peirce Papers must be reorganized (and completed, if possible); and (3) the dates of composition of the manuscripts must be determined.

I was not at the Milford conference, but I see several flaws in the plan. It assumes that all the relevant Peirce Papers are found at Harvard, while, during the last several years, we have found thousands of manuscript pages and scores of letters in the most diverse places, including the National Archives, the New York Public Library, and the libraries of Princeton, Columbia, Johns Hopkins, and Southern Illinois universities. It further assumes that reorganizing and dating the manuscripts is something to be accomplished in a matter of months. Finally, and perhaps most importantly, the plan's editorial principles do not address the question of how the texts are to be edited. I presume that editing Peirce was assumed to remain essentially what it had been in the *Collected Papers* and what it is in several of the other editions I have mentioned. That editorial/textual policy is summarized in one sentence in the preface to the *Collected Papers*: "Whenever possible Peirce's punctuation and spelling have been retained."[34] Jo Ann Boydston has shown that today's editorial/textual policies are more elaborate and must be more critical, and Fredson Bowers has admonished us that "no reader should be asked to accept anything in the text on trust. In his introductions and apparatus the editor should place all his textual cards on the table—face up."[35] That is what editing Peirce means in Indianapolis, and that is why we have been able to produce, for the first time, authentic and reliable texts based on all the available documents and evidence. That is why our volumes carry the CSE seal of approval.

This is not a textual conference, though it is obviously a textual session. Still, I shall not vex you with such matters as copy-text and compositorial interference, substantives and accidentals, stemmatics and historical collations, diplomatic and genetic transcriptions, and authorial intentions and superseded authorial intention in pre-copy-text forms. But you should keep in mind the two major kinds of modern editions, the documentary and the critical. Don Cook defines them in the most recent issue of *Humanities*, the quarterly journal of the NEH. The documentary edition makes archival materials available to scholars by presenting accurate transcriptions, by explaining obscure references and annotations suggesting the context and significance of the documents, and by providing indexes and finding lists to guide the user through the volumes and the archives from which the documents are selected. The critical edition, on the other hand, aims to present a text that reflects the intention of the author at a chosen moment, even if there is no single extant document that perfectly embodies the text as the author wanted to see it in print. "The established text," Cook concludes, "rests on the editor's conscientious interpretation of all the discoverable evidence, supported by cogent argument. That, and only that, is what critical edition means."[36] We should also keep in mind what Cook says in another place, namely that a critical edition is merely a tool for further scholarship, "a tool designed by editors for use by non-editors."[37] Our *Writings* is such a tool: it is addressed not to textual editors but to scholars working in philosophy and logic, in mathematics and the sciences, and in semiotics and various other disciplines to which Peirce contributed. And though it is true that we give some preference to Peirce's more philosophical writings in logic and metaphysics, we always aim at representing the full range of his work and, by presenting these works in a chronological order, at encouraging and enabling the reader to trace the development of his thought.

Most of you have seen at least one of the three volumes of our *Writings* so far published. You therefore know that, following the text, there are editorial notes (explanatory notes, beginning with volume 4), a bibliography of Peirce's references, a chronological list of everything Peirce wrote and published during the years covered by the given volume, and a substantial textual apparatus consisting of an essay on editorial method, emendations, textual notes, historical collations, a list of word divisions, and a detailed index. Because this is not a textual conference, I propose that, if you wish to learn more about some of the specific textual problems we have encountered, you check the apparatus in our volumes. I will only mention that, in one way, our textual problems are not nearly as diverse and expansive as those encountered in the Dewey, James, and Santayana editions. There are three reasons: (1) few of Peirce's articles were published more than once, (2) there are very few fair-copy manuscripts of his published articles and reports, and (3) because of his particular working method, we often find in his writings discrete versions instead of collatable drafts of unpublished essays on a given topic. We have few difficulties with selecting copy-text, regularizations (like adding missing periods at the end of sentences or italicizing mathematical variables) are a matter of course, and even the matter of authorial intention generally becomes difficult only when Peirce did not complete his revisions. Why, then, you might ask—and some of you have asked—is the fourth volume of *Writings* still not in print? When will the last be published? By the end of the century, we hope (or shortly after); or, if that gives us more time, by the end of the millennium.

I will now spend the last two minutes of my presentation on the two or three reasons that make editing Peirce so slow and laborious a process. I do not wish to bore you with computers but will only say that both Wang and IBM failed Peirce's mathematics and science, as well as some of the logical symbols he invented. The Apple Macintosh Plus and SE have just passed the test, and, beginning with volume 5, all our work will be done on the computer. Our typesetting and proofreading should be easier and less time-consuming. What we still need, however, is all of Peirce in databases: of our edition and of his publications, manuscripts, and letters—and of Max Fisch, that is, the enormous amount of materials he has gathered during the last several decades, without which there might have been no editing Peirce in Indianapolis.

The most difficult, but also most important, part of editing Peirce is the reorganization and dating of Peirce's manuscripts, both those at Harvard and at other places. A number of greater men than we saw, or heard about, the Harvard Peirce Papers and despaired at the prospect. That list of men includes Royce,

Santayana, Morris Cohen, and C. I. Lewis (and, as you recall, Peirce himself). I could dismay you (but that would be another talk) with the history of the papers at Harvard (and at the Coast Survey offices in Washington), which includes "giveaways" of manuscripts as mementos or as scratch paper during paper shortages. It is these giveaways that in part explain the great disorganization of, and some of the gaps in, the papers.

In any case, with what we have, mostly in photocopies, from Harvard and the other places mentioned earlier (and still others I haven't mentioned), we have some one hundred thousand manuscript pages, only about a third of which are dated by Peirce. We have been able to complete many a manuscript, like MS. 282a described earlier (with pages from MSS. 280, 908, and 1043), and we have tentatively dated all that we have. The final dating, however—that is, the fine-tuning—can only be done when we actively and intensively work in the period for each successive volume. Knowing the dates of composition of manuscripts is obviously important for a chronological edition. It is especially important in Peirce's case, because some of his manuscripts involve questions of priority: he made fundamental discoveries in geodesy, in topology, and in several theorems and methods of formal logic. The dating process, I am sorry to say, is thus likely to go on until the publication of our final volume.

But my time is up—and I haven't even mentioned our selection process. Because we are editing a polymath and publishing somewhat less than half of what might be published, the process of deciding what should be included in each volume is (even with the assistance of members of our Advisory Board and numerous contributing editors) laborious and slow. In any case, editing Peirce is seventy-three years old now. If I must close with at least one reference to the theme of this conference, I should say that each volume published in previous editions has represented a new frontier and that the last and greatest is now being conquered in Indianapolis, in our own new edition—and, because Peirce's "utterances still have their lessons for the world, with wholesome influences for all plastic minds, he should be studied in a complete (or half-complete), correct, and critical edition."

Notes

1. Heather Joanna Jackson, ed., *Editing Polymaths: Erasmus to Russell*. Papers given at the Eighteenth Annual Conference on Editorial Problems, University of Toronto, November 5–6, 1982 (Toronto: The Committee for the Conference on Editorial Problems, 1983), p. 11.

2. This work was originally published in 1878 and is on the brightness of the stars in, and on the form of, our Milky Way. See Christian J. W. Kloesel et al., *Writings of Charles S. Peirce: A Chronological Edition*, 3 of 30 volumes published (Bloomington: Indiana University Press, 1982, 1984, 1986), vol. 3, pp. 382–493. Hereafter cited as *W* followed by volume and page numbers.

Editing Peirce 61

3. Charles Hartshorne, Paul Weiss, and Arthur Burks, ed., *Collected Papers of Charles Sanders Peirce*, 8 volumes (Cambridge, Mass.: Harvard University Press, 1931–58). Hereafter cited as *CP* followed by volume and page numbers.

4. Kenneth Laine Ketner and James Edward Cook, comp., *Charles Sanders Peirce: Contributions to "The Nation,"* 4 parts (Lubbock: Texas Tech University Press, 1975–88). Hereafter cited as *C* followed by part and page numbers.

5. Carolyn Eisele, ed., *The New Elements of Mathematics, by Charles S. Peirce*, 4 volumes (The Hague: Mouton, 1976).

6. These are published in microfiche.

7. Carolyn Eisele, ed., *Historical Perspectives on Peirce's Logic of Science: A History of Science*, 2 vols. (Berlin: Mouton, 1985).

8. Irwin C. Lieb, ed., *Charles S. Peirce's Letters to Lady Welby*, 2 vols. (New Haven, Conn.: Whitlock's, 1953); also Charles S. Hardwick, ed., *Semiotic and Significs: The Correspondence between Charles S. Peirce and Victoria Lady Welby* (Bloomington and London: Indiana University Press, 1977).

9. Charles Hartshorne, "Review of volume 1 of *Writings of Charles S. Peirce*," *Transactions of the Charles S. Peirce Society* 19 (1983): 63.

10. Ernest Nagel, "Charles Sanders Peirce, a Prodigious but Little-Known American Philosopher," *Scientific American* 200 (1959): 185.

11. Carolyn Eisele, "Peirce's Pragmaticism," in *Pragmatik: Handbuch pragmatischen Denkens*, ed. Herbert Stachowiak (Hamburg: Felix Meiner, 1987), part 2, p. 83.

12. These manuscripts are entitled "Valency." Manuscript [MS] numbers cited in the text and notes of this paper refer to manuscripts listed and numbered in Richard S. Robin, *Annotated Catalogue of the Papers of Charles S. Peirce* (Amherst: University of Massachusetts Press, 1967).

13. National Archives Record Group 23, containing the records of the U.S. Coast and Geodetic Survey. The Peirce letter cited is from entry 22.

14. This paper is publication P77 listed in Kenneth Laine Ketner, ed., *A Comprehensive Bibliography of the Published Works of Charles Sanders Peirce*, 2nd ed. rev. (Bowling Green, Ohio: Philosophy Documentation Center, 1986). "P" numbers cited in the text and notes of this paper refer to publications listed and numbered in this bibliography. The paper P77 is also published in *W* 3:114–3:160.

15. National Archives Record Group 23, containing the records of the U.S. Coast and Geodetic Survey. The Peirce letter cited is from entry 22.

16. P 167, forthcoming in *W* 4.

17. MS. 1600, forthcoming in *W* 4.

18. MS. 1178.

19. MS. 1181.

20. MS. 1221.

21. MS. 1204, but the three pages actually belong with MS. 1500, a review of B. Matthew's *The Spelling of Yesterday and Tomorrow*.

22. P 396, dated 9/26/1890; this is published in *C* 1:96.

23. P 539, dated 11/9/1893; *C* 1:198.

24. P 641, dated 11/25/1897; *C* 2:146.

25. P 723, dated 2/15/1900; *C* 2:236.

26. P 1101, dated 7/20/1905; *C* 3:233.

27. P 791, dated 8/1/1901; *C* 3:38.

28. MS. 302.

29. Manley Thompson, *The Pragmatic Philosophy of C. S. Peirce* (Chicago: University of Chicago Press, 1953).

30. Murray G. Murphey, *The Development of Peirce's Philosophy* (Cambridge, Mass.: Harvard University Press, 1961).

31. MS. 434.

32. Max H. Fisch, "A Plan for a New Edition," presented in October, 1973, in Milford, Pennsylvania (unpublished manuscript).

33. The writings published in *W* 3:242–3:374 are scattered in 3 of the 8 volumes of *CP*. The 1898 Cambridge Conferences on "Detached Ideas on Vitally Important Topics" are published in *CP* 5, and the 1903 Lowell Lectures "On Some Topics of Logic" are published in *CP* 7.

34. *CP* 1:vi.

35. Fredson Bowers, "Textual Criticism," in *The Aims and Methods of Scholarship in Modern Languages and Literatures*, ed. James Thorpe (New York: Modern Language Association, 1963), p. 42.

36. Don L. Cook, "Preparing Scholarly Editions," *Humanities* 9:3 (1988): 17.

37. Don L. Cook, "Some Considerations in the Concept of Pre-Copy-Text," in *Text 4* (New York: AMS Press, 1988).

Final Intentions, Social Context, and Santayana's Autobiography*

HERMAN J. SAATKAMP, JR.

Introduction

Philosophers, literary critics, and scholarly editors have written extensively on the concepts of intention. And although I believe considerable headway has been made in understanding these concepts, I shall not review past accounts[1] or introduce new categorial schemes. Instead, in this paper I (1) discuss the relationships between authorial final intentions and their social context, introducing a modest claim concerning their interplay; (2) provide an account of the textual history of Santayana's autobiography that illustrates the interplay between Santayana's intentions and the socio-historical context; (3) suggest a few descriptive categories for understanding the "final intentions" associated with Santayana's autobiography; and (4) recommend that professional organizations consider proposing critical editions of major, contemporary authors who could make informed judgments about the final state of their published works.

I. Final Intentions and Social Context

The term *definitive edition* has been subjected to careful and telling criticism, and some editorial scholars are now maintaining that the concept of "final intention," when carefully examined, is also inadequate as the basis for editorial decisions and should be abandoned.[2] Perhaps they are right, if only because the term *final intention* appears to be causing confusion. However, the arguments against using the term *final intention* seem to be flawed in at least two respects: (1) these arguments rest on a sharp distinction between authorial intention and the social context and, ironically, the interplay between an author's intentions and the publishing environment is neglected; and (2) little attention has been given to the role of the social context in requiring that an author's intentions have a central import in publishing a book.

A. Interplay between Authorial Intentions and the Social Context

Simply stated, a central argument used to support the demise of "final intentions" rests on three points:

> (1) a sharp distinction is drawn between authorial intentions and their social context (copyeditors, publisher's profit margin, amanuensis, scholarly editors);
> (2) it is noted, replete with editing examples, that the social context plays a legitimate, authoritative role in the writing and publishing of a work;
> (3) the social context therefore cannot be ignored, indeed can often be the decisive authority, when determining the final form of a published work.[3]

It has been emphasized that the force of this argument rests on the authoritative role of the social context in publishing. But it is also established on a sharp and, I believe, far too simple distinction between authorial intentions and the social context.

The importance of the social context in publishing is unquestionable, but this context is also intertwined with authorial intentions. Personal intentions and social contexts are distinguishable in thought, but in action they are dialectically intertwined such that crystalline distinctions between them seem manufactured. To focus on one, excluding their interplay, leads to unnecessarily incoherent and unrealistic positions. Borrowing a phrase from Alfred North Whitehead, it is "misplaced concretion" to consider in isolation either an author's intentions or the social context. The reality of the relationship between authorial intentions and social context is that they are distinguishable but not separable.

Instead of arguing for the primacy of either authorial intentions or the social context, I advocate a more modest approach: the interplay between authorial intention and social context is a complex but genuine aspect of publishing, and this interplay places authorial intentions at a critical point in the publication of a work, particularly that of a book of prose or poetry by a single author.

This approach is an attempt to recognize the importance of both authorial intentions and of the social context while at the same time avoiding, if possible, the more theoretical (and perhaps more enchanting) issues related to individual responsibility and social realities. Broadly described, the social context not only is a significant determining factor in what an author intends but also predisposes the author with certain preferences, e.g., the native language of the author. And if one is not careful in these considerations, one can be thrust into the foray of questions confronting personal and social ethics as well as issues about freedom and determinism, historical materialism, socio-biology, etc. These issues often rest on a sharp distinction between the individual and the society, and focusing on one prong of that distinction depends on whether one supports the primacy of the personal or of the social (or the biological). Avoiding the theoretical and possibly foundational questions of the primacy of the individual or of the social context, it may be sufficient to simply note that the social context is an integral part of the author's intentions and that the author's intentions are also an integral part of the social context of publishing.

The writer submits manuscripts to publishers for all manner of social reasons: the publisher is known to be amenable to particular types of publications, the author has been recommended to the editor, the author met someone from the press at a party, the author has decided on a random mailing, the editor is his uncle, or the press has published the writer's previous works. To understand the author's intentions, even his considered and mature intentions about a particular work, one cannot overlook the desire to publish, to reach a particular audience of readers, to earn royalties, to write in a style acceptable for the publishing market. Within the writer there are many crosscurrents broadly delineated as tensions between autonomy and homonomy, between being self-governing and being an accepted part of society. Publishers, copyeditors, publication methods, sales formulas, economic conditions, war and peace—all may play decided roles in an individual writer's intentions.[4]

Likewise, the social context is not without consideration of the author's intentions. Economic factors are a powerful determining reality in publication, but a part of that economy is the extent to which a publisher honors the author's intentions. Should a publisher have the reputation of insensitivity to authors, then, in a relatively stable and moderately competitive market, that publisher's economic future will be affected. As a result, publishers' files are filled with letters to authors explaining why specific wishes of authors can or cannot be met. These files are demonstrative evidence of the publishers' compliance with economic realities and market efficiencies, as well as of their respect for authors. The best copyeditors attempt to make clearer what the author intended to say, spending considerable time reading and determining the thrust, the "active intention"[5] of the writer.

If there are crosscurrents entwined and tensed between what we are simply characterizing as authorial intentions and social context, how can one hope to make a reasoned judgment concerning variant readings in published works? One approach is a practical solution, not theoretically embroiled in controversy over the primacy of the individual or of society. And the Gregg-Bowers-Tanselle tradition of final intentions offers just such a pragmatic solution without the dogmatic trimmings of ideological conviction.

This pragmatic solution seems ultimately to rest on the foundational claim that intentions may be coupled with the responsibility for actions and that an author has a principal responsibility for the form and content of her or his work. From this basis, two guidelines may be presented: (1) the author's responsibility for substantive content (words) is usually more distinct than for form; and

(2) the author's responsibility for form is normally sharper for accidentals (spelling, punctuation, capitalization, word division, paragraphing, and devices of emphasis) than for the presentational format of the work (type style, binding, single or double column).

Of course, if an editorial scholar turns the pragmatic notion of final intentions into ideological cant without recognition of the historical/social conventions and their interplay with authorial intention, then one might well recall Santayana's description of a fanatic: a person who has lost sight of his goals and redoubled his efforts.[6]

B. THE CENTRAL IMPORT OF AUTHORIAL INTENTIONS IN SOCIAL CONTEXT

Authorial intentions are inherent to the social context of writing and publishing a book. This is so merely because the act of writing a book for publication is a social act. The extent to which an author's intentions play significant roles in that social act determines their importance to the social framework. Hence, the social context of a work may include most authorial intentions, including final intentions. However, the social context obviously includes more than authorial intentions: the specific economics of publishing, printing techniques, conventions of publishing style and format, taste and preference of copyeditors and editors, and sometimes events of a far broader nature such as national taxation policies, diplomatic relationships, and issues of public acceptability and of national security.

Within the broad reaches of the social context, authorial intentions, including final intentions, play a central role. The social act of publishing a work by a single author is just that: the publication of a work by an author. Ideally, the conventions and circumstances of publishing enable an author to publish her or his work with the clearest content and in a presentable and appealing format. This ideal is seldom fully realized, and when it can be demonstrated that an author's intentions conflict with the prevailing conventions, acquiescence to necessity cannot be taken to mean that the author intended a particular form or content of publication.

The social act of publishing a work focuses on the goal of making available the work of a particular author, and when conditions distort that goal, the scholar needs to determine, if possible, what best represents the considered and mature judgments of an author. Of course, the author's judgments may be in accord with publishing conventions and circumstances. If they are, it is the accord of the social context with the *author's* intention that validates the conventions, not the reverse.

Even if the term *final intentions* were to drop entirely from usage in scholarly editing—a prospect I think unlikely—there would still remain the necessity of attempting to determine the considered and mature judgments of authors regarding their works.

C. The Paradigm of Final Intentions

The paradigm of authorial final intentions consists in determining the considered, mature, and documented judgments of an author concerning the form and content of her or his work as it is to appear in published form. The practical value of the paradigm is ascertained by its clarity and fruitfulness. It must accurately represent enough instances to be useful, and it should provide interpretive meaning for the nonparadigmatic cases instead of discount them.

In general, this paradigm of final intentions appears to be quite fruitful when applied to the publication of a book by a single author but less fruitful, sometimes considerably less, when applied to works that have a significant performance aspect, such as ballads, plays, and operas. Performance-oriented literature may have authorial intentions as its springboard, but its form and content are shaped and altered by the flux of staging, performing, and acting as well as reviews and audience response. For example, the social significance and historical development of the ballad has broader relevance to the "active meaning" or illocutionary aspect of the ballad than does the intention of the original author. With the ballad, the author's mature and considered intentions, if they can be known, may have historical or literary significance, but they would most likely not take precedence over the historically and socially defined form and content.

Even in the case of books written by a single author, there are practical and circumstantial issues that may make it difficult and even impossible to apply the paradigm of final intentions. An example is a case where the only available evidence may be the editions and impressions of the published work or, worse yet, only fragments of these. Absent any clear evidence of an author's intention independent of the published work, the editorial scholar must simply rely on what is available and produce the most accurate critical edition within her or his powers. But such operational difficulties alone do not turn the paradigm belly-up. They may limit its application, just as geometries are limited to particular spatial applications, but they do not discount its value. It may well be that the highest value of the paradigm rests with books written by individual authors whose intentions are documented in holographs, letters, annotations, publishers' files, other publications, and recorded conversations. And this in turn may mean that the paradigm has a much higher value for nineteenth- and twentieth-century works than for works of earlier periods.

As a nineteenth- and twentieth-century author, Santayana is an archetype for the application of the paradigm of final intentions to his works. After resigning his professorship at Harvard in 1912 (age forty-nine) in order to become a full-time writer, Santayana took consistent and considerable care to document his intentions for his works, including collected editions that might come after his death (he died in 1952 in his eighty-ninth year). For example, Santayana wished to have British spelling in all his published works. He wrote the holograph of his autobiography using the British forms, he clearly stated his preferences in letters and annotations, and he frequently requested that his publisher honor these preferences. But in a clear conflict with Santayana's intention, the publisher altered the spelling to acceptable American forms. Ironically, because the British edition of the work is set from the American edition's sheets, even the British edition has the American forms. In such a setting, the editorial scholar would be remiss if the social conventions were given priority over the expressed intent of the author. On the other hand, these conventions could justifiably be given priority over authorial intention if a scholar determined that Santayana reconsidered his earlier preference and expressly endorsed the American forms, i.e., his final intention differed from his earlier one. Apart from the social conventions being in accord with Santayana's final intention, it is difficult to see another justification for the social convention receiving primacy over earlier authorial intention.

II. Santayana's Intentions and the Textual History of His Autobiography

The concept of final intentions provided clarity and interpretive usefulness in the editing of Santayana's three-part autobiography, *Persons and Places*. And given the tragic publishing history of this work, the intelligibility of the concept was most welcome. Santayana expressed his disappointment with the initial publication of his autobiography in the following words:

> I regard this edition of *Persons and Places* as a mutilated victim of war, and dream of a standard edition, which probably I shall never see, in which the original words, the omitted passages, and the marginal comments (not headings, as in the Triton Edition) shall be restored, and the portraits and other illustrations shall be well reproduced. (Santayana to Cory, March 14, 1945)[7]

From composition to publication, few modern textual documents have suffered more than Santayana's autobiography. The monogenous stemma[8] of the autobiography began in 1920, when Santayana was fifty-seven. He began writing down reminiscences, which by the late 1930s comprised four notebooks of jottings that were reasonably well organized but significantly quilted with deletions, insertions, false starts, and partial completions. In 1940 he began his fair-copy holograph. Intended as a one-volume work to be published posthumously, it was published instead as three individual works. Only the third book was published posthumously in 1953; the other two were published in 1944 and 1945, respectively.

The circumstances of the early 1940s caused Santayana, for the moment, to set aside his ambitions for his autobiography. After an unsuccessful attempt to leave Italy for Switzerland, Santayana lived in Rome for the duration of World War II, trapped by circumstance and by his age. At the same time, Santayana's friend Daniel Cory was stranded in New York without any clear means of support. To assist his friend, Santayana arranged for the royalties of his autobiography, whenever it was published, to be paid directly to Cory. In addition, Santayana's publishers, particularly Scribner's, were eager to issue what would become a Book of the Month Club best-seller, and they urged that the autobiography be published piecemeal instead of as a whole. Furthermore, there was an undercurrent of fear that the manuscript might be destroyed or lost during the war. These circumstances convinced Santayana to permit the publication of his autobiography in three parts and to allow the first two parts to be published before his death.

The typescript for book one was spirited out of Rome and delivered to Scribner's *sub rosa*, and likewise the typescript for book two was privately carried from Rome to the United States when official mail and other channels would not permit it to be brought in otherwise.[9] Following these adventures, the fate of the first portions of his autobiography was fully in the hands of his publishers and editors because Santayana could not receive galleys or communication from the United States or England. These circumstances contributed to what Santayana termed the "mutilation" of his memoirs. Publishing was difficult, and corners had to be cut. Some of Santayana's remarks seemed to his editors, and even to Santayana, too hard or too frank for the times. The publishers feared lawsuits, and Santayana was concerned that his friends and family might be upset. As a result, editors were charged with "softening" the text as well as deleting material difficult to print in restrictive times (for example, 717 marginal headings).

On October 14, 1941, Santayana, then nearly eighty years old, found refuge in a convent-clinic in Rome. The war cut him off from the United States, from his financial resources, and from his publishers. Not until the liberation of Rome did Santayana see a copy of the earliest book of his autobiography. Similarly, he saw the second book only after it was published in 1945. Unable to read the galleys or proofs for any of the publications, he could only chide his publishers and editors for the state of his autobiography, and he did so with his usual ironic wit.

Santayana to Cory, March 14, 1945: "I see by your letter of Jan. 29th, that you have been officially debasing my pure and legitimate English to conform with the vernacular." On April 8, 1945, Santayana says that Wheelock of Scribner's has promised him "English spelling" in volume two and that "ultimately all three volumes will be bound in one." But that, he says, "is not at all my dream of the final illustrated and completed edition!. . . You must manage to have, some day, an edition deluxe, to appease my Shade." To Otto Kyllmann on August 23, 1947, Santayana says, "I wrote these memoirs intending them to be posthumous; when circumstances led me to publishing them, I made some excisions."[10] And throughout it all his ironic sense of humor had its say: "I counted on dying, so that my indiscretions would all have acquired the impersonal authority of historical documents. I rely on Scribner to issue an edition deluxe eventually, if they think they can make money out of it. My idea had been, on the contrary, to help finance an edition that would have been a work of art."[11] But in earnest, he repeatedly expressed his hope for a grander, unexpurgated edition.

III. Final Intentions and Santayana's Autobiography

Santayana's final intentions for his autobiography can be descriptively categorized as (1) documented, (2) demonstrated, and (3) partial.

A. Documented Intentions

His documented final intentions are those found in such sources as letters, annotations to his copies of the published work, and errata lists. For example, all of Santayana's marginal notes or headings (he refers to them as marginal comments) were omitted from all published versions except the recent critical edition. Probably the difficulty of setting type for these headings was a principal reason for eliminating what had been an accepted nineteenth- to early twentieth-century publishing practice. Santayana repeatedly asks in letters to friends and to his publishers that the marginal headings be reinstated in any future editions. They never were, though the first part of the autobiography went through numerous reprints—it was a Book of the Month Club best-seller—and there was a new edition of the work published in celebration of Santayana's one hundredth birthday. Santayana's decided intention to include the headings is well documented. In addition, the actual placement and format of the headings is chronicled in Santayana's correspondence with his American publisher, Scribner's, and with his English publisher, Constable. In 1896, *The Sense of Beauty* was published with the marginal headings appearing to the flush left or right of their corresponding paragraph, depending on whether they were on the verso or recto page. On June 20, 1896, Santayana explicitly requested that this pattern be abandoned for left-hand appearances only. When the Triton edition of his works began appearing in 1936, Scribner's suggested that the marginal headings be removed from the left-hand margins and placed at the beginning of the respective paragraphs, similar to chapter headings. Scribner's recommendation was probably the result of considerations for typesetting ease. At first, Santayana thought these headings deserved such prominent placement, and he praised Scribner's foresight. However, after the publication of the centered headings, he abandoned his support for this new placement and requested that his volumes retain the left-hand marginal "comments" instead of "headings" as in the Triton edition.

As noted earlier, another example of documented intentions is Santayana's usage of British spelling and punctuation. In 1889[12] Santayana adopted the British forms and repeatedly requested that his publishers, both American and British, use the British forms. Not until he was a widely recognized author could he persuade the American publishers to honor his wishes, as in the Triton edition, for example (but only in the spelling, and then not fully consistently). The effect of his clear and repeated intentions on his American publisher was tied directly to his public standing as a writer and philosopher. From the 1920s through the 1930s his public recognition increased considerably. His public status was firmly established when he appeared on the front of *Time* in 1936 and when, in 1944–45, his autobiography was one of the best-sellers in America. Only then did his American publishers begin to publish his works with British spelling.

B. Demonstrated Intentions

When there is no documented evidence for authorial intention, one may convincingly determine authorial intention by a careful examination of authorial practice. Here, the necessity for data and good judgment must be emphasized. This is not a place for one and one-half truths, that is, a place where an editor makes a judgment about what a reading *ought* to be, beyond the limits of evidence. The use of computers and available software programs such as Word Cruncher and the Oxford Concordance Program makes it possible to demonstrate authorial practices in an easier and more readily accessible manner than ever before.

In examining Santayana's holograph, the following examples of authorial practice can be demonstrated. Santayana carefully distinguishes between "forever" (continually) and "for ever" (always). This distinction is uniform throughout the holograph, but the publishing convention was to collapse this distinction to "forever." Santayana also distinguished carefully between "whiskey" (Irish, U.S.) and "whisky" (Scotch). Interestingly, in conjunction with proper names Santayana used the American form of the initial capital in "Aunt" or "Uncle" when speaking of his American family, but he followed the Spanish form of not capitalizing "aunt" or "uncle" when referring to his Spanish family: "aunt Mariquita" and "uncle Nicolas Santayana." Although his publishers followed house style and uniformly capitalized "Aunt" and "Uncle" in conjunction with proper names, the evidence that these forms were not his normal practice is apparent in the holograph.

Perhaps one can make the claim that normal practice is related to intention in a manner similar to the relation between habitual action and intention. If I walk across the room, even though I am not conscious of all aspects of my doing so, I can still be said to have intended to go across the room. In part because they are habitual, the precise forms of my walking (gait, speed, etc.) may not have been individually intended, but I did intend to walk and therefore in some sense determined the individual forms. This suggestion is not without its difficulties. The relationship between habitual action and intention is by no means clear, nor is the relationship between responsibility and habitual actions. If one is inclined to accept a relationship between habitual action and intention, then the term *final intention* may not seem out of place in describing the writing habits of an author. But if one is inclined to deny such intention in habitual acts, then the term is likely to strike one as inappropriate.

Another descriptive classification may be called indirect demonstration. For example, all references to Spinoza were omitted from Santayana's autobiography. Santayana's comments about Spinoza were critical, but he also praises Spinoza as "my master and model." Santayana's intention to have the sections on Spinoza published can be documented by their appearance in the holograph. And even though these sections were omitted from all published forms, one can infer from Santayana's letters that he intended them to be published in the final "unexpurgated" edition of his autobiography. He repeatedly notes that he would like the omitted passages to be published, though he does not specifically mention the Spinoza sections, and he frequently comments that the holograph is to be used as the basis for a "good illustrated and unexpurgated edition of the whole three parts"[13] of his autobiography.

C. Partial Intentions

In some instances Santayana's intentions are explicit but incomplete. For example, Santayana wrote a chapter titled "We Were Not Virtuous" about his family, and he expressly intended it not be published until after his death. Although a part of the holograph, it was not included in any published form until the critical edition. However, Santayana's intention for the exact placement of this chapter in the holograph is not clear. It stands alone as an unnumbered chapter, and in the Columbia University collection it is physically located between chapters 12 and 13. It is not clear whether this location was by Santayana's design or a happenstance of the transfer of the holograph from Santayana to Cory to Columbia. Because it is not numbered as a chapter (although it is titled as one) and its content does not seem to belong between chapters 12 ("First Friends") and 13 ("The Harvard Yard"), the editors decided to include it as an addendum to the first part of the autobiography. That it should be published is clearly demonstrated in Santayana's correspondence, but where it belongs was only partially, and, for the editors, unclearly, designated.[14]

IV. Conclusions

A. Because of the dialectical interplay between authorial final intentions and the social context for writing and publishing a book, one cannot understand the concept of final intentions or the concept of social context in isolation: these notions are distinguishable in thought but not separable in activity. Indeed, the social context for writing and publishing a book places extreme importance on the role of authorial intentions.

B. The Gregg-Bowers-Tanselle tradition of final intentions offers a pragmatic solution to the problems of establishing an accurate and documented text. This solution can be turned into ideological cant but need not be. Its proper aim is to provide a paradigm whose interpretive value is established by its fruitfulness. The paradigm of final intentions is not a categorical principle applying to all cases and circumstances. Its limits are those of evidence and of relevance: are there documents and evidentiary bases for determining what an author intended the form and content of his work to be? Are the considered and final judgments of the writer of central importance for the final form and content of the work?

B.1. The paradigm has apparent value when applied to the works of a single author, particularly nineteenth- and twentieth-century writers for whom a scholar may gather considerable evidence for documenting, demonstrating, or inferring the mature and considered authorial judgments. Correspondence, annotations, publisher's files, and other records indicating writing habits and style provide an evidentiary base for decisions in modern, critical editing.

B.2. The value of the paradigm diminishes as the evidentiary base or the relevance of authorial intentions declines. In cases where there is little or no evidence to distinguish such intentions from the historical/social context of publishing, the paradigm may be of little value. The paradigm also seems less applicable to performance-oriented publications such as plays, operas, and ballads. Here the historical and social context is usually the more dominant factor in determining the final form and content of a work. The original author's final intentions, if they can be determined at all, may be of literary and historical interest, but they may not have the central import for the final form and content of the work in the way they would for a published book by a single author.

C. Santayana's work serves as a prime example for the application of the paradigm. Spending the last forty years of his life as a dedicated full-time writer, Santayana was careful to document his intentions. Because much of his correspondence, personal library, manuscripts, notes, and publisher's files has been preserved, the scholarly editor has information rarely available in such abundance. This is *not* to say that establishing the text for Santayana's works is not routinely complex and difficult, but that after disciplined and consistent research, a scholar can normally provide reasonable justification for decisions about the content and form of Santayana's works based on the evidence available.

V. Recommendation

All critical editors must wonder if their editorial judgments actually correspond with the author's intentions. Most of us have at one time or another fantasized about being able to present crucial editorial questions to our authors, but unfortunately this is not an option for any critical editions now underway because the authors are no longer living.

I recommend that the textual societies in conjunction with other professional associations consider proposing critical editions for eminent scholars who are now living. Such editions would employ all modern editorial practices in determining the form and content of the text, but the author would be able to make decisions concerning the final nature of these editions. Such editions would permit the eminent scholar to clear up matters that may have long plagued the publishing history of her or his work, and it would bring out variants that the author has been indifferent to. Furthermore, the determination of variants between editions and impressions may be a matter of appropriate computer software and compatibility because many contemporary texts are already on magnetic tapes.

This recommendation may seem a natural outgrowth of critical editing, but its implication and value are not fully clear. Could such editions even be classified as critical editions? The term *critical* implies that editorial judgments have been made in determining the text, but in the proposed editions, these judgments would be augmented and possibly overridden by those of the author. Perhaps these editions could be called critical authorial editions, and would they be closer to the paradigm of modern critical editions? The role of the editor would certainly be altered, however. The editor's scholarly abilities would still play a marked role in the quality and content of the editions, but would the editor not be more like scholarly copyeditor?

The author's involvement could result in editions that should be considered distinct from previously published editions—horizontal editions, as Tanselle refers to them. This would certainly change the nature of the editions, but it could further scholarship in a dramatic and engaging manner.

How would specific authors be chosen for critical authorial editions? No simple question, but perhaps various professional organizations could be asked to propose and support editions for the leading figures in their fields. No doubt this could lead to considerable partisan heat, but already there are examples of comparable efforts,[15] and most scholars can provide a listing of the top figures in their discipline. The problem of the judgment of history is perhaps a more serious difficulty. We may be able to arrive at a judicious consensus regarding contemporary eminent scholars, but will our present judgment stand through the rapidly changing methodologies, approaches, and focuses of our disciplines?

Although the import of the recommendation for critical authorial editions is not fully clear, I believe it is worth considering even if it serves only to highlight the differences between the role of editors in critical editions as opposed to critical authorial editions.

Notes

*Previously published in *Text: Transactions of the Society for Textual Scholarship*, volume 4, ed. D. C. Greetham and W. Speed Hill (New York: AMS Press, 1988), pp. 93–108.

1. G. Thomas Tanselle has given an initial account of philosophical and literary approaches to the concepts of intention in his "The Editorial Problem of Final Authorial Intention," in *Selected Studies in Bibliography* (Charlottesville: The University Press of Virginia, 1979), pp. 309–53. Reprinted from *Studies in Bibliography* (29 [1976]: 167–211).

2. See Jerome J. McGann, *A Critique of Modern Textual Criticism* (Chicago and London: The University of Chicago Press, 1983), pp. 37–49, 55–80, esp. p. 67.

3. This argument is summarized by Jerome J. McGann: "The fully authoritative text is . . . always one which has been socially produced; as a result, the critical standard for what constitutes authoritativeness cannot rest with the author and his intentions alone." (McGann, p. 75.)

4. Following John L. Austin's distinctions of locutionary, illocutionary, and perlocutionary, one might be able to draw distinctions between the writing of a work, the performative aspect of authoring a work, and what is brought about by the writing and publishing of a work. See *How to Do Things with Words*, (New York: Oxford University Press, 1965), p. 108.

5. Michael Hancher, "Three Kinds of Intention," *Modern Language Notes* 87 (1972): 827–51. "Active intentions characterize the actions that the author, at the time he finishes his text, understands himself to be performing in that text (p. 830)."

6. George Santayana, *Reason in Common Sense* (New York: Charles Scribner's Sons, 1905), p. 13. The precise quote is, "Fanaticism consists in redoubling your effort when you have forgotten your aim."

7. Unpublished letter to Daniel Cory. Santayana's letters to Cory are in Butler Library, Columbia University.

8. For a full description see the textual commentary of *Persons and Places: Fragments of Autobiography*, volume 1 of *The Works of George Santayana* (Cambridge and London: The MIT Press, 1986), pp. 582–610.

9. The first full account of the conveying of these transcripts from Rome to New York is given in the new critical edition of *Persons and Places: Fragments of Autobiography*, pp. 591–98.

10. Unpublished letter to Otto Kyllmann, housed in the Temple University Library.

11. Unpublished letter in the collection of Robert Shaw Sturgis.

12. See John McCormick, *George Santayana: A Biography* (New York: Knopf, 1987), p. 360.

13. This quote is cited in a letter from Harry A. Freidenberg to John Hall Wheelock, October 16, 1952, in the archives of Charles Scribner's Sons, Princeton University Library.

14. See the critical edition of *Persons and Places*, pp. 610–11, for a discussion of this. This chapter was probably omitted from publication because of its unattractive portrayal of Santayana's half-brother, Robert Sturgis.

15. For example, *The Library of Living Philosophers*.

THE NATURE OF PHILOSOPHY

The Modern Relevance of the Mathematical Philosophy of Charles S. Peirce

CAROLYN EISELE

Peirce once characterized his work in the following words: "My philosophy may be described as the attempt of a physicist to make such conjectures as to the constitution of the universe as the methods of science may permit. . . . The best that can be done is to supply a hypothesis, not devoid of all likelihood, in the general line of growth of scientific ideas, and capable of being verified or refuted by future observers."[1] He insisted that philosophy requires exact thought, and all exact thought is mathematical thought. By 1894 he announced that his special business was to bring mathematical exactitude into philosophy and to actually apply the ideas of mathematics in philosophy. He meant in part the construction of diagrammatic representation from which consequences of the hypothesis might be deduced intuitionally. And during 1894, Peirce read papers at each of two meetings of the American Mathematical Society at Columbia University. The society had been founded in 1888, and Peirce was invited to join the organization in 1891. It must now bring great satisfaction to all Peircean scholars to learn that his mathematical status will be further recognized by that society at the upcoming centennial celebration of its founding in August of this year (1988). A paper telling of his activity and publications in mathematics and in its history is included in volume 1 of the *Proceedings* of that congress.

In recent years, ongoing research on the writings of C. S. Peirce makes it ever more evident that his mathematical philosophical stance has a modern relevance. His general philosophy, colored by wide scientific experience, requires of necessity a mathematical approach to its conceptual bases. For example, the prevailing element of probabilism in Peirce's epistemology reflects the spirit of fallibilism in his astronomical and gravitational researches for the United States Coast and Geodetic Survey. The mathematical groundwork is evident in the rich mathematical allusions of his later writings: in the mathematical terminology, the diagrammatic explication, the very methodology induced by appropriate mathematical symbolism and procedure. Now it is possible to confirm the suspicion of Peirce's essentially mathematical cast of mind that spawned the philosophy he has bequeathed to us. For *The New Elements of Mathematics, by Charles S. Peirce*[2] offers at last a knowledge of that mathematical grounding. An inspection of some of the examples of Peirce's mathematical dependence will confirm these claims.

An obvious illustration is Peirce's invention of the existential graphs. He claimed to have extended Boolian practice to enable him to take into account ideas of relationship, or at least of existential relation. Peirce had invented different systems of signs to deal with relations, and he came to prefer the "diagrammatic syntax" that became the tool underlying the construction of his existential graphs in 1896. He maintained that the syntax is truly diagrammatic, for "its parts are really related to one another in forms of relations analogous to those of the assertions they represent, and that consequently, in studying this [diagrammatic] syntax, we may be sure that we are studying the real relations of the parts of the assertions and reasonings, which is by no means the case with the syntax of speech."[3] The graphs, incidentally, were probably the outgrowth of the topological investigations he had been making in the writings of J. B. Listing before that time.

Another illustration of the modern geometric cast of Peirce's thought is found in the description of his philosophical continuum in terms of the mathematical linear continuum, which was the subject of much mathematical revolutionary controversy during the latter half of the nineteenth century. Although Peirce had always expressed great admiration of Cantor for having brought the infinite within discussible reach as was the finite, he claimed to have worked out his own conceptions independently of Cantor and Dedekind. Evidence for the truth of this claim may be found in Peirce's early use of a sign quite different from Cantor's aleph to represent an infinite set analogous to that of Cantor. Peirce assumed later that the various orders of infinity that he developed in a unique way were of the same magnitude as Cantor's successive alephs, although he was somewhat uncertain because he had not proved them to be so. When describing the temporal or the arithmetic aspect of the continuum problem, Peirce related it to the line continuum. But in his philosophy he had need of a continuum far in excess of the magnitude of that corresponding to the numbers of the real number system. His denumerable set of positive integers and his abnumeral set of real numbers in his logical development of orders of the infinite begot ever greater multitudes where the aggregate of all possible combinations of the elements in each order leads to the next higher order. All lead in turn finally to the denumerable set of combinations of abnumeral sets, which no longer contains individual elements but represents what Peirce called "the continuum."

Peirce was well aware of Cantor's construction of successive alephs and noted that no one had tried to apply Cantor's ideas to infinitesimals. That sentiment foreshadows a statement made by Kurt Goedel in 1973 when he deplored the failure to introduce an infinitesimal theory after the number system had been extended to include rational, irrational, and negative numbers. Goedel considered it an "oddity" that it had taken three hundred years for this to happen in the work of Abraham Robinson. In his time Peirce was one of the last standouts for the existence of a Leibnizian infinitesimal element in the foundations of the calculus, insisting that "every part of space, no matter how small, consists of extended spaces quite innumerable."[4]

Peirce's need for such a concept in his work is seen in this statement: "It is difficult to explain the fact of memory and our apparently perceiving the flow of time, unless we suppose immediate consciousness to extend beyond a single instant. Yet if we make such a supposition, we fall into grave difficulties, unless we suppose the time at which we are immediately conscious to be strictly infinitesimal. There are other reasons . . . but such questions belong to physics, not mathematics."[5]

It is of interest to note briefly the work of the late Abraham Robinson and that of H. Jerome Keisler in the field of nonstandard analysis. Robinson argued that the theory of Leibnizian infinitesimals can be vindicated; and, using modern mathematical logic, he has proceeded to do that.[6] His disciple, Keisler, has published as of 1976 an elementary calculus in which the infinitesimal approach is acceptable.[7] Moreover, ranges of real numbers appear within ranges of real numbers to produce hyperreal numbers, hyperintegers, and infinite hyperintegers. Modern needs for such extension arise for Keisler in quantum theory and in economics. Peirce's need arose from the explication of logical and philosophical problems. Peirce would have welcomed Keisler's present approach to the calculus. It is unfortunate that Peirce did not have at his disposal the logical tools that Robinson used in his *Non-Standard Analysis* to establish the validity of his own infinitesimal stance.

Another example of Peirce's diagrammatic thinking, now with respect to the new geometry of the late nineteenth century, shows his geometric need for the infinitesimal. For he wrote, "As an example of the convenience of thinking about infinitesimals, supposing the idea does not involve any contradiction . . . , I may mention the conception of a translation as an infinitesimal rotation."[8] And Peirce proceeded to describe the movement so implied in non-Euclidean geometry using the absolute as an element of reference.

In volume 2 of *The New Elements of Mathematics*, one finds Theorem 47 on p. 184 stating that "every continuum without singularities returns into itself."[9] So, too, Theorem 5 on p. 277 highlights the demonstration of "every simple line without furcation, and not having two free extremities, returns into itself."[10] One not versed in Riemannian spatial ideas must be confused in Peirce's philosophical writings by the constant reference to elements that return into themselves. An illustration in Theorem 47 describes the horizon returning into itself ring-wise, for as a ray it must return into itself. "But what you call moving round the horizon is identical with its opposite. What you call the sphere of the heavens is the firmament twice over. The whole of it appears above the horizon. Yet the horizon is not the boundary of it. *So* regarded the firmament is nothing but a bounded artiad surface. The firmament, like any perissad surface, may be regarded as two bounded artiad surfaces pasted together. So our ribbon surface [Moebius strip] results from the pasting together of two surfaces of paper. And it is the union of these surfaces of the two which come into contact that makes a perissad surface."[11]

Throughout his writings in later life, Peirce's spatial conception was of a non-Euclidean cast. He was deeply influenced by the work of Cayley and the latter's creation of the concept of the absolute. He often refers glowingly to Cayley's sixth memoir of 1859 on quantics, in which memoire affine and metric geometry become special cases of projective geometry. He was familiar with Felix Klein's paper of 1871 in which Klein identified Cayley's generalized theory of geometry with the non-Euclidean geometry of Lobachevsky, Bolyai, and Riemann, so that the real, imaginary, or degenerate forms of the absolute determine the nature of the geometry as hyperbolic, elliptic, or Euclidean. Peirce believed space to be non-Euclidean, and for some time, in pragmatic fashion, he actually attempted to prove space to be hyperbolic by establishing a negative curvature for it in the course of an astronomical investigation and use of observed data. Unfortunately, the data proved to be unreliable.

Cayley's absolute became a conceptual device for Peirce in all areas of his thought. He wrote explicitly: "Let me tell you that when unbelievers tell you that the Absolute of mathematics is not that of metaphysics, they are blinded by their own disinclination to believe in the Absolute. They are the same; only the method of the mathematicians and their use of diagrams enable them to get distincter notions of the matter than the metaphysicians have. The mathematical Absolute is confined, it is true, to space. But it bears the same relation to attainable space as the metaphysical Absolute ought to bear to concepts of the Relative. At any rate it is approximately so."[12]

Peirce's approach to the solution of problems in geometry itself was also through the gateway of non-Euclidean representation in projective geometry. Moreover, although some theorems are handled in synthetic fashion—and that in a Peircean notation that is particularly fruitful in uncovering intrinsic relationships—Peirce utilized the analytic tool called the "barycentric calculus" of Moebius. The real number system is extended to include infinity, and it is represented on a line in a net of rationality. In several theorems, Peirce employs homogeneous coordinates to identify individual points.

Peirce believed that a similar mathematical procedure was applicable in his philosophical demonstrations. In a letter to William James, he explained that for a considerable time he "was much occupied by the question whether or not a notation similar to this [the barycentric notation] would not represent the modes in which concepts are, or should be, represented as compounded in definitions, with a leaning to the affirmative."[13]

Peirce thought that existing logic is defective in taking no notice of the limit between two realms. "I do not say that the Principle of Excluded Middle is downright false; but I do say that in every field of thought whatsoever there is an intermediate ground between positive assertion and positive negation which is just as real as they.... To recognize such a mode of composition of concepts as that of the barycentric calculus would be one way of recognizing the idea of lower dimensionality between any two mutually exclusive fields."[14] Again Peirce explained that he had long urged "that, in itself considered, any one concept is just as simple as any other. Now if we recognize that concepts are compounded to make other concepts in the same way, or in any analogous way with that in which in the barycentric calculus two points are compounded to make a point is to recognize that."[15] Peirce's recognition of that intermediate ground between positive assertion and positive negation led him to a workable triadic logic by 1909.

The above is but one illustration of the conversion of the elements under discussion in philosophy to symbolic form in Peirce's logical treatment of basic materials. Mention must be made here, too, of Peirce's frequent references to that form of inference that he called "theorematic," in the second step of which he seemed to find the element of ingenuity that makes possible originality in establishing proof. "Theorematic inference" gave Peirce a procedural model in his investigative reasoning in setting up an initial diagram, introducing new elements into it to reach valid secondary conclusions helpful in attaining the final conclusion and eliminated when the conclusion is reached at last. In the sign-world of mathematics, Peirce proved himself to be a master semiotician.

Another topological problem that engaged Peirce's attention over the years was that of the Four-Color Map Conjecture, which recently has been resolved at last by computer. We have evidence of his interest in the problem at a meeting of the Scientific Association at Johns Hopkins University on November 8, 1879, when during the discussion Peirce attempted to show "by methods of logical argumentation that a better demonstration of the problem than the one offered by Mr. Kempe is possible."[16] Now Peirce mentions in the course of his writing that "about 1860 DeMorgan, in the *Athenaeum*, called attention to the fact that this theorem had never been demonstrated; and I soon after offered to a mathematical society at Harvard University a proof of this proposition extending it to other surfaces."[17] This hitherto unknown reference to DeMorgan was traced recently and mentioned in *Graph Theory, 1736–1936* by R. J. Wilson, E. K. Lloyd, and N. L. Biggs.[18] Peirce apparently had indeed read the article in the *Athenaeum* (14 April 1860), which is the first known printed reference to the conjecture. Wilson, Lloyd, and Biggs say that "it is quite possible that he [Peirce] was the first American to interest himself in the problem."[19] In his attempt to demonstrate the truth of the conjecture, Peirce had used it as a "landmark to test the progress of his own skill."[20] For he came to believe he had applied his logical theory to the demonstration of several mathematical problems with success and that "the same method has only to be pushed a little further to solve the map-problem."[21]

As the writer has had occasion to note some time ago, when Peirce's message is finally clarified in terms of its mathematico-scientific orientation, we shall find that America's intellectual history will have been enriched by a chapter celebrating a native son as important to America as Leibniz has been to Germany and Poincaré has been to France. It brings some satisfaction to know that a scholar as reliable and prestigious as C. P. Snow classed Peirce, "the analytical philosopher,"[22] with J. Willard Gibbs as one of the two most original abstract thinkers to have been born in America. It is a sad comment to note that Snow felt compelled to add, "It is uncommon to meet an American student who has heard of either of those two great names."[23]

Notes

1. Source of Peirce quote unidentified. [Editor's Note: This paper was submitted by Caroline Eisele without identification of the sources for most of her references. Before she was able to fill in her documentation, Professor Eisele fell seriously ill and became unable to provide documentation for her sources. She has certainly been one of the greatest, perhaps *the very* greatest, Peirce scholar of our times, and there is not the slightest reason to question her reliability. It was decided, therefore, to publish her paper without attempting to provide documentation for her.]
2. *The New Elements of Mathematics, by Charles S. Peirce*, 4 vols., ed. Carolyn Eisele (Mouton, The Netherlands, 1976).
3. Source of Peirce quote unidentified.
4. Source of Peirce quote unidentified.
5. Source of Peirce quote unidentified.
6. Abraham Robinson, *Non-Standard Analysis*. Documentation not further provided.
7. H. Jerome Keisler. Documentation not further provided.
8. Source of Peirce quote unidentified.
9. Eisele, *The New Elements of Mathematics*, vol. 2, p. 184.
10. Ibid., p. 277.
11. Ibid., p. 184.
12. Source of Peirce quote unidentified.
13. Source of Peirce quote unidentified. James letter unidentified.
14. Source of Peirce quote unidentified.
15. Source of Peirce quote unidentified.
16. Source of Peirce quote unidentified.
17. Source of Peirce quote unidentified.
18. R. J. Wilson, E. K. Lloyd, and N. L. Biggs, *Graph Theory, 1736–1936*. Further documentation not provided.

19. Wilson, Lloyd, and Biggs, *Graph Theory*. Further documentation not provided.
20. Source of Peirce quote unidentified.
21. Source of Peirce quote unidentified.
22. Source of C. P. Snow quote unidentified.
23. Source of C. P. Snow quote unidentified.

Can Philosophy Have a Nationality?

GERARD DELEDALLE

Can philosophy have a nationality? In other words, is there an American philosophy, just as there are European philosophies: English, French, German? As early as 1917, John Dewey answered the question: "I do not see how any one can question the distinctively national color of English or French or German philosophies." And his conclusion was, "I believe that philosophy in America will be lost between chewing a historic cud long since reduced to woody fibre, or an apologetics for lost causes (lost to natural science), or a scholastic, schematic formalism, unless it can somehow bring to consciousness America's own needs and its own implicit principle of successful action."[1]

I am not going to question John Dewey's answer but try to qualify it. Can a national philosophy pretend to have the universality philosophy is supposed to have?

Let us go back, first, to Greek philosophy. Its universality has never been questioned until recently, and then it was to contrast it with Eastern philosophies; one can then say that there is a general agreement on the universal character of the philosophy that prevailed in antiquity in the countries around the Mediterranean Sea. Was this philosophy nationally Greek? It is difficult to give an affirmative answer, because the idea of "nationality" was not born yet. The Greek language was used very often, but the Latin language was later used together with the Greek. Of course, Roman philosophy is Greek philosophy in translation. So will be still later Arabic philosophy. But in no sense can those philosophies be said to be nationally Greek.

I do not want to minimize the impact of religion on philosophy, but if Christianity or Islam did change in one way or another the contents of philosophy, they did not affect its methodology, which was founded on reason, on *logos*: on a rational discourse. An attempt by Laberthonniere in France in the nineteenth century to oppose "Christian realism" to "Greek idealism" failed. As Jacques Chevalier pointed out: if it is true that "for the Fate of the Greeks, for that eternal, immutable order, born of the analytical ideal of human intelligence, always self-reflecting, and unaffected by time or true duration" Christianity substitutes "an order conceived by God, intended by him . . . and which has a history,"² "there are fundamental philosophical truths *presupposed* by Christianity." Thus Christianity detracts "in no way from the autonomy of philosophy" nor from its universality.³ So down to the twentieth century there is, properly speaking, no national philosophy. Philosophy is universal. And I do not mean geographically universal in the so-called Western world but logically universal.

The idea of a geo-philosophy appears in the nineteenth century, and the idea is German. Philosophers still discuss the problem today and with reason, because one cannot link a philosophy and a nationality and at the same time pretend that one can philosophize aloofly without interference of the nation that has produced this philosophy. Let us examine this question from a historical point of view.

The quarrel was at its pitch in the United States in the First World War when George Santayana wrote his *Egotism in German Philosophy* and John Dewey his *German Philosophy and Politics*. "Egotism—subjectivity in thought and will in ethics—" writes Santayana, "is the very soul of German philosophy."⁴ That is why "the German people, according to Fichte and Hegel, is destined, by the decision of Providence, to occupy the highest place in the history of the universe."⁵

But this philosophy could not be produced by a free observation of Life and Nature, as was Greek philosophy. It is Protestantism rationalized, not by individualities but by nations and institutions.⁶

Read Fichte's *Address to the German Nation*, says Santayana, and you will understand: "If the people is not inclined to obey the idea, the government must compel it to do so. All the faculties of all the citizens must be at the State's service."⁷

John Dewey said roughly the same thing in his *German Philosophy and Politics*.

> The premises of the historic syllogism are plain. First the German Luther, who saved for mankind the principle of spiritual freedom against Latin externalism; then Kant and Fichte, who wrought out the principle into a final philosophy of science, morals and the State; as conclusion, the German nation organized in order to win the world to recognition of the principle and thereby to establish the rule of freedom and science in humanity as a whole.⁸

Dewey tries to explain somewhere else why he had been fascinated by German philosophy. It is the result of the unfortunate way in which the history of philosophy is written apart from its social context. The expositions may be scholarly and technically accurate, but the systems described could have been elaborated and have flourished anywhere: "Greece, Turkey, the moon, or Mars."⁹

The First World War was a terrible shock to Dewey, who reread Kant and Hegel no longer as abstract philosophers but as German propagandists: "Kant's faithful logic compels him to insist that the concept of duty is empty and formal. It tells men that to do their duty is their supreme law of action, but is silent as to what men's duties specifically are."[10]

The Germans knew better, as a quotation by Dewey from Bernhardi's *Germany and the Next War* shows: "The assertion of the rights of the individual leads ultimately to individual irresponsibility and to repudiation of the State. Immanuel Kant, the founder of the critical philosophy, taught, in opposition to this view, the gospel of moral duty, and Scharnhorst grasped the idea of universal military service."[11]

The abrupt jump from ethical considerations to military applications is no less unbearable than the Hegelian justification by a Cologne newspaper of the sinking of the *Lusitania*. The quotation given by Dewey was sent to him, together with a quotation from Hegel, by Alex Sachs. I am quoting both.

Cologne *Gazette*:

> We base that deed [the sinking of the *Lusitania*] on the claims of the higher humanity which is the foundation of every national life. What appears inhumanity to the Americans was in the higher sense humanity. . . . National self-respect demands that a state shall not lay aside its holy duties, even if their fulfillment seems to involve harshness or cruelty. Would that the Americans could grasp this conception of humanity.[12]

Hegel:

> In the history of the world this nation ["whose natural principle is one of the stages of the world-spirit"] is for a given epoch dominant. . . . It has the highest right of all and exercises its right upon the lower spirits in world-history. . . . In contrast with the absolute right of this nation to be the bearer of the current phase of the world-spirit the spirits of other existing nations are void of right, like those whose epochs are gone, count no longer in the history of the world.[13]

The First World War ended in 1918. Exactly seventy years later in France in 1988, we are still discussing the same question. The only thing is that Heidegger has replaced Kant, Fichte, and Hegel. Can a national philosophy still be a universal philosophy? Before answering the question, I should like to deal with French philosophy for a short while.

In 1968, twenty years ago, a French-American philosophers' conference took place at the State University of New York at Oyster Bay. Jacques Derrida gave a lecture on *The Ends of Man*, which raised the question I am trying to make clear. Is there a French philosophy? And, if so, what is it? Nobody ever doubted that there existed a movement of thought called Cartesianism. Does it define French philosophy?

That is another matter. Louis Lavelle wrote, "It is characteristic of the French to believe that there is a natural light which illuminates all minds, to distrust feeling when it is not a subtler means of understanding and, as it were, a refinement of reason, and to prefer order and moderation to the unruly impulses of instinct and passion."[14] In other words, rationalism, which is wider than Cartesianism, would be the national philosophy of the French.

However, when one reads French philosophical literature, the philosophers referred to are not very often Fontenelle or Descartes—who are the typical French philosophers, according to Louis Lavelle—but Kant, Hegel, and, since the last war, Husserl and Heidegger. French philosophy draws heavily from the German source. That fact struck all our American colleagues who met at the Oyster Bay Conference I mentioned. According to Derrida—and I can assure you that he is right—French humanism has its sources not in Descartes but in Hegel, Husserl, and Heidegger.

That explains the present debate in France concerning Heidegger's Nazi ties. I am not going to enter into the discussion here, although it could be of interest for the academic world in America, concerning the question of politics and deconstruction, especially in literary criticism, of which Jacques Derrida is the pivot.

What I need to say is only that Heidegger proposed a philosophy that is a national philosophy and that, if one adopts Heidegger's philosophy, one must accept the idea of Hegel concerning the duty for a philosopher (as for any person) to submit to the domination of the German nation. Hegelian humanism denounced by Dewey is the same as that which Heidegger promoted and on which he based on two premises: (1) the German language is the only philosophical language, and (2) The German nation has an obligation toward humanity to convey to the world, in any suitable and efficient way, its message.

Let me say the same things in Heidegger's terms: "Only the German language can express the being of Being." Athenian (not Greek) thought introduced into the Western world the oblivion of Being. The Germans are the people "of Thought. And it is necessary that there be men who are thinkers."[15] At long last, with the National Socialist Revolution, the Western world "comes back to the essence of Being."[16]

At the Oyster Bay Conference, Richard Popkin in answer to Derrida insisted that, contrary to French philosophy, American philosophy "came from a deeply-felt need to reject the whole kind of formal metaphysical complex that this Hegel represented, and the strange hold his interpreters had on certain levels of institutionalized thought. We are still living in this world in which Hegel is the enemy, the force of darkness constantly to be rejected in favor of the clear light of pragmatism, empiricism and common sense."[17] Husserl, many of whose students came to America, has hardly found "a hearing of sorts." Heidegger is "untranslatable into our philosophical world."[18] That may explain, as Peter Caws pointed out, why "philosophy in France has never come to terms with the revolt against Hegel represented by pragmatism and logical empiricism and linguistic analysis."[19]

Pragmatism! This is the key word. It defines American philosophy. Is it just another philosophy proposed by Peirce, James, Dewey, and so many American philosophers until today, to fulfill, as Dewey said, "America's own needs and its own principle of successful action"?

My answer is no. I do not question the fact that pragmatism was born in America. I question the opinion that it is another national philosophy for a nation that had previously no philosophy of its own. Let me explain what I mean. I am not the first one to advance the idea. Alexis de Tocqueville, on the very first page of his chapter "On the philosophical method of the Americans" in *Democracy in America*, wrote, "It is easy to see . . . that almost all the inhabitants of the United States have the same ways of thinking, and the same processes of reasoning; that is to say that they possess, although they have never taken the trouble to define its rules, a certain philosophical method which is common to all of them." And this was rendered possible because they were able "to escape from the spirit of system, from the yoke of habit, from family maxims, from class opinions, and, up to a certain point, from *national prejudices*."[20]

Let us remark that the philosophical expression of this method was elaborated in a multinational country and also that it was developed in two completely different environments: Cambridge, Massachusetts, and Chicago, where America's needs were different. In both places, however, they were, properly speaking, neither material nor spiritual needs but intellectual needs: how to solve the question of the relation between science and religion in the new context of Darwinism and experimental science, in New England Cambridge; and how to cope with the social problems in the context of the wild industrial explosion in New America Chicago. Peirce's pragmatism was more theoretical, Dewey's instrumentalism more practical, but the former did not propose new creeds nor the latter new recipes. They both proposed the same method of approaching problems, any problems.

This was not entirely peculiar to America. At the same moment or soon after in Europe—France, Italy, Germany—scientists and philosophers discovered the same principle of action or rather of methodological action. But they did not succeed in imposing this new method, because the weight of adverse national traditions was too heavy. America had not that burden on her shoulders, and, in spite of the huge problems she had to solve, she succeeded in bringing to maturity the philosophy of successful action: pragmatism. She built a philosophy, but not a national philosophy—a new universal philosophy. Its universal character is more evident now than ever after the collapse of nationalism in Europe and the failure of philosophical movements like existentialism and structuralism. The "pragmatic turn" of thought in Europe is spreading rapidly in philosophy, in linguistics, and in social sciences in general. I cannot here be more explicit on this fact or give a more elaborated comment.

In conclusion, this philosophy—pragmatism—is not a national philosophy, although the two reasons why it is not rest on the philosophies of two American philosophers. It is not a national philosophy because it is the philosophy of Peirce's Community of Inquirers and the philosophy of Dewey's Common Man, a philosophy for which an idea is not true because it is imposed on me by myself, by the state or an institution, or by Reason, which is often a national or an institutional disguise. An idea can be asserted as true by the community of the Common Man to which philosophers as well as scientists belong, if and only if it has passed the public test to which it is put in a laboratory, be it a research center, a school, or a society.

Pragmatism is the new universal philosophy, because it is the philosophy of experience and democracy that is any nation's "manifest destiny."

Notes

1. John Dewey, "The Need for a Recovery of Philosophy," 1917, in *The Middle Works*, vol. 10 (Carbondale: Southern Illinois University Press, 1980), p. 47.

2. Chevalier, Jacques, *Histoire de la pensee*, vol. 2, *La Pensee chretienne* (Paris: Flammarion, 1956), p. 27. Translated by the author of the paper.

3. Ibid., p. 24, n. 1.

4. George Santayana, *Egotism in German Philosophy* (New York: Scribner, 1916), p. 17. French version under Santayana's supervision was *L'Erreur de la philosophie allemande* (Paris: Nouvelle Librairie Nationale, 1917).

5. Ibid., p. 32.

6. Ibid., p. 35.

7. Ibid., p. 107.

8. John Dewey, *German Philosophy and Politics,* (1915), in *The Middle Works*, vol. 8 (Carbondale: Southern Illinois University Press, 1979), pp. 181–82.

9. John Dewey, "On Understanding the Mind of Germany," *Atlantic Monthly* 117 (1916): 251–62; republished in *Characters and Events*, ed. Joseph Ratner (New York: Henry Holt and Co., 1929), vol. 1: 130–48, with title "The Mind of Germany," p. 138.

10. Dewey, *German Philosophy and Politics*, p. 163.

11. Ibid.

12. Dewey, "The Mind of Germany," pp. 135–36.

13. Alex Sachs to John Dewey, Columbiana Collection, Columbia University.

14. Louis Lavelle, *Universalia*, quoted in *Le Corpus des oeuvres philosophiques de langue francaise* (1988), pp. 431–32.

15. Martin Heidegger, *Erlauterungen zu Hoelderlins Dichtung* (1951); in French (Paris: Gallimard, 1962), p. 36.

16. Martin Heidegger, *Bekenntnis zu Adolf Hitler*. Translated by the author of the paper, 1933.

17. Richard Popkin, "Comments on Professor Derrida's Paper," in *Language and Human Nature* (St. Louis: Warren H. Green, Inc., 1969), pp. 209–10.

18. Ibid., p. 210.

19. Peter Caws, "On Self-Reference: Comments on Derrida," in *Language and Human Nature* (St. Louis: Warren H. Green, Inc., 1969), p. 219.

20. Alexis de Tocqueville, *De la Democratie en Amerique*, vol. 2 (Paris: Gallimard, 1961), p. 11.

EXISTENTIALISM AND PHENOMENOLOGY

Pragmatism And Heidegger: A Common World

SANDRA B. ROSENTHAL

Though the classical American pragmatists refer to "the world" quite frequently throughout their writings, they do not explicitly focus on its pervasive and crucial role within the context of the pragmatic position.[1] Thus, "the world" has too often been interpreted in a common-sense way with "what is the case" or "what there is." This unquestioned common-sense identification accounts in part for the historical alienation of the position of classical American pragmatism and the philosophy of Martin Heidegger, for the denial of this identification is central to his thought. Uncovering their similar conceptions of world, then, can provide a crucial focal point for grasping the basic affinities between these seemingly disparate positions. Further, this endeavor can help both to highlight the foundational nature of world as found in pragmatic thought and to provide an expansive context for understanding the function of world within Heidegger's philosophy. The ensuing discussion will turn first to a sketch of the concept of world within the context of pragmatism.[2]

Meaning, for the pragmatist, comes to be in our behavioral rapport with that which gives itself in experience. Meaning is already there for conscious acts, because conscious acts emerge within a meaningful world. This does not mean, however, that we discover meanings already metaphysically embedded in the world in the spectator-realist sense. Instead, the world is the world of perception in which things emerge as meaningful within experience, a world in which noncognitive, prereflective acts take place and within which reflection arises. Such a world is the level at which sense emerges in experience, for meaning begins to emerge at a level prior to that of conscious acts. And it is what it is only in relation to the human. Such a world is, to greater or lesser degree, implicitly operative throughout the pragmatic vision, but it is best brought into explicit focus through the concreteness of our everyday worldly engagement in Mead's development of "the world that is there."

The world that is there is indeed "there"; yet for Mead "there is no absolute world of things."[3] Instead, the world that is there and the things[4] that emerge within the world are what they are in relation to the meanings embodied in and expressive of purposive activity,[5] while the distinctive character of the individual's experience is dependent upon its peculiar relation to such a world.[6] As James expresses this relatedness, "The world experienced (otherwise called the 'field of consciousness') comes at all times with our body as its centre.... Where the body is is 'here'; when the body acts is 'now'; what the body touches is 'this'; all other things are 'there' and 'then' and 'that.'"[7] The significance of these positional words is that they "imply a systematization of things with reference to a focus of action and interest which lies in the body."[8] Or, as he elsewhere summarizes, "The world of living realities ... is thus anchored in the ego considered as an active and emotional term."[9] This ego, as an active and emotional term, is the vehicle by which a pluralistic universe becomes a meaningfully organized world.[10] Prereflective lived experience in its behavioral rapport with the world, then, provides the meaningful context within which perception of things takes place. Perception involves acts of adjustment between humans and their world, and within such acts of adjustment things and their qualities function in experience. Thus, while experienced qualities are always qualities of the "thing," the "thing" is always a "thing in the world."

The interrelation of the above account of our behavioral relation to the world with the dynamics of perceptual experience can be seen in Dewey's description of the disintegration of the perceptual situation because of the frustration of an ongoing act. "Generalized, the sensation as stimulus is always that phase of activity requiring to be defined in order that a coordination may be completed. ... The search for the stimulus is the search for the exact conditions of action. ... Similarly, motion, as response, has only functional value. It is whatever will serve to complete the disintegrating coordination."[11] All problematic contexts emerge within the context of the world, and within the problematic situation, data and verification instances gain their meaning and significance through the meaningful, interwoven network by which they emerge from the concrete matrix of possibilities of experience there for discrimination. Experience is first had in a world about which there is neither doubt nor conscious belief, and questioning cannot occur without the world as the context within which the doubt and questioning make sense. Thus, the pragmatic understanding of the dynamics of experience requires the world as the backdrop of all that takes place in perception.

This emergence of things or facts from the backdrop of a human-world relationship, expressed above in terms of concrete human behavior, is developed by Peirce and Lewis as an examination of the way in which that meaningful projection that is the world provides the backdrop for the rigors of more sophisticated awareness rooted in sense experience.[12] The foundationally real world, for Peirce and Lewis, as for the other pragmatists, is the world of everyday concrete experience.[13] What becomes clear in the general context of their respective but parallel discussions of worldly experience is that worldly possibilities are a unity of humanly projected possibilities[14] with a rich matrix of possibilities provided by that which is independently there.[15] The real world is characterized by both Peirce and Lewis as the world of perceptual facts,[16] but facts are not independent of the intentional unity between knower and known.[17] The grasping of the sensible with respect to a system of meanings is what Peirce intends by saying that the sensible world is but a fragment of the ideal world.[18]

Further, the system of meanings in some sense limits the facts that may occur "in the world," for "we know in advance of experience that certain things are not true, because we see they are impossible. . . . I know it is not true, because I satisfy myself that there is no room for it even in that ideal world of which the real world is but a fragment."[19] As Lewis notes, there is a "plurality of equally cogent systems which may contain the same body of already verified propositions but differ in what else they include."[20] And what else they include is not merely what facts will be but also what facts conceivably may be. Thus, at any time, a range of what is possible to occur may be determined ideally or logically, though what specific possibility will in fact be actualized in the future cannot be determined in this manner, for there are of course real "future contingents."[21]

Although what may occur "in the world" cannot be understood apart from humanly projected possibilities, this does not lead to a conventionalism, for these possibilities must mesh with the possibilities available within that independent thereness that presents itself within the context of world.[22] Thus, the real world is that "which sufficient experience would tend ultimately . . . to compel reason to acknowledge as having being independent of what he may arbitrarily, or willfully, create."[23] Conversely, what the possibilities of this independent being can consistently be held to be is partially determined by the range of meaningfully projected possibilities within which facts can consistently emerge.

The world as the horizon for all experience cannot itself be exhaustively known, both because of the nature of meaning projections and the concreteness of the independently there. Thus, though there is a possible world for every self-consistent system,[24] Lewis asserts that "no conceivable knowledge can ever be adequate to a world."[25] A fixated system of meanings can never be exhaustively known because any meaning has its own implicated meanings that limit the range of possibilities of experience—though of course they do not determine which possibility will become actual. Although the projection of a meaning system limits the alternatives possible within it, the richness of the possible alternatives thus fixed can never be fully grasped. And just as knowledge cannot be adequate to a world, in that it cannot exhaust the constituted richness of its content (and, mutatis mutandis, the independently there concreteness of its content),[26] so a world cannot be totally adequate to that which is independently there. For a system of meanings that constitutes our orderly world of experience is that perspective of the indefinitely rich, independently real matrix of possibilities for ordering that has been disclosed by a system of meanings. While the concrete richness of the matrix for possible discrimination of things (a matrix which, in Peirce's terms, "swims in indeterminacy" because of the indefinite richness of its possibilities)[27] is independent of our meanings and the possibilities they allow, the manner in which things are delineated is partially determined by the range of meaningful interrelationships within which perceived things can emerge.

As can be seen from the above discussion, this world is ontologically one with the independently real matrix of possibilities within which it emerges. Yet such a world is dependent upon the human projection or constitution of meanings in a way in which that which is independently there is not. Such a world, then, opens in one direction toward the structures of the independently there and the possibilities it presents, and in the other direction toward the structures of our modes of disclosing it and the possibilities such modes of disclosing allow. What this clearly indicates is that within pragmatic philosophy, "things" cannot be understood in terms of substance or underlying essence but with respect to a unified functionality within the encompassing meaningful context of world. Peirce expresses this in his seemingly cryptic claim that "there is no *thing* which is in itself in the sense of not being relative to the mind, though things which are relative to the mind doubtless *are*, apart from that relation."[28]

In the interactional unity that constitutes our worldly experience, both poles are manifest: the independently there otherness onto which worldly experience opens, and the structure of the human way of being within whose purposive activity worldly experience emerges.[29] There is thus a two-directional openness in experience. What appears within experience reflects both the character of the independently there and the character of our mode of disclosing it, for what appears within experience is a structural unity formed by the interaction of these two poles. In light of this brief sketch, the ensuing discussion will turn to the central role of world in Heidegger's philosophy.

The significance of world as related to the human mode of being, which is implicitly operative in pragmatic philosophy, is brought into sharp focus in its foundational significance in Heidegger's position. Heidegger moves from the world of second-level objects of reflection and their manner of being to an understanding of everyday being-in-the-world or the concrete world of everyday involvements. From there he proceeds to the foundational level, to the conditions of possibility of any world, to the worldhood of the world as rooted in the structure of the human way of being. The worldhood of the world, its nature as a significant whole or a meaningful totality, makes possible the human, everyday "work world," as well as derived worlds of second-level reflection. For Heidegger, the very structure of the human way of being is world-founding or world-projecting. The human is ontologically defined as worldly: it is being-in-the-world.

"So far as the Dasein *is*, it is in a world."[30] Conversely, "World is only, if, and as long as a Dasein exists."[31]

The world is not an object of conscious belief; instead it is "'there' before all belief."[32] Doubt can occur within the world but not about the world. To try to prove the world is a misunderstanding, according to Heidegger, for "such a questioning makes sense only on the basis of a being whose constitution is being-in-the-world. It is absurd to wish to subject to a proof of existence that which founds in their very being all questioning of a world and all attempts to prove and demonstrate that the world exists. World in its most proper sense is just that which is already on hand for any questioning."[33] For Heidegger, then, world as a significant whole, which is necessary for any beliefs or questioning about things within the world or aspects of it, is founded in the holistic nature of knowledge and experience, and the structure of the possibility of such holistic awareness is at once the ontological structure of the human mode of being. The ensuing discussion will turn to the explication of the other dimension of world, its openness onto that which is independently there.

The question of the famous turning in Heidegger's thought, and the debate as to whether it constitutes a rupture or a continuity between the earlier and the later Heidegger, is by now a well-ploughed field. The following discussion, based on the latter alternative, proposes to examine Heidegger's understanding of world as involving the two-directional openness developed above in the context of pragmatism and Heidegger's earlier and later works as concerned respectively with these two poles.

The early Heidegger, in his concern with the openness of world onto our modes of disclosure, describes being itself as the "total meaningfulness of the world" projected by the human. The coming to pass of being as the luminosity of the world in *Being and Time* occurs through human "care." As he summarizes and emphasizes what is a seemingly subjectivistic position, Being "is dependent upon the understanding of Being."[34] Heidegger himself, however, attempts to correct the implications of his numerous statements in *Being and Time* that seem to conflate being with the human lighting of world. Thus he queries, "But does not *Being and Time* say on p. 212,[35] . . . 'Only so long as Dasein is, is there Being'? To be sure. It means that only so long as the lighting of Being comes to pass does Being convey itself to man. But the fact that the . . . lighting as the truth of Being itself, comes to pass is the dispensation of Being itself. . . . This sentence does not say that Being is the product of man."[36]

In the later Heidegger, the nature of humans as world-founding becomes explicitly understood in terms of the broader context of being in which they are participants. Indeed, being provides thinkers with the very being by which they are able to think. Here being, as that which gives possibilities, is not the being of the human as world-founding but is that which grounds the human mode of being in a broader context. This is expressed in Heidegger's discussion of that-which-regions.[37] That-which-regions provides the open-ended availability of possibilities. It grounds all that is and all the ways of being and is itself present in all that appears within the world.[38] It grounds the human mode of being and provides the possibilities that allow the functional unity of things to emerge in relation to human creative, purposive activity. The human emerges within this context as that manner of being in reference to which that-which-regions is disclosed via the mediation of world.[39] The world, as a significant, unified whole, is the horizon of meaningful experience. As Heidegger observes, however, "The horizon is still something else besides a horizon. Yet after what has been said that something else is the other side of itself, and so the same as itself."[40] As the "side facing us" it reveals, but even as it reveals it conceals. It is not exhausted in its horizonal relation to the human. The concreteness of the possibilities engendered by this extantness of being[41] can never be exhausted by human disclosive activity. It makes possible both disclosedness and its "other side," opacity.

The human horizons of interpretation must be grounded in extant being, which has its own potentialities for being disclosed as exhibiting certain types of structures. Thus, Heidegger can emphasize a certain essential "powerlessness" of the human mode of being.[42] Yet, worldly significance cannot be understood through the disclosedness of essential natures, for worldly significance is not independent of the projections of the human. The "natures" or "essences" of things in the world reflect the character of human activity within an action-oriented world, a world of praxis. And, just as world is not a collection of intraworldly things but is instead the context of meaning within which worldly things can reveal themselves in their significance, so the extant matrix of being, as having its own potentialities for exhibiting certain types of structures, is not a collection of individual things having essential natures.[43] Instead, it is that indeterminately rich matrix of possibilities for ordering that unveils itself through the emergence of individual things as it enters the horizons of significance or the horizons of human purposive activity. Things as they emerge within the context of world are a function of the intertwining of the matrix of being, having its own developing potentialities and the possibilities projected through the structure of human activity. Only through meaningfully directed activity does the matrix of being let itself stand out as individual things; likewise, in our encounter with individual things we are experiencing the being of these things.

Without world horizons there can be no meaning to that which is independently there or to independent possibilities for entering into worldly significance. As Heidegger observes, even "resistance is a phenomenal character which already presupposes a world."[44] Indeed, the meaningfulness of "resistance as well as bodily presence find their ground in this, that worldhood already is."[45] But there can be no world and no intraworldly things without extant being that grounds both the being of humans and the world that they project, without the matrix of extant possibilities for entering into worldly significance. And the brute facticity of this extant matrix of possibilities must be adequately incorporated within the contours of world if world is not to soar out of sight[46] but instead "is to ground itself on a resolute foundation."[47]

The above discussion has attempted to show that for pragmatism and Heidegger alike, the things within our everyday world do not copy the independently there but instead emerge through our modes of disclosing its rich matrix of possibilities for ordering. Nor do the modes of disclosing via which emerge the things within our world copy the independently there; instead, they allow to emerge in a meaningful way its indeterminate richness. Finally, the world within which specific meanings and beliefs arise, and within which things or facts emerge for conscious awareness, is not a copy of that which is independently there—nor is the world identical with it in its character as independent. Instead, such a world is the encompassing frame of reference or field of interest of human purposive activity, the ultimate backdrop of significance within which emerging things are situated, the "outermost" horizon of meaningful rapport by which humans are actively unified with that which is independently there. Thus, our world is a function of the interplay of meanings and independent possibilities for ordering and, as a function of both, mirrors neither exactly, though it reflects characteristics of each. What occurs in the world must conform to the possibilities available within the world we have projected through our action-oriented meaning bestowing activity, although the world we have projected has itself risen through the intertwining of our purposive activities with what is there as possibilities for worldly disclosedness.

For Heidegger and pragmatism alike, then, the sense of both the structure of the human mode of being and the being of the extant, or the independently there, is rooted in the phenomenological features of a worldly experience that is a function of the intertwining of each dimension. Thus, the sense of worldly experience in its two-directional openness provides a common foundation for the exploration, within the positions of pragmatism and Heidegger, of the human way of being and of that larger context within which it is immersed and from which it has risen. With such a common foundation for this two-directional exploration, it can well be anticipated that mutually illuminating insights are to be found throughout their respective results.

Notes

1. By "classical American pragmatism" is intended that position incorporating the works of its five major contributors: Charles S. Peirce, William James, John Dewey, C. I. Lewis, and G. H. Mead. That these philosophers provide a unified perspective is assumed in this essay, but this claim is defended at some length in my book, *Speculative Pragmatism* (Amherst: The University of Massachusetts Press, 1986).

2. The brief sketch presented in the following discussion is examined and supported in some depth in Rosenthal, *Speculative Pragmatism*.

3. George Herbert Mead, *The Philosophy of the Act* (Chicago: University of Chicago Press, 1938), p. 331.

4. At this point, a potential language problem should be anticipated. Pragmatists tend to use the terms *objects* and *things* interchangeably, referring to the objects of the second-level reflections of science as a different kind of object than the objects of common sense. Heidegger, however, distinguished between objects and things, reserving "things" for that which comes to presence within primary experience and "objects" for the content of the abstract focus of science. Thus, I have chosen to use the term *thing* in my discussion of pragmatism. Even here, however, there is a possible point of confusion. When Heidegger discusses "the thing" in his most famous work in this area— namely, Martin Heidegger, *What Is a Thing?* trans. W. Barton and V. Deutsch (Chicago: Regnery Press, 1967)—he is dealing with the Kantian concept of a thing, which corresponds most closely to his own use of "object." This Kantian concept of 'thing', however, is not appropriated by Heidegger in his own use of 'thing'. See, for example, Martin Heidegger, "The Thing," in *Poetry, Language, Thought*, trans. William Lovitt (New York: Harper and Row, 1971); see also Martin Heidegger, "The Turning," in *The Question Concerning Technology and Other Essays*, trans. William Lovitt (New York: Harper and Row, 1977).

5. Mead, *The Philosophy of the Act*, pp.116–17.

6. Ibid., p. 35.

7. William James, *Essays in Radical Empiricism: The Works of William James*, ed. Frederick Burkhardt (Cambridge, Mass.: Harvard University Press, 1976), vol. 1, p. 86n.

8. Ibid.

9. William James, *Principles of Psychology: The Works of William James*, ed. Frederick Burkhardt (Cambridge, Mass.: Harvard University Press, 1977), p. 926.

10. Such a pluralistic universe is the precondition for the interactionally unified world of pragmatism, for with a pluralistic universe, "so far from defeating its rationality, as the absolutists so unanimously pretend, you leave it in possession of the maximum amount of rationality practically attainable by our minds. Your relations with it, intellectual, emotional, and active, remain fluent and congruous with your own nature's chief demands." William James, *A Pluralistic Universe: The Works of William James*, ed. Frederick Burkhardt (Cambridge, Mass.: Harvard University Press, 1977), p. 144.

11. John Dewey, "The Reflex Arc Concept in Psychology," in *The Works of John Dewey: The Early Works*, ed. Jo Ann Boydston (Carbondale and Edwardsville: Southern Illinois University Press, 1969–72, 1979), vol. 5, pp. 107–108.

12. This difference in levels of focus reflects no difference in the relationship intended. Instead, the human-world relation can be expressed through a focus on concrete activity or through a focus on the level of functioning of more consciously grasped interrelationships rooted in such concrete activity.

13. Charles Sanders Peirce, *Collected Papers*, vols. 1–6, ed. Charles Hartshorne and Paul Weiss (Cambridge: Belknap Press of Harvard University, 1931–35), vol. 3, p. 527; C. I. Lewis, *Mind and the World Order* (New York: Dover Publications, 1929), app. A.

14. Peirce here distinguishes between what he calls the essentially or logically possible and the substantially possible, while Lewis distinguishes, in parallel fashion, between absolute possibility and relative possibility (C. I. Lewis and C. H. Langford, *Symbolic Logic* [New York: Dover Publications, 1959], pp. 160–61; Peirce, *Collected Papers*, vol. 4, p. 67, and vol. 3, p. 527).

15. C. I. Lewis, "Replies to My Critics," in *The Philosophy of C. I. Lewis*, ed. P. A. Schilpp, *Library of Living Philosophers Series* (La Salle, Ill.: Open Court, 1968), p.

660; C. I. Lewis, "Facts, Systems, and the Unity of the World," in *Collected Papers of C. I. Lewis*, ed. John. D. Goheen and John L. Mothershead, Jr. (Stanford: Stanford University Press, 1970), pp. 383–93; Charles Sanders Peirce, *Microfilm Edition of the Peirce Papers*, Harvard University, catalogue by Richard Robin (Amherst: University of Massachusetts Press, 1967), sect. 647, p. 8; Peirce, *Collected Papers*, vol. 4, p. 68, and vol. 3, p. 527.

16. Lewis, "Facts, Systems, and the Unity of the World," pp. 383–84; Peirce, *Collected Papers*, vol. 2, p. 141.

17. Lewis, "Replies to My Critics," p. 660; Peirce, *Microfilm Edition of the Peirce Papers*, sect. 647, p. 8.

18. Peirce, *Collected Papers*, vol. 3, p. 527.

19. Ibid.

20. Lewis, *Collected Papers of C. I. Lewis*, p. 306.

21. Peirce, *Collected Papers*, vol. 4, p. 67.

22. Ibid., vol. 3, p. 527.

23. Ibid.

24. Lewis, "Facts, Systems, and the Unity of the World," p. 390.

25. Ibid.

26. Ibid., pp. 387–90.

27. Peirce, *Collected Papers*, vol. 1, pp. 171–72.

28. Ibid., vol. 5, p. 311 (emphasis added).

29. The character of both poles that enter into world must be understood in terms of temporality. The development of this point, however, lies beyond the scope of this paper.

30. Martin Heidegger, *The Basic Problems of Phenomenology*, trans. Albert Hofstadter (Bloomington: Indiana University Press, 1982), p. 169.

31. Ibid., p. 170.

32. Ibid., p. 216.

33. Martin Heidegger, *History of the Concept of Time*, trans. Theodore Kisiel (Bloomington: Indiana University Press, 1985), p. 215.

34. Martin Heidegger, *Being and Time*, trans. John Macquarrie and Edward Robinson (New York: Harper and Row, 1962), p. 255.

35. Ibid.

36. Martin Heidegger, "Letter on Humanism," in *Basic Writings*, ed. David Farrell Krell (New York: Harper and Row, 1977), p. 216.

37. Martin Heidegger, *Discourse on Thinking*, trans. John Anderson and E. Hans Freund (New York: Harper and Row, 1966), pp. 66ff.

38. Heidegger rejects the notion of a suprasensible reality that grounds appearances as in substantive realism or that houses them as in modern subjectivistic epistemology. Worldly appearances are the appearances of that which is independently there as revealed within the contours of human disclosive activity.

39. As is the case within the context of pragmatism, the character of both poles that enter into world must be understood in terms of temporality. The development of this point, however, again lies beyond the scope of this paper.

40. Heidegger, *Discourse on Thinking*, p. 64.

41. The concept of extantness, of that which is independent of humans and their world, is not to be found in *Being and Time*. However, it is brought into clear focus in the early Heidegger in *The Basic Problems of Phenomenology*. See, for example, Heidegger, *The Basic Problems of Phenomenology*, pp. 169, 286, 294–97. It can also be found in Martin Heidegger, *The Metaphysical Foundations of Logic*, trans. Michael Heim (Bloomington: Indiana University Press, 1984). See, for example, pp. 156–57 in the latter work.

42. Heidegger, *The Metaphysical Foundations of Logic*, p. 125.
43. Although the human mode of being is not substantive even in Heidegger's *Being and Time*, this work still allows for the existence of substances other than the non-substantive human way of being: substances that ground the more abstract functional concepts, although this point is essentially irrelevant for Heidegger's concerns there. See, for example, *Being and Time*, pp. 118–22. However, in the later Heidegger, when his concerns turn explicitly toward the independent dimension that enters into the character of experience, the unity not just of second-level objects of abstract reflection but also of the things of everyday experience lies in their functionality. (See his analysis of the jug in "The Thing," in *Poetry, Language, Thought*, pp. 166ff.
44. Heidegger, *History of the Concept of Time*, p. 222.
45. Ibid., p. 222.
46. Heidegger, *Basic Writings*, p. 175.
47. Ibid., p. 175

Pragmaticism Is an Existentialism?

KENNETH L. KETNER

"You misspelled part of your title," said a loyal and diligent proofreader. "It's pragmatism."

So one day when I was doing nothing in particular in the library I looked for the word in the 1958 edition of Webster's unabridged dictionary. Here is what I found on page 1938: "Pragmaticism. The philosophic doctrine of C. S. Peirce; adopted by Peirce to distinguish his philosophy from other forms of pragmatism."[1]

Where and when did he adopt the strange word? It happened in 1905, in an article for *The Monist* entitled "What Pragmatism Is."[2] There Peirce recalled his introduction of pragmatism in the Metaphysical Club at Cambridge in the 1870s. Peirce had virtually lived in a laboratory since age six. So, it was an experimentalist's theory "that a *conception*, that is, the rational purport of a word or other expression, lies exclusively in its conceivable bearing upon the conduct of life; so that, since obviously nothing that might not result from experiment can have any direct bearing upon conduct, if one can define accurately all the conceivable experimental phenomena which the affirmation or denial of a concept could imply, one will have therein a complete definition of the concept, and *there is absolutely nothing more in it.*"[3]

That, of course, is a version of the pragmatic maxim—that is, the pragmaticistic maxim—one of the jewels of American technical philosophy, a way of finding the meanings of concepts. A common erroneous tendency is to regard this maxim as an early form of logical empiricism, erroneous because logical empiricism is inconsistent with Peirceian realism and his notion of open inquiry, not to mention being inconsistent with semiotic. Moreover, Peirce explicitly denied that it was a kind of positivism.[4] Perhaps that is why, if our eyes are lifted toward the more human elements of those remarks, we can detect a statement by a man struggling through the cosmos, as we all must do—to the effect that life is an experiment, with nothing guaranteed in advance and no sure path except to continue experimenting, correcting our errors as best we can as we push toward future interpretations. That is hardly the stance of a foundationalist, whether of the Cartesian or sense-datum variety.

Peirce is often understood only as a technician in philosophy. But consider that passage from a wider perspective. Doesn't the phrase *finding the intellectual purport of conceptions*, which is the utility of Peirce's maxim, begin to bring to mind the possibility that alongside words like "argument" or "reality" he is also thinking of the intellectual purport of "happiness" or "community" or "person"?

Why did he adopt the strange term? In the interval since the public announcement of the philosophical conception of "pragmatism" in a lecture by William James in 1898,[5] until Peirce's article in 1905, multiple versions of "what pragmatism is" had appeared in the United States and elsewhere. The situation was about as varied then as it is now. Now, as then, it is difficult to keep track of all the pragmatists, especially when the list contains persons as diverse as Henry Kissinger, Richard Rorty, or Lee Iacocca. One is tempted to observe that pragmatism has become too successful. Peirce reflected that the situation had become so bad that his brat "pragmatism" was even beginning to appear in literary journals, "where it gets abused in the merciless way that words have to expect when they fall into literary clutches."[6] Peirce then made a radical decision: "The writer, finding his bantling 'pragmatism' so promoted, feels that it is time to kiss his child good-by and relinquish it to its higher destiny; while to serve the precise purpose of expressing the original definition, he begs to announce the birth of the word 'pragmaticism,' which is ugly enough to be safe from kidnappers."[7]

This result appeased my proofreader. But in the course of sifting the foregoing material, certain other questions came to me. Why, more than eighty years later, is this name for Peirce's work still so little used? Surely not because it is ugly, or that Edwardian kidnappers have a stronger stomach than their contemporary comrades—which is to say that many more ugly bastards have been kidnapped since 1905. Moreover, why is Peirce's work, by any name, still less well known today and less used now, even by those among us who are identified as pragmatists? Why are philosophers and academicians today, similar to those of 1905, likely to know nothing of pragmaticism, the overall philosophical doctrine of C. S. Peirce, the founder of pragmatism as a philosophic movement?

I can't give complete answers in this short compass. Some evidence relevant to these issues is already generally available. But I can offer a hypothesis, which, if correct, will be relevant.

Abruptly expressed, it has occurred to me that pragmaticism is an existentialism. If that were true, because existentialism is rather out of fashion among the majority of philosophically inclined intellectuals in North America, it would tend to answer my questions about pragmaticism and its relative nonabsorption into American and English intellectual life. It would also tend to explain the rather curious fact that Peirce is more generally appreciated in Europe than in his native Massachusetts. Behold, the fate of prophets!

If pragmaticism is an existentialism, there should be some recognizable consequences of that claim. At least we ought to be able to find some parallels with some of the existentialist thinkers. But the first problem encountered there is that the existentialists are about as varied as the pragmatists! Probably the best I can do here is to select some writers who are generally acknowledged as good representatives of existentialist tendencies. I will use an inductive sample of two: Walker Percy and Jean-Paul Sartre. And I limit the sampling to just a few points.

One general character in common between the existentialists and Peirce is recognition of the reality of persons: acting, choosing, suffering, living, searching, interpreting, dying beings. This factor in Peirce's thought sometimes is obscured by his proper emphasis upon community and his disgust with Cartesian subjectivism *in science*. But there is a strong, not well-known, personalist strain in Peirce's general system (which is wider than his account of science and philosophy). You will have to accept my promissory note for a defense of that claim on another occasion.

To descend to more particular similarities, we might first notice that when we initially come to realize our personhood, we find that we are in a *world*, as Percy phrases it,[8] as opposed to just an *environment*. An environment, in his sense, is a setting in which only efficient causal relations are to be found. A world, on the other hand, along with environmental factors, also includes significance, meaning, interpretation, understanding, and selves. These additional factors Percy places under the heading of triadic behavior, or sign use. Percy's discovery was that such triadic relations cannot be reduced to conglomerates of dyadic relations. Or, worlds are not reducible to environments. In this point Percy is actually an independent rediscoverer of the almost identical principle noticed by Peirce about 1866.[9] I have traced aspects of these two parallel discoveries elsewhere in considerable detail.[10] It is a major confirmation of my thesis that Dr. Percy, after a period of intense immersion in the literature of existentialism, rediscovered this point independently. Only later did he come to realize that Peirce had worked it out almost a century earlier.[11] That the two thinkers are so close on this fundamental point is a major confirmation, and hence perhaps the principal point of comparison that tends to support pragmaticism's really being an existentialism.

This world of triadic phenomena, in which we first come to recognize ourselves, has a fundamental place in Peirce's late work. I think that there is only a terminological difference between it and related topics in existentialism. He referred to it as "common sense." All of his mature philosophical elaborations arise from his belief that the world of common sense is a fundamental guide to all philosophizing, a process he understood as only a task of clarifying in a controlled way what in a vague form we already accept as residents of the common-sense world. There is also much in Peirce's semiotic that can be brought forth to bolster the notion of a world (but not today).

The very definition of existentialism can be seen as a way of claiming this same point. My favorite example of this is from Sartre.[12]

> What [the existentialists] have in common is simply the fact that *existence* comes before *essence*—or, if you will, that we must begin from the subjective. . . .
> There is at least one being whose existence comes before its essence, a being which exists before it can be defined by any conception of it. That being is man or, as Heidegger has it, the human reality. What do we mean by saying that existence precedes essence? We mean that man first of all exists, encounters himself, surges up in the world—and defines himself afterwards. If man as the existentialist sees him is not definable, it is because to begin with he is nothing. He will not be anything until later, and then he will be what he makes of himself. Thus there is no human nature.

This passage provides the opportunity for an interesting experiment. Suppose we rewrote it using the terminology of pragmaticism? Would we get something that the existentialists would accept, at least those who savvy Peirce's lingo? "What do we mean by saying that man's reality comes before man's nature or significance? We mean that first of all the human mind acquires the power of interpretation, then begins to engage in interpretation, including interpretation of self. Thus a person will be what his or her interpretation of self creates. There is no a priori human nature: yet there is an 'image of man' which is but the collective consequence of many individual instances of interpretive actions, or semeioses."

That is, a pragmaticist would urge that Sartre could have made his point more accurately by means of Peirce's existence/reality distinction. Instead of "existence precedes essence," it would have been more accurate to explain that "the reality of the process of semiosis precedes any actual interpretations." In other words, for Peirce, existentialists might be better identified as "realistentialists." Peirce might have agreed with Sartre that man is nothing, in the sense of "no thing" but could have gone on to elaborate that not being a thing (not being a *res cogitans*, or just a collection of banging, wiggling molecules), man is a process of semiosis or system of relations, the central feature of which is the action of interpreting. This is the upshot of Peirce's essay, "Man's Glassy Essence," the title referring to our mirror-like essence.[13] By this allegory of mirrors I take it that Peirce was imagining one of us looking in a mirror and thinking, "That is me." That is to say that the essence of a self is that it interprets, even itself, and that the very reality of a self is as a continuing process of interpretation and self-interpretation.

Existentialists of all varieties are widely known for their emphasis upon human freedom. There are few clear statements in Peirce about that topic. However, consider this one:[14] "My account of the facts you will observe leaves a man at full liberty, no matter if we grant all that the necessitarians ask."

This infrequency of comment on the subject is, I believe, somewhat misleading. Peirce is well-known as an exponent of interpretation. I think this is but a somewhat logically oriented way of asserting the same point for which Sartre, for instance, is widely known—the claim that man is "condemned to be free." There are occasions in Sartre's prose when for him to continue to talk of choosing causes reader nonresonance, leading one to wish that he would switch over to interpretation-talk, for his point would make more sense that way. For example, his dictum that "in choosing for myself, I choose for all mankind" would on the face of it be more plausible if it were, "In making an interpretation I am aiding in forming the idea or general image of humanity."

In another location we can catch Sartre making the switch himself, for there he virtually accepted "interpret" as an explication of his sense of "choose."[15] "No rule of general morality can show you what you ought to do: no signs are vouchsafed in this world. The Catholics will reply, 'Oh, but they are!' Very well; still, it is I myself, in every case, who have to interpret the signs."

A bit later on the same page, Sartre made it clear that each of us bears full responsibility for the "decipherment of signs," that each of us decides the meaning of our being through interpretation. Coming to knowledge of this brings with it the experience of one of those Sartrian emotions, "abandonment," the feeling that we are inevitably separated from any a priori source that will create our person. An accompanying feeling is anguish, brought about through the realization that each of us and no other is responsible for the interpretations we make. One familiar with semiotic who reads these sentences in Sartre will find it difficult to escape the conclusion that Sartre's enlarged conception of "choice" is very much more than likely equivalent to Peirce's notion of "interpretation." Thus, the slogan widely associated with Sartre can be restated in equivalent Peirceian language: "We are condemned to interpret."

For Peirce, the first move out of the world of common sense is a major person-forming choice—selection of a method of resolving doubt. In typical existentialist manner, he is aware that there is nothing guiding or forcing the choice of the objective or rational method versus any of the nonobjective or egocentric approaches (authority, tenacity, fashion). He described that choice, on which all his later intellectual work was based, in ringing prose that is reminiscent of the focus and tone of Sartre and Percy.[16]

> Such are the advantages which the other methods of settling opinion have over scientific investigation. A man should consider well of them. . . . Upon such considerations he has to make his choice—a choice which is far more than the adoption of any intellectual opinion, which is one of the ruling decisions of his life, to which, when once made, he is bound to adhere. . . .
>
> Yes the other methods do have their merits: a clear logical conscience does cost something—just as any virtue, just as all that we cherish, costs us dear. But we should not desire it to be otherwise. The genius of a man's logical method should be loved and reverenced as his bride, whom he has chosen from all the

world. He need not contemn the others; on the contrary, he may honor them deeply, and in doing so he only honors her the more. But she is the one he has chosen, and he knows he was right in making that choice.

Which of the two concepts, "choice" or "interpret," is more encompassing? I can but guess now that the answer is "neither," that a more complete study would show that they are equivalent notions.

Let us end this exercise as we began it, by thinking of the maxim of pragmaticism. Instead of being some vague precursor of the verification principle, Peirce stated on a number of occasions that it was but a corollary of the theory of signs, a corollary of semiotic, which is in effect a theory of interpretation. Presented in the semiotic mode, the pragmaticistic maxim might read in general that the meaning of a concept lies in future intrepretations, in particular those interpretations on which we will be prepared to act. That suggests that it might be plausible for us to summarize our results by modifying a well-known philosophical graffitum:

>To be is to interpret.
>Peirce
>
>To be is to do.
>Sartre
>
>Do be do be dooo.
>Sinatra

Notes

1. *Webster's New International Dictionary of the English Language* (Springfield, Mass.: G. and C. Merriam Co., 1958).
2. Charles Sanders Peirce, "What Pragmatism Is," *The Monist* 15 (1905).
3. Ibid., p. 162.
4. Charles Sanders Peirce, "On the Natural Classification of Arguments," *Proceedings of the American Academy of Arts and Sciences* 7 (1867): 283–84.
5. William James, "Philosophical Conceptions and Practical Results," *University Chronicle* 1 (1898): 287–310.
6. Peirce, "What Pragmatism Is," p. 165.
7. Ibid.
8. Walker Percy, *Lost in the Cosmos: The Last Self-Help Book* (New York: Washington Square Press, 1983), pp. 97f.
9. Documented in Walker Percy, "The Delta Factor: How I Discovered the Delta Factor Sitting at My Desk One Summer Day in Louisiana in the 1950's Thinking about an Event in the Life of Helen Keller on Another Summer Day in Alabama in 1887"; reprinted in Walker Percy, *The Message in the Bottle: How Queer Man Is, How Queer*

Language Is, and What One Has to Do with the Other (New York: Farrar, Strauss and Giroux, 1975), pp. 3–45.

10. See Kenneth Laine Ketner, "Peirce's 'Most Lucid and Interesting Paper': An Introduction to Cenopythagoreanism," *International Philosophical Quarterly* 26 (1987): 375–92.

11. For example, in Charles Sanders Peirce, "On a New List of Categories," *Proceedings of the American Academy of Arts and Sciences* 7 (1867): 287–98; Charles Sanders Peirce, "Questions Concerning Certain Faculties Claimed for Man," *The Journal of Speculative Philosophy* 2 (1868): 103–14; Charles Sanders Peirce, "Some Consequences of Four Incapacities," *The Journal of Speculative Philosophy* 2 (1868): 140–57.

12. Jean-Paul Sartre, "Existentialism Is a Humanism," in *Existentialism from Dostoevsky to Sartre*, ed. Walter Kaufmann (Cleveland: Meridian Books, 1956), pp. 289–90.

13. Charles Sanders Peirce, "Man's Glassy Essence," *The Monist* 3 (1892): 1–22.

14. Charles Sanders Peirce, "The Papers of Charles Sanders Peirce," Department of Philosophy, Harvard University, Houghton Library, MS. 448:25.

15. Sartre, "Existentialism Is a Humanism," p. 298.

16. Charles Sanders Peirce, "The Fixation of Belief," *Popular Science Monthly* 12 (1877): 14.

To Create the Absolute Edge

DAVID G. LEAHY

> *Like William James, I too believe that experience grows by its edges. By nature, the child comes into the world on edge, on the qui vive, with a penchant for making relations.*
>
> John J. McDermott
> Streams of Experience[1]

> *Beginning itself is becoming a surd in our consciousness, a cipher without a code, the only code ready to hand being one which reverses our given identity of beginning by apprehending it as the beginning of the end.*
>
> Thomas J. J. Altizer
> History as Apocalypse[2]

The thing embodied is the essentially American philosophy of Pierce, James, and Dewey—the thing that is really where it's at: at a definite place indefinitely, or definitely at an indefinite place. This alternative is in fact the structure of the actual phenomenology of quantum mechanics in which Heisenberg's "principle of indeterminacy" says the observer may choose to know precisely *either* the position *or* the velocity of a particle but not both at once. Dewey welcomed the discovery of this principle as the "the acknowledgment, within scientific procedure itself,"[3] of pragmatism's understanding of the essential finitude of the intellectual organization of experience; an acknowledgment "of the fact that knowing is one kind of interaction which goes on within the world." The emergence of the principle of indeterminacy was for him the "final step in the dislodgment of the old spectator theory of knowledge";[4] in effect, the recognition of the inseparability of synthetic a priori judgments from active methodology and the acknowledgment that universal laws are but *instrumentalities* directed toward the "observation of a new phenomenon, toward an object actually experienced by way of perception," which is always an individual.[5] Dewey instantiates the philosophic understanding of the scientific enterprise as that which is ordered to the production of new individuals. The un-Aristotelian conflation of intellect with reason in European thought had been *formally* prepared in Aquinas's notion of the human intellect as "defective"[6] and essentially carried through in Descartes's *Meditations*.[7] When James insisted on substituting *things* for "ideas" in the psychological doctrine of association[8] and, analogously, when he translated the "meaning" of pragmatism from the realm of Peirce's transcendental habits to the world of percepts,[9] he, in an un-Aristotelian direction, restored qua species, as Peirce had qua universal, the Aristotelian irreducibility of intelligence to reason.[10] In his *Logic*, Dewey completed this restoration qua individual,[11] producing in American thought a scientific Aristotelian realism without the latter's *transcendent* intuitionism: a new perception is essentially a construction of the acting mind within the actual world. There remains, however, in Dewey, for whom *mind* is the active background abiding change,[12] an *immanent* intuitionism, the reversal of Aquinas's negative "defect" of intellect (the fact that it "is more easily led by what is known through natural reason")[13] to the mind's positive ability to undergird "consciousness" as the Aristotelian active intellect was to reason, or, in Hegelian terms, as a "higher continuity" of self is to the point of contact where self and world interact. But this "mind," unlike its predecessors, is a thoroughly naturalized product of "prior interactions" of the self "with environment."[14] The implicit indefiniteness of origins in this account is fundamental to pragmatism. Pragmatic objectivity first had been Peirce's divine analogue of mind,[15] the operational understanding of which we do not possess, a matter of instinctual belief, although we can "catch a fragment" of its thought in science. Then it was James's pluralistic universe of intelligent existents, constituting "the wider life of things" to which we are "tangent," a matter of the "proofs of religious experience"[16]; but finally it became Dewey's synthesis of Peirce and James: the ideal/instinctual and the particular/emotional realms embodied in the "mysterious totality of being," a matter of constructive imagination, the "matrix" of "ideal aspirations" and the "source" of "moral values," "the encompassing scope of existence the intellect cannot grasp," the mystery of existence in which we are "enmeshed."[17] As Dewey says, the fact that "the object of knowledge is a constructed, existentially produced, object" is a "tremendous" "shock" to traditional notions, which fact, however, clearly and effectively "installs man, thinking man, within nature."[18] But not only is "thinking man" comprehended in Dewey's pragmatic objectivity: the "Almighty," the "Creator," is installed analogously, by way of Dewey's synthesis of Peirce and James, in the existential mystery of the "totality of being" as, in effect, the imagination's symbolic analogue of the mind of the finite *creator*. Where the Torah says "In the beginning God created the heaven and the earth," Dewey, in *Art as Experience*,[19] takes the creation of heaven and earth to be an act of *self-expression* on the part of the Creator. "Even the Almighty took seven days to create the heaven and the earth, and, if the record were complete, we should also learn that it was only at the end of that period that he was aware of just what He set out to do with the raw material of chaos that confronted Him. Only an emasculated subjective metaphysics has transformed the eloquent myth of Genesis into the conception of a Creator creating without any unformed matter to work upon."

But the textual epitome, *bereshit bara' elohim*, relates the beginning of the *totality* of the universe to divine creating. The "seven days" of creating comprise this beginning of "heaven and earth." Indeed, *bara'*, "to create," is spoken exclusively of divine creation,[20] exactly to distinguish it from the human making that is "the prolonged interaction of something issuing from the self with objective conditions, a process in which both of them acquire a form and order they did not at first possess."[21] It is not that the Creator creates "without any unformed matter to work upon" but, more precisely, that the Creator creating transcends the matter/form distinction, that *the distinction matter/form is created*. The notion of the "mysterious totality of being" supports the otherwise clearly unwarranted projection onto the creation of the universe as a whole of a process of subjective-objective identification actually experienced only as interaction with a universe that by its very nature is partial. The "mysterious totality of being" is the cosmic counterpart to pragmatism's essential way of having *and* not-having the *individuality* that for Dewey is *the* necessity. The "mysterious" is the soft underbelly of a thinking that essentially, if not formally, continues to take seriously the a priori other and, therefore, will have, but not *finally* have, the existence of the individual. Dewey's objective subjectivity, essentially a form of pragmatism's infinite self-postponement of consciousness, confronts the divine with *chaos*. "Chaos" is the "raw material," the "objective condition" confronting "a self not consciously known," a self itself—for chaos is inexhaustible—inexhaustibly not-consciousness. But "to create," *bara'*, is objectivity itself: to create is the absolute edge upon which cannot be projected any a priori thing, (any)thing from before the edge of the totality of being, (any)thing of mystery, (any)thing of that most subtle residue of European subjectivity in American thought, the a priori other, the matter a priori, the unformed matter not in fact experienced but *affirmed to be*, self-projectedly, present at the edge of totality. But strike out pragmatism's projective "nature," the a priori other, strike out the "mystery" of pragmatism, strike out the dogmatic assumption of a postponed reality *finally* intelligible self-referentially, jettison at last that final remnant of Cartesian dualism, the "functional" self[22]: then the edge of totality is *necessarily* the edge of creation, the edge of existence *ex nihilo*. In the thirteenth century Thomas Aquinas distinguished the meaning of *ex nihilo* in a way ignored for the most part until now: on the one hand, that the universe had a beginning (where *ex nihilo* means *out of* nothing).[23] Aquinas *denied* that when the world is said to be made from nothing this signifies the material cause. Dewey with "chaos," like Heidegger with "nothing,"[24] is caught up in an argument absent both from Aquinas and the Torah, an argument projected indirectly or directly from the essentially unhistorical self-reception by consciousness of

To Create the Absolute Edge

the fundamental historical facts of faith, Creation and Incarnation.[25] Indeed, Aquinas's own historically conditioned share in the essentially reactive self-consciousness prevented him from being able to understand the "species" or essence *except* as "abstracted from *here* and *now*,"[26] so that he was not able to *think* what now begins essentially to be conceived *in the wake of the actual Death of God*—when the essence is now understood to be *existence* "here and now," when time is now the absolute totality of being—namely, that the Torah speaks with perfect intelligibility of the perfect beginning of the universe as "an integral part of history";[27] in effect, speaks essentially of an absolutely historical universe.

But where *is* the point of contact with the world within the world? The meshing takes place at the edge. The mesh is the place where we tangle with the world. But we are "on edge," "enmeshed" in the world. What of the edge? The edge is not before the thing. The edge is not after the thing. The edge of a definite thing is an indefinite thing. But the edge of an indefinite thing is a definite thing. Definition: *the edge is the essentially narrow part of the thing* (as the *surface* is the essentially *thin* part of the thing).[28] The edge separates the greater part of the thing from not-the-thing. The edge of a thing is not to be confused with what is *at* the edge of the thing. The bank of a stream is not the edge of the flow. The edge of the stream is precisely that essential narrowness of the stream by which it separates itself from the emptiness-of-the-flow that is the land. The edge of the land interacting with the edge of the stream is the real indefiniteness of the respective edges of definite stream and definite land, reflecting the functionally irreducible distinction of perception and conception (the latter, in turn, a function of an irreducibly "functional" self), respectively, the indefinite edges of two definite things at the point of contact supported by their infinitely indefinite separation (= almost nothing between) and, conversely, the definite edges of two indefinite things at the point of contact supported by their absolute separation (= nothing between). But now for the first time "nothing" is no more. Now, for the first time, "almost nothing" is no more. Now in history the beginning of the *conception* of resistance is *identical with* the zero-resistance of the medium to the flow. What now actually exists is the elimination of the necessity of reducing the motion of the world to "nothing" or to "almost nothing" in order to defeat the consequences of an inertial framework. The construction of the frame of reference is the essence of motion *ex nihilo*; that is, *following* nothing, *not* "not made out of anything," not made *out of* nothing (European consciousness), but also not made doubly redundantly of matter, not "not made out of almost nothing." That is, not "not created but fashioned" (American consciousness) but the unprecedented construction of the frame of reference made out of actual existential matter: motion beginning to be constructed (New World consciousness). Now conceived for the first time: the reduction to "nothing" or "almost nothing" of the elimination of motion identically the perfect ordering of motion: neither the ideal definite, "nothing," nor the real indefinite, "almost nothing," at the *vanishing* of the points between edges, respectively, of two indefinite and two definite things, but the infinitely shared edge, the existence itself of order. The threshold of a new universe is traversed for the first time.

But the final frontier of American thought is the bifurcation: either "almost nothing" or "nothing": the polarity of subjective edge and edgeless subjectivity; the polarity, at once, of consciousness and mind. In McDermott, American thought experiences the Death of God as the death of an *empty* belief in the Finite God; i.e., experiences the Death of God as the disappearance of an Emptiness, a leaving behind of the divine symbol, Dewey's "eloquent myth" relegated to the past. In Altizer, American thought transcends the disbelieving belief of McDermott (the mere belief in the reality of Death of God), experiences the Death of God *as the reality*, experiences the *total* collapse of the ungraspable environment, the collapse of the "mysterious totality of being" into emptiness *in the wake* of the divine disappearances, and, believing belief that it is, experiences *the unreality of the emptiness*, the presence of the totality of the body remaining after the disappearance of divinity. The American theology of the Death of God takes the form of the self-separation of the edge from the thing for the first time, or the actual elimination of the edge of the self of the thing, but not for the first time. In the form of the inversion of the abyss itself, the edge is not the abyss. Before now the realization of the Death of God is the edge of not-the-abyss, the furthest possible extension of modernity, at once the impossible of pragmatism made possible. The residue of the disappearance is at once *the disappearance of the possibility of reconstructing the world*. It turns out, in the final extremity of modernity, in the American death, that the *existential* embodiment of the "principle of indeterminacy" is *existence or a beginning, but not both at once*. Altizer chooses beginning without existence, substituting for the latter precisely the unknown "presence." Beginning itself is "apprehended" as the beginning of the end: not as the beginning of the other at the point of contact but as the beginning of the other at the edge itself of our separation from self, which, because it is at a beginning that cannot be our own beginning, *inessentially* is our own beginning: the beginning in reserve, the beginning *as* the beginning apprehended. Altizer writes in *Total Presence:*[29] "Genuine solitude is a voyage into the interior, but it is a voyage which culminates in a loss of our interior, a loss reversing every manifest or established center of our interior so as to make possible the advent of a wholly new but totally immediate world. The joy of solitude comes only out of a breakthrough releasing us from our own interior, a breakthrough and a joy which is clearly present when we fully listen to music, and it is no less present in the presence of another, but only when that other has no point of contact with our own within."

"Absolute solitude" embodies the pragmatic extreme of modern skepticism[30] in the paradoxical form of an *Epicurean rationalism* that actually *experiences* a new universal humanity in the only way open to it in its perfect withdrawal as "a humanity which we can neither conceive nor define":[31] this is the oxymoronic depth of the immediate world: the essentially mute acknowledgment of a newly intelligible universality: the purely material elimination of the a priori other in the form of "our own."

In McDermott, the other extreme of the modern disbelieving reason reduced to belief is embodied in a *sensible Stoicism*,[32] which, facing Altizer's "eternal death of Jesus,"[33] or absolute death, seizes upon "the journey itself" as the embodiment of the perpetual challenge of experience. Faced with the necessity of existentially embodying the "principle of indeterminacy," McDermott chooses existence without a beginning, substituting for the latter "transience." He writes in *Streams of Experience*:[34]

> We are the species *Homo viator*, persons on a journey, human travelers in a cosmic abyss. Actually, in my judgment, transients is a better word than travelers, for the latter often connotes a definite goal, an end in view, or at least a return home. A transient however is one who is passing through. The meaning of a transient's journey is precisely that: the journey itself. . . . We should make our journey ever alert to our surroundings and to every perceivable sensorial nuance. Our journey is a kaleidoscope of alternating experiences, mishap, setback, celebrations, and eye-openers, all undergone on the *qui vive*.

For the radical experiences of the Death of God, the inversion of the *rational* abyss wherein is glimpsed "a new world in the very advent of a new and universal humanity," the only possible question is "whether or not that humanity is our own."[35] The ultimate answer embodied in this reversal of "our given identity of beginning" is that our own humanity is not our own. The alternative to this absolute advent of a new humanity, the alternative to the *interior* arrival of the Death of God, the alternative to the arrival of an actually novel reality, the alternative to the *owning* separating itself from the novelty of the world in the form of "total presence" is McDermott's absolute journeying: nonarrival absolutely prescinding arrival. While denying the world's novelty,[36] it prescinds the advent of an abysmal *reason*, inverts the *cosmic* abyss to the ideal of making ours what is *originally* not ours, inverts the *exterior* abyss to the ideal of making ours "every perceivable sensorial nuance," inverts the nothingness of experience, the inevitability of our death, to our ideal "capacity" "to eat experience": inverts the fact of death to "personal growth" as "the only sure sign that we are not yet dead,"[37] *believes* in Altizer's "absolute solitude" but experiences it as *not yet*. For McDermott the perpetual challenge of life certifies we are *not yet* absolutely alone. In the return to an original primitivity in a new situation is embodied the attempt at the self-postponement of self-postponement—indeed, the reduplication of the very essence of pragmatism: at once *after Dewey* a return to James: precisely, a Deweyan retreat to James that identifies mind with consciousness, the aesthetic with the rhythmic "run" of things,[38] Dewey's "ordered movement of the matter of . . . experience to a fulfillment"³⁹ with the *essential* forsaking of fulfillment: a post-Deweyan pragmatism reducing the meaningful to the *search* for meaning: indeed, purely theoretical *existence*: beyond Dewey, the *final* existence of the individual in the form of the pre-Deweyan untheoretical existence of the a priori other, in the form of the purely theoretical elimination of the a priori other. Thus, the final extremity of European-American consciousness, the total undergoing of the "immediate world," is split down the middle: *either* the appetite for the satiable experience of relational, i.e., human-made, novelty, the "passing through" on the edge of the same, the relation-making prehension of the same, the perpetually new seizing of the same old world, the perpetually *formal* fulfillment, *or* the insatiable satiety of the experience of a new humanity in the depths of the individual, the perpetual arrival of the totality, the seizing upon, the securing of sameness, taking possession of the new in the name of the same: the *material* fulfillment prescinding the matter/form distinction in the form of unreserved anticipation.

But for the first time, just in time, the edge of mind is a consciousness, the edge of which is absolute. The edge is essentially perfect as never before. For the first time in history, the fact is perceived that the essentially narrow part of mind is the edge of consciousness now after nothing. Mind is absolutely edged out of the edge after nothing. The edge is actually the totality of Identity *after* nothing. As never before the edge of the ocean is the edge of an absolute stream: the explosion of the universe itself, the advent of genetic engineering, the beginnings of the practicability of superconductivity, the incipient technology of thinking: there is not land the stream passes through, no same, neither in imitation of the stream to "pass through," nor to occupy in refusing to imitate the stream, neither to seize upon nor to seize: the banks are identical with the stream for the first time: in the cosmological flood of the stream of consciousness both banks flow as the stream itself flows: there is neither the possibility of an *absolute* hanging back from a sameness, the same "hanging back from," nor the possibility of "participating in the flow," which possibility as already too much of a "hanging back,"⁴⁰ a hanging back *from* the flow *in the relationship to* the flow, the same "taking part." Now, for the first time in history, the Christ is the god of the stream: thought in essence for the first time, the Christ of the stream eliminates the "eternal death of Jesus": not the god of this or that stream but the god of the stream of existence itself beginning the absolute elimination of the Death of God. As never before the divine flows absolutely. In this flow every notion of self is completely dissolved. The nakedness of the species is essentially eliminated. There remains the "almost nothing" enveloped in the pure "nothing." The consciousness of man is the creating edge. The essentially narrow part of man, the narrow itself of man—the edge by which man grows is existing *ex nihilo*. What now actually occurs is the perfect envelopment of the beginning of which the Torah speaks essentially. The *totality* of being *after* nothing, the totality *not* after (either) being (or) nothing (the totality of being *not* after "either nothing or"), i.e., not *from* nothing, is the absolutely existing edge, the edge every part of which is identical with the edge itself.

What now for the first time is conceived essentially is the apocalyptic vision: there is no temple in the city (*Revelation* 21:22), nothing whatsoever is hidden, the body itself *is* clothing itself, clothes do not cover the body but reveal the essence of the body, manifest the essentially artifactual structure of the body, reveal the world to be such a novelty that men cannot stand even so much apart as to be a participant, so as to (merely) *take* part in the creation of the world, avoiding thereby the absolute responsibility of creating a new world. The literal truth of the fact that the body is the temple of the divine spirit now begins to be understood: because the divine spirit, qua first-time experience of the perfect edge of the other, takes up no room whatsoever, there is no end to the artifactual surface of the body in the so-called "interior depths." The essentially thin part of the artifactual body (surface) is its essentially narrow part (edge) infinitely after nothing. The reality of the body is the absolutely unconditioned exteriority of the world. Humanity can hide no longer in its clothes or in its nakedness: everything begins to be fabricated. For the first time, the network is absolute. The essentially narrow part of existence, *ex nihilo* exists everywhere. The edge of consciousness begins to be an essential objectivity: not the edge of mind, but the edge sharing the edge of the other for the first time, the edge of the mind of the other, transcending the "functionally" self-referential polarity of the definite/indefinite vanishing of separation by sharing the edge *after* nothing of the essentially different reality of the other, experiencing the other as identical with the novelty of every part of the edge. *For the first time* the transcendental is absolutely separate from the edgeless. Thought is the edge of the thing. Consciousness, at once absolute, begins to *share* the edge of the mind of another consciousness. *After* nothing the absolutely *form*-less totality: for the first time the perfect elimination of the space of time:[41] no possibility of the essential redundancy of placing time: *whether* inside an exterior space ("a totally present objectivity" "dissociated from all ... interior identity"[42]) or outside an "interior space" that has been made "our place."[43] Time is *absolutely* the place. For the first time the *Ego*, minus the a priori, transcendental other, is absolute *act*. To create the absolute edge is to begin to operate *essentially* without reference to self: time *after* nothing is neither "our" now nor "our" place. The infinitely shared edge has no within to be eternally outwardized, and *a fortiori* no within to transform existence into a body in the absence of the divine spirit ideally interiorizing the world. The absolute exteriority of time-consciousness is the resurrection itself of the Body of the Finite God absolutely at the disposal of another.[44] For the first time the clearly perceived reality is that objectivity is to create objectivity itself. Time itself for the first time is *ho topos*, The Place, in which we live and move and exist, *zomen kai kinoumetha kai esmen*,[45] in which we have not "our being" but the being of the other being at the disposal of another. The temporality of time is The Place that we, embodying, intimately comprehend as the pure "at the disposal of another." *Qui vive?* The person who begins to fabricate an *essentially* new world.

Notes

1. John J. McDermott, *Streams of Experience: Reflections on the History and Philosophy of American Culture* (Amherst: University of Massachusetts Press, 1986).
2. Thomas J. J. Altizer, *History as Apocalypse* (Albany: State University of New York Press, 1985).
3. John Dewey, *The Quest for Certainty*, ed. Jo Ann Boydston (Carbondale and Edwardsville: Southern Illinois University Press, 1984), p. 163.
4. Ibid.
5. Dewey, *The Quest for Certainty*, p. 165.
6. Thomas Aquinas, *The Summa Theologica of St. Thomas Aquinas*, vol. 1. trans. Fathers of the English Dominican Province (New York: Benziger Brothers, 1947), pp. 1, 2, and 5; also D. G. Leahy, *Novitas Mundi: Perception of the History of Being* (New York: New York University Press, 1980), pp. 57ff.
7. René Descartes, *Meditations on First Philosophy*, trans. J. Cottingham, in *The Philosophical Writings of Descartes*, vol. 2 (Cambridge, U.K.: Cambridge University Press, 1984), pp. 16ff., 76ff.
8. William James, The Principles of Psychology, vol. 1, ed. F. Burkhardt (Cambridge: Harvard University Press, 1981), pp. 522–23.
9. Charles Sanders Peirce, *Collected Papers*, vol. 5, ed. Charles Hartshorne and Paul Weiss (Cambridge: Harvard University Press, 1934), p. 343.
10. Leahy, *Novitas Mundi*, pp. 41ff.
11. John Dewey, *Logic: The Theory of Inquiry*, ed. Jo Ann Boydston (Carbondale and Edwardsville: Southern Illinois University Press, 1986), pp. 125ff. and passim.
12. John Dewey, *Art as Experience*, ed. Jo Ann Boydston (Carbondale and Edwardsville: Southern Illinois University Press, 1984), p. 270.
13. Aquinas, *Summa Theologica*, pp. 1, 2, and 5.
14. Dewey, *Art as Experience*, p. 269; also John Dewey, *Experience and Nature*, ed. Jo Ann Boydston (Carbondale and Edwardsville: Southern Illinois University Press, 1981), pp. 229ff.
15. Charles Sanders Peirce, *Collected Papers*, vol. 6, ed. Charles Hartshorne and Paul Weiss (Cambridge: Harvard University Press, 1935), pp. 338–53.
16. William James, *Pragmatism*, ed. Frederick Burkhardt (Cambridge: Harvard University Press, 1975), pp. 143–44.
17. Dewey, *Art as Experience*, p. 56.
18. Dewey, *The Quest for Certainty*, p. 168.
19. Dewey, *Art as Experience*, p. 71.
20. *The New Jerusalem Bible*, ed. H. Wansbrough (Garden City, New York: Doubleday & Co., 1985), p. 17. [Editor's note: I have substituted Roman script for the original Hebrew script of the passage that the author quotes from *Genesis* 1:1 and whose meaning is, "In the beginning God created." I have also so treated—here and later in the text—the Hebrew word for "(he) created," which third-person-singular perfective Hebrew verb-form the author here and later translates by the infinitive "to create."]

21. Dewey, *Art as Experience*, p. 71.
22. McDermott, *Streams of Experience*, pp. 53–54.
23. Aquinas, *Summa Theologica*, art. 45:1–3.
24. Martin Heidegger, "What Is Metaphysics?" trans. A. F. C. Hull and A. Crick, in *Existence and Being* (Chicago: Henry Regnery, 1949), p. 345.
25. Leahy, *Novitas Mundi*, passim.
26. Aquinas, *Summa Theologica*, art. 46:2.
27. *The New Jerusalem Bible*, p. 17.
28. But see Avrum Stroll, *Surfaces* (Minneapolis: University of Minnesota Press, 1988), pp. 204ff.
29. Thomas J. J. Altizer, *Total Presence: The Language of Jesus and the Language of Today* (New York: The Seabury Press, 1980), pp. 106–107.
30. Leahy, *Novitas Mundi*, pp. 340ff.
31. Altizer, *Total Presence*, p. 106.
32. McDermott, *Streams of Experience*, p. 198.
33. Thomas J. J. Altizer, *The Descent into Hell: A Study of the Radical Reversal of the Christian Consciousness* (New York: Seabury Press, 1979).
34. McDermott, *Streams of Experience*, p. 165.
35. Altizer, *Total Presence*, p. 89.
36. McDermott, *Streams of Experience*, p. 168.
37. McDermott, *Streams of Experience*, p. 166.
38. McDermott, *Streams of Experience*, pp. 138ff.
39. Dewey, *Art as Experience*, p. 334.
40. McDermott, *Streams of Experience*, pp. 166–67.
41. G. W. F. Hegel, *Philosophy of Nature*, vol. 1, ed. and trans. M. J. Petry (New York: Humanities Press, 1970), pp. 236–37.
42. Altizer, *Total Presence*, pp. 91ff.
43. McDermott, *Streams of Experience*, pp. 132ff.
44. Leahy, *Novitas Mundi*, pp. 341–96.
45. [Editor's note: I have substituted Roman script for the original Greek script for the Greek word for "the place" and for the original Greek of the passage that the author quotes from *Acts of the Apostles* 17:28, whose meaning is, "We live and we move and we exist."]

SANTAYANA

Santayana: Spirited Spirituality[1]

MORRIS GROSSMAN

I recently read this: "It is said that Kurt Goedel, perhaps the greatest logician who ever lived, long refused to become an American citizen and pledge allegiance to the principles of [the Constitution] because it was, to his eye, so obviously internally inconsistent."[2]

The search for consistency and completeness in our vision of the nature of things, and in our lives, is at once heroic and pathetic. For what if such a laudable vision—sometimes called seeing life steady and seeing it whole—is not, in the nature of things, attainable? What to do then? It is possible to descry the Constitution and to refuse to be an American. But is it possible to refuse to be human? Isn't some inconsistency inevitable? Indeed, would philosophy be at its best without some uncertainty, humanness, and incompleteness? Don't things have to end—papers, the Constitution, even life itself—before they are properly completed?

The noble demand for dialectical precision conflicts, then, with the human need for dramatic largeness and openness. In Santayana's examination of spirit and spirituality the tensions between drama and dialectic are very keen.[3] What follows is a very brief, and certainly incomplete, look at the issues involved, with the help of some selected texts. My references are limited. Although it is good critical procedure to look at everything—usually a great variety of things—Santayana has said about any particular subject, I can only claim a fair sampling. My examples focus on the conflicts, indeed the ongoing drama, associated with the tasks of both defining spirit and living the spiritual life. They involve perspectives that cannot be molded into a consistent outlook, though there is an unspoken, behind-the-scenes perspective of perspectives. Santayana's occasional self-deprecatory remarks, that he momentarily took a transcendental point of view or that he "skirted psychologism," sound dismissive of himself but are themselves voices among ongoing voices.

The tension between defining or clearly specifying what is meant by spirit on the one hand, and living the spiritual life on the other hand, led Santayana to puzzle and agonize over attributing existence to spirit. He confesses his perplexities in the frankest and most disarming fashion. One might say that the decision about attributing existence to spirit turned out to be, for Santayana, at once an intellectual puzzle and an agonizing "existential" dilemma.

As an intellectual problem it involved a search for the essence of spirit. But as an "existential" problem it had to do with moral claims and possibilities, with old-fashioned questions like, What is it to live life well and what is it to convey effort and care? There was the paradox, pervasive and for Santayana always tantalizing, that spirit ultimately perfected accomplishes its own extinction, or nonexistence.[4] Spiritual effort might be furthered by logical clarity, but clarity gained never undid the need for further effort. The clarity and the effort were not the same, and clarity alone did not suffice. The spiritual life might involve the vision of seeing things under the form of eternity, but it was not a life that passed into eternity or that ceased its precarious existence. In one instance, Santayana says that the subtlest form of spirit's distraction is "when it torments itself about its own existence."[5] This is certainly autobiographical, and there is considerable evidence of such torment. In the Santayana manuscripts, his indecisions about attributing existence to spirit jump from the pages—with the word *exists*, on occasion, written and then crossed out. It is, for Santayana, a problem that must persist: its facile resolution, one way or another, would be an evasion of something important. It is as though Santayana could not, in good conscience, escape the horns of his own dilemma.

I propose that it is helpful, and appropriate, to see this Santayana problem as nontemporal and to look at the texts from different periods for what they have in common. For one cannot dispel the difficulties, even the contradictions, by careful attention to the chronology of various statements and by presuming, or claiming, that Santayana's views changed. It is not as though at one time he clearly said this, and at another time he clearly said that. The myth of two Santayanas is indeed that, created by critics who (like Goedel) cannot accommodate to contradiction. So the dilemmas of the spirit are not limited to the elderly Santayana, the result (as has been suggested) of a geriatric transformation in his thinking. His reflections on consciousness, as early as *The Sense of Beauty*,[6] prepare for and parallel his later thoughts, dilemmas, and paradoxes.

That early work lays the groundwork for and anticipates, with a slightly different vocabulary, the writings that followed. In *The Sense of Beauty* there is the distinction between consciousness as purely intellectual (comparable to nonexisting spirit) as opposed to "emotional consciousness," (comparable to existing spirit). This discussion long anteceded Santayana's eventual substitution of the word *spirit* for consciousness, but the words, and the problems associated with them, are essentially the same. Santayana's definition of beauty (as "pleasure objectified") is an early attempt to deal with the two kinds of consciousness or spirit already alluded to, one emotional and human, the other a kind of transcendent consciousness. In *The Sense of Beauty* he attempts to imagine the transition from emotional consciousness (possessed of feeling, will, and change) to consciousness purified, in which pleasure is no longer felt but rather known and transcended. It is the spiritual life, seen in aesthetic terms. It is the move from passion felt to passion Platonically overcome, in the constant or modal refrain of Santayana's attempts, logical and moral, at a passionately passionless, or a spiritedly spiritual, life.

Indeed, the phrase "pleasure objectified," on the face of it, is an oxymoron. Pleasure, or emotion, is subjective. What can be seen in its objective clarity is a term or an essence, which is not the same as having a human emotion. (The essences of surprise and anger, for example, are not the same as being surprised and angry.) The only way to interpret the blatant contradiction of the phrase *pleasure objectified* (as with the phrase *spirited spirituality*) is to see it as a depiction of an always imperfect and uncompleted process, a human happening that cannot be fully seized. The same with "spiritual life," which as a *life* cannot be purely spiritual and, were it to attain purity, would no longer be a life.

In his persistent quandary about the existence of spirit, and in the language that followed *The Sense of Beauty* (where "consciousness" eventually became "spirit"), Santayana wavered between denying the possibility of pure spirit on the one hand and affirming as a viable option an active furtherance of a spiritual life on the other. Thus, pure spirituality, godly omniscience, would preclude the actualities of spirit that occur as phases or moments of human life. Those actualities include intent, care, belief, surprise: in a word, the instabilities of existence.

Surprise, about which Santayana has some words, could not be known by an omniscient spirit. The definition could be known, but surprise as surprise could not be experienced by such a being. "To know surprise by experience is the only way of knowing its essence," Santayana writes.[7] Surprise can't be known by a spirit that sees all things under the form of eternity. Or, surprise defined is not the same as surprise experienced. And the same applies to spirit's existence. ("Knowing its essence" is the problematic phrase here, which is why, later, intuiting essences is not the same as knowledge.)

"The idea of final union with anything specific, even with omniscience or with pure Being, therefore contradicts the very nature of spirit."[8] Of course, what it contradicts is spirit seen as existing, as on the wing, as affiliated with psyche, as longing, as music felt. It does not contradict that other, that greater-than-human sense of spirit that can be defined, and which needs to be defined, but which cannot be achieved. Santayana's strategy (eventually, if not at the outset) is to deal with the interplay, dramatic and poignant, between these aspects of spirit.

Some further remarks might help us to get at the drama and the interplay. "If spirit in us could be entirely dominant we should esteem everything in nature as if it were the inmost part of ourselves, and everything in ourselves as if it were the remotest and the least part of nature. But the actual life of spirit is all compromise, being continually stopped in its flights, and enslaved by some particular passion or illusion. To that extent spirit is not spiritual and exists only in a thwarted effort to be born."[9]

Spirit is known, then, by being imagined, by the thought or specification, of its clearly defined termination. It has its essential nature. But it is also "known," or needs to be known, by the unclear actualities and experiences of pursuit and mortal effort. The spiritual life is not a life of mere philosophical precision and consistency. It is a life of difficult seeking, lighted by the vision of a goal but never attaining the precision of that vision. Spirit is "known" the way existence is known, by the felt stress and distraction of it instead of by its perceived or intuited clarity. This gets at the winged evasiveness of spirit and at the logical futility of trying to capture it frozen and motionless. That effort will inevitably be thwarted. But the logical futility of a task (and it is time to say this) certainly does not rule out the desirability of logical effort—especially for a philosopher. Rendering the futility of that logic required *failed logical effort as a phase of the larger task*! There's a difference between failing and not trying; also, between merely failing and stopping as opposed to failing and then reflecting constructively about why the failure occurs.[10]

Another passage about spirituality. "Such triumphs over nature and human nature can never be complete, and the moments in which it *almost* exists are rare."[11] Notice the "almost" in the above. Again, what is conveyed is a defeated movement. And it could only be conveyed by being defeated; that is, by being attempted *and* failing.

Santayana is Heraclitean in his constant insistence on two simultaneous phases. "Were there less change there would be no spiritual realization of repose, for eternity lies above or beneath life, and even to *pass* into eternity . . . is still an act and a transition. If time were ever arrested, the experience and the thought of eternity would be abolished."[12] So much for any practical claims about living *in* the eternal, which Santayana only proclaimed ironically. But living in pursuit of the eternal, and in changing approximation to it, is another matter and is always possible. Intellectually delineating that pursuit and humanly exemplifying the effort were what Santayana's career was about.

Again, "Spirit lives by transcendence from its center."[13] Note that what is meant here is not transcendence accomplished but, as I have been suggesting, transcendence ventured and imperfectly approached.

There are times when Santayana seemed to affirm a spiritual state, as though transcendence was arrived at and accomplished (though some irony in the claim is usually evident). But consider this spirited scolding of spirituality: "Shall we detach our love altogether from existing beings and platonically only worship universal Ideas of the Beautiful and the Good? This might be wisdom or spiritual insight, but is it love? And can such sublimation really be professed without hypocrisy?"[14]

In the above self-directed taunt, a bit surprising in isolation, we again see

Santayana's rational naturalism in conflict with his other self and chiding the claims of spirituality. Hypocrisy is a strong accusation. At times he was more charitable toward himself—less Goedel-like and dialectical, may we say, about the inevitability of professing conflicting sentiments and needing to live with such professions.

Santayana bravely sought to define certain elusive things, like "feeling" and "existence," as clearly as he could. Feeling he called the intuition of the inarticulate, and existence was specified in terms of external relations. But there is something unsatisfactory—and Santayana knew or felt it—about bringing a pseudoprecision, a clarificatory essence, to that which needed to be experienced in its imprecision and in its obscure movement. This caused the wavering and the drama. Definitional clarity is not the same as moral accomplishment. Giving spirit some definition was important, but doing something else—getting at, celebrating, and conveying the moral feel of spiritual effort—was also important. They had to be done together: each properly depended upon the other, though they pulled in different directions. "Logic and morals": this phrase, this juxtaposition, I believe, appears an astonishing number of times in the Santayana corpus—for reasons I hope I have been suggesting.

Once again: "Spirit is not a reality that can be observed. . . . Spirit can never be observed the way an essence is observed, not encountered the way a thing is encountered. . . . The essence of spirit can be described only circumstantially, and suggested pregnantly."[15]

Essences, ordinarily, are precisely what they are, unchangeable and definable. Is the essence of spirit different from all other essences? Is there an essence of spirit, in view of its recalcitrance to definition? As I have suggested, we need to note Santayana's ungainly attempts to define existence, motion, feeling. These attempts tend to be paradoxical and elusive. Some things are "essentially" defined as undefinable: like man's nature, by existentialists.[16] Especially existence, whose essence is to elude essential capture. "Existence is a surd. . . . Nothing accurate can be said of a thing supposed to bridge two moments of time. Yet to bridge two moments, in some sense, is indispensable to existence."[17] The same applies to spirit. Spirit eludes accurate description for the same reason that existence does. Santayana prefers to live with the paradoxes and the drama as over against a vacuous and nonhuman clarity.

"Spirit is a category, not an individual being."[18] But, of course, it only exists in its instances or individual occasions. "In intent, in belief, in emotion a given essence takes on a value which to pure spirit it could not have."[19] This is connected with Santayana's early thoughts about aesthetics and emotional consciousness. The notion of an essence "taking on a value," however, is clearly problematic. Essences don't change; even the essence of change undergoes no change.

"All this intuition of turbulence and vitality, which a cold immortal spirit could never know, fills the spirit of man, and renders any contemplation of essences in their own realm only an interlude for him or a sublimation or an incapacity. It also renders him more conscious than a purer spirit would be of his own spirit."[20]

It's like knowing surprise better than God knows surprise. The cold immortal spirit is the godlike idea of nonexisting spirit. Existing spirit, in man, is precarious, on the move, with only intimations of pure spirit. Morally, *in this passage*, Santayana used derogatory words like "sublimation" and "incapacity" (not as derogatory as "hypocrisy") to characterize this impulse toward self-transcendence. *In this passage*, I noted. For on other occasions Santayana reverses his moral perspective and sees the impulse to transcendence not as a sublimation in any negative sense, nor as an incapacity, but as a mode of moral fulfillment—certainly one of life's greater moral options.

The evidence that Santayana is dramatizing conflicting viewpoints is overwhelming. To isolate one of Santayana's voices to the neglect of other voices, or to present one voice as contradicting another voice, is a failure of criticism. The textual evidence, in its fullness, should keep us from this. And if we still had any doubts about the matter, there are the frequent passages where Santayana does not hold a second voice in abeyance, or hidden from us, but he presents the voices juxtaposed, in a transparent rendering of them as dramatic alternatives.

Consider the following: "If I am spiritually proud and choose to identify myself with the spirit, I shall be compelled to regard my earthly person and my human thoughts as the most alien and the sorriest of accidents; and my surprise and mortification will never cease at the way in which my body and its works monopolize my attention. If on the contrary I modestly plead guilty to being the biped that I seem, I shall be obliged to take the spirit within me for a divine stranger, in whose heaven it is not given me to live, but who miraculously walks in my garden in the cool of the evening."[21]

Here, side by side, are existing and nonexisting spirit. Given such passages, and there are many of them, how can Santayana be faulted for taking a dogmatic, or a spirited, stand in favor of spirituality? He displayed the drama, and his spiritual detachment is ironically, and indirectly, revealed by his refusal overtly to opt for spirit in the very moment of that remarkable detachment.

Once more. "But the existence of spirit really demands an explanation; it is a tremendous paradox to itself, not to say a crying scandal. . . . Spirit, since it *can* ask how it came to exist, has the right to put the question and to look for an answer. And it may, perhaps, find an answer of some sort, although not one which spirit, in all its moods, will think satisfactory."[22]

Santayana sometimes talks about taking the "point of view" of spirit, which would be different from the point of view of psyche. But there are large dramas and smaller ones, and here we see that even spirit has its moods and some varying moral propensities.

It sometimes passes as scholarship to go behind the backs of philosophers and to presume to reveal them, as it were, to themselves. We are pleased if we can show that they missed some important implications of what they said, or indeed that what they said here was contradicted by what they said there. Such an approach is sometimes useful and sometimes even appreciated. I do not myself find many such opportunities in Santayana. What he said here might indeed contradict what he said there—but not for want of remembrance. As I have indicated, his repeated *deliberate* juxtapositions of conflicting viewpoints ought to remove all doubts about such viewpoints when they are spread out and not juxtaposed. They ought also to keep us from presuming logical carelessness on Santayana's part.

When they are juxtaposed, we can sense some element of pain and dilemma in the moral predicament. We can see greater and lesser success in dramatizing the viewpoints in question. But I know of no instance where what is at stake is logical failure, where Santayana could not see what he was about.

Santayana had extraordinary self-knowledge. He was not at the mercy of, and there is little evidence of, logical or psychological perplexity. There is, however, much evidence of the kind of dramatic wrestling and rewriting that accompanies the effort of good writing.

Consider the following, which might serve as a prime, and here a final, example of Santayana's overt grappling or wrestling with his dilemma: "For a man, and especially for a philosopher, to suggest that spirit does not exist may accordingly pass for a delicious absurdity, and the best of unconscious comedy. If it had been some angel that denied it, because in his serenity and selflessness he could not discover that he was alive, we might regard the denial of spirit as the highest proof of spirituality: but in a material culture struggling to see and to think, and tossed from one illusion and passion to another, such a denial seems not only stupid, but ungracious. . . . Nevertheless I think that those who deny the existence of spirit, although their language is rash and barbarous, are honestly facing the facts, and are on the trail of truth."[23]

So much for the "existence" of spirit (its precarious existence, one might say), which agonized Santayana and which involved him in so many richly dramatic affirmations and denials.

What more can one do with the paradoxes of spirit than display them? Even so, there are some (the earnest logicians, the Goedels) who will persist in missing the message. Santayana at one point made a remark, most unspiritual and unphilosophical, even with a touch of pique, about terminating his efforts. Although he did not adhere to his own declaration, let me use his words as an excuse to bring my own remarks to a close. "I will not pursue this topic: if the reader does not understand, he probably never will."[24]

Notes

1. Some ideas for this paper were generated by reflections on Victorino Tejera's paper "Spirituality in Santayana, and the Critique of Calculative Reason." I commented on that paper at the annual meeting of the Society for the Advancement of American Philosophy, at Pennsylvania State University, March 4, 1988. My title, "Spirited Spirituality," is an oxymoron, and it is intended to be in the spirit (may I say) of Santayana's awareness of the ambiguous and even contradictory senses of "spirit" in his philosophy.

2. Kenneth McKenna, *The New York Times*, April 25, 1988.

3. These categories, I have argued elsewhere, are particularly useful in studying all aspects of Santayana's achievement.

4. Santayana saw that this was the case in Indian philosophy, which intrigued him endlessly, and against which he bounced off his own reflections.

5. George Santayana, *Realms of Being* (New York: Scribner's Sons, 1942), p. 742.

6. George Santayana, *The Sense of Beauty* (Cambridge, Mass.: The MIT Press, 1988).

7. George Santayana, *Scepticism and Animal Faith* (New York: Scribner's Sons, 1923), p. 276.

8. Santayana, *Realms of Being*, p. 817.

9. Ibid., p. 612.

10. Some would see this approach to dialectic as the pervasively hidden, and at times not so hidden, Platonic refrain and message. Santayana, as we know, constantly disparaged logic, while never relinquishing the search for logical clarity. In the dialogue "The Vortex of Dialectic," he dealt in specific fashion with the thwarting, albeit necessary, futility of logic.

11. Santayana, *Realms of Being*, p. 647 (italics added).

12. Ibid., p. 694.

13. Ibid., p. 696.

14. Ibid., p. 782.

15. Santayana, *Scepticism and Animal Faith*, p. 272.

16. Though I have been suggesting connections with the existentialist tradition, there is no evidence that Santayana cared much for the writers in this tradition.

17. Santayana, *Scepticism and Animal Faith*, p. 273.

18. Ibid., p. 275.

19. Ibid., p. 276.

20. Ibid., p. 277.

21. Santayana, *Realms of Being*, p. 278.

22. Ibid., p. 284.

23. Santayana, *Scepticism and Animal Faith*, p. 286.

24. Santayana, *Realms of Being*, p. 280.

Animal Faith: Santayana and Strawson

EDWARD S. SHIRLEY

One of the puzzles of Santayana's *Scepticism and Animal Faith* is his two-fold claim to undermine traditional Cartesian skepticism and at the same time to establish a more all-embracing form of skepticism. How does he undermine traditional skepticism? What is the form of the new skepticism with which he replaces it? There are two conflicting answers to these questions. One maintains that Santayana undermines traditional skepticism by reducing it to solipsism of the moment, which is the new, more all-embracing form of skepticism. The other maintains that Santayana refutes traditional skepticism by refuting the foundational view of knowledge of which traditional skepticism is a form and replacing it with "animal faith." According to the first view, Santayana merely narrows the foundation of knowledge to solipsism of the moment, from which we escape only by a leap of "animal faith" in which we acquiesce in our instinctive propensity to believe in an external world. Let us call this the foundationalist (F) interpretation. For instance, Douglas Greenlee claims Santayana's doctrine that infallibility is limited to intuition of sensory "essences" ("data") has the result "that the mind is screened from the world by appearances," for such essences "play the role in knowledge of the external world only of signs posited as representations of objects and events."[1] It follows there is "no cognitive exit from the given" because "what we know in sense perception are only the immediately given essences."[2]

The second view maintains that instead of arguing that there is a foundation of knowledge, though it is limited to solipsism of the moment, Santayana is contending that the very notion of an incorrigible foundation of knowledge is incoherent because, although we are indeed infallibly aware of sensory qualia, this awareness does not constitute a form of knowledge and so cannot be construed as a foundation for our supposed knowledge. Greenlee is misled by the term *intuition*. Intuition isn't a form of knowledge for Santayana. Santayana's point is that if we were to refrain from interpreting sensory experience in terms of animal faith, all that would be left would be a purely aesthetic, noncognitive experience of sensory qualia that can have no logical connection with any possible knowledge claim. There can be no foundation apart from (or prior to) animal faith. Santayana's skeptical regress argument serves two purposes: first, to show that such a regress does not lead to an infallible form of knowledge but instead to a noncognitive aesthetic experience; and to isolate and introduce us to one type of essences—namely, sensory essences—that can only be reached in this way. Knowledge and aesthetic contemplation of essences are alternative, incompatible states of mind that have nothing to do with one another. With regard to our supposed knowledge, Santayana is merely setting out the content of animal faith genetically, beginning with the sense of "shock" we experience in our contact with the things of the external world. When he speaks of skepticism as a possibility that can only be rejected by a decision, he means only that we could theoretically choose to spend our life in aesthetic contemplation of essences, though no one will do so.[3] Let us call this the antifoundationalist (AF) interpretation.

The issue seems to revolve around whether Santayana conceives of intuition as a form of knowledge. The AF interpretation is correct in that Santayana doesn't *call* intuition a form of knowledge. However, the reason Santayana doesn't term the intuition of essences knowledge is that he restricts the application of "know" to claims about existences, and, in his technical sense of the term *exist*, essences do not exist. "Existence" is restricted to items that have external relations to other items or, what supposedly comes to the same thing, to items that exist in space. Essences don't exist, because they don't have external relations to anything else nor are they in space. They lack relations to anything else, because they're given in intuition, and intuition isn't aware of an external world, of an intuiting subject, or even of the act of intuition itself: it is only aware of the object of intuition, the essence. Hence, the essence isn't given as having any (external) relation to anything else. Through a process of imagining or reasoning out what would be left if we deliberately suspend or set aside absolutely *all* of our beliefs (both conscious and unconscious), we can isolate a residual sort of awareness that wouldn't include self-awareness or awareness of the world (or of itself): "If I confine myself to the given essence without admitting discourse about it, I exclude all analysis of that essence, or even examination of it. I must simply stare at it, in a blank and timeless aesthetic trance."[4]

However, if the mind does incorrigibly grasp the essences in intuition, and this isn't called knowledge only because essences don't exist and Santayana restricts knowledge to cognizing of existences, then the supposed difference between Santayana and the foundationalists turns out to be merely verbal.

There is another way of interpreting Santayana's denial that makes the difference between the two more than verbal, however. According to Herman J. Saatkamp, Santayana is claiming that knowledge requires a judgment (proposition) about the essence, but "to make . . . a judgment about the given one would have to recognize the identity of the given, and such recognition (such as 'Blue now') is subject to error because 'identity . . . implies two moments, two instances or two intuitions, between which it obtains.' If identity involves this sort of temporal relation then it is conceivable that one may be mistaken about identifying that which is now intuited with what was intuited (if only an instant before)."[5] But the fact that the identification of two essences intuited at different times as the same essence is not infallible does not show that each of the two essences was not infallibly known by the mind at the time it was intuited. It merely shows that one of the reasons such infallible intuitions of essences don't provide any knowledge of the world is that they don't render an infallible basis for the meaning of our terms or for analysis of concepts (or for Santayana's dialectic). Even the belief that we know what it is that we are talking (or thinking) about rests upon animal faith. The person assumes he is "perusing the *same* essence, or returning to consider it. Without this postulate it would be impossible to say or think anything on any subject. . . . Yet this necessary belief is one impossible to prove or even to defend by argument, since all argument presupposes it. It must be accepted as a rule of the game, if you think the game worth playing."[6] What this argument is intended to show is that a leap of animal faith is required to get from the intuitions of essences to reasoning and discourse. It isn't intended to prove that the intuited essences aren't cognized.[7] To be sure, we cannot cognize essences through judgments about them in which we apply concepts to them (that is, take them as instances of certain concepts), if only because the concepts themselves originate in our intuitions of essences; that is, intuitions precede the concepts. However, in denying that essences are known in this way, Santayana is merely denying that we have knowledge by description of them. It doesn't follow that we do not have knowledge by acquaintance of them, because that is nonjudgmental. In fact it is essential to his position that essences be cognized, for it would be ridiculous to introduce essences as what is left after one performs the skeptical reduction but add that what one has left is unknowable.[8] Since they aren't taken as instances of concepts, it may be that such essences are ineffable, but this doesn't mean unknowable, merely inexpressible. Earlier, Santayana said, "any intuition gives *knowledge by acquaintance* with an essence, not subject to error, since the intuition . . . asserts no existence of that object."[9] He never abandons this position but merely stresses even more that this yields no knowledge of any existence. This is done by limiting the term *knowledge* to knowledge by description.

Santayana analyzes perception into two processes: the first consists of the intuition of an essence and the second of the addition to it of psychological *intent* (a part of animal faith), in which the essence is taken as purporting to be a sign (or appearance) of something existing in the external world. "In order to reach existences intent must transcend intuition, and take data for what they mean, not for what they are."[10] Again, "I have absolute assurance of the character of some essence; the rest is . . . interpretation added by my animal impulse."[11] The essence is infallibly cognized; the possibility of error arises only with the interpretation given the essence by animal faith. The idea is that to take an essence as (say) red is to take it as the same color as things that are red, which opens the way to error, for I may be mistaken about what color *is* the color of things that are red or mistaken in believing there are any red things.

Does this mean the foundationalist interpretation is correct? No, for foundationalism must maintain that the foundational data are appearances or signs of things in the external world and at the same time experiences in the mind of the person. While essences are known by acquaintance, when they are so known they are not known as appearances (or signs) of things in the external world or as experiences in the mind of the person in question. They must be known both as appearances and as experiences, because the foundational data must be such that they can be used as a jumping-off point for reaching the external world, if not by influence then at least by a leap of faith. As intuited, essences can't serve this function because, unlike appearances, they contain no implicit reference to an external world and, unlike experiences, they contain no implicit reference to an observing mind.[12] Greenlee's error lay not in assuming we know the essences but in describing them (as intuited) as "appearances," for to do so is to confuse them with signs of things or properties.

At this point it is helpful to compare Santayana with P. F. Strawson's argument that the Cartesian questioning of the existence of the external world already presupposes such a world. The similarity may not be apparent because Strawson misstates the conclusion of his argument. His avowed aim is to establish the stronger Kantian "thesis that for a series of diverse experiences to belong to a single consciousness it is necessary that they should be so connected as to constitute a temporally extended experience of a unified objective world."[13] However, we shall see that all his argument shows is that *if* we are to *assume* (in animal faith) the data are being viewed by a consciousness, we must also *assume* that at least some of them are experiences of a unified objective world.

In a nutshell, Strawson's argument is that to have the concept of experience, persons must be able to refer different data to themselves as the "one identical subject of them all."[14] To be able to do this, they must make a general distinction between their experience of the object and the object of experience; otherwise, the data would be experienced as objects in themselves and as such could not belong to them. Because when viewed as objects in themselves (that is, in Santayana's terminology, when viewed as essences) they cannot belong to them, it is only if persons distinguished between the objects that they experience and their experience of them (that is, in Santayana's terminology, take the essences as signs or appearances of things in the external world) that they can have something which they can assign to themselves (take as belonging to them). To be conscious, or believe, that they are having an experience, the persons must (1) be conscious or believe that they exist, and (2) be conscious or believe that there is an object that they are experiencing. (For an experience must be an experience *of* something.) There is another step to the argument, of which Strawson doesn't make enough: the general distinction between the object experienced and our experience of the object, in turn, presupposes that we sometimes experience (perceive) physical and not just sense-data. We can distinguish within our experiences between the object experienced and our experience of it only if, sometimes at least, we regard the object as transcending, both temporally and metaphysically, our experiencing of it. For the object to transcend our experience of it, it must be such that we can encounter it more than once and identify it in different encounters as the same thing experienced in different situations at different times. For the object to transcend our experience of it, it must be *possible* for the object to be other than we experience it (that is, to appear to us to be other than it is). If the object is to be other than we experience it, it must be capable of having properties it doesn't seem to have and of not having properties it seems to have (that is, we can be mistaken about it). Only physical objects, not sense-data, transcend our present experience, for only they can have properties other than they seem to have, seem to have properties they don't have, or be encountered more than once. Because we cannot be mistaken about sense-data, they must have *all and only* the properties they seem to have; because their *esse* is *percipi*, they cannot transcend the experiencing of them and so cannot be experienced more than once. Persons who made nothing except judgments about sense-data (that is, who never took themselves to perceive physical objects) could not distinguish between the object experienced and their experience of it. If they couldn't do this, they *could not think of* themselves as having experiences, for we've seen that this presupposes the distinction between the object experienced and our experience of it. Strawson's notion of the role of transcendent physical objects, together with the notion of minds or selves, is included in Santayana's "animal faith," because the latter is roughly our everyday, common-sense view of the world.

Santayana makes the same point as Strawson when he says that the object of intuition is not given as existing. To exist, he maintains, is to stand in relation to other things or experiences. "Existence or fact, in the same sense which I give to these words, cannot be a datum at all, because existence involves external relations . . . ; whereas, however complex a datum may be, with no matter what perspectives opening within it, it must be embraced in a single stroke of apperception and nothing outside it can belong to it at all. The datum is a pure image."[15] In denying the datum exists, Santayana is denying that it is given as having a relation to anything else, including the persons themselves. This means that the datum is not given *as an experience*, for to be an experience is to belong to a mind, and no mind is given in the experience.[16] Because no self or mind is given in experience, no experience is given *as* experience: "The complement added to the datum when it is alleged to exist . . . is the finding, the occurrence, the assault, the impact of that being here and now; it is the *experience* of it. But what can experience be . . . ? And what meaning can I give to such words as impact, assault, occurrence, or finding, when I have banished and denied my body, my past, my residual present being, and everything except the datum which I find?"[17] Hence when I think of the datum as existing, I am adding something to it. The datum's "presence is not an experience, for there is . . . no watchful spirit to appropriate it."[18] Santayana's point is that to be given as an experience the datum would have to be given as belonging to me, but only that which is a qualitative character of a datum can properly be said to be given, as opposed to being merely a belief. But belonging to me cannot be a qualitative—that is, sensory—character. Consider a visual datum—say, of a red, round shape. As a visual datum it can only have *visual* properties, such as being red, round, perhaps having a size (e.g., being large), etc. However, belonging to me (or being mental) is not the sort of thing that can be a visual characteristic and hence cannot be included in the datum. The same argument applies to the data of all the other senses, because being mental or belonging to me isn't any kind of sensory quality.

The only way to avoid this conclusion would be to reject Santayana's restriction of the given to sensory qualities. One might claim to have a nonsensory intuition of the self. However, Santayana would dismiss this as a mere belief. And he would have a point. To allow the given to include propositions about more than that which is presented in sensory images or qualia is to adopt a psychological criterion of the given in which the given is simply those beliefs of which we feel most certain. But to begin with that of which we feel most certain would be to begin *within* the sphere of animal faith. Santayana's whole point is that this is where we must begin.

To put it another way, Santayana states that if we eliminate *all* beliefs whatsoever (conscious or unconscious), the only elements left—the only ones that cannot be merely a product of beliefs—are momentary sensory qualia.[19] Santayana's aim is to establish what would remain if we eliminate, by argument, all that can only be a matter of belief: "The point is, in this task of criticism, to discard every belief that is a belief merely."

When we do this, the object of awareness (datum) ceases to be a sign, representation, or appearance of anything; it is, so to speak, simply an object in itself, not purporting to have any connection with anything else. "By being . . . treated as a signal for I know not what material opportunity or danger, the given image is taken up into the business world. . . . Remove this frame . . . and . . . the datum ceases to be an appearance, in the proper and pregnant sense of this word, since it ceases to imply any substance that appears or any mind to which it appears."[20] If the datum is not an appearance of anything else, if it doesn't purport to refer to an external, extramental world, then obviously the question of the existence of such an external world cannot arise. That is, unless we have already assumed (in "animal faith") there is an external world, the question of whether there is such a world could not arise. Until we've made this assumption, there can be for us neither experiences nor appearances. Hence, Santayana agrees with Strawson.

However, while Strawson claims to prove "that for a series of experiences to belong to a single consciousness it is necessary that they should be so connected as to constitute a temporally extended experience of a unified objective world," all his argument shows is that *if* a being is to be *conscious of itself* as having any experiences, it *must think of* them as experiences of an external world of transcendent objects (which is all Santayana claims). Clearly, persons do not need to have the *concept* of experience before they can have experiences. The concept of experience is only necessary for them to be self-consciously aware of themselves as having experiences. Cats and dogs probably have experiences without being consciously aware of them *as experiences*. The most that can be proved by an argument to the effect that self-knowledge presupposes we perceive objects that transcend our experiences of them is that *we must take ourselves* to perceive such objects. That is, the most Strawson shows is that knowledge rests upon faith. However, this is sufficient to dislodge skeptics from their position, because if they are to raise the question of the existence of the external world, the skeptics must presuppose that they have in their mind sensory experiences that purport to refer to things in the external world (that is, which are appearances, not mere essences in Santayana's sense). Moreover, they must assume they know this *without needing to know anything else*. As Peter Brueckner, a representative critic of Strawson, puts it: "I typically come to know that a current experience is mine simply by *having* it. . . . My knowledge that a current experience is mine is not based upon my knowledge of some ground."[21] This is correct *only upon the assumption* that *our conceptual scheme* is correct—that is, that it is part of "animal faith" and hence not an assumption to which the skeptic is entitled. As Santayana points out, mind or self is no more given in intuition than is the external world: all that is given is the datum, which isn't *given as* an experience (because it isn't given as belonging to a mind) or as an appearance (because it isn't given as a sign of anything else).

Moreover, in animal faith's postulation of the existence of a mind (self) and an external world, there is a sense in which the world has priority. For to distinguish between appearances in our mind and an external reality they purport to represent, we must distinguish between external reality and our ideas of it. "Thought becomes obvious when things betray it; as they cannot have been false, something else, which we call thought, must have existed and must have had a different status from that of the thing it falsified. Error thus awakens even the laziest philosophy from the dream of supposing that its own meanderings are nothing but strands in the texture of its object."[22] But to take one belief as erroneous, one must take some other belief as true. The point is that one cannot conclude certain data do not belong to the external world unless one makes certain assumptions about the nature of the external world. The reason why is simple: the only reason I can have for concluding that a datum I'm inclined to believe is part of a physical object is not part of the actual physical object is that I take another "datum" to be a part of the object, and I believe that both cannot be a part of the object. To assume that both cannot be a part of the physical object, I must assume that both cannot be a part of the physical object's nature. In effect, I must treat a datum as illusory or hallucinatory when it doesn't fit into the pattern of types of data that I have assumed are causally connected with the nature of that type of physical object. If I consider the bent-image of a stick half in and half out of water to be an illusion because when I pull the stick out it is straight, I'm assuming sticks don't suddenly change their shapes or are not so flexible that they bend when placed in water. When Macbeth concludes that the datum of a dagger he seems to see floating in the air in front of him isn't part of an actual dagger because when he tries to grasp it his hand doesn't encounter anything solid, he is assuming that daggers are solid (unlike clouds) and cannot disappear suddenly. What Richard Rorty says of sense-data must be true of essences: "All that 'sense-datum which does not cohere with other sense-data' can mean is 'unfamiliar sense-datum.'"[23] The fact that a datum does not belong to a familiar pattern that I expect to be repeated does not mean that it does not belong to the physical object in question, for it is always logically possible that the physical object has properties I have not observed before, or it may acquire new properties in these circumstances or simply manifest different properties under different circumstances. Only the assumption that I know enough about the nature of that type of physical object to exclude the possibility that it might manifest certain properties could license me to conclude that any datum doesn't belong to a physical object and so must be subjective (in my mind) and not part of the external world. That is, to treat any supposed perception as illusory or hallucinatory, we must assume that we know a lot about the world and so know what to expect from it, for it is only when our expectations are disappointed that we consider a supposed perception illusory or hallucinatory. The point is that we must not only have certain concepts of physical objects; we must assume that these concepts *are correct*—that is, that they correspond to the way these objects actually are.

If taking the data or essences as appearances or experiences in our minds already presupposes we know at least something about the world, then there is no possibility of any foundation outside the sphere of animal faith.

Notes

1. Douglas Greenlee, "The Incoherence of Santayana's Scepticism," *Southern Journal of Philosophy* 16 (1978): 54. See also John Lachs, "Santayana's Philosophy of Mind," *The Monist* 48 (1964); John Lachs, "The Proofs of Realism," *The Monist* 51 (1967); and Sidney Grossman, "The Scepticism of George Santayana," *Tulane Studies in Philosophy* 18 (1969).

2. Greenlee, "Santayana's Scepticism," p. 54.

3. See Timothy L. S. Sprigge, "Santayana and Verificationism," *Inquiry* 12 (1969).

See also Herman J. Saatkamp, "Some Remarks on Santayana's Scepticism," in *Two Centuries of American Philosophy*, ed. Peter Caws (Totowa, N.J.: Rowman & Littlefield, 1980). For what seems to amount to the same view, see also Beth J. Singer, "Signs of Existence," *Southern Journal of Philosophy* 16 (1978).

4. George Santayana, *Scepticism and Animal Faith* (New York: Scribner's Sons, 1923), p. 12.

5. Saatkamp, "Some Remarks," pp. 138–39.

6. Santayana, *Scepticism and Animal Faith*, p. 114.

7. Saatkamp quotes Santayana that in intuition, all of the person's efforts "are concentrated on *not* asserting, and *not* implying anything, but simply noticing what he finds" (Santayana, *Scepticism and Animal Faith*, p. 16) and that such a person "would believe nothing" (ibid., p. 17). However, the context makes it clear that Santayana is thinking only of assertions, implications, and beliefs about things in the external world, not the essence: "Ideas become *beliefs only when* . . . they persuade me that they are signs of things." In refraining from asserting or implying anything, the person is merely exercising care not to slip into animal faith, "not to posit any of these fancied worlds, nor this ghostly mind imagined as viewing" the essences (ibid.). That is, he or she is refraining from unconsciously assuming there is either a world or a mind. It should be noted that noticing something is itself a cognitive act.

8. Perhaps this is why Saatkamp wishes "to distinguish the central thesis of his solipsism of the moment from his fully developed doctrine of essences" (Saatkamp, "Some Remarks," p. 138).

9. George Santayana, "Literal and Symbolic Knowledge," in George Santayana, *Obiter Scripta*, ed. Justus Buchler and Benjamin Schwartz (New York: Charles Scribner's Sons, 1936), p. 128 (italics added).

10. Santayana, *Scepticism and Animal Faith*, p. 65.

11. Ibid., p. 110.

12. The reason they cannot function as a jumping-off point must be something more than the mere fact that the person in question is in an "aesthetic trance" and so cannot frame the question of whether there is an external world (although some remarks of Santayana can be taken as suggesting this), because that would be only a psychological, not a logical, impossibility.

13. P. F. Strawson, *The Bounds of Sense* (London: Methuen, 1966), p. 97.

14. Ibid., p. 101.

15. Santayana, *Scepticism and Animal Faith*, p. 34.

16. "Experience has no conditions for a critic of knowledge who proceeds . . . from the vantage-ground of experience itself. To urge, therefore, that a self or ego is presupposed in experience . . . is curiously to fail in critical thinking" (ibid., p. 23).

17. Ibid., p. 37 (italics added).

18. Ibid., p. 39.

19. Santayana presents his arguments as if he is doing a form of phenomenology, merely paying close attention to what is actually given. "Just as inattention leads ordinary people to assume as part of the given facts all that their *unconscious* transcendental logic has added to them, so inattention, at a deeper level, leads the empiricist to assume an existence in his radical facts which does not belong to them" (ibid., p. 39 [italics added]). However, as the word *unconscious* shows, he was not assuming that what he claims to be the case is to be uncovered merely by paying close attention to what is presented to awareness; instead, when one considers his arguments, one finds that they are just that—arguments. For instance, he argues that our supposed knowledge that there are moments other than the present one cannot be a datum but merely a belief: "At one moment I may *believe* that there are or have been or will be other moments; but evi-

dently they would not be *other* moments, if they were data to me now, and nothing more" (ibid., p. 4 [italics added]). He is arguing that what many take to be simply given is such that it is logically impossible for it to be given, so it must instead be a product of belief, though an instinctive, unconscious belief. In fact, belief—his "animal faith"—is even prior to intuition or experience. "Animal faith, being a sort of expectation . . . is earlier than intuition: intuitions come to help it out and lend it something to posit" (ibid., p. 46). So Santayana would not be disturbed by contemporary claims, such as that of Fodor, to the effect that the "module" that unconsciously governs perception assumes the existence of three-dimensional physical objects, so we cannot by psychological introspection locate a level of awareness below (or prior to) such assumptions. (See Jerry Fodor, "Observation Statements," *Philosophy of Science* 51 [1984].) Hence, it is irrelevant to protest that we are not normally consciously aware of what purports to be an appearance or experience of something. It is precisely because we are not aware of them that they must be introduced by his skeptical reductive analysis.

20. Santayana, *Scepticism and Animal Faith*, p. 39.
21. Peter Brueckner, "Transcendental Arguments," *Nous* 2: 206.
22. Santayana, *Scepticism and Animal Faith*, p. 123.
23. Richard Rorty, "Strawson's Objectivity Argument," *Review of Metaphysics* (1980): 212–13.

Pragmatism and Irony in Santayana

HENNY WENKART

In the spirit of our exploration of the roots and edges of American philosophy, I shall indicate some eight ways in which Santayana, often characterized as an "edge" philosopher, draws deeply from some of the strongest American roots yet always with a difference.

(1) His materialism is American in its emphasis upon striving and movement and a kind of unconscious teleology in matter. It differs from the other American views in its neglect of attention to creative interaction between society and individual in the achievement of material goals. (2) On the other hand, its view of organisms as a kind of "habit" in matter is very American. (3) With respect to evolution, Santayana is impressed with the surplus generated by nature but rejects the evolution-theory corollary of the discarding of nonuseful characteristics through natural selection. (4) He goes along with the thought that mind is a product of evolution but rejects the corollary that therefore it must be useful. (5) His view of mind is like Dewey's in distinguishing between "having" and "knowing" but unlike it in rejecting any interaction between mind and matter. (6) The good for mankind, the goal of aspiration, for Santayana as for the other Americans, is no static approximation to a prior standard, no object of desire, not even a state of affairs, but instead continuing activity. The activity that is the goal of *his* aspirations is, to be sure, idiosyncratic: it is the peaceful intuition of essences. (7) He rejects the pragmatic theory of truth of William James. On analysis, however, we shall find that he holds a double theory of truth: one theory that approximates Peirce's view and one that bears a deep resemblance to that of James. (8) Like the other Americans he gives importance to the role of chance and probability, but unlike them he does not calculate mathematical probabilities or think statistically.

His teachers at Harvard were Royce and James. Like James and the other pragmatists, he is moving sharply away from Royce. His critique of the pragmatists is that their metaphysics remains caught in the idealist confusion between knowing and the known, between experience of matter and matter raw. When the pragmatists think that they have accounted for interaction between the material world and the conscious agents within it, their description fails: it still cashes out as a picture of bits of experience relating to other bits of experience.

> The pragmatist's reliance on facts does not carry him beyond the psychic sphere; his facts are only his personal experiences. . . . It is abundantly clear that the effort to distinguish fact from theory cannot be successful, so long as the psychological way of thinking prevails.[1]
>
> James was . . . carried . . . by a subtle implication of his method. This implication was that experience or mental discourse not only constituted a set of substantive facts, but the *only* substantive facts.[2]

Santayana develops his own metaphysics, steering clear of absolute idealism on the one hand and positivism or radical empiricism on the other, embracing both consciousness and universals while excluding the Absolute Mind. Like all his most serious work, *Realms of Being* is best seen as an immense prose poem—in this case, a parable in which with typical deadpan irony he employs the image of separate "realms" to stand for incommensurate activities: the various kinds of philosophic activity demanded by the task of describing all there is. We shall return to this notion when we come to discuss theory of truth.

In the preface to *Character and Opinion in the United States*, Santayana says that he is not an American except by long association, although it has been an acquaintance with America and American philosophers that has chiefly contributed to clear and settle his own mind. In metaphysics he says he is a materialist, perhaps the only one living.[3] But what an astonishingly American materialism this is, full of endeavor, full of directionality.

The natural state of matter is motion and continuous change; it is a continuous flux, composed of internally controlled "natural moments" of varying duration, continually generating one another. Each of these moments is a kind of valve: "It contains a reference to the direction in which matter may flow through it. The moment exists only in act, when the valve is a valve in function; and at that crisis it yields to pressure coming from one side only, while it opens out and empties itself only towards the other side."[4]

There is no difference in kind between animate and inanimate matter. There is an "observable endeavor in things of any sort to develop a specific form and to preserve it."[5] Matter tends to become more and more complex. It moves into repetitive patterns that in turn form superpatterns of ever-increasing complexity, until at last they spin off seeds to reproduce the parent pattern. Matter has become alive; indeed, only inimical lateral tensions could prevent it from achieving animation. The active, powerful pattern of events driving each organism is given the mythical name "psyche." (More about myth later.)

> In the individual, in whom actual preference has its only possible seat, ultimate sincerity presupposes a definite psyche, with assignable aspirations. . . . Yet

... she successively develops and outgrows functions which are essentially temporary. In her origin she was a new equilibrium that changing circumstances had rendered possible; and her organism remains always potentially plastic and internal to the flux of nature at large.[6]

She slept at first in a seed; there, and from there, as the seed softened, she distributed her organs and put forth her energies, always busier and busier in her growing body ... reacting from the centre ... upon events at her frontiers ... and what we sometimes call her plan, which is only her propensity, may be developed and transformed, if she finds new openings, until it becomes quite a different plan.[7]

The psyche invents new organs for her organism in response to needs and opportunities, all without any *conscious* planning: that is the materialism in this view. Santayana would have been very pleased with some facts detailed in an article by Robert Wright in the current issue of *The Sciences*,[8] describing the work of the psyche (Wright does not call it that of the bacterium *Escherichia coli*). It seems that when *E. coli* finds itself in an environment with little or no energy-giving carbon, it will synthesize a molecule called cyclic AMP, whose manufacture would have been inhibited by the presence of carbon. AMP attaches itself to a protein, and together they bind to *E. coli*'s DNA, altering its expression so that it causes the bacterium to produce flagelli, which begin whipping around and transporting it to a different environment. The physical DNA is what Santayana would have called *E. coli*'s psyche, which is "essentially generative and directive" and is "capable of existing unconsciously and of exerting material energy."[9]

The psyche, in its moral unity, is a poetic or mythological notion, but needed to mark the hereditary vehement movement in organisms towards specific forms and functions.[10]

This psyche is the specific form of physical life, present and potential, asserting itself in any plant or animal. ... Such a moving equilibrium is at once vital and material, these qualities not being opposed but coincident. Some parcels of matter, called seeds, are predetermined to grow into organisms of a specific habit, producing similar seeds in their turn. Such a habit in matter is a psyche.[11]

This is mythology with an evolutionary cast, very much in the classical American pattern, implying as it does the superior adjustive power of organisms that can "react upon events at their frontier" and respond to new "openings" by adjusting their habits. Peirce, James, and Dewey all hold variations of this view of the organism as a set of habits. In such a view, every goal achieved at the same time sets up a new task. Santayana's sympathetic description of pragmatism in *Winds of Doctrine* rings with overtones of psyche's particular kind of energy: "There are in pragmatism echoes of various popular moral forces, like democracy, impressionism, love of the concrete, respect for success, trust in will and action, and the habit or relying on the future, rather than the past, to justify one's methods and opinions. Most of these things are characteristically American."[12]

Santayana's picture of the operations of a living organism is like Dewey's, who says, "All life operates through a mechanism, and the higher the form of life the more complex, sure, and flexible the mechanism."[13] It seems that if indeed Santayana is no American, his philosophical creation, the psyche, certainly is one: active, directional, absorbed in her work, full of momentum, vigor, and love of achievement—hope made animate.

But as I shall be pointing out in various connections, Santayana's view is American with a difference. Missing in his treatment of the psyche's exploration of and response to the environment is the American emphasis upon the crucial importance of the social environment. Society is mentioned, but only glancingly and by-the-by. It is part of the environment, perceived as friendly or inimical, to be embraced or avoided as far as possible, but never as the partner in an interaction. Even where Santayana acknowledges that he is using the singular when he ought to be speaking the plural, he is still viewing society as a simple multiplicity of individuals instead of as an organic complex: "I speak of the American in the singular, as if there were not millions of them. . . . Of course the one American I speak of is mythical; but to speak in parables is inevitable in such a subject."[14]

This contrast is sharpest, of course, vis-a-vis the view of Dewey. For in Dewey the society is not merely a source of opportunities and threats: Dewey's picture is of interaction of society and the individual as partners, active upon one another. In *Human Nature and Conduct* he says that natural operations like breathing and digesting and acquired ones like speech are functions of the surroundings as truly as of a person. They are things done *by* the environment by means of organic structures or acquired dispositions. The same is true of characteristics such as malice, courage, honesty, and so forth: "They are working adaptations of personal capacities with environing forces. All virtues and vices are habits which incorporate objective forces. They are interactions of elements contributed by the make-up of an individual with elements supplied by the out-door world. They can be studied as objectively as physiological functions, and they can be modified by change of either personal or social elements."[15]

Dewey gives pride of place to group action as the primary element in habit formation. Santayana recognizes the importance for habit formation of both the physical and the social environment, but he recognizes it, as it were, from the point of view of the individual psyche, whose needs are largely predetermined by heredity: "This partial predetermination of life—which in man is especially imperfect, and dependent on the chances of education and experience—is the source of the generic. . . . Every living creature aims at and needs something generic, not anything in particular: *some* food, *some* shelter, *some* mate, *some* offspring, *some* country, *some* religion."[16]

Next the environment does its part, as the generic preferences of the psyche are "rendered precise and irrevocable by habits formed under the pressure of circumstances."[17] And then, *"Not this, not all this, not merely this,* says the psyche at every turn; and her sustenance leaves her half-disgusted and half-hungry."[18] Precise preferences are established through interaction with the environment. Established by experience, *preferences* become *norms*: "Acquaintance with facts ... narrows ... generic native demands into specific requirements ... only *this* food ... *this* mate, *these* children, *this* country, *this* religion. In the same way the mind, when indoctrinated, will suffer only *this* physics, and only *this* logic. Nevertheless, any given world or any given flow of imagination is an accident."[19]

Dewey says this too. But while Santayana takes the individual as his point of origin, Dewey starts out from the group.

> We must start with grouped action, that is, with some fairly settled system of interaction among individuals. The problem of origin and development of the various groupings, or definite customs ... is not solved by reference to psychic causes, elements, forces. It is to be solved by reference to facts of action, demand for food, for houses, for a mate, for some one to talk to and to listen to one talk, for control of others, demands which are all intensified by the fact ... that each person begins a helpless, dependent creature.[20]

Santayana's and Dewey's lists of needs overlap substantially, with important differences: Dewey's sociable demands for "some one to talk to and to listen to one talk" and also for "control of others" are absent from the list drawn up by the solitary Santayana, who talks about groups of people one person at a time.

Let us return now to the active psyche—seeking, testing, developing fresh organs in response to new needs, and selecting among its own accomplishments in order to discard failures and reinforce successes. Each success is merely a brief resting place, defining and pointing the direction of the next task. In response to its success in achieving locomotion, the psyche identifies the need for information at a distance and develops sense organs and fresh brain capacity for processing their input. Along with all of this comes consciousness. James tells a similar story but with quite a different slant. Both men are impressed by the science of evolution, although they draw different conclusions from it in detail. Evolutionary theory teaches that a great surplus of species and characteristics is produced. James sticks closely to the corollary, that of these characteristics the useful will be the ones to survive. Therefore, because consciousness survives, it must have proved useful: it must have interacted with matter in a way beneficial to the organism.

But Santayana insists that consciousness is completely impotent and epiphenomenal. It *is* the fruit of nature's "generosity" in producing a surplus of kinds of things and characteristics. But *it is not useful* for bodily survival. Indeed, the situation is the reverse: from the perspective of consciousness, which is of course *the only possible point of view*, it is the body that is *useful* and good instrumentally, while consciousness alone is good categorically.

James, says Santayana, was too sentimental and soft-hearted to carry through a tough, consistent epiphenomenalism, although he began correctly by characterizing emotion as purely bodily sensation and the mind as a total shifting sensibility.

> To pursue this path, however, would have led him to admit that nature was automatic and mind simply cognitive, conclusions from which every instinct in him recoiled. He preferred to believe that mind and matter had independent energies and could lend one another a hand, matter operating by motion and mind by intention. This dramatic, amphibious way of picturing causation is natural to common sense ... but James was insensibly carried away from it.[21]

Like all the Americans, Santayana speaks often of "predicaments." Now he says that consciousness, which he calls "spirit," is epiphenomenal: it is the voice of the psyche talking to itself about the predicament of being alive. When Santayana talks about predicaments, we can assume that what he is giving us is an ironic dyshyperbole: for the psyche, being alive is one big predicament.

Spirit possesses no causative power whatever. It is pure content, the psyche insofar as psyche is conscious; we must avoid hypostatizing it. Even in the long passages in *The Realm of Spirit* where it is difficult to see how this can go through, we must treat references to the actions of spirit as cases of metonymy. For "spirit" read "psyche qua conscious." The mechanism is all in the physical psyche—there is no mental machinery. In the *Apologia* of the Schilpp volume he says that he regards the mind as purely expressive: he speaks of "the element of intensity in all moments of spirit, which are essentially moments of life, not collections of data, essences, or objects."[22] In "The Progress of Philosophy" he declares:

> It is utterly impossible to free the spirit materially, since it is the voice of matter, but by a proper hygiene it can be freed ideally, so that it ceases to be troubled by its sluggish instrument, or conscious of it.... The spirit, viewed from within, is omnipresent and timeless.... Spirit calls itself a stranger, because it finds the world strange; and it finds the world strange because, being the spirit of a very high-strung and perilously organized animal, it is sensitive to many influences not harmonious with its own impulses, and has to beg its daily bread.[23]

He explains this kind of utterance in more matter-of-fact language in the *Apologia*: "When the physical impressions have been successive in fact, they should appear as successive in a single intuition.... It is such an intuition that is an instance of spirit in act.... It will last as long as the vital interest that calls it forth.... Things as they exist can not be data ... being given they have become ideas."[24]

We have remarked earlier that except in their radically different approaches to the role of society, the views of Santayana and Dewey have much in common. Here is another instance. Santayana notes that his distinction between intuition and belief is Dewey's between that which is "had" and that which is known.[25] But the difference in temperament that separates Santayana from the pragmatists appears here also: where for them beliefs are primarily tools for the construction of the future, he adds that they are that and are also the source of pleasant relief from anxiety.

> The pleasure of seeing is one, and the pleasure of believing is quite another; the first liberates our senses and fills the present with light; the second directs our conduct and relieves our anxiety or doubts about the past and future. When the spectator bethinks himself of destiny as well as of beauty, his sensibility becomes tragic, it becomes intelligence. Every picture is then regarded as a sign for the whole situation which has generated it or which it forebodes. The given image, for intelligence, expresses a problematic fact; and intelligence invents various grammatical forms and logical categories by which to describe its hidden enemy or fascinating prey.[26]

Whole situations, problematic facts, hidden enemies, and fascinating prey are very familiar pragmatic preoccupations, but the issue of all this, in pragmatism, is supposed to be action within and upon the environment. And Santayana's psyche, employing the intelligence insofar as it is a physical complex of capacities separate from any consciousness of these, does in fact act on its environment in accordance with unconscious "beliefs"—which are, in the pragmatist way, sets and potentialities of behavior. But the "action" of intelligence that chiefly interests Santayana is mental: its invention of forms and categories for use in descriptions.

This brings us to the most striking similarity-with-a-difference between the pragmatists and Santayana. The similarity is that of goals: for each, the goal to be desired is no object, no conformity with imposed or prior standards, no steady-state situation, but instead the freest possible exercise of a particular favored kind of activity. Dewey states this goal in a somewhat quixotic form, as a definition of "democracy."

> Democracy is the faith that the process of experience is more important than any special result attained, so that special results achieved are of ultimate value only as they are used to enrich and order the ongoing process ... faith in democracy is all one with faith in experience and education. ... Experience is that free interaction of individual human beings with surrounding conditions, especially the human surroundings, which develops and satisfies need and desire by increasing knowledge of things as they are. ... Need and desire—out of which grow purpose and direction of energy ... —continually open the way into the unexplored and unattained future.[27]

For Santayana, on the other hand, the favored activity whose free and abundant exercise in the ultimate goal is all mental, it is the undisturbed intuition of essences by the spirit. Anything done "by spirit," which in itself is impotent, is really done by the psyche qua conscious, we remember. But as we read many passages in *The Realm of Spirit*, it is hard work to keep remembering that. The spirit is often portrayed as such an independent character in this drama that its "sympathy" with itself qua psyche is actually called "vicarious":

> Not that spirit trembles for its own being. . . . What torments it is no selfish fear but a vicarious sympathy with its native psyche and her native world, which it cannot bear to feel dragged hither and thither in tragic confusion, but craves to see everywhere well-ordered and beautiful, *so that it may be better seen and understood*. This is the specific function of spirit, which it lives by fulfilling, and dies if it cannot somehow fulfill. But as it is unresisting yet indomitable in its existence, so it is resourceful in its art, and ultimately victorious.[28]

Now the four "realms" in *Realms of Being* are to be read not as cosmological regions but instead as cosmological symbols for an ontological situation. Santayana says: "My system . . . is no system of the universe. The Realms of Being of which I speak are not parts of a cosmos, nor one great cosmos together: they are only kinds or categories of things which I find conspicuously different and worth distinguishing."[29] The "realms" are, then, realms of application of various techniques of description, realms for the various jobs of philosophers.

It is not unusual for Santayana to speak in parables when he is most serious. On the contrary, he often tells us that this is exactly what he does. If we take his major systematic philosophical works as long prose poems, then we can turn to his self-critical essays, such as the *Apologia* of the Schilpp volume and the even later "The Idler and His Works" (but note the sharp irony even in these titles) for their explication.

> The looseness and variety of my language indicate my sense of the seriousness of my subject, and my respect for it. I do not delude myself into thinking that I can thrust it bodily into my pocket or into my mind. When on the contrary I choose to be literal . . . I am consciously playing with definitions, ramifying transcendental "problematics," like the Italian idealists, and laughing up my sleeve.[30]

And again:

> That [my views] should often be misunderstood is rather my fault, because I have clothed them in a rhetoric that, though perfectly spontaneous and inevitable in my own thoughts, misleads at first as to their character. . . . I am a Scholastic at heart, but I lack the patience and the traditional training that might have enabled me to discuss every point minutely, without escapades or ornament or exaggeration or irony. . . . The truth is not impatient; it can stand representation and misrepresentation. The more we respect its authority, the more confidently and familiarly we may play round its base.[31]

Parable is the only available medium for describing accurately the relationship between mind and matter. All other attempts are bound to lead to contradiction, or to the false description of one due to the attempt to force it into the language appropriate to the other.

In this parable the fourth book, *The Realm of Spirit*, must be read as a work of phenomenology. "In this book I am deliberately taking the point of view of spirit fully awake, contrasting itself with other things, and aspiring to its own freedom and perfection."[32] On the other hand, just as *The Realm of Spirit*, being about mental experiences, must be read from the point of view of consciousness, *The Realm of Matter*, which is about material facts, must be read as though from the point of view of a neutral or omniscient observer: "In regard to the realm of matter I propose no theories, but only ask a preliminary question, namely: What presuppositions do we make in pursuing knowledge of anything? And I reply: We presuppose that there is some real object or event to be known or reported, prior or subsequent to the report that reaches us. In other words, we presuppose existent facts about which our affirmations may be false or true."[33]

That is his rejection of idealism. And *The Realm of Essence* is his rejection of nominalism. Ironically naming them "a term in scepticism," he slips in that essences *are actual*. "Essence is not an object of faith, but a least ultimate term in scepticism, showing how little evidence there can be for faith of any sort, since all data are in themselves dream-data, actual in that we evolve them like a pain, but false in that they do not otherwise exist."[34]

These three "realms," then, are really ways of describing, of talking about what there is. But what is the "realm" of truth? It is a stroke of irony that, while this is the one "realm" to which he has given a name referring to discourse, it is the one actual *realm* in his system. It is "the total history and destiny of matter and spirit, or the enormously complex essence which they exemplify by existing."[35] Or, put another way, it is the world of facts, where certain essences and not others are instantiated at various times in matter, and various essences and others are experienced in minds. He says that it is only "by accident" that the same essence will be intuited in mind and instantiated in matter at the same time—in other words, that anybody knows the truth about something that happens in the material world. What he does not address is a deeper question about the ontology of essences: what do essences instantiated in matter have in common at all with essences intuited in mind, in addition to the name of "essence" that he gives to them?

In any case, it is clear *The Realm of Truth* is Santayana's rejection of the Jamesian theory of truth. In *Character and Opinion in the United States* he says, "In striving to prove the being of truth, the young Royce absurdly treated it as doubtful, setting a bad example to the pragmatists."[36] This is also what he had said earlier, in *Winds of Doctrine*, where he complains about the pragmatists that what they call facts can be made by thinking, that our faith in them may contribute to their reality, and may modify their nature; in other words, these facts are our immediate apprehensions of fact, which it is indeed conceivable that our temperaments, expectations, and opinions should modify. Thus the pragmatist's reliance on facts does not carry him beyond the psychic [in Santayana's mature terminology, this would have been "spiritual"—he means mental, not physical] sphere; his facts are only his personal experiences. Personal experiences may well be the basis for no less personal myths; but the effort of intelligence and of science is rather to find the basis of the personal experiences . . . and this . . . basis of experience is what common sense calls the facts, and what practice is concerned with.[37]

In his completed system, thirty years later, Santayana still identifies the nonmental facts of the material world as the proper realm of activity for the intelligence, now identified as a nonmental activity of the nonmental psyche. What has changed is his valuation of personal myths. What he says now is that the realm of application of those myths is the realm of "moral," or "ultimate," truth.

Santayana's mature system carries a double theory of truth. Truth$_F$ is part of a correspondence theory about the facts of the material world. Santayana does not calculate probabilities mathematically, but he does go along with contemporary probabilistic views to the extent of holding that it is only by chance that the deliverances of intelligence correspond with material facts. He goes further: while there are facts to be known, and knowledge of these facts is possible, so that it is possible to be in possession of factual truth, it is never possible *to know that* we are in possession of it. This is his skepticism. A leap of animal faith is required of us before we can believe ourselves in possession of some truth$_F$.

This theory of truth is much closer to that of Peirce than that of James, except that Santayana does *not* conceive it possible, even in an infinitely long time, to arrive at complete truth$_F$ and to know that you have gotten there. Truth$_F$ is truth from the point of view of the omniscient observer who is the protagonist of *The Realm of Matter*.

But in Santayana's mature view there is another brand of truth altogether, which he calls "ultimate" truth, or sometimes "moral" truth. Let us call it truth$_M$. Santayana calls it "ultimate" for two reasons: first, because concerning truth$_M$ we can achieve certainty; second, because what is true$_M$ is of ultimate importance to some "living interest" of some conative being. It is also of ultimate importance to him, because he is also a conative being. He acknowledges that his philosophical view is always relative to his own preferences in a remark he makes in *The Idler and His Works* with reference to *The Life of Reason*: "I intended . . . to be a consistent naturalist, and I ought to have smiled a little at my casual enthusiasms, seeing that all ideals are but projections of vital tendencies in animal organisms. Therefore, since animal organisms are of many and variable sorts, the direction and goal of progress always remain optional and subject to revision."[38]

Truth$_M$ is close to much that James says in *Pragmatism*, although it is not identical to his pragmatic theory of truth. In the first place, truth$_M$ is about events in the mental realm only, while James's view, at least in intention, is "amphibious." Truth$_M$ is truth from the point of view of the protagonist of *The Realm of Spirit*. Santayana specifically identifies the "moral" plane with the plane of consciousness: "Nature reproduces itself by generation or derivation on the material plane. When it creates feeling or thought it passes on to the moral plane of comment and enjoyment."[39] And because consciousness itself is the "cry," the emotional exclamation, which the "predicament" of being alive wrings from the organism, the conscious plane as a whole is that which some living being radically cares about. The "moral" is so from one specific view at a time; its referent is simply what is *important* to a specific organism. And a judgment is called "true morally" when it expresses "the bias of human nature."[40] Because the mind is the expression on the part of the body about its situation in the world, every mental act is inherently emotional, and every "moral" truth is an emotional truth. A desire on the part of the psyche will turn out to have been a "false" desire if its satisfaction does not bring real satisfaction to the psyche. "The original demand for change or reform, though prophetic of what was about to happen, would have been morally an illusion, since that desired possibility, when realised, was not the blessing expected."[41]

So to verify *that* something is true$_M$ we wait for the long run. But truth$_M$ does not *consist* of this verification. What is true$_M$ is a statement that a particular state of affairs is congenial to the psyche. It can be known for certain because it is introspective.

And obviously this is very close to James, one of whose definitions of truth for the pragmatist is expressed as follows: "The pragmatist clings to facts and concreteness, observes truth at its work in particular cases, and generalizes. Truth, for him, becomes a class-name for all sorts or working-values in experience."[42] Again: "Ideas (which themselves are but parts of our experience) become true just insofar as they help us to get into satisfactory relation with other parts of our experience . . . any idea that will carry us prosperously from any one part of our experience to any other part, linking things satisfactorily, working securely, simplifying, saving labor."[43]

Ideas that are "true morally" for Santayana are not exactly this, but that is because labor-saving is not one of his most radical desires. But truth$_M$ consists of precisely those views that most truly describe the spirit's situation and most closely express its desires. "Moral," for Santayana's mature view, means "radically important to some living mind." What is radically important to James is the assimilation of the novel in his experience to his beliefs in stock, and therefore James declares, "I must both lean on old truth and grasp new fact. . . . That new idea is truest which performs most felicitously its function of satisfying our double urgency."[44] And for Santayana, also, that idea is true$_M$ that best satisfies the deepest urgency of the spirit—in the case of his spirit, that will be the urgency for expression.

Finally, we find that what Santayana has said about his own expression of what is most important for him applies to truth$_M$ in general. "Ultimate truths are more easily and adequately conveyed by poetry than by analysis."[45] And, "The deeper the passion that selects and transmutes . . . images, the truer the picture becomes to the heart. . . . In the realm of myth . . . what matters . . . is . . . the courage and pathos of human life in its essence."[46] That is from *The Idea of Christ in the Gospels*, where he also says the following: "[The] criterion of truth is not evidence or probability: it is congruity with the faith, fittingness, significance, edification. Things have been ordered by God as it is beautiful that they should be ordered; and it is on this ground that true reports are to be distinguished from false ones."[47]

In *Realms of Being* Santayana says,

> A man may be conscious of his passion . . . but the passion itself is a force, a physical automatism let loose within him, and altogether other and deeper than his consciousness of it. If he attempts to put it into words, or to conceive its proper nature, he is driven to dramatic fictions . . . he is driven to myth . . . the truth facing his passion, as he is best able to conceive it, is a dramatic truth. . . . Dramatic intuition, or apt myth . . . may be true of the world without being parts of it . . . . Dramatic fiction may thus reveal to us the gist of existence, as . . . prosaic observation could never do.[48]

In *Some Turns of Thought in Modern Philosophy*, he remarks, "The myths of a wise philosopher about the origin of life or of dreams, though expressed symbolically, may reveal the pertinent movement of nature to us, and may kindle in us just sentiments and true expectations."[49] For pragmatists also, particularly for James, an expression will count as true if it kindles true expectations.

To one group of "wise myths," Santayana devotes an entire book: *The Idea of Christ in the Gospels*. In this book he summarizes "the course of moral and intellectual self-transcendence":

> When attention passes from a fact to an idea, both the psyche thinking and the fact confronted continue to exist: the intuition . . . and the essence which is its theme, are elicited by that substantial process and tension beneath, which probably continue beyond. Transcendence and sacrifice thus form a moral accompaniment to a particular cycle in the flux of existence. They do not imply a suicide followed by the inception of a new being. Vital continuity in the psyche is presupposed, carrying personal identity with it. . . . Vital feeling or stress takes a great leap when it forms images . . . and intelligence takes another, doubtless simultaneous, when it transcends these images and posits independent and dynamic ob-

jects beneath or beyond them. This is an invaluable progress from the point of view of conduct. . . . It adjusts action and sentiment to the real forces on which existence depends.⁵⁰

This much, again, is very congenial to what James has to say. But Santayana names something more desirable still, because it is more congenial to the spirit. This is the step the spirit takes when it reverts enthusiastically to the cult of ideas—and *this* crowns its life.

> For what profit is there in discovering the order of nature or the history of mankind except that we may thereby protect and sweeten the transit of the soul through the world, and choose eternal objects of study and love? The idea of Christ, with the corresponding theory of a soul in man, puts this conclusion before us in a dramatic myth, where the changed affections of the enlightened spirit are represented as a life lived or to be lived in other worlds. The illusion that may attach to this is innocent and the truth conveyed is important.⁵¹

However, Santayana warns, it is also important not to kick away the ladder—truth about material facts—by means of which the mind has ascended to this higher and more deeply satisfying position; for "that a man should remain man is the first condition of God's coming to dwell in him."⁵² Expressed in the form of myth, this is Santayana's statement of his important theory of two kinds of truth. He identifies several other important myths in the Gospels:

> The idea of God as Lord and Lawgiver represents dramatically the contact of spirit with all external powers. Respect for these powers is wisdom. . . . When we pass to the idea of God as Creator and Father what is dramatised is rather the dependence of spirit upon the vital powers that generate it: an agitated and troubled dependence, because not all psychic movements are favourable to spirit. . . . The idea of Christ thus represents the intrinsic ideal of spirit; that is to say, the acme of disinterested intelligence and disinterested love. . . . Life when it has arisen begins to pursue certain contingencies and to tremble at others; and spirit inherits this moral and dramatic sensibility. Yet its own impulse is to transcend that agitation.⁵³

These myths are true$_M$. They are also true in the sense James intends, for they carry the spirit prosperously from one part of her experience to another part. The parable of realms of being is also true$_M$ for the same reason. Santayana says: "The only authority in existence is the *authority of things*. I like the irony and the blessedness of this: that since only *things* have any authority there is, *morally*, no authority at all, and the spirit is free in its affections."⁵⁴

Notes

1. George Santayana, *Winds of Doctrine* (Gloucester, Mass.: Peter Smith, 1971), pp. 126–27.
2. George Santayana, *Character and Opinion in the United States* (New York: Norton, 1967), p. 70.
3. George Santayana, *Scepticism and Animal Faith* (New York: Scribner's, 1923).
4. George Santayana, *Realms of Being* (New York: Scribner's, 1942), p. 282.
5. Santayana, *Realms*, p. 607.
6. Ibid., p. 481.
7. Ibid., pp. 335–36.
8. Robert Wright, "The Life of Meaning," in *The Sciences* (New York Academy of Sciences, May/June 1988).
9. Santayana, *Realms*, p. 330.
10. Ibid., p. 570.
11. Ibid., p. 331.
12. Santayana, *Winds*, p. 124.
13. John Dewey, *Human Nature and Conduct* (New York: Modern Library, 1930), p. 70.
14. Santayana, *Character*, p. 167.
15. Dewey, *Human Nature*, p. 16.
16. Santayana, *Realms*, p. 97.
17. Ibid., p. 99.
18. Ibid., p. 135.
19. Ibid., p. 99.
20. Dewey, *Human Nature*, p. 62.
21. Santayana, *Character*, p. 70.
22. George Santayana, "Apologia Pro Mente Sua," in Paul Arthur Schilpp, ed., *The Philosophy of George Santayana* (La Salle, Ill.: Open Court, 1951), pp. 578–79.
23. George Santayana, *Soliloquies in England and Later Soliloquies* (Ann Arbor: University of Michigan Press, 1967), p. 212.
24. Santayana, "Apologia," p. 575.
25. Ibid., p. 573.
26. Santayana, *Soliloquies*, p. 127.
27. John Dewey, "Creative Democracy—The Task Before Us," in James Gouinlock, *Excellence in Public Discourse* (New York: Columbia University Press, 1986), p. 151.
28. Santayana, *Realms* pp. 567–68.
29. Santayana, *Scepticism*, p. vi.
30. Santayana, "Apologia," p. 576.
31. Ibid., p. 604.
32. Santayana, *Realms*, p. 659.
33. Ibid., p. 826.
34. Ibid.
35. Santayana, *Realms*, p. 827.
36. Santayana, *Character*, p. 105.
37. Santayana, *Winds*, p. 126.
38. George Santayana, *The Idler and His Works* (New York: George Braziller, 1957), p. 15.
39. Santayana, *Realms*, p. 539.
40. Ibid., p. 480.
41. George Santayana, *Dominations and Powers* (New York: Scribner's, 1954), p. 51.
42. William James, *Pragmatism* (Indianapolis: Hackett, 1981), p. 34.

43. James, *Pragmatism*, p. 30.
44. Ibid., p. 32.
45. Santayana, *Idler*, p. 16.
46. George Santayana, *The Idea of Christ in the Gospels* (New York: Scribner's, 1946), pp. 4–5.
47. Santayana, *Idea*, p. 4.
48. Santayana, *Realms*, pp. 467–68.
49. George Santayana, *Some Turns of Thought in Modern Philosophy* (Freeport, N.Y.: Books for Libraries Press, 1933), p. 931.
50. Santayana, *Idea*, pp. 247–48.
51. Ibid., p. 248.
52. Ibid.
53. Ibid., pp. 252–53.
54. George Santayana, *Persons and Places* (Cambridge, Mass.: The MIT Press, 1986), p. 284.

Santayana: Objective Overreach?

ANGUS KERR-LAWSON

Santayana can variously be read: by some as extreme realist, and by others as skeptical philosopher. Both of these readings are legitimate findings of two strands present in his writings. These strands are unified by his usual account of knowledge, which takes faith as central and takes correctness of descriptive detail as secondary; our conviction in the objective reality of the world is confirmed by animal faith; our representation of this reality, although it yields a symbolic truth and a utility, is nevertheless in all likelihood not literally true and is vulnerable to skeptical argument if taken to be literally true. However, in Santayana's view, skepticism about the literal truth will lead to full-fledged doubts about the existence of an external reality only through a mistaken account of knowledge, modeled too closely on the kind of formal knowledge proper to ideal topics like mathematics.

Santayana speaks with a remarkable objective detachment, little swayed by a compulsion to utter empirically verifiable statements. He speaks of the essence of the world, for instance, meaning the constitution of the entire cosmos, a radically unmanageable notion. (Today, some modal logicians do speak in similar terms.) This detachment is of course tied to his doctrine of nonliteral knowledge. For if even the simplest perceptions fail to yield literal truth, it becomes idle to require of factual assertions with much less empirical affinity an unspecified reduction to empirical terms. If the table in front of us has an essence that we cannot intuit, we do not therefore desist from discussing it; why then must we refrain from discussing the essence of the world? As he frequently points out, all that is assumed with this terminology is that the world has some definite nature.

I shall call Santayana's sense of reality substrative, following Walter Watson and David Dilworth. Those with a substrative view hold "that reality as encountered or perceived is not the reality.... What is really real is the object as it is in itself, apart from its effect on us."[1]

The substrativist is prepared to give good reasons, often based upon certain presuppositions in science, or in a materialist philosophy, for doubting the exact representational status of our knowledge. What he or she is not prepared to do is to relinquish their beliefs in the underlying substratum, however little we may know about it; they do not accept ideas or appearances as substitute objects of belief. "Good sense," says Santayana, is not misled by the verbal identification of appearances with things, "unless a sophistical attempt at accuracy trips up its honest intentions."[2]

He describes a certain "Mania for accuracy" that he finds in epistemology, something alien to a true understanding of the function of knowledge as a symbolic interaction between animals and their surroundings. Objections can be expected to this realist doctrine, not merely attacks on its correctness but even doubts about its coherence, and I focus on this aspect of a possible defense. No criticisms from particular philosophers will be considered here, because I wish to treat the issue of incoherence in its generality. Objections of the following kinds could most certainly be anticipated, however.

The above two strands do not permit any unification but must stand in extreme opposition: the aseptic is antirealist and converse. The notion that one can sensibly discuss things-in-themselves as hidden and wholly unknown objects has long since been exposed either as empty or incoherent. The discussion of existing objects in Santayana has an objective veneer, but this is deceptive and only betrays the lack of any detailed analysis of the nature of these objects. Finally, the suggestion that accuracy in philosophy is a mistake is ridiculous.

Critics will defend attempts at accuracy against the charge that they will say that this talk of loose connections between appearance and substratum is itself intolerably loose discourse and unacceptable. I shall use the terms *analysis* and *analyst* narrowly here to refer to the doctrine (and its advocate) that the above-mentioned loose connection permits and demands minute clarification, as a minimum requirement of sound philosophical technique. The analyst, as here understood, treats with weary contempt any mention of things in themselves. My suggestion will be that this devotion to logical clarity can serve as a front for reductivist thinking.

Matters are not easy for the defender of a substrative sense of reality in the face of attacks from the analyst, who insists that no harm can come from the effort to clarify the terms used to designate external objects. Would it not be preferable, for instance, for Santayana to say more precisely what is meant by a term such as *physical time*? The defender must point out that his imprecision is a studied one, not a result of his incompetence in logic. Santayana in fact considers many clarifications—only none is taken to be definitive: there is sentimental time, mathematical time, specious time, absolute time. However, the term *physical time* must be retained, to denote the real thing; dropping it in favor of mathematical time (or any of the other terms with exact descriptive content) leads regularly to a hypostasis of the mathematical continuum (or of some other concept) and brings on serious difficulties.

I wish to side with Santayana. It is perfectly coherent to refer to objects without being able to define them. While it may seem unprofessional to advocate looseness of discourse, a certain looseness is nevertheless forced on us by circumstances, because of the fragility of our knowledge. When philosophers insist on an account of knowledge that extends past the natural bounds forced on us by our ignorance, faulty inferences can follow, as I shall attempt to show.

For the philosopher steeped in verificationist doctrine, here characterized as analyst, the marked objectivity found in Santayana poses difficulties and may be dismissed as objective overreach. I draw the term *objective overreach* from *The View from Nowhere*,[3] in which Thomas Nagel raises the question of whether his own objectivity and realism may not be seen as extreme. Perhaps some do not find extreme any mention of a view from nowhere; however, there will be no criticism here of his moves toward objectivity and away from verificationism and reductionism. Reservations are expressed only on the point that his principles could well lead him to carry these moves further.

Several of the issues raised in Nagel's book suggest parallels with themes from Santayana. One such is Nagel's willingness to take skeptical arguments seriously. He notes that the idea of objectivity seems to undermine itself, and he observes that responses to this problem are of three possible types: skeptical, reductive, and heroic. The reductive he views with distaste and looks instead to a combination of the skeptical and heroic for the solution.[4] Enter skepticism and animal faith! Santayana bases his combination of the two on the notion of literal and nonliteral knowledge. His skepticism about literal knowledge is complete, and animal faith is made useful and functional by the mediation of nonliteral or symbolic knowledge. Nagel does not go so far, but both harbor a strong antipathy toward the "reductive substitutes" to which some have been led by skeptical argumentation.

Another similarity with Santayana is Nagel's decision to tag as forms of idealism theories that accept various reductive substitutes in place of natural objects; their authors feel driven to this by their imperfect knowledge of the causal objects, whereas the ideal substitutes are perfectly clear. It is easy, but it is incorrect, to see Santayana's incessant attack upon idealism and empiricism as a critique of ideas long since rejected. A closer look at the text shows that he has in mind much more recent versions of reductionism, versions that often present themselves as anti-idealist doctrine. Like Nagel, Santayana groups together and accuses of idealism all those who attach epistemological criteria on what there is or what there might be. For both of them, any test of the real inspired by epistemological consideration is a sign of residual idealism.

Nagel asks "how far we can go in forming the idea of a world with which our minds cannot make contact,"[5] and he maintains, against the analytic critics, that beyond what we can and do know with precision, there may be other parts of the universe that are quite unknowable. The much more radical position of Santayana holds that the forms of knowing that have evolved in animal life yield representations that are probably incommensurate with the actual facts, even under immediate and ideal conditions. This doctrine places him at the opposite extreme from idealism, as characterized by Nagel; for it gives an objectivity to objects and their real properties that detaches them entirely from both their perceived and their theoretically understood properties. Epistemology here surely does not dictate to metaphysics. This reinforces Nagel's point that a close tie exists between objectivity and skepticism, for here Santayana's wholesale objectivity is tied to his wholesale skepticism.

As far as I can see, arguments of incoherency, such as propounded by our analytical critics, have their inspiration in a rather simple, almost linguistic intuition, which sees contradiction in any claim to discuss, or refer to, or have cognitive awareness of things that we do not know. According to the intuition, this would involve in some way the absurdity of knowing the unknown. It is useful to consider this intuition in its simplicity, detached from the technical complexities of a particular example. In fact Santayana's doctrine forces one to do just this, it being innocent of any technical detail. He holds that one can indeed "know the unknown" of objects whose true nature is hidden from us. Presented in these stark terms, both the charge of incoherency and the possible naturalistic retort are seen more clearly than in cases complicated by technicalities and by complex theory.

As one example of this simple intuition in action, we cite Russell's doctrine of acquaintance and his theory of logically proper names. To Russell, true knowledge is inconceivable without at some level of analysis a direct connection to the external, which in turn gives a foundation in meaning and validity to further knowledge claims. Later thinkers have declared that knowledge is fully conceivable, without the Russellian apparatus.

Typically, a particular explanatory link between mind and reality is abandoned, without at the same time dropping the requirement that there must be some specific link. Another theory with its own precisely defined link follows and in its turn is seen to be obviously faulty, once the initial enthusiasm abates. This requirement rules out a position like Santayana's, which rejects all such specific links in advance and limits itself to general pragmatic descriptions about the validation of knowledge by animal successes and failures in encounters with reality.

A more recent such link is provided by Kripke's rigid designators, which offer a direct connection between language and things, somewhat like logically proper names. Here we may note that Kripke's teaching lends important support to the doctrine of the substrativist: that we can and do talk effectively of things in the absence of full knowledge or understanding of them. Of course, Kripke does not conclude that we must settle for a loose connection between names and things. Quite the contrary—the weakened descriptive connection to things is replaced by a direct referential link that is rigid and absolute. I believe that the assumption of this absolute link leads to various difficulties.

In my estimation, neither the link offered by Russellian names nor that of rigid designators provides any satisfactory explanation of how we interact with things. Neither is much superior in real explanatory force to what Santayana calls "a friendly concomitance between material events and the free symbolism proper to animal sense or imagination."[6] And Santayana's language is less misleading, for it expresses the true assertion that knowledge arises from poorly understood interactions between animal life and their physical surroundings.

The analytical critic of Santayana's substrative view will have many questions to pose, always appealing to logical standards of clarity. If something is to be called knowledge but is denied literal truth, can it be knowledge at all? And in what manner can it be useful, if it is false? An elaboration of what is special about some kinds of nontrue knowledge, which sets them apart from other nontrue knowledge and renders them useful, is called for. The analyst holds that it is no more than good philosophy to pose these and other questions. A doctrine that cannot stand up to such scrutiny is worthless.

Substrativists, however, are apt to take a rather different view. They will see the insistence on the application of analytic technique here not as a requirement of good philosophy but instead as an instrument in the reductionist enterprise. According to the substrative view of what is open to literal knowledge, nothing better than a loosely defined connection with external realities is available; the insistence on further analysis can only be an attempt to subvert that doctrine. Of course the questions posed by the analyst are good ones, and answers to them would be welcome—but no such answers seem to be forthcoming.

It is not commonly held to be incoherent to admit that one does not know something. Why then must it be incoherent to question the literal truth of all knowledge of physical fact? Would Nagel, an eminently coherent writer, become incoherent, were he led to question his belief in primary qualities and our knowledge of them? It is not easy to take seriously this charge of incoherency. Still, the demand for some clarity and detailed explanation of what nonliteral knowledge may be does not seem unreasonable. What then are Santayana's reasons for holding that this demand cannot be met and that we should not go beyond a "friendly concomitance"?

The reasons he gives for resisting this clarification are, to a large extent, psychological ones. In his view, those who identify knowledge with correct representation seem always to misdirect the psychological forces of belief and to point them mistakenly at ideal objects instead of at the material things of which these ideal objects are mere imperfect descriptions. The doctrine of animal faith is meant to avert this problem and to allow knowledge without exact representation. Of course, clarifications are acceptable, so long as they are not taken too seriously. Santayana appears to be correct: the attempt to make epistemology precise frequently does lead to theories that are taken more seriously than they merit, leading often to bad arguments. Nagel considers and rejects a number of arguments against his objective view. I look very briefly at two of these, one skeptical and one antiskeptical, from the standpoint of a substrative sense of reality. In each case the argument loses much of its force and takes on an a priori aspect.

One class of arguments attempts to show that a proper analysis of our own discourse makes it impossible for certain types of skeptical argument to be correct. If we were brains in a vat, for instance, our use of designating terms would be radically different than it is in fact.[7] For a brain in a vat, the term *vat* does not refer to vats.[8] The case is made, on the basis of this linguistic discrepancy, against the viability of the skeptical argument that we might in fact merely be brains in a vat. These arguments can be countered, as in fact Nagel does. However, I wish to consider only this general form of argument from the substrative standpoint.

Seen from this perspective, the use of rigidity, or something very similar, to disqualify skepticism cannot be justified. It assumes a bond between thing and name that has incorrectly been assigned an absolute status, and from a failure of the bond, it assumes there must follow an incoherency. For one who accepts the world as it is in itself, independent of our understanding of it, any argument appealing to technicalities such as this, to dismiss doubts about our knowledge of that reality, must be seen as inadequate and naive.

Consider next the Wittgensteinian case against any use of rules having application to an infinity of cases. His skeptical conclusions, in Nagel's words, "seem to imply that nothing can make sense which purports to reach beyond the outer bounds of human experience and life."[9] But for Santayana, the posits of animal faith already lead us beyond any descriptive accounts stemming from experience, all of which are imperfect. The additional imperfections to which Wittgenstein calls attention may hurt the general coherence and effectiveness of our knowledge but do not destroy that knowledge, for its validity has a different source. "Only the demand for literal knowledge makes knowledge impossible."[10]

With skeptical arguments, like that of Wittgenstein, there is one sense in which the argument must be accepted, for it is because of such arguments that Santayana is led to give his revised account of natural knowledge. These arguments are conceded by him in advance, if they are seen as directed against the possibility of literal knowledge. A general feature of the attacks considered by Nagel against his version of objectivity is their appeal to incoherency. In all such cases, the argument is powerless against a doctrine that sets the world as it is apart from our theories about that world. The incoherency, if it exists, touches only a certain theory, without destroying our knowledge of that world. An entire class of epistemological argument is rendered suspect, in Santayana's eyes; these arguments assume that with knowledge there must be a specific and precise link with reality, and they seek to show that contradictions are generated by that link.

With a severe skepticism like that of Santayana, it is not surprising that much must be sacrificed. However, his view that we do possess nonliteral knowledge serves to limit what must be abandoned to just the above class of philosophical arguments. Intelligent activity is preserved and retains a sound explanation. As well, our belief in science can also be rationally maintained, so long as we strip it of its claim to literal truth (as many scientists in fact do). Indeed, the credibility of science is enhanced, because the revolutionary shifts in scientific theory that occur from time to time are readily understood, once the pretension of literal truth is dropped.

For Santayana, the nature of our knowledge is truly described by his account. If he is correct, philosophers face the difficult task of reconciling their powerful analytic techniques with their subject matter.

Notes

1. See Walter Watson, *The Architectonics of Meaning: Foundations of the New Pluralism* (Albany: State University of New York Press, 1985), p. 50. I am grateful to David Dilworth for several discussions on this subject.

2. See George Santayana, *Realms of Being* (New York: Scribner's, 1942), p. 66.

3. Thomas Nagel, *The View from Nowhere* (New York: Oxford University Press, 1986), p. 108.

4. Nagel, *The View from Nowhere*, p. 68.

5. Ibid., p. 97.

6. Santayana, *Realms of Being*, p. 411.

7. See, for instance, Hilary Putnam, *Reason, Truth and History* (Cambridge: Cambridge University Press, 1981).

8. Nagel, *The View from Nowhere*, p. 72.

9. Ibid., p. 105.

10. See George Santayana, "Apologia Pro Mente Sua," in *The Philosophy of George Santayana*, ed. Paul Arthur Schilpp (Evanston, Ill.: The Library of Living Philosophers, Northwestern University Press, 1940), p. 518.

Santayana and the Many Faces of Realism

HENRY SAMUEL LEVINSON

I want to suggest that the writings of George Santayana play out a dialectic that we currently see in pragmatists like Richard Rorty, on the one hand, and realists like Hilary Putnam, on the other. Fleshing out this argument entirely would take a book. But the point is this: Rorty's pragmatism is realistic and Putnam's realism is pragmatic, and they tend to converge in a position similar to one occupied by Santayana.

I characterize Rorty's pragmatism as realistic because his efforts to see language as part of the coping behavior of human beings living their way through contingent predicaments, instead of as a mirror reflecting nature as it understands itself, demands a material backdrop. He not only presumes that there is extralinguistic stuff or "bits of the universe"[1] that make the solving of problems and the management of difficulties indispensable parts of our repertoire of distinctively human behaviors. He also argues that, so far as arts and sciences have been normalized, material truth conditions exist by which parties to dispute may come to presumptive settlements.

I accept Putnam's own characterization of his realism as pragmatic.[2] His three commitments to conceptual relativity, to taking "our familiar commonsense scheme, as well as our scientific and artistic and other schemes, at face value, without helping itself to the notion of the thing 'in itself' "[3] and to the view that such descriptive schemes "reflect our interests and choices,"[4] all point toward an understanding of philosophy as "a study of the comparative advantages and disadvantages of the various ways of talking which our race has invented"— which is Rorty's pragmatic view.[5]

One way to display an overlap, at least, in their realisms is to say that Rorty and Putnam are both committed to the views (1) that there are material conditions (including material human conditions) we do not just legislate, and (2) that, given this or that tradition of thought and action, there are some facts internal to it that may be discovered.

One way to characterize their common pragmatism is to say that they agree (1) to an account of language that collapses any *metaphysical* distinction between fact and value, though permitting a *phenomenological* distinction between these two things, (2) to a nonfoundational view of knowledge, and (3) to a nontranscendent picture of rationality. They both profess that every human language, including human language used to indicate facts, is evaluative, expressing determinable human interests; that knowledge is constituted by sound opinion; and that, when it comes to ironing out disagreements, we have no recourse to some science capable of settling all controversy but only to judgments and methods of arriving at judgments, which themselves might well be placed in critical jeopardy.

Where they appear to disagree most is over the role that truth plays in human discourse. Rorty has said that "truth . . . is not a profitable topic"[6] and that he follows Wittgenstein's "resistance to the entire cultural tradition which made truth—the successful crossing of the void which divides man from the world—a central virtue."[7] Putnam responds, implicitly anyhow, by saying that "we may come to think of history and politics as nothing but power struggle, with truth as the reward that goes to the victor's view. But then our culture—everything in our culture that is of value—will be at an end."[8] On this view, truth appears to be a central virtue indeed.

But here, I think, it is crucial to characterize the dispute in the right sort of way if we are ever to figure out what difference, if any, it makes to accept one of these views over the other. This is so for a number of reasons. First, to some extent, I believe that Rorty and Putnam are talking past one another; but second, in another way, I think there is a difference here that makes a difference. And finally, I believe that, whatever this difference is, it is important to consider the view that if truth *is* a virtue indispensable to culture, it is, for all that, capable of distracting us from other virtues if we give it more than its due.

As I indicated to begin with, I think that reflection on Santayana's writings may clarify these three issues. This is so because Santayana accepted both a realism and a pragmatism that Rorty and Putnam could share. He both rejected the notion of truth understood as "the successful crossing of the void between man and world" and defended love of the truth as a virtue indispensable to culture. And finally, he attempted to characterize the discipline or virtue of truth within a broader spiritual context that both made it indispensable and curbed its pretensions.

I will assume there is no need to persuade anybody that Santayana maintained that we are born into material conditions we do not just legislate or that, having adopted a way of speaking about those conditions, there are facts to be discovered about them. But I will provide a brief sketch of the more contentious view that Santayana developed a kind of pragmatism (despite his own disclaimers).

There are four strands in Santayana's writing—especially, I would argue, his post-Harvard work—that suggest his pragmatism. Take *Realms of Being* and its introduction, *Scepticism and Animal Faith*, as exemplary. First, these books abandoned foundational epistemology for a characterization of knowledge and understanding that is grounded in variable human practices and that collapses the distinction between *doxa* and *scientia*.

Second, these books departed from metaphysics for reflection on the conditions that let the human spirit flourish. They accepted the Romantic view that philosophy, the arts, the sciences, and religious meditation are alternative languages that function to manage life's difficulties and articulate human aspirations instead of special intuitions revealing the really real. Both works urged us to accept the fact that "all thinking is originally poetic in texture."[9] But they both also rejected the Romantic claim that poetry, instead of some other sort of discourse, was metaphysically revelatory. Exercises in satirical irony, *Scepticism and Animal Faith* as well as *Realms of Being* not only rejected the idea of metaphysical disclosure but the very idea of metaphysical presence that it presumed.

Third, they retained Santayana's earlier view that reason must be characterized as a life articulated and constrained by the disciplines or human institutions of common sense, social practice, religion, art, and science. Reason was constituted by an intricate pattern of human institutions that constrained one another within the context of material conditions that were largely out of human control. Reason was *not* simply a set of logical rules or a list of applicable but abstract principles and protocols.

Finally, Santayana's mature works rejected the distinction between necessity and contingency. "In a contingent world," Santayana argued, "necessity is a conspiracy of accidents."[10] Every condition that permits or fosters human well-being is contingent. Any claim to the contrary, he said, "foolishly parades the helplessness of the mind to imagine anything different" and fuels vicious dogmatism.[11] We know, to be sure, that now and again Santayana rejected identification with pragmatism. He said he prided himself on remaining James's disciple when it came to his understanding of reason and knowledge and the spiritual character of philosophy but that he "could not stomach" the way his mentor spoke about truth in his lectures in *Pragmatism* or the way he apparently collapsed pragmatism into a kind of idealistic metaphysics in his *Essays in Radical Empiricism*.[12] With regard to Dewey and his followers, he was unwilling to accept the outright identification of philosophy with social policy formulation, on the grounds that philosophers were as much concerned with solitude as with society. Not one of Santayana's criticisms of James and Dewey, however, disturbed the strands in his work that make it both realistic and deeply pragmatic. But they do prefigure some of the disagreements, especially over the role of truth, that now exist between philosophers like Putnam and Rorty; and finally, they do place questions about the virtue of truth within a broader spiritual context.

Now I have noted that Santayana followed James's lead in dumping an allegiance to truth understood as the virtue that let people transcend the void separating them from the world. More clearly than James, though, Santayana attempted to reduce to absurdity the notions on which this putative virtue depended: there simply was no void separating the human psyche and the material world, or break between necessary and contingent truths, or distinction between principles or facts that were given and formulated judgments. On his view, the psyche was a structure of material behaviors in the world. We might stipulate necessary relations among logical terms or definitions, but the applicability of this or that logic to the ways of the world was a matter of contingent fact. Finally, we could intuit given essences or qualities or functions (like "rocking" or "nausea"[13]), but only by *withholding* any belief, assertion, or implication whatsoever, not by establishing an *indubitable ground* for knowledge or claims to truth. The given was constituted, Santayana argued, by "illusion."[14] Because this was so, the given *per se* simply had no role in resolving epistemic disputes.

The trouble with maintaining truth understood as the virtue letting us link up our presumptively charmed circle of thoughts with an external world—in other words, by letting us intuit things or possess them just the way they are—was that this discipline was irrelevant to the demands of scientific, moral, and spiritual life. Prefiguring the later Wittgenstein, Santayana's meditations in *Scepticism and Animal Faith* concluded, among other things, that "if all data are symbols and all experience comes in poetic terms, it follows that the human mind, both in its existence and in its quality, is a free development out of nature, a language or music the terms of which are arbitrary, like the rules or counters of a game."[15]

Following this line of thought, Santayana asserted that "all [the] insecurity and inadequacy of alleged knowledge," that is, knowledge construed as a privileged (because literal) intuition of things, was "almost irrelevant to the natural order of the mind to describe natural things." Epistemology understood as permitting a God's-eye view of the world, or even as revealing invariant norms by which to settle any controversy, was a setup for failure, because it was based upon "a false conception of what would be success." "Our worst difficulties," Santayana went on, "arise from the assumption that knowledge of existences ought to be literal, whereas knowledge of existences has no need, no propensity, and no fitness to be literal. . . . It fulfills its function perfectly—I mean its moral function of enlightening us about our [well-being]—if it remains symbolic to the end."[16]

It is, I think, Santayana's insistence that "truth is a moral . . . good,"[17] that the function of our allegiance to truth is essentially moral, clarifying both the dangers impeding and the chances for attaining our ability to flourish humanely, that establishes the appropriate context for understanding the dispute between philosophers like Putnam and Rorty over the role of truth in human discourse as well as the limits of truth as a virtue. Put most perspicaciously, the dispute seems more a matter of will or courage than one of matter of intellect alone.

According to my way of interpreting them, neither Santayana nor Putnam nor Rorty sees truth understood as the virtue that overcomes the void separating humankind from the world, because for all three of them, truth understood this way functions to solve a pseudoproblem. If anything, allegiance to truth understood this way is a vice: something that Santayana characterized as a spiritual distraction that actually impeded the realization of human joy by sidetracking us intellectually the way a cramp sidetracks us physically.

Overcoming the void separating humankind from the world *is not a profitable topic*, at least from the vantage points of these philosophers, because there is no such void. And yet, it would be cavalier, I think, to claim that the dispute between Rorty and Putnam is bogus once we make this clarification, because a significant issue still appears to divide the two.

For Rorty, "truth" is just an honorific or eulogistic term we give to the claims that competent people now happen to have, constrained by the relevant conversations they happen to have held. Putnam does not deny that opinion alone constrains the course of controversy. But he does insist that our most significant conversations, those that turn on disclosing moral or material circumstances to help settle an issue one way or another, dispose us to reporting what has actually gone on—to searching out some aspect of the truth. The sheer honorific use of the term *true* keeps conversation wobbling between smug quietism and Nietzschean assertion. It eclipses the truth understood pragmatically as the unknown we yet need to discover if we are to get things right. The cash value of the term *true*, understood as *limit concept* (in Putnam's term) or as an *ideal ideal* or *immaterial sort of being* (in Santayana's terms), demands a presumption that there is a gap between whatever we claim to know, now or whenever, and the truth of the matter: between the ways we signify things knowledgeably and the ways we might give a complete description of what happens (in any modality).

The point is that, on both Putnam's and Santayana's view, knowledge-claims (of whatever garden variety, because we only have garden varieties) are more or less versionary and fragmentary, capable of indefinite revision. The truth that anchors realism has many faces, each of which constitutes a physiognomy of plural traditions of thought and action. This point accounts for Santayana's disappointment in James's pragmatism. James's "truth"—and Rorty's—appear to discount the (pragmatic) discipline, to play on one of Quine's phrases of pushing and pulling ourselves towards objectivity.[18] So does James's "radical empiricism" if, as Santayana claims, it is established to permit some metaphysical disclosure. The project of metaphysical disclosure upends allegiance to truth by suggesting that there is a "view in which truth is contained once for all and without qualification."[19]

As limit concept, "the truth" ironically fixes the presumption that our best current claims, whatever and whenever, are corrigible, fallible, always open to criticism and refinement. In Santayana's view, the distinction between "essence" of truth and the "existence" of knowledge-claims captured the intuition voiced by James in his own time and by Rorty in ours: that we idolize our knowledge-claims, we eulogize them, whenever we count them as literally mirroring the way things are.

When we do this, we commit what Santayana called the first false step in philosophy[20] and what Quine would eventually call philosophical "original sin, coeval with the word," namely, the confusion of sign and object.[21] Santayana noted that "the truth posited by animal faith, in action or in curiosity, is posited as unknown, as something to be investigated and discovered, and truth in this transcendent sense can never be denied by an active mind," living as it does in utterly contingent material conditions that constitute it no less contingently.[22] "But," Santayana continued, "when animal faith has already expressed itself in conventional ideas, its own further actions find those ideas obstructive. Truth has now been rashly posited as known. An idea, an idol, has taken the place of the god [the strictly ideal ideal] originally and intrinsically invoked by the mind and posited as unknown."[23] The truth, then, that critics like Rorty deny, is "itself a blasphemy," and in denying it, Santayana argues, they are "secretly animated by the love of truth."[24]

Allegiance to truth, then, remains a central virtue in our culture, according to Santayana. But it is one that not only recognizes that the Platonic quest to capture some intellectual intuition of the whole universe is a vice; it also demands that we recognize how fragile our knowledge claims are and how revisionary we must always be prepared to be, given the variable and modifiable faces of material power that make up our own lives and the environments in which we live.

Allegiance to the truth, in Santayana's view, is clearly a central virtue, the discipline that undercuts the monumental deceit involved in maintaining that our words call themselves or anything else into existence, that our thinking or wishing or willing make things so. But, for this very reason, allegiance to the truth can never stand alone and, just as surely, can run amok.

Sufficient attention to truth sanely fixes the (modifiable and variable) horizons within which we can hope to overcome the things that impede human joy. But, as Santayana wisely noted, "merely being true does not make things worth knowing."[25] Again, "the real problem is moral; and even if science presents truth more honestly than the humanities, we should still have to ask whether these scientific truths were the most important, and even whether the knowledge of truth is the ultimate goal or good of mind. Frankly," Santayana asserted, "it is not when the mind is free."[26]

When the mind is free, when matters let life be liberal, the point is not simply to pursue the truth but instead to pursue the good, as Santayana put it, that our natural world "suggests, approaches, and misses."[27] To be sure, such poetic freedom is "premature, and even criminal, when the psyche is living at cross-purposes with the possibilities of life."[28] But once we have taken sights on such possibilities, we are left to balance our contrary spiritual interests as best we can with what creativity we have at our disposal. Only as we raise the vexing issues concerned with doing this, I suggest, can we pragmatic realists or realistic pragmatists raise with clarity the reasons why and how truth is a virtue.

Notes

1. Richard Rorty, *The Consequences of Pragmatism* (Minneapolis: University of Minnesota Press, 1982), p. xliii.
2. See, for example, Hilary Putnam, *Realism and Reason: Philosophical Papers, Volume Three* (Cambridge: Cambridge University Press, 1983), p. 225; see also Hilary Putnam, *The Many Faces of Realism* (LaSalle, Ind.: Open Court Press, 1987), p. 17.
3. Putnam, *The Many Faces of Realism*, p. 17.
4. Ibid., p. 37.
5. Rorty, *The Consequences of Pragmatism*, p. xl.
6. Ibid., p. xliii.
7. Ibid., p. 35.
8. Putnam, *The Many Faces of Realism*, p. 71.
9. Paul Arthur Schilpp, *George Santayana: The Library of Living Philosophers, Volume Two* (LaSalle, Ind.: Open Court Press, 1940), p. 539.
10. George Santayana, *Realms of Being* (New York: Scribner's Sons, 1942), p. 291.
11. Ibid., p. 417.
12. Schillp, *George Santayana*, pp. 14–16.
13. George Santayana, *Scepticism and Animal Faith* (New York: Scribner's Sons, 1923), p. 92.
14. Ibid., p. 99.
15. Ibid., p. 98.
16. Ibid., pp. 101–102.
17. Santayana, *Realms of Being*, p. 551.
18. See Willard Van Orman Quine, *Word and Object* (Cambridge: MIT Press, 1960), pp. 5–8.
19. Santayana, *Realms of Being*, p. 536.
20. George Santayana, *The Birth of Reason and Other Essays* (New York: Columbia University Press, 1968), pp. 148ff.
21. Willard Van Orman Quine, *Ontological Relativity and Other Essays* (New York: Columbia University Press, 1969), p. 15.
22. Santayana, *Realms of Being*, p. 536.
23. Ibid.
24. Ibid.
25. Ibid., p. 441.
26. Ibid., pp. 440–41.
27. Ibid., p. 833.
28. Ibid., p. 443.

DEWEY

Dewey, Virtue, and Moral Pluralism

JAMES GOUINLOCK

I wish to draw attention to a feature of Dewey's moral philosophy that is both important and neglected. I have in mind his emphasis on the cultivation and exercise of certain virtues in the conduct of life. In this neglected feature we find one of the most valuable of his ideas. I want also to suggest that this emphasis on virtue is the key to finding a happy medium between absolutism and relativism in moral thought. It is well known that Dewey was the enemy of all forms of absolutism. He did not mean to say that there might be moral absolutes, but we just can't be sure that we know them; he meant that there are no invariable ends or norms of conduct. He was equally opposed to relativism, according to which there can be no rational basis for intersubjective agreement on moral norms. Dewey's rejection of both absolutism and relativism is not incoherent, for here, as elsewhere, he rejects the premise that these two positions exhaust the alternatives. He held a distinctive view, pluralism, which will be characterized below. In my conclusion, I will indicate the merit of Dewey's position, but I will also suggest that it requires significant modification.[1]

Section I

The element of Dewey's ethical philosophy that has received the most attention is his insistence that ethics can be scientific. But the sense in which science is utilized in the moral life has been poorly grasped by admirers and critics alike. At the same time, he is widely respected as a philosopher who undertook a reconstruction of the meaning of democracy. He frequently urged, indeed, that democracy be adopted as a way of life. A casual observer might be perplexed by the juxtaposition of these two themes: how can ethical discourse be at once scientific and democratic? Scientific discourse forces conclusions upon us whether we like them or not, but democratic discourse is a procedure that rests ultimately on the uncoerced preferences of the participants. In identifying the role of virtue, however, we shall see how moral discourse can be both scientific and democratic.

Although he does not discuss virtue systematically, Dewey repeatedly appeals to the necessity of various traits of character, or habits, in the moral life. He will urge the importance of courage, sensitivity, impartiality, flexibility, cooperativeness, receptiveness, creativity, perseverance, integrity, and the like. He often sums up the virtues with such expressions as "intelligence" or "being scientific," and this has been misleading. He seems to be reductive, for example, when he says in *Freedom and Culture*, "The future of democracy is allied with spread of the scientific attitude."[2]

Yet if Dewey sometimes uses, say, "intelligence" as an omnicompetent virtue, he does so as well with "democratic." "Democracy," he writes, "is a *personal* way of individual life; . . . it signifies the possession and continual use of certain attitudes, forming personal character and determining desire and purpose in all the relations of life."[3] He likewise urges that democracy as a way of life "provides a moral standard for personal conduct."[4]

The unity of the scientific and democratic attitudes will be within reach once we dismiss the assumption that for Dewey the point of "scientific" ethics is to solve the "is/ought" problem. I have in several writings argued that this interpretation is without merit, but I cannot review the argument here.[5] Let it suffice to assert that there is not so much as a sentence in Dewey's writings that supports this view. It was gratuitously read into him by Morton White and others, who took it as axiomatic that the basic enterprise of moral philosophy is to show a logical relation (if there could be one) between descriptive and normative statements.

Dewey did urge that we use scientific ideas to direct conduct. Such ideas would function in the moral life in the same way that they direct the behavior of the scientific investigator. Scientists hypothesize that if certain variables are introduced under particular conditions, and if they are manipulated in specified ways, then certain consequences will be observed to occur. They test their hypothesis by undertaking action just as prescribed, and if the predicted events occur, their hypothesis is warranted.

With qualifications and additions to be mentioned, Dewey would have this be the model for addressing morally problematic situations. With the same scrupulous analysis of a situation that an experimenter must adopt, we formulate a plan of action that would address the specific conditions that make a moral situation problematic. The plan of action is a prediction that if the problematic conditions are reconstructed in the manner specified, the situation will no longer be troublesome. Hence, the hypothesis directs conduct just as it does in the obviously scientific situation. If we are addressing the conflicts in Central America, for example, we must determine the nature of all the relevant conditions there. We cannot proceed prejudicially and just ignore what is uncongenial to our initial convictions. Then we are prepared to formulate working hypotheses that predict outcomes contingent upon particular reconstructions of that situation.

No scientific procedure proves or demonstrates that we ought to follow any particular prescription. Science does not prescribe ends. Instead, the prescription is instrumental in meeting the actual demands of ongoing experience. Inasmuch as there may well be several ways in which a situation can be reconstructed, the parties to the situation often differ as to the preferred alternative. Even an exhaustive use of scientific method, as such, is not in itself sufficient to resolve such differences—although it may well bring us to revise many of our original intentions. At this juncture (if not sooner), distinctively *democratic* qualities would be effective in addressing the problem. The democratic attitude would be expressed in the deliberate and mutual attempt to find adjustment or unification among conflicting aims, instead of remaining intransigent. The attempt is to seek accommodation and shared solutions instead of stay fixed in an adversary relation. This is a difficult procedure, demanding great virtue, and it by no means guarantees success, but Dewey believed it was better suited to the flourishing of individual and social life than any method tried hitherto.

Dewey's position can be amplified by summarizing the minimal virtues of the "democratic mind," as we might call it. The most pertinent virtues can be digested to three: first, being scientific; second, being willing to communicate: and third, showing respect for other persons.

Being scientific means that one tries conscientiously to become well informed regarding the constituents of the moral situation. (This is so rarely done that its observance alone would bring a vast improvement to our discourse.) It also means that one entertains a variety of hypotheses for the reconstruction of the situation. The scientific attitude entails further that one regards both oneself and one's ideas as fallible. In being scientific, one is, therefore, open-minded: we regard our convictions as subject to experimental test and revision; we are susceptible to instruction from others and from experience. We recognize that our knowledge is incomplete, subject to error and prejudice, and that the remedy for these deficiencies is in further inquiry and communication. Everyone has strong moral convictions, but to convert them into unquestionable absolutes is to declare them beyond criticism. Thus intolerance and fanaticism are reinforced, and competing absolutes stand in irreconcilable antagonism. These are not just the absolutes of, say, the Bible-thumper. They are the absolutes of Rawls, Nozick, Hare, Gauthier, and many others, each of whom has settled on an exclusive moral criterion.

I just mentioned communication. Willingness to communicate is the second virtue to analyze. Everyone recognizes that communication is an indispensable constituent of scientific inquiry. More than any other philosopher in the western tradition, Dewey urged the centrality of communication in the moral life. The isolated mind is impotent in scientific inquiry; it is likewise impotent in moral controversy. The individual who would aspire to intersubjective agreement in moral situations must proceed by way of sharing knowledge, communicating concerns, and consulting others to determine possible plans of action. Unless we regard ourselves as morally perfect and cognitively flawless, we cannot settle moral controversy subjectively, even though we might disguise such attempts by appeal to abstract reason. Moral discourse, in brief, must be colloquy, not soliloquy, if it is to be effective in problematic situations.

The last virtue to be discussed, respect for persons, is necessarily vague. It implies no specific rules of conduct, and it presupposes no arcane concept of the person. We are talking here of concrete beings of nature and history, in their diverse ways, with respect to whom we have no utterly fixed rights or obligations. Dewey frequently insists, however, that democratic persons show a positive regard and active support for one another's concerns.[6] At a minimum, what is suggested is a sense of moral equality: each person has his own needs, aspirations, biases, and convictions, just as we do, and no person is abstractly entitled to a privileged position relative to anyone else. For Dewey, this means that any individual is as entitled to his "day in court" as anyone else. The demands of each person are taken seriously and would be given a full and even-handed hearing, and each such person would give a like hearing to others. This is not to prejudge what the outcome of the hearing might be. Actual moral discourse takes place in a living context, in which there already exists a plurality of deeply felt moral relations. Respect for actual persons can hardly ignore this context. Democratic discourse is not Cartesian: it does not begin with the hypothetical eradication of the concerns and convictions of the persons who have reached a moral impasse.

Even if all these virtues are exercised in a moral situation, there can be no assurance of agreement between the engaged parties. Unlike, say, the phantoms of Rawls's original position, real people are not replicas of each other. The moral life has its irreducibly plural dimensions. On the other hand—and this is a crucial point—practicing the virtues of democratic intelligence excludes antisocial or otherwise vicious behavior. Those who possess the democratic virtues in some measure are not murderers, liars, terrorists, or thieves. Most of our serious interpersonal problems come at the hands of deliberate parasites and exploiters. Without them, life would still be vexing and hurtful in many ways, but it would be a veritable transfiguration compared to the conditions posed by the willfully negligent and malignant.

In a rough way, we see how Dewey's position is pluralistic. The varieties of moral criteria are not reducible to one; there is not one right answer to a moral dilemma. So Dewey is not absolutistic. But he is not relativistic, either. That is, his philosophy obviously rules out the wide, if indeterminate, range of behavior that is inconsistent with the democratic virtues. To recast the ancient expression a bit, there are but a few forms of good but an infinity of forms of evil.

Section II

Philosophers respond to the moral condition in extreme ways. The way of absolutism persistently makes itself ridiculous. In just the few years since the publication of Rawls's *A Theory of Justice*, we have witnessed a succession of demonstrative moral systems, each one refuting, or just ignoring, the others. The more precisely absolutists formulate their principles, the more vulnerable to criticism they are. At the same time, there have been persistent relativists.

One of the virtues of Dewey's virtues, if I may put it that way, is that there is a *limited permissiveness* about them. They are not demands for rigidly specified rules of behavior. This characteristic makes them very attractive in a way that neither absolutism nor relativism can be. The absolutist tells us that we must accept a certain well-defined position without reservation or exception. This position threatens, therefore, much that we cherish in the moral life—and for that reason, any given system will have very few subscribers. It leaves us no room to modify it in favor of even a qualified version of our own convictions. From the pluralistic point of view, we conscientiously reject the system. If our choice is to take it or leave it, we leave it. We must be reminded, in addition, that confirmed absolutists remain at odds with each other; social action short of force is therefore stymied.

The relativist tells us that there is no preferable view beyond the preference that we just happen to have—no matter how many and how polyglot they happen to be. Entertained seriously, this philosophy, like absolutism in its way, deprives us of one of our most essential values: a community of endeavor. Life requires more or less stable and predictable relations between persons, and a reasonably satisfying life requires a community that can be counted upon for forms of mutual support and affection. Even if we accept the dreary assumptions of a Hobbes, we recognize, as he did, that the forces that draw us together are usually stronger than those that drive us apart. Accordingly, a thoroughgoing relativistic position cannot be pursued in the moral life.

In contrast to these extremes, Dewey provides the means for carrying on the moral life. His way, happily, makes demands on us, but limited and flexible demands. It is possible to subscribe to Dewey's philosophy without placing nearly so much in jeopardy as one would in subscribing to either absolutism or relativism. One is at the same time accepted as an equal in ongoing moral deliberation. No doubt, of course, there will always be absolutists and relativists in some number, just as there will be plenty of more or less immoral people; I therefore don't make the argument that Dewey's position will be convincing to everybody. I just make the claim that it is likely to be more widely acceptable than any of the alternatives.

Section III

I have proposed that the democratic virtues are highly effective conditions for moral deliberation and action and that they escape the liabilities of both absolutism and relativism. Nevertheless, the nature of these virtues is subject to question in some ways. I will attend to those of being scientific and showing respect for persons.

Dewey should have been more pluralistic in regard to the nature of rationality. There are many models of rationality about. Even when we confine ourselves to forms of rationality in indisputably cognitive inquiries, we find that they are not reducible to one. When we consider norms of *moral* rationality, we will not find even one that is morally neutral. A given philosopher defines moral rationality in a way that has a remarkable aptitude for yielding prescriptions of the sort he or she already prefers. To minimize question-begging, I propose a definition of rationality that might count as a minimum condition for anyone who would support any notion of rationality at all.

For the virtue of rationality, I would ask no more than a sincere attempt to seek the truth relevant to a given moral situation. If the expression *truth* is too quaint, then I would accept something more technical: "a sincere attempt to achieve assertibility" or—to get down to business—"a sincere attempt to get at the facts." The operative term here is *sincere*. The crucial need is that individuals engaged in moral controversy be willing to make an honest effort to get at the facts that are to be evaluated. Then we have at least eliminated the dogmatist, ideologue, and deliberately irrational. That alone would constitute a great advance in our discourse. In such an environment, we could establish a further tenet of rationality: namely, that everyone is fallible. In this day, how could anyone who claims to be rational also claim to be infallible? Recognition of our fallibility is a major accomplishment, for it tends to encourage open-mindedness and a willingness to entertain other points of view.

Dewey's notion of respect also needs to be more permissive. As he sketches it, it requires positive good will, "effective regard" for the well-being of others, and this is unrealistic. Such a condition does not and cannot exist on a wide scale, and a moral theory that demands it should be greeted with skepticism.[7] Although respect would not call for universal brotherly love, it would still perform invaluable moral functions. It is inherently unfriendly to *disregarding* the claims of others and, as previously noted, to willfully antisocial or negligent behavior. Discourse and conduct that demonstrated such virtue would be a singular achievement and a massive improvement in the moral life.

If I were to consider Dewey's position further, I would take up the matter of courage, whose roles in deliberation and conduct he seriously underestimates. But space has not permitted, and in any case I prefer to end on a more positive note.

Dewey's moral philosophy—and this account of it—are not predicated on an analysis of the conceptual adequacy of alternative theories. They are animated by a concern with what seem to be the characteristic problems of the moral life and the discourse attendant to it. Dewey frequently observed that the point of philosophy is not to study philosophy but to use it to address the problems of men. Accordingly, the point of reflecting on his ideas is to consider their adequacy for addressing the problems of our historical situation. I know of no other philosophy that even approaches Dewey's in this regard, and I urge you to consider the merits of his thought according to this criterion.

Notes

1. Today, the relativist argument typically takes the form of historicism, according to which there can be no interculturally intelligible moral norms. Historicism is not identical to relativism, for the latter does not necessarily imply that competing moral principles are incommensurable. The distinctively historicist thesis is worthy of attention, but this paper will not address it. In my judgment, it does not constitute an insurmountable barrier to intercultural moral discourse.

2. John Dewey, *Freedom and Culture* (New York: G. P. Putnam's Sons, 1939), p. 148.

3. John Dewey, "Creative Democracy: The Task Before Us," in S. Ratner, ed., *The Philosopher of the Common Man: Essays in Honor of John Dewey to Celebrate His Eightieth Birthday* (New York: G. P. Putnam's Sons, 1940), p. 222.

4. Dewey, *Freedom and Culture*, p. 130.

5. See in particular my "Dewey's Theory of Moral Deliberation," *Ethics* 88 (no. 3, 1978): 218–28.

6. *Democracy and Education*, for example, is replete with such demands. See especially the concluding chapter.

7. I do not ignore the fact that Christianity, for example, requires its adherents to love their neighbors as themselves. But the prescription is never met, especially if it is thought to demand universal benevolence. It is not an enforceable requirement and hence cannot intelligibly be regarded as a duty. On the other hand, the virtue of respect for persons does not prohibit or discourage altruistic conduct. Respect, as conceived herein, is one of the *minimum* conditions of morality.

John Dewey's Limited Humanism:
The Sectarian Stance of America's Philosopher of Holism

MICHAEL ELDRIDGE

American humanists have long claimed John Dewey as one of their own. As a member of the American Humanist Association (AHA) and the First Humanist Society of New York, a financial contributor to these organizations, an occasional literary contributor to *The Humanist*, intellectual mentor to many prominent secular humanists, signer of the 1933 Humanist Manifesto, and the first recipient (albeit posthumously) of the AHA's Humanist Pioneer award, Dewey's place in the humanist galaxy would seem to be secure.[1] Many historians and other intellectuals have also taken him to be not only representative of humanism but supremely so. Historian Donald H. Meyer, for instance, once observed that Dewey was "humanism's most notable spokesman."[2] The religious right, of course, includes Dewey on its list of devils. In the fall of 1986, Pat Robertson declared, "We have taken the Holy Bible from our young and replaced it with the thoughts of Charles Darwin, Karl Marx, Sigmund Freud, and John Dewey."[3] Robertson and others regard Dewey as the father of progressive (which they now call humanistic) education and hold him responsible for the destruction of Christian America's public schools.[4] In this rush to humanize America's most noted philosopher of the first half of the twentieth century, however, little attention has been paid to those statements in which he made clear that his endorsement of humanism was a limited one, confined to his participation in the battles with supernaturalist and sectarian religion. He refused to describe his own philosophy as humanist, contending that he was best understood as a naturalist. As we shall see, this naturalism was a form of holism, the attempt to understand physical and social reality as connected wholes. Thus, it is ironic that a philosopher who sought an undivided world was a participant in the humanist struggles with traditional religion and has now become an icon in the ideological warfare between secular humanism and the religious right. Perhaps it is inevitable that one who would overcome metaphysical and social divisions and who would be active in public affairs falls victim to the sectarianism that he deplored. In a divided world, even a holist apparently cannot escape being a partisan.

In this paper, I will first establish Dewey's relationship to humanism by quoting extensively from his correspondence with Corliss Lamont. Then I will consider Dewey's religious proposal and his own faith, apart from his sectarian involvements, before pondering the question of the necessity of sectarianism for the religious person.

The Dewey-Lamont Correspondence

John Dewey surprised many people in 1934 and even upset some of his closest associates by using the term *God* affirmatively in his Terry lectures at Yale University, published later that year as *A Common Faith*.[5] Many theists mistakenly thought they had found a new ally in an old enemy. On the other hand, Sidney Hook, who assisted Dewey in the preparation of the manuscript for publication, later wrote that "the only thing" in *A Common Faith* on which he "disagreed with" Dewey "was his use of the term 'God' for faith in the validity of moral ideals."[6] In 1940 Lamont, one of humanism's foremost spokesmen, wrote Dewey, questioning him about his use of "God" and his reluctance to use the term *humanism* to describe his philosophy. In the ensuing correspondence, Dewey chided Lamont for this "'squeamishness' about the use of the word 'God'"[7] and explained that he was not recommending that the term be used but, if it were used, then that for which it should stand is the process of ideals being realized in this world through human action.[8] Then Lamont confronted Dewey about the latter's reluctance to use the term *humanism* in reference to his philosophy. In a letter dated August 30, 1940, Lamont wrote:

> Since in 1933 you signed the Humanist Manifesto . . . I am wondering why you have not used the word "Humanism" more to describe your own philosophy. Though I realize this term "Humanism" is open to misconception, it is certainly far less formidable for the average person, whom you wish philosophy to reach, than the term Pragmatism or Instrumentalism or even Naturalism. And of course these latter words have also given rise to plenty of misunderstanding.[9]

Dewey replied a week later. His response is worth quoting at some length, because in it Dewey clearly states in which context he was willing to use the term.

> There is a great difference between different kinds of "Humanism," as you know; there is that of Paul Elmer More, for example. I signed the humanistic manifesto . . . because it had a religious context, and my signature was a sign of sympathy on that score, and not a commitment to every clause in it.
>
> "Humanism," as a technical philosophy is associated with Schiller; and while

I have a great regard for his writings, it seems to me that he gave Humanism an unduly subjectivistic turn. He was so interested in bringing out the elements of human desire and purpose neglected in traditional philosophy that he tends . . . to a virtual isolation of man from the rest of nature.

I have come to think of my own position as cultural or humanistic Naturalism. Naturalism, properly interpreted, seems to me a more adequate term than Humanism. Of course I have always limited my use of "instrumentalism" to my theory of thinking and knowledge; the word "pragmatism" I have used very little, then with reserves.[10]

The Humanist Manifesto was an affirmation of a religious humanism, and it was, at least from Dewey's point of view, a salvo in the sectarian battles of the time. He did not mean for it to be taken as representative of his philosophical position, which could best be described as a humanistic naturalism. Even in the opening paragraphs of the revised version of *Experience and Nature*, where Dewey uses the phrase *naturalistic humanism*, he makes clear that his intent in the book is to locate human experience or culture within the realm of nature. Dewey rejected any approach that would separate human experience from nature.[11] Lamont was not satisfied with Dewey's response, protesting in a letter the following week:

Though Naturalism is probably clearer to professional philosophers, it is certainly confusing to the average person, who considers a Naturalist one who, like John Burroughs, makes a specialty of birds and flowers. Also since Humanism as a word has real warmth and on the face of it indicates concern with humanity, I firmly believe that it would be more appealing and intelligible to the plain man. . . . You have always been in favor of bringing philosophy out of the confines of academic discussion and university circles so that it would mean something to the ordinary citizen. And I think you would have the best possible chance of succeeding in this aim with your own philosophy by calling it "Humanism" or perhaps "naturalistic Humanism."

Furthermore, even for philosophers you would be able to make your meaning of "Humanism" clear and drive its association with people like More and Schiller into the background. As a matter of fact, you are actively involved in the Humanist movement by being a member of the Advisory Board of Dr. Potter's First Humanist Society.[12]

Dewey replied promptly, as was his habit:

I don't see I have anything to add to what I wrote you the other day. I note that you prefer the word "Humanism" as a name for my philosophy. I do not, and have definite objection to it save as an adjective prefixed to Naturalism, and I suppose I must be the judge in the case of my own philosophy.

Since it is a philosophy in question and since philosophers from the time of Aristotle—and before—have used the word "Nature" in a fundamental sense, I can't see the force of your objection about Naturalism having a philosophical sense. As to the Humanistic Society, as I told you before, I limit my acceptance of Humanism to religious matters where its meaning in opposition to supernaturalism is definite in significance.[13]

This correspondence establishes firmly that Dewey understood himself to be a philosophical naturalist but a humanist only in a limited sense. He was willing to associate with organized humanism in order to oppose the supernaturalists. He was not willing to call his philosophy a humanistic one.

Dewey's Religious Holism

To avoid the risk of just tossing around labels, let me develop Dewey's holistic perspective as it can be seen in his religious proposal. Then I can show that his religious proposal—as distinct from his own practice—provides a nonsectarian way to be religious.[14]

Dewey's opposition to dualisms is well known. Typically, he criticized some philosophical views because they embraced a dualism or because they represented an extreme position. His standard practice was to compare and contrast two positions he saw as one-sided, then to put forth what he regarded as a fuller, more adequate one. Dualisms that he encountered in other philosophers' work were regularly transformed in his analysis into unified wholes. This mediating tendency is present in Dewey's approach to religion, as developed in *A Common Faith*. There is no preface or introduction to this little book on religion, but Dewey stated his purpose in the opening paragraphs. He observed that there were two opposing groups: supernaturalists and militant secularists. Both identified the religious with the supernatural, viewing them as being inextricably tied together. His intention, against both, was to free the religious from its identification with the supernatural[15] and from those who claimed access to it—the various organized religions.[16] Dewey, in brief, proposed a naturalistic reconstruction of religion that, characteristically, sought a middle way between atheism and religious supernaturalism, providing an alternative to sectarianism.

As a philosophical naturalist it was incumbent upon him—if he were to make room for religion—to find a place for it within experience. This he does by fastening on those attitudes often associated with the various religions, attitudes that bring about "a better, deeper and enduring adjustment in life."[17] He looks to the "ethical and ideal content" of religion[18] but concludes that the truly religious attitude is "broader than anything indicated by 'moral' in its usual sense."[19]

Dewey's hostility toward both supernaturalism and sectarianism sprang from his holism, a holism that survived his turning away from an early attraction to

Hegel. As a young philosopher he had been impressed with the Hegelian synthesis of God, man, and nature. Later, he rejected Hegel's approach but retained the "emphasis upon continuity and the function of conflict,"[20] which can be seen in his continuing valuation of "unified wholes." His naturalized Hegelianism set him against the discontinuities of a nature-supernature world-view and of competing groups, each claiming special access to the other world. He sought to live in a one-order universe with a common faith that was the condition and product of intelligence. Thus his antagonism to supernaturalism and sectarianism was a principled one, firmly situated in his holism.

Dewey's most forthright statement of what religion comes to is in a discussion of the role of intelligence early in the second chapter of *A Common Faith*. He argues that the scientific method—the "one method for ascertaining fact and truth"—cannot disturb "the faith that is religious." He then continues with this significant, defining statement: "I should describe this faith as the unification of the self through allegiance to inclusive ideal ends, which imagination presents to us and to which the human will responds as worthy of controlling our desires and choices."[21] Note the pragmatic or functional character of this approach. He was in effect saying, If you want to know what religion is, look at what it does. And what it does is to integrate the self through loyalty to values that are suggested by imagination but which are also inclusive and worthy of being regulative. We develop the possible out of that which exists, setting aims for ourselves. These possibilities govern what we do to realize them. They are regulative. To the extent that they inform our whole lives, integrating us as individuals, they are religious.

But, metaphysically, the most important feature of the Deweyan ideal is its natural origin and setting. To call attention to this, Dewey speaks of the actual and ideal being in relationship. "We are in the presence," he wrote, "neither of the ideals completely embodied in existence nor yet of ideals that are mere rootless ideals, fantasies, utopias. For there are forces in nature and society that generate and support the ideals."[22] Although the ideals are appropriated initially by our imaginations, we must not conclude that they are fabricated out of thin air. Dewey, as a holist, resists the subjective-objective split. He wants to say they are both found and reworked by us. They are neither wholly external nor internal.

Dewey's attitude toward nature is indeed one of reverence, for he thought that only through "a thorough-going and deep-seated harmonizing of the self with the Universe" could the self be unified.[23] Both supernaturalism and militant atheism isolate man from nature. Both pass lightly over "the ties binding man to nature that poets have always celebrated." A truly religious attitude, however, senses the "connection of man, in the way of both dependence and support, with the enveloping world that the imagination feels is a universe."[24] Earlier he had declared: "Natural piety is not of necessity either a fatalistic acquiescence in natural happenings or a romantic idealization of the world. It may rest upon a just sense of nature as the whole of which we are parts, while it also recognizes that we are parts that are marked by intelligence and purpose, having the capacity to strive by their aid to bring conditions into greater consonance with what is humanly desirable."[25]

This natural piety kept Dewey from identifying too closely with the humanist movement, or at least a humanism that "excludes our relation to nature." Certainly, he did not want to deify humanity or isolate it from nature. Toward the end of the second chapter of *A Common Faith*, he wrote, "A humanistic religion, if it excludes our relation to nature, is pale and thin, as it is presumptuous, when it takes humanity as an object of worship."[26] Quite aside from labels and institutional affiliations, Dewey was humanistic in a broad, nonpartisan sense: he had a profound faith in "shared experience." He could speak of it in almost mystical terms: "When the emotional force, the mystic force one might say, of communication, of the miracle of shared life and shared experience is spontaneously felt, the hardness and cruelty of contemporary life will be bathed in the light that never was on land or sea."[27]

This is poetic language indeed for the plain-spoken Dewey. More straightforwardly he says in *Experience and Nature*, "Shared experience is the greatest of human goods."[28] Shared experience is what Dewey usually had in mind when he spoke of democracy. He was aware of the decision-making procedures and the political processes that are a part of democracy, but these often receded into the background in his thinking. What is usually in the foreground is a noninstitutional sense, a vision of democracy as shared experience. "A democracy," he once wrote, "is more than a form of government; it is primarily a mode of associated living, of conjoint communicated experience."[29] In a democratic society people collaborate together, using their intelligence to solve the "problems of men." The experimental method was not for him the activity of an isolated scientist. It was a method by which individuals could solve their problems and resolve their differences.

The Escape from Sectarianism

To those who think that one must have a religion, that one cannot be religious in the abstract and so must affiliate with some sect, Dewey has an ingenious proposal: stop thinking of the connection between organized religion and the religious in experience as a necessary one. It is possible to be religious without being an adherent of some institutional religion. If we free ourselves of the notion that the religious must occur in organized religion, then we will be able to find it wherever it occurs in society.

Dewey, of course, abandoned the church for the school. Public schools ideally do not exclude participation on the basis of race, sex, creed, or national origin. They are public, fully a part of the community. But even more importantly, schools—public and private, primary, secondary, and collegiate—are, or at least should be, places where one can reconstruct his or her experience. Schools are intended to be places where education occurs explicitly. Dewey goes so far as to ascribe to the school the integrative task that has often been associated with religion.

> The school has the function . . . of coordinating with the disposition of each individual the diverse influences of the various social environments into which he enters. One code prevails in the family; another, on the street; a third, in the workshop or store; a fourth, in the religious association. As a person passes from one of the environments to another, he is subjected to antagonistic pulls, and is in danger of being split into a being having different standards of judgment and emotion for different occasions. This danger imposes upon the school a steadying and integrative office.[30]

This "steadying and integrative office" is a role often assigned to religion. *Religere*, from which *religio* may have been derived, has among its senses "to bind or fasten to" and "to tie together." "Religion," then, has been taken to mean either a "being bound to something" or a "tying together of life." Dewey assigns religion the role of being bound to something,[31] and as the above citation indicates, he gives education the integrative role.

I have taken some space for this discussion of Dewey, schools, and education to make concrete his contention that we can be religious without participating in a "religious institution." Of course, we must be a part of some group, organization, institution, or culture, but it does not have to be a "religious" one—if by "religious" we mean "concerned with the supernatural." We are not condemned to supernaturalism and sectarianism. We can engage in the ordinary, common activities and institutions of life in such a way that our participation may be said to be religious. Dewey was not only suspicious of anything that would divide nature and society, he was hostile toward it, because he valued nature and shared experience. In spite of Dewey's antisectarian religious proposal, he himself did not escape sectarianism. As we saw earlier, his natural piety and devotion to shared experience led him to become involved in a variety of humanist organizations. Thus, Dewey did not fully realize his own religious proposal; he can fairly be accused of occasional sectarian behavior.

Some would argue that one cannot escape partisanship: we are condemned to particularism. Whatever our universal aspirations, we must be part of a particular group at a particular time. Sectarianism is our common lot. Admittedly, we are "condemned" to particularism. But just because we must act in a particular way does not mean we must be sectarian. Particularity and sectarianism are not equivalent to one another. I must use some language to communicate, but a language is not necessarily sectarian. English, for instance, is the language of a culture, not of a sect. Of course, in using English I am using a particular language, but I am using one that is more or less shared by Jerry Falwell and Norman Lear.

I do not say we should never be partisan, but I will say that we do not, in being religious, *have to be* sectarian. Religiosity, if Dewey's proposal is correct, is not necessarily oriented toward other-worldly beings that have to be approached through separatist groups. To be religious is to respond to what one regards as ultimately important in such a way that one becomes who he or she is. This can be done in nonsectarian and nonsupernatural ways. A teacher or an artist who works within the common forms of society to respond to what he or she thinks is of overwhelming significance is doing so in a way that is not sectarian and not necessarily supernaturalistic. Yes, Dewey became sectarian in his humanist involvements. But it is not necessary for an antisupernaturalist and antisectarian to join a religious group in order to battle supernaturalism and sectarianism. There are many avenues open to one, other than to become a member of the American Humanist Association or the Unitarians. One can be a teacher, writer, or artist who is committed to wholeness without joining a religious group.

I need to spell this out, for it is central to the understanding of Dewey's proposal for a common faith. Dewey is suggesting that our society provides forms—activities, practices, occupations, organizations—that enable one to respond to what is of inclusive value, becoming through this loyalty who one is. These cultural forms, by virtue of being common to the wider group, are nonsectarian. One does not ordinarily have to be sectarian to be a fire fighter, teacher, artist, rehabilitation therapist, investment advisor, or parent. Admittedly, at any given time one will be a member of some fire department or teach a certain subject, but one, in being particular, is not separating oneself from others by holding to an exclusive belief or engaging in an excluding practice. If, and this is a big if, one through this practice is responding to what is ultimately important, then that person is being religious.

The virtue of this approach is that it escapes sectarianism. One is living in a nonexcluding manner. But, of course, there is a downside as well. By limiting one's religious practice to what is common, one runs the risk of having a very attenuated faith, or at least so the traditional believer will think. The quip of Dewey's fellow philosophical naturalist, Santayana, is relevant here. Santayana, who remained a Roman Catholic, supposedly reacted to Dewey's book, *A Common Faith*, by noting that it was "a right common faith indeed!" Secular religionists who limit themselves to common activities and beliefs cannot call on supernatural help or rely on the rich liturgical resources of, say, the Eastern Orthodox Church. They cannot call down the wrath of God on the "me" generation or appeal to the private insights of the mystic. They are limited to those practices that are commonly shared. For some of us, this will be enough; for others, it will not.

Notes

1. Corliss Lamont, "John Dewey and the American Humanist Association," *Voice in the Wilderness: Collected Essays of Fifty Years* (Buffalo, N.Y.: Prometheus Books, 1974), pp. 31–37. First published in *The Humanist* 20 (January–February, 1960): 3–10. All of the humanist ascriptions in the text come from Lamont except the mentorship one. I have in mind the connections of Lamont, Sidney Hook, and Paul Kurtz to Dewey. Lamont, author of *Humanism as a Philosophy*, 6th ed. (New York: Frederick Ungar Pub. Co., 1982), and editor of *Dialogue on John Dewey* (New York: Horizon Press, 1959), everywhere acknowledges his debt to Dewey. Hook is considered by some to be Dewey's foremost disciple. See Paul Kurtz, ed., *Sidney Hook: Philosopher of Democracy and Humanism* (Buffalo, N.Y.: Prometheus Books, 1983), pp. xf., 6, 18, and 27–29. See also George Dykhuizen, *The Life and Mind of John Dewey* (Carbondale: Southern Illinois University Press, 1973), p. 297. Kurtz, Hook's student and later literary collaborator, was the editor of *The Humanist* when the second Humanist Manifesto was published in 1973 and later became the editor of *Free Inquiry*, which published "A Secular Humanist Declaration" in 1980. He is also the author of *In Defense of Secular Humanism* (Buffalo, N.Y.: Prometheus Books, 1983).

2. Donald H. Meyer, "Secular Transcendence: The American Religious Humanists," *American Quarterly* 34 (Winter, 1982): 532. Meyer's survey is admirable, but, I shall argue, his portrayal of Dewey as a humanist, while accurate within a limited context, is ultimately misleading.

3. Dudley Clendinen, "Robertson Sets Conditions For Making a Run in 1988," *The New York Times*, national ed., Thursday, September 18, 1986, p. 16.

4. See Tim LaHaye, *The Battle for the Mind* (Old Tappan, N.J.: Fleming H. Revell Co., 1980), pp. 43–45 and 97; Homer Duncan, *Humanism: In the Light of Scripture* (Lubbock, Tex.: Christian Focus on Government, 1981), p. 52f.; James Hitchcock, *What Is Secular Humanism?* (Ann Arbor, Mich.: Servant Books, 1982), p. 12f.; and John Whitehead, *The Stealing of America* (Westchester, Ill.: Crossway Books, 1983), pp. 16–18 and 86f. Almost all of the expert witnesses called by the plaintiffs in the secular humanism textbook case (tried in October, 1986, in Judge W. Brevard Hand's federal court in Mobile, Alabama) spoke of Dewey as the archetypal secular humanist.

5. For the occasion of and reaction to *A Common Faith*, see Milton Konvitz's introduction and Ann Sharpe's textual commentary in Jo Ann Boydston, ed., *John Dewey: The Later Works, 1925–1953*, vol. 9 (Carbondale: Southern Illinois University Press, 1986).

6. Sidney Hook, *Pragmatism and the Tragic Sense of Life* (New York: Basic Books, Inc., 1974), p. 114. Hook not only disagreed with Dewey, but, if this characterization of Dewey's theism is any indication, Hook also misunderstood his teacher. For Dewey, God is the process whereby ideals become realized in our lives—not a disposition, such as Hook's use of "faith" implies. In *A Common Faith*, Dewey declared that it is the "*active* relation between ideal and actual to which I would give the name 'God'" (Boydston, ed., *John Dewey*, vol. 9, p. 51).

7. Corliss Lamont, "New Light on Dewey's *Common Faith*," *The Journal of Philosophy* 58 (January 5, 1961): 25.

8. Ibid., p. 24.

9. Ibid., p. 26.

10. Ibid., p. 26f.

11. John Dewey, *Experience and Nature*, 1925; 2nd ed., 1929; reprint (New York: Dover Pub., 1958), p. 1a and following. Originally published in 1925, *Experience and Nature*, one of Dewey's major works, was revised in 1929. The Dover edition is a reprint

of the second edition. Dewey normally used some variation of the term *natural* to describe his mature philosophy. In 1933 he did use the phrase *a secularized humanism*, but its meaning is that of "a naturalized humanism." His point is that we can rely on the whole range of a naturalized human experience, for "it is impossible to confine any longer what is regarded by religionists as of authoritative value to limited and exclusive organs, channels and objects," that is, to church, scripture, and a supernatural god (Boydston, ed., *John Dewey,* vol. 9, p. 221).

12. Lamont, "New Light," pp. 26ff. Along with Irving Babbit, More was a leader in the new humanism, an American movement in literary criticism that was prominent in the 1920s. Its dualistic and conservative tendencies were unacceptable to Dewey. F. C. S. Schiller was an Oxford philosopher who was influenced by William James. Charles Francis Potter, a former Baptist and later a Unitarian minister, was the founder and leader of the First Humanist Society of New York. He was also a signer of the Humanist Manifesto.

13. Ibid., p. 27.

14. My purpose in this paper is twofold: (1) to show what sort of humanist Dewey was and (2) to show that there is a way, suggested by Dewey's work, to be religious without being sectarian—even though Dewey himself did not always take it.

15. In another context, Dewey said he addressed the book "to those who have abandoned supernaturalism" in order to show them "that they still have within their experience all the elements which give the religious attitude its value" (Paul Arthur Schilpp, ed., *The Philosophy of John Dewey* [Evanston, Ill.: Northwestern University, 1939], p. 597).

16. John Dewey, *A Common Faith* (New Haven: Yale University Press, 1934), p. 1f. Reprinted in Boydston, ed., *John Dewey,* vol. 9, p. 3f.

17. Ibid., pp. 14, 11.

18. Ibid., pp. 8, 7.

19. Ibid., pp. 23, 17.

20. Jane Dewey, ed., "Biography of John Dewey," in *The Philosophy of John Dewey,* ed. Paul Arthur Schilpp (Evanston and Chicago: Northwestern University Press, 1939), pp. 3–45.

21. Dewey, *A Common Faith*, p. 33. Reprinted in Boydston, ed., *John Dewey*, vol. 9, p. 23.

22. Ibid., pp. 50f, 34.

23. Ibid., pp. 19, 14.

24. Ibid., pp. 53, 36.

25. Ibid., pp. 24, 18.

26. Ibid., pp. 54, 36.

27. John Dewey, *Reconstruction in Philosophy*, 1920; enlarged ed., 1948; reprint (Boston: Beacon Press, 1957), p. 211.

28. John Dewey, *Experience and Nature*, p. 202.

29. John Dewey, *Democracy and Education: An Introduction to the Philosophy of Education*, 1916; reprint (New York: The Macmillan Co., 1965), p. 87.

30. Ibid., p. 22.

31. Dewey, *A Common Faith*, p. 23. Reprinted in Boydston, ed., *John Dewey*, vol. 9, p. 16.

AMERICAN PHILOSOPHY AND ORIENTAL THOUGHT

Internal and External Frontiers of Classical American Philosophy:
Santayana's Differences from James and Dewey in World-Perspective

DAVID A. DILWORTH

Peirce's Theory of Mind

C. S. Peirce wrote of the transmission of thought as a self-forming and self-continuing process. Amplification, ramification, and generalization, Peirce noted, are immanent tendencies in the universe at large and are vividly illustrated in the histories of human sciences, arts, and crafts. The growth of mind from the mere accidentality of what he called "certain one idea'd philosophies," which fill in available niches in an ephemeral landscape, to enduring habits of higher civilization exemplifies the same developmental process.[1]

Peirce's concept of the growth of mind, I submit, is just right for our conference. The frontiers of which we speak are philosophical. Such frontiers are both boundaries and openings. They are definite and yet vistas on the wider world of our multiple intellectual heritages.

Implicit in Peirce's formulations is the thought that the world's enduring philosophies are the very substance of our own higher mental life. Authentic intellectual activity clarifies but does not break with the achievements of the past. Instead, we repossess the qualitative perceptions of the traditions in our own active intellection of the possibilities of contemporary life. We do so through the self-developing forms of our sciences and arts, but especially and more fundamentally by reenacting the major philosophical and religious theories in modern forms.

Given the synechistic character of all higher mental life, we need to produce a hermeneutical model that does justice to the rich variety of good philosophical texts in our multiple heritages of world-civilization. Every good philosophy indeed has its final *raison d'etre* by participating in the substantive field of mind that the world-history of philosophy discloses.

These programmatic reflections, however general, have a direct application to the work of our conference. Our convocation here affords us a timely opportunity to view the classical American philosophers as having their places not only in a late nineteenth- and early twentieth-century intellectual environment of the modern West but in relation to the world traditions of philosophy, including those of the East.

Contributing only minutely to this vast research topic, the present paper seeks to promote an approach to viewing the classical American philosophers in a perspective suggested by Peirce's theory of the generality of mind. To this end, I will argue that the American philosophers must finally be seen as world-philosophers, in the company of and in comparison with the best thinkers of all time. I will key this thought by first referring to the career-text of Santayana, perhaps the most cosmopolitan of the classical American philosophers. The catholicity of Santayana's thought confirms for me the approach I venture to take. Then, in special reference to the variety of Asian philosophies and religions, I will briefly sketch certain lines of theoretical continuity obtaining among the exemplary Asian and American philosophical texts.

Santayana's Cosmopolitanism

In breadth of career, with its distinctive output and outreach, Santayana is a special resource, I think, among the classical American philosophers. He was the quintessential immigrant. He spoke and read in many tongues. He hobnobbed with Bostonians and achieved distinction on the Harvard faculty. And yet he was not of them, or for them. He remained a free spirit, at home in many realms of spirit. His mind ranged through the varieties of religion, philosophy, literature, and art. A rarity among our philosophers, he loved the classics and even ventured to write in their styles.[2]

Intellectually, Santayana was a multiperson. Impartially, he inhabited the new and the old. He inspected many of the frontiers of American thought, while retaining a deep commitment to his European memories. An admirer of Freud and Einstein and Proust, he retained a fondness for the ancient religious imagination, notably of the Hindus and the Catholics. He could probe his intellectual roots to another level—to Democritus, Lucretius, and the other pagans. His philosophy combined all these things, in subtle proportions.

The synechistic reaches of Santayana's text are worth emulating. If I may be permitted a personal observation—and one partially gathered from my students—the far-ranging pluralism of Santayana's mind provides a pedagogical model for the intellectual frontiers of Toronto, Boston, New York, San Francisco, Honolulu, and the other metropolitan areas today. The life of such cities, it has been noted, is the real frontier—the intercultural frontier—of our times. Not only does Santayana's life and thought directly reflect our complex European and Asian ancestries, his ideas combine a desired pedigree and civilized edge with a gentle compassion. They have a special relevance for the multiethnic populations of our American universities.

Catholicity, quality, criticism, and compassion are hallmarks of Santayana's writings, which combine assertive and exhibitive modalities of expression to a high degree. Soliloquizing scholar and world-traveler, he lived his own philosophy as well. All this reduces to the essential point that Santayana's career was that of an authentic American—as American indeed as Peirce, or James, or Royce, or Dewey, or any of the other prominent names. It is only that he may have embodied an even wider sense of "frontiers" than most.

Exemplary, therefore, for my own project are Santayana's words in the preface to his *Dominations and Powers*. Living in Rome and still writing at age eighty-eight, the American philosopher Santayana penned the following good sentences.

> Circumstances from the beginning had prepared me to feel this limitation of all moral dogmatism. My lot had been cast in different moral climates, amidst people of more than one language and religion, with contrary habits and assumptions of their political life. I was not bound to any type of society by ideal loyalty nor estranged from any by resentment. In my personal contacts I found them all tolerable when seen from the inside and not judged by some standard unintelligible to those born and bred under that influence. Personally I might have my instinctive preference; but speculatively and romantically I should have been glad to find an even greater diversity; and if one political tendency kindled my wrath, it was precisely the tendency of industrial liberalism to level down all civilizations to a single cheap and dreary pattern. I was happy to have been at home both in Spain and in New England and later to have lived pleasantly in England and in various countries frequented by tourists; even happier to have breathed intellectually the air of Greece and Rome, and of that Catholic Church in which the world and its wisdom, without being distorted, were imaginatively enveloped in another world revealed by inspiration. All this was enlightening, if you could escape from it; and I should have been glad to have been at home also in China and in Carthage, in Bagdad and in Byzantium. Had that been possible, this book could have been written with more elasticity. It is a hindrance to the free movement of spirit to be lodged in one point of space rather than another, or in one point of time: that is a physical necessity which intelligence endeavours to discount, since it cannot be eluded. Seen under the form of eternity, all ages are equally past and equally future; and it is impossible to take quite seriously the tastes and ambitions of our contemporaries.[3]

At age eighty-eight, you will say, he was entitled to that one. But in fact the passage is vintage Santayana. It's his usual style and chock full of his basic ideas and presuppositions.

Santayana goes on in that passage to say, "Everything gently impels us to view human affairs scientifically, realistically, biologically, as events that arise, with all their spiritual overtones, in the realm of matter."[4] In that regard, too, he was simply being true to the form of his perennial ontology.

The ancient *physis* philosophers, the Indians, and Spinoza, he wrote in *Scepticism and Animal Faith* and in other places, were right on the fundamental issues: the nature of the universe and man's relation to it.[5]

We need not address the details of Santayana's perennial ontology here. For present purposes it is sufficient to cite the preface to the same work, where he insists that his system is party to no current school of philosophy.[6] In such wise once again, Santayana, a genuine American philosopher, transcended all chauvinistic claims. To this writer he is reminiscent of such figures as Haydn, Mozart, and Freud, who are hard to categorize in nationalistic or stylistic terms. He was a world-philosopher, whose thought resonated with many strains of premodern philosophy.

But indeed, when we think of it, the works of James, Peirce, and Royce, although to a lesser extent than Santayana's, are cosmopolitan in their own distinctive ways. James's writings richly involve the European intellectual traditions of his day; those of Peirce establish important links with Kant and other major figures even while engaging in exhaustive researches into the methods of the logical, mathematical, and physical sciences; Royce's have all the latitude of the Hegelian imagination.

Once again, therefore, our "Frontiers in American Philosophy" theme allows us to begin to set their respective achievements in this enlarged perspective keyed to boundaries and openings. The chief American philosophers—James, Peirce, Dewey, and Santayana, among others—should all be read as world-philosophers. They realized essential possibilities of thought, in the company of the world-philosophers of all ages and cultures.

Internal Boundaries in American Philosophy

To this writer, one of the hermeneutical functions Santayana's career-text performs is its fifty-year-long internal criticism of the American philosophical schools of his day. We already see the seeds of this in Santayana's early letters to James when he (Santayana) was sojourning in Europe.[7] Santayana went on to lay the basis of his mature world-view while at Harvard, when he evidently developed a considerable repertory of historical and contemporary analyses.

Santayana's *Character and Opinion in the United States* (1920) represents only one version of his trenchant critique of a variety of American philosophical colleagues, most notably of James himself. Combing through Santayana's various letters and essays on James, we see that he consistently regarded James as defending a personalistic, existentialistic, and voluntaristic world-view.[8] Santayana differed, of course, on all these counts. A pure materialist in the Democritean mold, he regarded the surface life of psychological consciousness as supervenient—as the epiphenomenal play of free spirit subtended by the ever-dark forces of material psyche. Accordingly Santayana produced a devastating critique of the doctrine of "pure experience," while accusing James of a fundamental agnosticism in his own indomitable spirit.[9]

In *Character and Opinion in the United States* Santayana also wrote an incisive critique of Royce, whom he portrayed as a consummate patron of transcendental theater. True to the form of his own materialistic ontology, Santayana says of Royce's honest, California Hegelianism: "The performance may take place today and last one hour, while the fable transports us to some heroic epoch or to an age that never existed, and stretches through days and perhaps years of fancied time. Just so, transcendental thinking, while actually timeless and not distributed among persons, might survey infinite time and rehearse the passions and thoughts of a thousand characters. Thought, after all, needs objects, however fictitious they may be."[10]

Santayana's power of objective delineation of philosophical types was always accompanied by the reflexive function of his own ontology. I will call his own text *substrative* in its fundamental perception of the solid reality of material existence.[11] James, we saw, was an *existentialist*; Royce, by contrast once again, was an *essentialist* in the Hegelian style.

The philosophy of Dewey, it turns out, was also of an essentialist type, albeit of a distinctively naturalistic strain. Dewey's methodic doctrine centers on a concept of consummatory human experience. Santayana sketched Dewey's type in the self-legislative function of his own text. His *Obiter Scripta* (1936) contains a trenchant essay, "Dewey's Naturalistic Metaphysics." The long and the short of it is that Santayana portrays Dewey's position as amounting to a "half-hearted and short-winded" kind of naturalism, committed as it is to "the dominance of the foreground" and other illusions of the merely dramatic scenes of human existence, which takes place against the impersonal backdrop of nature.[12] Thus, to Santayana, Dewey—as also Whitehead—philosophized in theatrical fashion in ways that were partially associatable with Royce's transcendentalism.

The more we probe the internal latticing of classical American philosophy the more confirmed we will be in the view that its conspicuous strains of thought are irreducibly plural. Each of the exemplary philosophers satisfies Kant's definition of the philosopher himself. The philosopher, Kant says, legislates for human reason.[13] He privileges the first principles of his discourse. Simultaneously, he subordinates the principles of all other actual and potential discourses to his own. That is precisely why all philosophical discourses—even those claiming to be non-foundational—are foundational discourses.

It follows that the philosophers themselves provide the best articulations of their differences from one another. Dewey, as another example, ubiquitously critiqued the rationalistic assumptions of the Greek and early modern philosophical traditions. He also engaged in direct debate over fundamental issues with such philosophical contemporaries as James, Peirce, Royce, Bradley, Santayana, Russell, and Whitehead.[14]

For a third, and palmary, case of how one American philosopher disagreed with the governing assumption of another, I would cite Peirce's series of exchanges with James.[15] Their letters reveal that Peirce criticized James's pragmatism in general, while attacking his essay "Does Consciousness Exist?" in particular. Peirce also took the pains to present the essential gist of his own system. "But I seem to myself," he writes in one letter, "to be the sole depositary at present of the completely developed system, which all hangs together and cannot receive any proper presentation in fragments" (November 25, 1902).[16]

James replied in his own fashion. To one such epistelatory explication of his system, James responded to Peirce two days later, "I have to confess that I don't understand a word of your letter" (September 28 and 30, 1904).[17] This was all good philosophical fun, and nice work if you can get it.

But we can't leave it at that, for Peirce's further rejoinders represent a serious effort at foundational discourse. Thus, on July 23, 1905, Peirce wrote again to James. "It is . . . entirely inscrutable to me why my three categories have been so luminous to me without my being given the power to make them understood by those alone who are in a condition to see their meaning,—i.e. my fellow-pragmatists. It seems to me that you all must have a strange blind spot on your mental retina not to see what others see and what pragmatism ought to make much plainer."[18] Concerning James's radical empiricism, Peirce went on to write: "What you call 'pure experience' is not experience at all and certainly ought to have a name. It is downright bad morals so to misuse words, for it prevents philosophy from becoming a science. . . . My 'phenomenon' for which I must invent a new word is very near your 'pure experience' but not quite since I do not exclude time and also speak of only one 'phenomenon'" (October 3, 1904).[19]

In a later explication of his position to James, Peirce wrote that his own conception of Phaneroscopy, which describes what does appear before the mind, articulates three different kinds of consciousness, ranked under three headings: "First, 'Qualisense,' which means that element of Feeling which consists in consciousness of the Quality of Feeling. . . . Second Heading: what I call Molition, which is volition minus all desire and purpose, the mere consciousness of exertion of any kind. Third Heading: the recognition of Habit of any kind in consciousness" (December 17, 1909).[20] I read this as further to his letter of October 3, 1904.

The net effect of these letters is to show that Peirce offered James many such synoptic versions of his system of the Three Categories. James consistently turned Peirce down, for reasons of the fundamental assumptions of his own text. Peirce, it turns out, was another essentialist: he believed in gradations of mental life, in the universe at large, as interpreted in the degrees of generality of his Three Categories. James, we saw, was a radical empiricist, or existentialist.

Radical Continuities with Asian World-Views

Although I have only touched the surface of this research project, I think I have indicated some lines along which the classical American philosophers differ from one another. James (and later Buchler) were existentialists; Santayana was a materialist; Peirce, Royce, and Dewey, in differing versions, were essentialists. In synoptic fashion I intend now to generalize the analysis, to establish the interface between these American strains of thought and their Asian counterparts. It is here where a synchronic analysis is both necessary and possible.

To reduce a much longer discussion to essentials, I submit that we can distinguish four coexistent ontological paradigms in the annals of Asian philosophy, literature, and art:

> (1) an existential paradigm corresponding in ontological focus to James's concept of "pure experience." The conspicuous representatives of this in Asian thought are the various Buddhist traditions, as many scholars have already pointed out. From the text of the Indian philosopher, Nagarjuna, through most Chinese and Japanese forms—Tendai, Shingon, and Zen, for example—down to the eighty-year-old literature of the present-day Kyoto School, the mainstreams of Mahayana Buddhism have defended existential theses for the purposes of their own soteriologies of human freedom. (The existential sense can take a secular form as well, as in Sei Shonagon's *Pillow Book* and other literary classics.)
>
> (2) a not-of-this-world religiosity, as exemplified by Hinduism in India, and another form of Buddhism, a Pure Land or Amidist variant, which originated in the Mahayana sutras of India and spread among the populaces of China and Japan. This is a noumenal kind of spirituality having many analogues in the Platonic, Christian, neo-Platonic, and Islamic traditions of the West. There is no major representative of it in the classical American tradition, although individual American thinkers—Thomists, Spinozists, Leibnizians, Kantians, Kierkegaardians—bear witness to this ontological sense in their own several versions.
>
> (3) a this-worldly, moral-and-political essentialism, exemplified in the rich legacies of Confucian and neo-Confucian teachings and practices for more than two thousand years of Chinese and Japanese civilizations. In comparative hermeneutic, the different versions of essential ontology in Peirce, Royce, and Dewey clearly fall under this generic type.

(4) a naturalistic, substratively materialistic strain.

By this last item, I mean to indicate once again a strain of ontological perception that refers the deceiving surface of psychological consciousness to an underlying, but always concealed, flow of material forces, vital powers, and the like. In India, the Carvaka school expounded such a materialistic ontology. In China and Japan, such a perception of true but hidden natural causes typically takes the form of Taoist and Shinto religious naturalisms. It can also be thematized in quite secular ways—as the erupting force of human instinct and passion, for example. I think some of the erotic, nostalgic, sexually unrelieved, kharmically retributive, and *yugen*-type texts of Japanese culture—from the *Manyoshu* through Saigyo, many of the *no* and *kyogen*, the *Hagakure*, *ukiyo* art and literature, up to such writers as Nagai Kafu, Kawabata Yasunari, and Yukio Mishima—can be accounted for in these terms. This substrative sense appears to be a feature of the Japanese arts centering on masks and puppets. The substrative sense is again conspicuous in some Chinese political texts, from the *Tao Te Ching* to the Legalist classic of *Han Fei Tzu* to Chinese Marxism. Another version is found in the writings of the Han dynasty critic Wang Ch'ung, whose text is reminiscent of Santanaya's in some ways.[21]

By the next-to-last item, I refer to centuries of East Asian traditions that centered on the historical transmission of certain essential ethical and political values. This is of course one of the major traditions of Chinese and Korean civilizations. This would again be true of the medieval Japanese samurai cultures, the social dynamics of which underwrote the emergence of *bushido* ideals already evident in the Kamakura and Muromachi periods, to say nothing of the Edo. The samurai classes clearly achieved aristocratic structures of their own, with attendant standards of social rank and moral and aesthetic performance. The evidence of this is in the various House Laws of the military lords and the ethical testaments they left their heirs.

Here I will simply cite the conspicuous evidence of this strain of Confucian and neo-Confucian thought disclosed in literary form though the historical *novellae* and biographies of Mori Ogai. Generally set in late Muromachi and Edo times, Ogai's exhaustively researched stories repossess with consummate clarity a whole range of enduring Japanese concerns for the highest standards of love, loyalty, filiality, sincerity, intellectual assiduity and honesty, independence of spirit, perseverance, caution, discretion, discernment, temperance, frugality, economy, the beauty of virtue, and aesthetic ritual.[22]

A lot more can be said of the Mahayana strains, both existentialist and Amidist as well. But I cannot spell out all the dimensions of this problematic here. My general and essential point is that these four ontological paradigms, taking different forms and names, will be found to be comprestly interwoven into the fabric of each of the major historical epochs of Indian, Chinese, and Japanese civilizations up to the present. Such is the rich diversity of the Asian cultural traditions.

The discrimination of such a variety of paradigms of higher Asian civilizations will yield, I submit, many interpretive dividends. For various networkings of such paradigms, in specifiable relationships, can be found in any developed epoch of world-civilization: the ancient Greek, Roman, Indian, Chinese, and the early modern or contemporary Western, for example. The great texts of classical American thought rightfully belong in this community of world-philosophy. As long as we take individual career-texts as our common currency of analysis, comparative—as distinguished from contrastive—studies in philosophy, religion, and the literary arts are possible.

We can pursue such intertextual relations in both the diachronic and the synchronic, or structural, approaches. In all such cases it is possible to establish both an essential variety of basic philosophical types and their coexistence in given historical epochs. A further point is that these ontological types form continuities in both diachronic and synchronic patterns of relationship. Thus they exemplify Peirce's concept of synechism in exemplary ways. And the complex set of such relationships establishes a networking of new "frontiers" for classical American philosophy. The general, and theoretically normative, implications of this are worth pondering.

Notes

1. See C. S. Peirce, "The Architecture of Theories," in *Philosophical Writings of Peirce*, selected and ed. with intro. by Justus Buchler (New York: Dover Publications, 1955), p. 315; also *Collected Papers of Charles Sanders Peirce*, 8 vols., ed. Charles Hartshorne, Paul Weiss, and Arthur W. Burks (Cambridge: Harvard University Press, 1931–58), vol. 6, paragraphs 7–25. Hereafter cited as CP, followed by a volume number and paragraph number. When Peirce came to name his own philosophy, he said that Tychism, or Firstness, is subsidiary to continuity, or Thirdness, and thus he called it Synechism (CP 6.202). The governing assumption of Peirce's synechism is what he called "the principle of Habit," or "the self-development of Reason," or again, "thought as an active force in the world" (CP 1:337, 1:340, and 1:348). The principle of habit as the mind's—and the universe's—generalizing tendency undergirds his various formulations of the spread, plasticity, and insistency of ideas, which are manifestations of evolution in the widest sense (CP 1:390, 1:409, 1:615, 1:621, 1:140, 6:204, and 6:289). This law of the growth of mind functions in turn as the *lumen naturale*, the guiding light of active intellection in Kepler's instinctive judgments in science (CP 1.80, 6.10). Synechistic evolution in this sense accounts for the very possibility of abduction, hypothesis-making, or retroductive reasoning rooted in the connaturality of mind and universe (CP 1.81, 5.172, 7.46). In this paper I focus Peirce's concept of Thirdness on the sphere of philosophies—philosophies as distinct kinds of Thirds, or general mental formations—and employ it to make sense of their historically realized forms and their various actual and possible continuities and combinations.

2. See George Santayana, *Persons and Places*, critical edition, ed. William G. Holzberger and Herman J. Saatkamp, Jr. (Cambridge, Mass.: MIT Press, 1986), subtitle: "In Boston But Not of It." "These things befell after Susana's time in Boston. For her the

Iasigis and the Homers were friendly households, nests of marriageable girls, where she could break away from the restraints of polite hypocrisy and could take comfort in feeling that her religion was no anomoly but perfectly natural, traditional, and a matter of course. It was the Bostonians who were eccentric and self-banished from the great human caravan. I found the same comfort in ancient literature and philosophy, which carried me beyond the Church and beneath its foundations. It is all a *Santa Maria sopra Minerva*. But towards Boston and Protestantism Susana and I had exactly the same feelings" (pp. 85–86).

3. George Santayana, *Dominations and Powers: Reflections on Liberty, Society, and Government* (New York: Charles Scribner's Sons, 1951), pp. vi–vii.

4. Ibid., p. vii.

5. George Santayana, *Scepticism and Animal Faith* (New York: Dover Publications, 1955), p. viii. "The first philosophers, the original observers of life and nature, were the best; and I think only the Indians and the Greek naturalists, together with Spinoza, have been right on the chief issue, the relation of man and of his spirit to the universe."

6. Ibid. "My system, finally, though, of course, formed under the fire of contemporary discussions, is no phase of any current movement. . . . It is not unwillingness to be a disciple that prompts me to look beyond the modern scramble of philosophies: I should gladly learn of them all, if they had learned more of one another. Even as it is, I endeavor to retain the positive insight of each, reducing it to the scale of nature and keeping it in its place; thus I am a Platonist in logic and morals, and a transcendentalist in romantic soliloquy, when I choose to indulge in it. Nor is it necessary, in being teachable by any master, to become eclectic. All these vistas give glimpses of the same wood, and a fair and true map of it must be drawn to a single scale, by one method of projection, and in one style of calligraphy." Santayana presents the image of himself as a "soliloquist" and "wandering scholar" in his various writings. But in net effect his works, in thirty volumes, may well amount to the most comprehensive and radically hermeneutical commentary on the multiple philosophical, religious, artistic, and literary world-traditions to be found in a twentieth-century author.

7. See references to William James in the index to *The Letters of George Santayana*, ed. Daniel Cory (New York: Charles Scribner's Sons, 1955), p. 448, esp. the letters on pp. 30, 61, 67, 76, 78, 81, and 372. On Dec. 6, 1905, the young Santayana wrote James from Paris: "You are very generous; I feel that you want to give me credit for everything good that can possibly by found in my book [*The Life of Reason*]. But you don't yet see my philosophy, nor my temper from the inside" (p. 81). Years later, from Rome on March 12, 1948, Santayana wrote to another party: "You are right in saying that from William James I got my strong sense of the 'contingency' of all facts and of their primacy in the order of discovery; but he thought momentary feelings were the ontological basis of the universe, in the order of genesis and causation; and this I wholly rejected, having always been a naturalist in belief. . . . It is possible to be interested in a play at the theatre, without forgetting that we are sitting in the stalls" (p. 372).

8. It goes without saying that the ontological focus of James's text is "radically empiricist," which is also to say existential. Thus, to James, "pure experience" is always "the instant field of the present" (William James, *Essays in Radical Empiricism and a Pluralistic Universe* [New York: Longmans, Green and Co., 1955], p. 23). It is only a collective name for "all these sensible natures" (ibid., p. 27) of the empiricist universe that float and dangle like those dried human heads with which the Dyaks of Borneo deck their lodges (ibid., p. 46). They do not float and dangle in any essential order. Pure experience is instead "the stream of concretes, or the sensational stream," indefinitely multivariate in character, in which the conjunctive and the disjunctive parts are perfectly confluent (ibid., p. 95). It can figure "twice, thrice, or four times, or any number of times,

by running into as many different mental contexts, just as the same point, lying at their intersection, can be continued into many different lines" (ibid., p. 80). Simultaneously, James's text presupposes a volitional principle and in that respect asserts its relationship to the traditions of American biblical theology. In James's vision, the world is still pursuing its adventures, and novelties are forever leaking in; the creation is still going on, and thus we are actively collaborating with God in the making of fact. We experience this "front edge" of pure experience in the lived immediacy of our own individual, energetic lives (ibid., pp. 181–82). He argues that such an existential philosophy harmonizes best with a radical pluralism, with novelty and indeterminism, moralism, theism, and humanism (ibid., p. 90).

9. Santayana's chapter, "William James," in *Character and Opinion in the United States* (Doubleday: Anchor Books, n.d.), pp. 39–59, first appeared in 1920. It is a critique of James's "agnostic" individualism and existentialism of the psychological flux. Santayana repeated the gist of this critique in his miniature portrait of James, subtitled "William James: He Inspires Trust but Creates Insecurity," in *Persons and Places*, pt. 2 (1947; critical edition, ed. Wm. G. Holzberger and Herman J. Saatkamp, Jr., Cambridge, Mass.: MIT Press, 1986), p. 401–402. We may assume that earlier, in his *Three Philosophical Poets* (Cambridge: Harvard University Press, 1910; 5th impression, 1935), Santayana was obliquely referring to James's doctrine as he repudiated Goethe's Faust's turn to a life of "pure experience" (see pp. 198–99, 203).

10. "Josiah Royce," in Santayana, *Character and Opinion*, pp. 60–85. The cited passage is on p. 82.

11. This nomenclature is adapted from Walter Watson, *The Architectonics of Meaning: Foundations of the New Pluralism* (Albany: SUNY Press, 1985), pp. 42ff. and passim.

12. George Santayana, *Obiter Scripta*, ed. Justus Buchler and Benjamin Schwartz (New York: Charles Scribner's Sons, 1936), "Dewey's Naturalistic Metaphysics," pp. 213–40.

13. See Immanual Kant, *Critique of Pure Reason*, trans. F. Max Muller (Garden City, New York: Doubleday Anchor Books, 1966). A:838 = B:866, pp. 533–34.

14. See Ralph W. Sleeper, *The Necessity of Pragmatism* (New Haven: Yale University Press, 1987).

15. CP 8:186–213.

16. Peirce to James, Nov. 25, 1902, CP 8:255.

17. James to Peirce, Sept. 28, 1904, CP 8:279–85 and CP 8, fn. 31, pp. 198–200.

18. Peirce to James, July 23, 1905, CP 8:262. Compare Peirce's complaint with Santayana's remark on James in *Persons and Places*, pt. 2: "I, for instance, was sure of his goodwill and kindness, of which I had many proofs; but I was also sure that he never understood me, and that when he talked to me, there was a mannikin in his head, called G. S. and entirely fantastic, which he was really addressing. No doubt I profitted materially by this illusion, because he would have liked me less if he had understood me better; but the sense of that illusion made spontaneous friendship impossible" (critical edition, ed. Wm. G. Holzberger and Herman J. Saatkamp, Jr., 1986, pp. 401–402).

19. Peirce to James, Oct. 3, 1904, CP 8:301.

20. Peirce to James, Dec. 17, 1909, CP 8:303.

21. See Wang Ch'ung, *Lun Hung*, 2 vols., pt. 1: *Philosophical Essays of Wang Ch'ung* and pt. 2: *Miscellaneous Essays of Wang Ch'ung*, trans. Alfred Forke (London: Luzac, 1907–11). The *Lun Hung* was written in the first century A.D.

22. See *The Historical Literature of Mori Ogai*, 2 vols., vol. 1: *The Incident at Sakai and Other Stories* and vol. 2: *Saiki Koi and Other Stories*, trans. and ed. David A. Dilworth and J. Thomas Rimer (Honolulu: The University Press of Hawaii, 1977).

Democracy and Feudalism

ZHU XINMIN

The last dynasty of China was overthrown in 1911. No one can actually become an emperor any more in modern China; however, a few short-lived "emperors" did appear in the twentieth century. This is the dilemma that China has been confronting since 1911. Why does this dilemma exist in modern China? My view is that the tradition of Chinese culture has only been modified, but not to the extent that it can back up a democratic government. That is to say, it still provides the ground for the possibility of having an emperor. On the other hand, in addition to the impact of Western democracy, Chinese people, especially intellectuals, have realized that the feudalism of dynasties has prevented the progress of China, so the actuality of an emperor's ruling China does not exist any more. This paper is an attempt to show that Dewey's philosophy played a special role in this dilemma, although it is not the only cause. Specifically, Dewey's idea of democracy stimulated the thoughts of Chinese people, and its impact made it impossible for anyone to become an emperor in China. But his philosophy did not reveal that democracy was a historical outcome of the spiritual tradition of the West. Democracy is impossible without this type of tradition. Instead, Dewey thought that the keys to solve the problems that China confronted after the last dynasty were to introduce science into China, to establish a democratic government, and to popularize education. The weakness of his philosophy in this respect helped someone to be a short-lived "emperor." I will try to show in this paper that his suggestions result from the methodology of pragmatism.

Dewey arrived in China on May 1, 1919. This was an important year in the modern history of China. It has been called the period of the May Fourth Movement. Dewey said, "Simply as an intellectual spectacle, a scene for study and surmise, there is nothing in the world today—not even Europe in the throes of reconstruction—that equals China. History records no parallel."[1] The most important question that he wanted to investigate was, "Can an old, vast, peculiar, exclusive, self-sufficing civilization be born again?"[2] Hence, Dewey's lectures in China focus on social and political philosophy. In his lectures on these topics, the first question that Dewey asked was whether social and political theories can be a means toward the cure of the social diseases or whether it can merely describe their symptoms. Before offering any answer, Dewey pointed out the defects of two antithetical points of view; that is, idealism and materialism. The idealist emphasizes the ideal, holding that everything results from theory. On the other hand, the materialist maintains that a theory is an effect, not a cause. It results from something but cannot result in anything. According to the materialist, slogans such as "freedom and justice" and "making the world safe for democracy" to which the leaders of the allied nations appealed are only catchwords. Then, Dewey proposed a third view: a pragmatic view. It insists that a theory is, in its initial stages, the result instead of the cause of practice, but as soon as a theory is formed, it becomes part of the practice that produces it. Dewey argued that theories can and do influence human actions. The first function of theory is to give permanence to something that is initially temporary or accidental, to provide stability for ways of thinking and doing that are wavering and shaky. He cited an example from Chinese intellectual history: Confucianism has stabilized many Chinese institutions. However, now it results in rigidity instead of stability and interferes with progress. Thus, theories can become dangerous. The second function of theory is that in time of crisis it can generate faith. People will sacrifice their property, and even their lives, for something in which they believe deeply. I believe that Dewey's basic point on the relation between practice and theory is right.

After clearing up the confusion about the relation between theory and practice, Dewey discussed the ways in which a theory produces its effect. Generally speaking, social and political philosophies fall under two broad categories, the radical and the conservative. Radicals are dissatisfied with and sharply critical of existing social institutions. They do not intend to improve what exists but to replace it with something entirely new and different. Conservatives are also dissatisfied with existing institutions, but they recognize that each institution evolves to serve a human need. Hence, a given institution may have deteriorated because people lose sight of the purpose it was originally intended to serve; the conservative always looks for the original meaning instead of a way to replace the institution. Confucius is a conservative, who holds that all institutions have their ideal purposes; if men could rediscover and act upon them, there would be no need to destroy the institutions. Dewey believed that mankind has fallen into the trap of "either-or," either radical or conservative. However, "What mankind needs most is the ability to recognize and pass judgement on facts. We need to develop the ability (and the disposition) to look for particular kinds of solutions by particular methods for particular problems which arise on particular occasions. In other words, we must deal with concrete problems by concrete methods when and as these problems present themselves in our experience. This is the gist of what we call the third philosophy."[3] The characteristics of this third philosophy can be formulated as follows: (1) emphasis on experimentation, (2) emphasis on application of knowledge and intelligence to social change, and (3) emphasis on the study of individual events. Dewey reminded people that only after the scientific spirit has been introduced into social philosophy could the third philosophy come into being, so his philosophy is scientific. So far, Dewey had presented his methodology of social philosophy. Following this methodology, he naturally reached the conclusion that the reform of China was not the replacement of the tradition and the structure of the society but the solution of some particular problems, such as the form of the government and education. In a word, social reformation is retail business, not wholesale. It is made piecemeal, not all at once.

Dewey suggested that three aspects of Chinese society can be reformed right now. First of all, a feudal government can readily be modified into a democratic one. Secondly, China can achieve democracy by popularizing education. He said, "The reconstruction of society depends, to a very great extent, upon the school. The school is the instrument by which a new society can be built, and through which the unworthy features of the existing society can be modified."[4] Finally, Chinese scholars and scientists should pursue specialized knowledge and devote their research to special problems.

I believe that Dewey intended to introduce American democracy into China so that this old civilization would be reformed. He mentioned that democracy in any true sense of the word must have a grassroots social basis. It must be part of the fabric of the lives of people and begin in every village and in every city block. Discussions concerning cabinet organization, parliamentary organization, and even about centralism versus federalism were unreal so long as the people as a whole were not thoroughly imbued with democratic attitudes and did not participate in the processes of a democratic life. However, he did not make it clear that democracy was a historical outcome of the profound spiritual disciplines that had given the West its inner form of life and that still determined, to a large degree, the course of the development of the West. This was because he did not clearly realize that Chinese civilization and Western civilization were so different that democracy had no roots in the former. As a matter of fact, there were no such words as assembly, senator, and citizen in the ancient Chinese language. Dewey mistakenly claimed that the Chinese had an instinctive attraction to a democratic political order. He said, "Although this democracy is articulately held only by a handful who have been educated, yet these few know and dumb masses feel that it alone accords with the historical spirit of the Chinese race. For Bolshevism there is no preparation and no aptitude in China."[5] Therefore, Dewey did not emphasize that the tradition of Chinese culture was the main obstacle to the reform of China. Instead, he called people's attention to some concrete problems. The question is how these problems can be solved without changing the tradition. Here, by the tradition, I mean the fundamental assumptions of Chinese culture.

A comparison between Chinese and Western civilizations will make our point clear. The mental life of Western Europe and America can be traced to three main sources: (1) Greek culture, (2) Jewish religion and ethics, and (3) modern industrialism, which itself is an outcome of modern science. Plato, the Old Testament, and Galileo may be taken as representing these three elements. None of these elements has had any appreciable part in the development of Chinese tradition. This tradition has its own origins, which happen to be very different from the sources of Western spirit. Because of these, Western society in the modern era is composed of individuals acting as independent units, and its laws and ethics tend to protect individual freedom and rights. John Locke's theory of contract begins with the assumption that a primitive social community consists of individuals as basic units. Only in such a society is democracy possible. On the other hand, Chinese society, even in the modern age, consists of families as basic units. An individual is regarded merely as a member of the family and not as an independent unit in the society. This feudalist structure of Chinese society is the result of Confucianism, which has dominated Chinese minds for two thousand years. The fundamental ethical principle of Confucianism, filial piety, upholds the traditional family system, and at the same time it becomes the basis of the principle of loyalty to the sovereign. Filial piety is defined in Confucian classics as a duty beginning with serving one's parents, developing in serving the emperor, and ending with benefitting oneself. *The Book of Filial Piety* says, "A gentleman who serves his parents with filial piety may transfer it to his loyalty to the emperor." And the committing of an unfilial act is the severest crime among three thousand categories of the five classes of punishment. The way in which Confucian emphasis on filial piety prevents the growth of public spirit is illustrated by the following story. One of the feudal princes was boasting to Confucius of the high morality in his own state. "Among us here," he said, "you will find upright men. If a father has stolen a sheep, his son will give evidence against him." "In my part of the country," replied Confucius, "there is a different standard from this. A father will shield his son, a son will shield his father. It is thus that upright man will be found." It is interesting to contrast this story with that of Euthyphro's prosecution of his father for homicide in the dialogues of Plato.

As a result of the theory of filial piety, Confucianism supports a castle system and the inequality of the status of individuals in the society. The sovereign, father, husband, and officials are superior, and ministers, sons, wives, and other people are inferior. The distinction between the superior and the inferior cannot be abandoned. In this way, Confucius advocated unlimited authority for the monarch and government by man instead of by law. He identified the emperor with heaven, a being to be checked by nothing save his own conscience.

Now the core of the tradition, Confucianism, had not been replaced at the time that Dewey stayed in China. It still prevailed in the society. Hence, the key to reform China is to change the tradition. Partly because of Dewey's influence, many outstanding intellectuals of China judged that the power of the West lay not in the spiritual tradition but in its understanding and control of the material world and its democratic government. They had an illusion that the West had first formed the new society by its development of scientific knowledge and democratic institutions, but China was without these things. The best hope of China seemed to be in following the West in these areas. They had little awareness of from which sources a democratic political system was developed. They did not see the necessity of changing not only a political institution but a form of life and a set of fundamental values. It seem to me that to solve these concrete problems such as changing political institutions is difficult, but to change the core of Chinese culture—Confucianism and its corresponding individual and social virtues—is the real challenge. To solve practical problems is very important, but to keep the task of changing the tradition in the mind and try to accomplish it has at least the same importance.

Although many intellectuals believed that Dewey was right, a few scholars held a different view. In 1923, there was a debate of science versus metaphysics. This debate, I think, reflects both the influence and weakness of Dewey's philosophy. Carson Chang, who was a philosopher, indicated that science differed in many ways from a view of life, which was a person's attitude toward his relation with the outside world. The characteristics of the former were objective, logical, and causative, whereas the latter were subjective, intuitive, and unique. Consequently, no matter how far science developed, it was not able to solve the problems of a view of life. That is to say, science could scarcely solve the problems of China, because science had nothing to do with a view of life, which, by his definition, included most of the social sciences, ethics, religion, and philosophy. On the other hand, some leading philosophers, including Hu Shih, who was the most famous disciple of Dewey, argued that a view of life was governed by scientific method. And although it was not unified at the present, it would be in the future. Science could save China. This debate lasted about a year. There were many issues involved in this debate, and the arguments on both sides appeared confusing in many respects. This is not the place to assess those arguments. However, it is evident that the philosophers who were on the science side basically borrowed their view and method from Dewey's pragmatism. The philosophers who were on the metaphysics side had some insight about the reform of Chinese society, although their view was not completely correct. They realized that Dewey's suggestions could not solve the problems of China unless people paid enough attention to reform their view of life. Unfortunately, not many people recognized that point, partly because of Dewey's impact. That is to say, they wanted to industrialize China and to set up a democratic government within the framework of Chinese tradition. They paid enough attention to the concrete problems but forgot that they should fight against tradition at the same time. The dilemma of China in recent history results in part from this. The following historical facts can prove this view.

Jiang Jian-che gained control over China with the help of Russians in 1924.

Although he sometimes shouted the slogan "freedom and democracy," he wanted to be "an emperor" of China. Basically, he set up an authoritarian institution. The theory that he used to justify his actions was Confucianism. However, an ideal democracy had become a constant influence and had affected the political life of the country. For example, the legislative assembly was established for the first time in the history of China, although it was responsible to the government, not the government to the assembly. That is to say, the political system of China at that time was not democratic in the real sense. The interesting thing to note is that Dewey has been blamed by some scholars in Taiwan after 1949 for paving the way for the Communists. At the same time, he has been criticized by the Chinese Communists for his opposition to Marxism. How can that happen? First of all, as we have mentioned already, what Jiang Jian-che advocated was not democracy but Confucianism after he controlled the government. The form of the government that he set up was semifeudal. But the slogan that the Communists used to unify Chinese people, especially the intellectuals, in the fight against Jiang's dictatorship was "democracy and freedom," which Dewey proposed to the Chinese people. The Communists promised to the people a society of freedom, democracy, and equality. Although this was a tactic that the Communists used in the struggle, it was attractive to the people. As a matter of fact, a great number of intellectuals did believe that a democratic China would be born after Jiang Jian-che was defeated. They did a lot to help the Communists fight against Jiang. Hence, essentially the destruction of Jiang's government was the victory of the ideal of democracy. That is to say, what motivated most people was the ideal of democracy. At any rate, this ideal has made Jiang's dream of being an emperor impossible, but Confucianism as the core of Chinese tradition has made him a short-lived "emperor." Of course, the Chinese Communists do not really believe in democracy. After taking over the mainland of China, they gave up the slogan of "democracy and freedom" and criticized Dewey's philosophy.

Another interesting figure was Mao, who was educated in the tradition of Chinese culture. He had never been to other countries except the Soviet Union and knew the West only superficially. Because Marxism is a historic outcome of the Western tradition, how can a person who does not know Western culture very well know Marxism deeply? Mao was the person who really understood Chinese culture and the Chinese people. Hence, he knew pretty well how to manipulate the minds of the Chinese. He succeeded in making people believe that he was a perfect man who deserved to be worshipped. An overwhelming number of people were convinced that Mao was the sun rising from the East in the beginning of the so-called cultural revolution. It is not because the people were unbalanced or irrational at that time. Essentially, it was the hard core of the tradition that made the disaster of the cultural revolution possible. And it was the very same thing that made Mao a short-lived "emperor." However, even in the cultural revolution, the ideal of democracy is not dead. The Tiananmen

Square Event, which was a movement against the cultural revolution during which many persons were arrested because of their dissenting political views, was good evidence that the ideal of democracy was alive in the people's hearts at that time. After the death of Mao, his dynasty clashed immediately. That shows that the ideal of democracy works again and that people need democracy badly.

It is worth noting that the slogan "science and democracy" has been used again in the current discussion of the reform of China. Philosophers' interest in Dewey's philosophy has revived. They seem to confront the question that Dewey asked sixty-five years ago: can an ancient civilization be reborn? Can the Four Modernizations solve the problems of China? The fate of Dewey's philosophy in China should give us some inspiration in the discussion of the reform of China. I firmly believe, in light of the historical lessons, that science alone cannot do the job unless political institutions and the value system are reformed at the same time. Of course, all of these cannot be done in a short period of time. What we can do is to solve one problem after another, but we have to remember that the hard core of Chinese culture is the ultimate and main obstacle to the reform of China when we deal with these concrete problems. The fight against Chinese tradition is a long-lasting but urgent battle.

Notes

1. John Dewey, "Old China and New," *Asia* 21 (May, 1921): 445.
2. John Dewey, "New Culture in China," *Asia* 21 (July, 1921): 642.
3. John Dewey, *Lectures in China, 1919–1920* (Honolulu: The University Press of Hawaii, 1973), p. 53.
4. Ibid., p. 213.
5. John Dewey, "The International Duel in China," *New Republic* 20 (Aug. 27, 1919): 112.

PHILOSOPHY AND LITERATURE

Josiah Royce:
Literature and Humanism

JOHN CLENDENNING

In the history of American thought, Josiah Royce is the supreme polymath. Remembered primarily, if not exclusively, for his pioneering work in traditional branches of philosophy—logic, epistemology, metaphysics, and ethics—he was also a novelist, historian, psychologist, social critic, and religious thinker. Although a few devoted scholars have kept Royce's philosophy alive, his contributions to literature—his "fugitive" essays, as Jacob Loewenberg characterized them—have been totally ignored. No book or article has given the slightest attention to Royce's frequent references to poets and novelists, and all of his literary allusions have passed through the minds of scholars with scarcely a flicker. But Royce was a profound student of literature. A collection of his literary essays would fill a substantial volume, and if taken holistically and seen in light of his philosophic commitments, these offer striking perceptions. No other American philosopher—from the Golden Age onward—provides an equal wealth of hitherto unexamined literary insight.

As an undergraduate at the University of California, Royce specialized in classics. He knew Latin, Greek, and Hebrew. He wrote a baccalaureate thesis on Aeschylus and a commencement address on Sophocles, and he published his first important essay, "The Aim of Poetry," on Aristotle's *Poetics*. Before his twentieth birthday Royce had articles published on Shakespeare, Poe, Tennyson, George Eliot, Hardy, Turgenev, and others. In Europe he studied German literature, especially Goethe and the romantics. His knowledge of German poetry was so exact that he often dazzled friends and audiences by quoting original texts effortlessly. In Germany he also learned Sanskrit, a study he continued at Johns Hopkins, advancing to the Bhagavad Gita, the Vedas, and the Upanishad. During his two years in Baltimore, Royce became increasingly committed to philosophy, but he did not abandon literature. Indeed, at no point in his life did he draw a sharp line between these two fields, or any fields, of humanistic study.

At Johns Hopkins his doctoral studies included a lecture series on romanticism, from which he published an early essay, "Schiller's Ethical Studies."

Royce began his teaching career as an English instructor at the University of California. Except for chance earned through effort, he might have remained in this position indefinitely. At Berkeley he wrote his first important essays in philosophy but kept up his literary studies with public lectures and articles. His concerns, then focused on the nineteenth century, yielded essays on romanticism and realism.

In an early unpublished lecture, "What Constitutes Good Fiction," Royce explored the art of the novel. Critics of the 1870s were just beginning to discuss realism; prose fiction was still primarily a popular, and not quite harmless, form of entertainment. Treating the novel seriously as an art form, Royce isolated its components—description, dialogue, plot, character—and proceeded to argue that the last component, psychological portrayal, is the hallmark of excellence in prose fiction. In insisting upon this point, Royce placed the novel, and indirectly also himself, in the tradition of humanism. "In properly studying character, the Novel accomplishes the end of idealizing human life. For in the evolution and the interaction of individuals consists the great active whole we call Life. To understand the individual lives is the stepping stone to the understanding of Humanity."[1] The American novelists who formulated the theory of realism, Henry James and William Dean Howells, emphasized the same criterion for judging fiction. Five years after Royce, James wrote in his seminal essay, "The Art of Fiction": "Humanity is immense, and reality has a myriad forms; the most one can affirm is that some of the flowers of fiction have the odor of it."[2] And three years after James, Howells offered this as a test of good fiction: "Is it true?—true to the motives, the impulses, the principles that shape the life of actual men and women? . . . In the whole range of fiction we know of no *true* picture of life—that is, of human nature—which is not also a masterpiece of literature, full of divine and natural beauty."[3]

The realist, for whom the portrayal of human experience is the primary aim of art, is essentially a humanist. Such writers favor the natural, the ordinary dimensions of life; they avoid the spectacular, parody the sentimental, resist dogma, and encourage critical inquiry. Erasmus and Montaigne were such men as these. So also was Josiah Royce. But adding his own dash of idealism, Royce stands apart from the others. Truthful portrayal is a necessary, but not sufficient, mark of excellence. The writer must also grasp the whole of life, must see the universal in the individual: must, in short, have the "synoptic vision." We return to this point repeatedly in Royce's literary essays. The novelist, the poet, the literary scholar becomes a philosopher by interest and a humanist by aim. In "A Neglected Study"—a piece written for the *Harvard Monthly* in 1890—Royce advocated an approach to literature modeled on classical philology—neither pure linguistics nor pure esthetics—whose subject is the "history of politics, of ethics, of morals, of society, of all civilization . . . and [whose] purpose is the comprehension of human life."[4] Again, in a very late lecture, "What Does Philosophy Mean to the Literary Man?" we find the same advice directed to the writer. "Without some . . . sense of what is deep, of what is permanently interesting about the tasks, the tragedies and the triumphs of human life, the literary artist is at the mercy of the whims and of the fads and the transient passions of his day, of his own social level, and of his party or his school. . . . The literary artist needs somehow to have won a sense of what is deep and true and universal about the issues of life."[5]

The literary humanist is an idealist in the general, nontechnical sense of the word. While we should include Royce within this category, we should also recognize that he was one of its severest critics: witness his frequent jabs at Francis Peabody, G. H. Howison, and G. H. Palmer and his devastation of F. E. Abbot. Most idealists irritated Royce because he found them overly enthusiastic and intellectually flaccid. Their grand visions appealed to the masses, but the visions were vague and the visionaries defenseless. For Royce the idealist must be rooted, shockproof, and tough-minded as any pragmatist. A mealy-mouthed idealism, he insisted, poses a threat to civilization. "I have a profound contempt for deliberate excesses in the work of reasoning . . . and a great hatred for the excessive use of formulas."[6]

I maintain that the concept of Roycean criticism is quite as meaningful as any criticism associated with a comprehensive theory. Reading as Royce reads literature provides a useful perspective and facilitates insights that otherwise are not available. I believe this will become clear through an examination of "Tennyson and Pessimism," an essay Royce wrote for the *Harvard Monthly* in 1887, one year after the publication of "Locksley Hall Sixty Years After."[7]

Tennyson's poem had been met with bitter disappointment. The young radical who had ignited a generation with the first "Locksley Hall" in 1842 now seemed little more than a grumpy old Tory. The first poem offered a stirring vision of the future:

> Not in vain the distance beacons. Forward, forward let us range,
> Let the great world spin for ever down the ringing grooves of change.[8]

This became, in the second poem, a sad echo:

> Gone the cry of "Forward, Forward," lost within a growing gloom;
> Lost, or only heard in silence from the silence of a tomb.[9]

Critics have always ranked "Locksley Hall" with the best poems of the nineteenth century. Its quotable lines are read in childhood and remembered long afterward:

> In the Spring a young man's fancy lightly turns to thoughts of love.[10]

On the other hand, "Locksley Hall Sixty Years After" is seldom anthologized and is discussed only as a despondent answer to the earlier classic.

Royce takes the unpopular position, claiming that the second poem is "healthier, more manly, more devout, and even more cheerful." He does not claim that it is aesthetically superior, but as a philosopher he finds it "ethically higher."[11] To grasp this point we need to examine the first poem and compare it to the second. It begins as the speaker—not Tennyson, but a young man who lives in Lincolnshire near the sea—asks to be left alone while he surrenders to a lover's complaint. We learn that he has been jilted by a young woman, Amy, who has chosen a wealthier, uncultured landowner, a man who can never be more than a clown or a beast. Suddenly the persona darts from this romantic theme to a series of extravagant fantasies. Having "dipt into the future," he has global visions of magnificent decades stretched ahead: a future energized by science, technology, commerce, empire, peace, world federation—all "rapt in universal law."[12] The tension that controls the poem is the persona's turbulence. At times he revels in his dreams, at times he is overwhelmed by doubts and remorse. Nevertheless, at the end in the midst of a storm, he resolves to leave Locksley Hall forever and to strike out:

> For the mighty wind arises, roaring seaward, and I go.[13]

Royce labeled these sentiments a disease, "the favorite disease of [Tennyson's] age."[14] Although he admired this spirit of worship and loyalty, he rejected it for two reasons. First, dreams of a perfected future resist definition. Ideals have ultimate value only when they can be known and experienced in concrete life. Mere escape from coarseness is insufficient; mere hope pinned on dreams is insubstantial. Second and more important, such dreams are treacherous because they lead invariably to pessimism. When hope fails, as mere hope must, the dreamer sinks into despair. Thus the young Tennyson, by his own agenda, was doomed.

This result was fulfilled in "Locksley Hall Sixty Years After." We learn that the persona has, after all, never left Locksley Hall. Instead, now in his eighties, he meets his grandson, Leonard, who, upon the death of the old squire, Amy's husband, will inherit the hall. The grandfather and the young man are the only survivors. Amy is dead; so is Edith, whom the persona subsequently married; dead also is their son, Leonard's father. The persona's energy is also gone.

> Gone the fires of youth, the follies, furies, curses, passionate tears,
> Gone like fires and floods and earthquakes of the planet's dawning years.
> Fires that shook me once, but now to silent ashes fall'n away.
> Cold upon the dead volcano sleeps the gleam of dying day.[15]

The earlier world vision of order, peace, and progress is now blasted by chaos, global violence, revolution, stupidity, mendacity:

> Chaos, Cosmos! Cosmos, Chaos! who can tell how all will end?[16]
> . . . .
> Forward, backward, backward, forward, in the immeasurable sea,
> Sway'd by vaster ebbs and flows than can be known to you or me.[17]

For Royce, Tennyson's late pessimism was inevitable, because the original optimism was false. But it was also healthy, because the path to redemption is the via dolorosa. Although the persona's losses cannot be ignored, he has learned courage and faith and, most important, he has become connected with real life. This becomes clear through the most dramatic revelation in the poem: the old squire, the youth's rival, turns out not to have been a philistine but a fine man—simple, straightforward, benevolent, a model for the grandson to emulate.

> . . . You, my Leonard, use and not abuse your day,
> Move among your people, know them, follow him who led the way,
> Strove for sixty widow'd years to help his homelier brother men,
> Served the poor, and built the cottage, raised the school, and drain'd the fen.[18]

A Roycean analysis of Tennyson's two poems argues in favor of the second against the first. Romantic enthusiasm and disembodied earnestness are symptomatic of the disease of "Locksley Hall." If "Locksley Hall Sixty Years After" sinks into pessimism, that itself is a sign of moral and intellectual health. The poet now understands the problem of evil, not exclusively in terms of personal suffering but as a condition of human experience in general. Accepting the tragedy, he urges us to seek some tangible good we can do in and for the world. "Take this commonplace life, and without denying it, without forsaking it, make it no longer narrow. Make it large and full, but keep it concrete."[19] Any Royce scholar will instantly recognize this analysis as an application of the philosophy of loyalty to literary exegesis—and a very good one indeed.

Having explored Royce's literary applications of his idealistic principles, I turn now to the second part of my inquiry: to show how the Roycean perspective may be applied in general. I hope to demonstrate that this perspective provides a useful tool that can highlight and clarify works that have been abundantly discussed—but not, without it, understood. I will illustrate my point with a single instance: Henry James's *The Ambassadors*.

What James knew about Royce's theories remains a mystery. He must have heard about Royce from his brother, William James, and as an active man of letters in the late nineteenth century he was certainly acquainted with contemporary thought. But philosophy was definitely not James's metier. Living outside of academic circles, James observed philosophers from a distance and without much sympathy. His snide reference to "the sandy plains of a history of German Thought"[20] tells us a lot about James's attitudes, and his description of Josiah and Katherine as "the ghastly Royce couple" confirms the appraisal. "I shall never . . . ," James promised, "embrace any man's philosophy till I have seen him—and above all till I have seen his wife."[21]

Nevertheless, there are striking parallels between Royce's philosophy and James's fiction. Especially relevant to this observation is the ethical idealism that Royce presented in *The Philosophy of Loyalty*. Indeed, James's novel can be read—with or without a claim for direct influence—as a critical examination of the status of loyalty as an ethical principle. The Roycean perspective does not exhaust the richness of *The Ambassadors*, but it does identify and keep in focus a theme that has not been sufficiently emphasized.

In the fictional world of Henry James, we repeatedly encounter shambles of broken ties and tragedies of missed opportunities. We find, moreover, in nearly every short story or novel, a character—sometimes two or three—who lives in and for the ideal, who is determined to "be true," and who actively submits to self-sacrifice. Such a person is Lambert Strether.

Strether is a handsome but worried middle-aged man from Woollett, Massachusetts, thirty years a widower. In more than half his life he has done virtually nothing except edit an obscure *Review*—whose green covers alone distinguish him—and attend to Mrs. Newsome, a wealthy New England widow, whom he hopes finally to marry. When we meet him, he has "come out on purpose" to Europe to "save" the lady's son, Chad, who has been enjoying a youthful fling in Paris.[22] Strether believes that Chad has been ensnared by a "base, venal" foreign woman.[23] As ambassador, Strether has an apparently simple mission: bring Chad home so he can join the family business and marry his brother-in-law's sister, Mamie Pocock. Thus far the plot and the protagonist's position in it seem a fair representation of Roycean loyalty. Strether is clearly one who engages in "the willing and practical and thoroughgoing devotion . . . to a cause."[24] His goal of constructing a network of loyalties—he to Chad and Mrs. Newsome, she to Chad, he to his mother, Mamie to Chad, and he to her—illustrates the highest good in Roycean ethics: loyalty to loyalty.[25] For himself Strether has nothing to gain except marriage with Mrs. Newsome and, more importantly, the satisfaction of knowing that he has done his duty.[26] Three factors help to make this banal situation complex and interesting. True, Strether is the prototypic loyalist. He lives for others, his life is "covered" in promises, he fears and distrusts his tendency toward disloyalty. But he also has a secret desire to escape entanglements. He wants deeply to live for himself, but his selfishness, as he sees it, has brought gloom. Now in Paris, he hopes to achieve redemption by surrendering to the good of others totally. Also, we learn that besides Strether and his young friend, Maria Gostrey, no one appreciates or subscribes to Strether's values. He becomes merely an easy tool they use in promoting personal success. Much of the comedy and pathos of the novel results from our watching "poor Strether" trying to put people in their places while they are scurrying about to get the upper hand. And to achieve this end, they mystify Strether by constantly covering their tracks and telling him lies. Finally, we discover, through Strether's growing awareness, that Chad's mistress, Madame de Vionnet, is a clever, charming, magnificently civilized woman; that Chad has not been corrupted but "improved" through her influence; and that Strether himself is on the brink of falling in love with her.

In Paris, with a new circle of attractive friends, Strether sees that his life has been stifled by provincial values and conventions, an insight he expresses in the most quoted sentence in the novel: "Live all you can; it's a mistake not to."[27] Instead of taking his own advice—"letting himself go"—he revises his mission and extends his commitments. When Madame de Vionnet asks a "favour"—a word that always endangers Strether—she drives a "little golden nail" into his conscience. After an intimate luncheon with her, he is determined to "save" her too—to save or at least satisfy everyone except himself.[28]

Not that he lacks opportunities: two women virtually throw themselves at his feet. But whereas Chad abandons his mistress to become the all-American ad man, Strether returns to Woollett in defeat, an untainted failure. Oblivious to his choices, he sees himself as "a helpless jelly" poured into "a tin mould." Loyalty is not an option for Strether but a necessity: he needs "to be right." "That, you see," he insists at the end of the novel, "is my only logic. Not, out of the whole affair, to have got anything for myself."[29] A Roycean will insist that, though Strether's tale is tragic, his tragedy does not in any way discredit loyalty. Royce never promised that the loyalist will succeed: only that by stepping beyond himself he will find himself, that by forsaking personal happiness he will find something better than happiness, that by weaving the social fabric he will become truly individual. Which is precisely what Strether achieves. His future, enhanced by loyal and invigorating months abroad, will be deepened by reflections on the meaning of his renewed life long afterwards.[30] No longer a mere "cover" or editor of other people's lives, nor a drifter—like those expatriots whom James knew and scorned—Strether will be a man, a man whose understanding admits him into the corridors of humanity.

The ancient house of humanism is immense. It contains many rooms and mixtures of styles. Royce's room in this house was furnished in a simple decor, full—perhaps too full—of familiar, serviceable objects. But like a cluttered parsonage its books, its desk, and straight chairs served a larger purpose. That purpose was to defend a faith in "the Spirit, the Beloved Community, the work of grace, the atoning deed, the saving power of the loyal life."[31] The octogenarian of Locksley Hall and the defeated Lambert Strether illustrate this faith, all of Royce's writings proclaim it, and nothing says it better than his "fugitive" essays on literature.

Notes

1. Josiah Royce, *The Papers of Josiah Royce*, Harvard University Archives, vol. 80.
2. Henry James, *Selected Literary Criticism*, ed. Morris Shapira (New York: Horizon Press, 1964), p. 56.
3. William Dean Howells, *W. D. Howells as Critic*, ed. Edwin H. Cady (London: Routledge & Kegan Paul, 1973), p. 101.
4. Josiah Royce, *Fugitive Essays*, ed. J. Loewenberg (Cambridge, Mass.: Harvard University Press, 1920), pp. 376–77.

5. Royce, *The Papers of Josiah Royce*, vol. 78.
6. Josiah Royce, *The Basic Writings of Josiah Royce*, ed. John J. McDermott (Chicago: University of Chicago Press, 1969) 2:1125.
7. Josiah Royce, *Studies of Good and Evil* (New York: D. Appleton and Co., 1898), pp. 76–88.
8. Alfred Tennyson, *The Works of Tennyson*, ed. Hallam, Lord Tennyson (New York: AMS Press, 1970), vol. 2, p. 49.
9. Ibid., vol. 6, p. 285.
10. Ibid., vol. 2, p. 35.
11. Royce, *Studies of Good and Evil*, p. 77.
12. Tennyson, *The Works of Tennyson*, vol. 2, pp. 44–45.
13. Ibid., p. 50.
14. Royce, *Studies of Good and Evil*, p. 77.
15. Tennyson, *The Works of Tennyson*, vol. 6, p. 282.
16. Ibid., p. 288.
17. Ibid., p. 296.
18. Ibid., p. 303.
19. Royce, *Studies of Good and Evil*, p. 87.
20. Henry James, *The Novels and Tales of Henry James* (New York: Charles Scribner's Sons, 1907–1909), vol. 3, p. 31.
21. Henry James, *Letters*, ed. Leon Edel (Cambridge, Mass.: Harvard University Press, 1974–84), vol. 2, p. 385.
22. James, *The Novels and Tales of Henry James*, vol. 21, p. 30.
23. Ibid., p. 55.
24. Royce, *The Basic Writings of Josiah Royce*, vol. 2, p. 186.
25. The triviality of this network and the exaggerated importance that Strether attaches to it perhaps underscore Royce's failure to establish a hierarchy of loyalties. Strether's efforts to collect a prodigal son for a puritanical mother hardly qualifies as a paradigm for a serious moral conflict. And yet Royce does cite obstreperous children who defy their mothers as examples of the tensions that concern him. See Royce, *The Basic Writings of Josiah Royce*, vol. 2, p. 868.
26. Strether should also secure his sense of moral individuality. Royce maintains that loyalty—that is, uncompromising commitment—does not weaken but strengthens the individual. "Disloyalty," he says, "is moral suicide" (Royce, *The Basic Writings of Josiah Royce*, vol. 2, p. 944). James seems to acknowledge this principle when he has Madame de Vionnet, in a curious echo of Royce's language, "renounce all claim to be an object of interest" (James, *The Novels and Tales of Henry James*, vol. 22, p. 281). By choosing disloyalty in order to gain personal happiness, she has ceased to be, in a meaningful sense, a person.
27. James, *The Novels and Tales of Henry James*, vol. 21, p. 217.
28. Ibid., p. 276.
29. Ibid., vol. 22, p. 326.
30. James sprinkles hints of Strether's reflective life throughout the text. A study of this "later" Strether is long overdue.
31. Josiah Royce, *The Problem of Christianity* (Chicago: University of Chicago Press, 1968), p. 404.

Reconstructing American Philosophy:
Emerson and Dewey

RUSSELL B. GOODMAN

What is a man born for but to be a Reformer, a Re-maker of what man has made.

*Ralph Waldo Emerson
in "Man the Reformer"*

In such essays as "Man the Reformer," "Circles," "Experience," and "Montaigne: Or the Skeptic," Emerson writes as a philosopher of flux, a Heraclitean, holding that "there are no fixtures in nature" and that "permanence is but a word of degrees."[1]

In "Circles" he portrays a typical pattern of change among our arts, empires, rites, and other forms of life: a circle of seeing and living forms, proving useful and insightful; but the circle hardens in time, the "wave" becomes a "ridge," and life is hemmed in. A new circle must then be drawn, breaking through the old one but carrying its message forward: "the result of today, which haunts the mind and cannot be escaped . . . will itself be included as one example of a bolder generalization."[2] All stages of the pattern of natural progression Emerson describes have a common center. This center represents the unchanging, unitary, neo-Platonic element in his thought, while the series of circles expanding into what he calls "the newness"[3] represents his Heraclitean emphasis on process.

My suggestion in this essay is that the canon of "classical American philosophy"—which has generally been taken to begin with Peirce or James—has itself become a hemmed-in circle and that we can expand our horizons without losing our center by connecting Emerson himself (as well as Thoreau) with James and Dewey. To use Emerson's circle metaphor again, we treat "pragmatism" and "transcendentalism" as circles with different centers. This is reflected in the fact that the great body of recent writing about Emerson and Thoreau is by professors of English and American Studies, while that about Dewey and James is mostly by philosophers.[4] Emerson and Thoreau play a minor role in standard histories and surveys of American philosophy.[5]

The full accomplishment of the project of relating transcendentalism to pragmatism is obviously beyond the scope of this paper. Here we shall trace some particular paths: first, from Dewey back to Emerson via Dewey's 1903 essay on Emerson; second, from Emerson forward to pragmatism via his focus on experiment and action; third, from the romantic respect for the child found in Wordsworth and Rousseau to the overlapping educational philosophies of Emerson and Dewey.[6]

Section I

Although the statement that Emerson is a neo-Platonist or a mystic is not incorrect, it is incomplete. Emerson is also a philosopher of experience, and of experiment. This is certainly the way Dewey reads him. "I fancy he reads the so-called eclecticism of Emerson wrongly," Dewey writes in his 1903 essay, "who does not see that it is the reduction of all the philosophers of the race, even the prophets like Plato and Proclus whom Emerson holds most dear, to the test of trial by the service rendered the present and immediate experience."[7] Dewey is thinking of Emerson's remark that the philosophies of Bacon, Spinoza, Hume, Schelling, Kant, or others are just "more or less awkward translator[s] of things in your consciousness, which you have also your way of seeing, perhaps of denominating."[8] The final test of ideas, for Emerson as for Dewey, lies in experience. Dewey takes even Emerson's so-called "idealism" to be an experiential matter. Idealism, Dewey maintains, "is to Emerson a narrowly accurate description of the facts of the most real world in which all earn their living."[9] In the conclusion to *The Quest for Certainty*, Dewey surveys three varieties of idealism. The first, plainly the Hegelian variety, attempts to present an ideal world "through purely intellectual and logical processes." The second "sets the measure of our ideas of possibilities that are to be realized by intelligent endeavor"; like Emerson's, it is based on experience: "the beauty and harmony of existence is disclosed in experiences which are the immediate consummation of all for which we long." This way of "idealizing the world" is, "while it lasts ... the most engaging," according to Dewey. But it is dependent on "fortune," and so "insecure." Dewey's third, pragmatic form of idealism starts from the insight that "nature is capable of giving birth to objects that stay with us as ideal," but it does not rest there. It sets human intelligence to work idealizing the world.[10] In such later works as *The Quest for Certainty*, *Experience and Nature*, and, especially, *Art as Experience*, Dewey works at developing the third form of idealism, always pressing home the Emersonian point that even our most authoritative ideals—truth, beauty, divinity—are rooted in human experience.

Emerson's idealism has elements of both Dewey's second and third types. It is, firstly, based on those specially authoritative experiences that, as Emerson puts it, have a "depth . . . which constrains us to ascribe more reality to them than to all other experiences."[11] The famous passage from the introduction to *Nature* is a case in point. "Crossing a bare common, in snow puddles, at twilight, under a clouded sky, without having in my thoughts any occurrence of special good fortune, I have enjoyed a perfect exhilaration. I am glad to the brink of fear."[12] Dewey correctly identifies Emerson's experiential emphasis, which is why he denies that Emerson is a transcendentalist, treating something that is "beyond or behind or in any way apart."[13] Secondly, Emerson's "idealism" contains more than a dash of incipient pragmatism in its experimentalism and its emphasis on transforming the world. Emerson maintains, for example, that "revelation, always a miracle . . . needs a vehicle or art by which it is conveyed to men."[14] In Dewey's terms, the second way of "idealizing the world" requires a third way to render its values secure. Emerson is thus not only a philosopher of thought or "ideas" but (like his follower Nietzsche) a philosopher of power. He calls our ability to make them live instead of "die with their subject" the "power of communication" or "expression." Power requires thought for Emerson, but also "a mixture of will, a certain control over the spontaneous states."[15]

Section II

Essential to pragmatism is a focus on action and on consequences of action. Dewey defines knowing, for example, as "a form of doing" and holds that we in part constitute the objects we know by the actions we take in knowing them.[16] Surprisingly enough, Emerson anticipates these positions. He writes in "Man the Reformer," for example, that "manual labor is the study of the external world" and holds in "The American Scholar" that without action, "thought can never ripen into truth." "Only so much do I know," he says again, "as I have lived."[17] Emerson's American Scholar is thus not only "Man Thinking" but "Man Acting." He discovers who he is by learning what he can do: "none but he knows what that is which he can do, nor does he know until he has tried."[18]

Emerson not only connects action and knowledge—something the pragmatists were to do more thoroughly later—but, again like the pragmatists, he stresses results, taking a forward-looking approach. "Genius looks forward," he writes; "the eyes of man are set in his forehead, not in his hindhead. Man hopes. Genius creates."[19] This anticipatory, creative, and constructive attitude permeates especially Emerson's early work. "The American Scholar," for example, is a paean to the promise of this new land, to "the rich possibilities" of a "new era" on American, not European, soil.[20] In *Nature*, he writes that "it is essential to a true theory of nature and of man, that it should contain somewhat progressive." The dwarflike, still emerging man Emerson there describes is just learning to guide the changes of nature: "we do not know the uses of more than a few plants, as corn and the apple, the potato and the vine."[21] In *Nature*'s chapters on "commodity," "economy," and "discipline," Emerson sets out the project of understanding nature by influencing it. And though he follows his romantic forebears Wordsworth and Coleridge in giving a primary role to the imagination, he gives it a practical cast. "The imagination may be defined to be, the use which the Reason makes of the material world."[22]

In his later essays, Emerson continues to ascribe not only insight to his heroes but power: "the thought," as he puts it, "and the publication."[23] When he calls for an "idealism of action that is devoted to creation of a future," for a "deeper and richer intercourse with things," and for "large and generous ideas in the direction of life," John Dewey thus travels a path already taken by Emerson.[24]

Section III

We have reaffirmed Dewey's insight that Emerson is an experiential philosopher, testing even philosophical notions by their import for "the present and immediate experience." But further, and again like Dewey, he develops an "experimental empiricism"[25] that acknowledges and accepts uncertainty, even as it strives to influence events. Emerson describes himself as "only an experimenter" in "Circles": "No facts are to me sacred; none are profane; I simply experiment, an endless seeker with no Past at my back."[26] Even when he offers a list of basic categories of experience in his great essay "Experience," he does so in an explicitly experimental spirit. "I name them as I find them in my way. I know better than to claim any completeness for my picture."[27]

Such a spirit takes a particularly modern and "pragmatic" form in this passage from Emerson's essay "Intellect": "God offers to every mind its choice between truth and repose. Take which you please—you can never have both. . . . He in whom the love of repose predominates, will accept the first creed, the first philosophy, the first political party he meets,—most likely, his father's. . . . He in whom the love of truth predominates, will keep himself aloof from all moorings and afloat. . . . He submits to the inconvenience of suspense and imperfect opinion."[28]

Emerson's conception of us as afloat reminds one of Neurath's famous picture of science as a boat continually reconstructed while underway. And Emerson's reconciliation to "imperfect opinion" is quite modern and un-

Platonic—at least if we are thinking, as Dewey is in *The Quest for Certainty*, of the Plato who valued certainty instead of the Plato who wrote myths and saw truth emerging dialectically.

Emerson's experimentalism infiltrates not only his religion and his metaphysics but his philosophy of language. "All symbols are fluxional," he writes in "The Poet," indicating the impermanence he sees even in those instruments with which we order change. He says too that "all language is vehicular and transitive, and is good, as ferries and horses are, for conveyance, not as farms and houses are, for homestead."[29] Language here is treated as an instrument needed for some result, not as mirroring some preexisting reality. Emerson's position is not distant from Dewey's views that ideas are operations to be performed[30] or that, as R. W. Sleeper puts it, "essences are provisional."[31]

Section IV

The romantic writers of the late eighteenth century saw children not as incomplete adults but as wise, original beings whose freshness of vision should be recaptured in adulthood. In the "Immortality Ode," for example, Wordsworth portrays the child as the "best Philosopher, . . . On whom truths do rest, Which we are toiling all our lives to find." Emerson, who traveled to England as a young man to meet Wordsworth, Coleridge, and Carlyle, often speaks of the autonomy, wisdom, and freedom of children. "Their mind being whole, their eye is as yet unconquered. . . . Infancy conforms to nobody; all conform to it; so that one babe commonly makes four or five out of the adults who prattle and play to it."[32] Children are not just self-reliant; they are wiser than many adults. "The idiot, the Indian, the child and unschooled farmer's boy," Emerson ends "History" by writing, "stand nearer to the light by which nature is to be read, than the dissector or the antiquary."[33] But the child, Emerson maintains, must be allowed his freedom to be what he is. He warns against "the cramping influence of a hard formalist on a young child, in repressing his spirits and courage, paralyzing the understanding."[34] And he advocates action, life itself, as the proper means of education. "Life is our dictionary," he writes in "The American Scholar." "Colleges and books only copy the language which the field and the work-yard made."[35] Even history is not best learned from books but from our own political and social experiences: "The student interprets the age of chivalry by his own age of chivalry, and the days of maritime adventure and circumnavigation by quite parallel miniature experiences of his own."[36] In such early works on education as "My Pedagogic Creed," published in 1897, Dewey too advocates that education not be separated from life. It is, he maintains, "a process of living and not a preparation for future living . . . that education which does not occur through forms of life, forms that are worth living for their own sake, is always a poor substitute for the genuine reality, and tends to cramp and deaden."[37] If Wordsworth finds the experience of the adult to be hollow and restricted, then Emerson and Dewey are saying that society should counter such forms of being-in-the-world early on, in its schools.

Dewey's thoughts about children were shaped not only by Emerson but by Rousseau. In *Schools of Tomorrow*, for example, he uses Rousseau's *Emile* to develop the importance of experience, of play, and of the body in education. Central to Rousseau's outlook (as it is to Emerson's) is a sense of the inherent powers of the child. "Rousseau said, as well as did, many foolish things," Dewey begins *Schools of Tomorrow* by writing. "But his insistence that education be based upon the native capacities of those to be taught and upon the need of studying children in order to disclose what these native powers are, sounded the key-note of all modern efforts for educational progress."[38] Dewey takes up Rousseau again in his educational magnum opus of 1916, *Democracy and Education*, where he praises him for encouraging respect for the natural aims and interests of the child and for emphasizing the body's role in developing them. But Dewey also criticizes Rousseau for equating the natural and the physical and for devaluing our intellectual practices. Dewey reveals a side of his thoughts too frequently missed by both his admirers and his critics when he maintains that children need guidance and that Rousseau erred in thinking everything can just be left to nature.[39] Instead of looking to Rousseau for a fully adequate position, Dewey turns to Emerson. Warning against "idealizing" childhood by accepting everything the child does as an end in itself but committed at the same time to respecting the child's "natural instincts," Dewey finds that "the true principle of respect for immaturity, cannot be better put, than in the words of Emerson," who wrote that one should "respect the child," and not be "too much his parent," but also that one should respect oneself. "The two points in a boy's training are, to keep his *naturel* and train off all but that; to keep his *naturel*, but stop off his uproar, fooling, and horseplay; keep his nature *and arm it with knowledge in the very direction in which it points*."[40] Dewey wants children interested and self-reliant so that they will learn, but he also sees such learning as the track left by a life absorbed in the values of the present. Learning, for Dewey, is not an end-product. In *Reconstruction in Philosophy*, published four years after *Democracy and Education*, Dewey defines education as "getting from the present the degree and kind of growth there is in it." This statement reflects the orientation of a section of *Democracy and Education* called "Education as Reconstruction," in which Dewey argues that the reorganizing effected by education is constant: its goal, the "chief business of life," is to "make living ... contribute to an enrichment of its own perceptible meaning."[41]

Whether figured as "reconstruction" in Dewey or as "remaking" in Emerson, the picture of a life of constant, interested, and creative education is a common theme in this "transcendentalist" and this "pragmatist." By tracing this and other connections between Dewey and Emerson, I hope to have given the sense that the links between our early and late nineteenth-century American philosophers are various and rich and that they constitute what Emerson calls an "undiscovered region of thought."[42]

Notes

1. Ralph Waldo Emerson, *The Collected Works of Ralph Waldo Emerson,* ed. Robert Spiller et al. (Cambridge, Mass., and London: Belknap Press, 1971), vol. 2, p. 189. Compare p. 204, where he places Heraclitus among a group, including Empedocles, Plato, and Proclus, of "grandees . . . so vast in their logic, so primary in their thinking" that their thought is "at once poetry, and music, and dancing, and astronomy, and mathematics."

2. Ibid. pp. 180–81.

3. Ibid., vol. 3, p. 40.

4. The current outpouring on the transcendentalists by professors of English includes B. L. Packer, *Emerson's Fall* (New York: Continuum, 1984); Sharon Cameron, *Writing Nature* (New York: Oxford University Press, 1985); David Van Leer, *Emerson's Epistemology* (Cambridge: Cambridge University Press, 1986); Evan Carton, *The Rhetoric of American Romance* (Baltimore: Johns Hopkins University Press, 1985); and Leon Chai, *The Romantic Foundations of the American Renaissance* (Ithaca, N.Y.: Cornell University Press, 1987). For recent writing on Emerson by philosophers, see Stanley Cavell, "Genteel Responses to Kant in Emerson's 'Fate' and Coleridge's *Biographia Literaria,*" *Raritan* (1983); Cavell, "Thinking of Emerson" and "An Emerson Mood," in Stanley Cavell, *The Senses of Walden, an Expanded Edition* (San Francisco: North Point Press, 1981); Darnell Rucker "Philosophy and the Constitution of Emerson's World," in Timothy Fuller, ed., *Something of Great Constancy* (Colorado Springs: Colorado College, 1979), pp. 76–101 (which both notes the tendency to treat Emerson as a nonphilosopher and works to correct it); John McDermott, "Spires of Influence: The Importance of James and Dewey for Classical American Philosophy," in *Streams of Experience* (Amherst: University of Massachusetts Press, 1986); and Russell B. Goodman, "Freedom in the Philosophy of Ralph Waldo Emerson," *Tulane Studies in Philosophy* (New Orleans: Tulane University Press, 1987), pp. 5–10.

5. See, for example, Elizabeth Flower and Murray Murphey, *A History of Philosophy in America* (New York: G. P. Putnam's Sons, 1977); Joseph Blau, *Men and Movements in American Philosophy* (Englewood Cliffs, N.J.: Prentice Hall, 1952); John Smith, *The Spirit of American Philosophy* (New York: Oxford University Press, 1963); and John Stuhr, *Classical American Philosophy* (New York: Oxford University Press, 1986). Sheldon Peterfreund calls Emerson a "quasi-philosopher" in *An Introduction to American Philosophy* (Rucker, "Philosophy and Constitution," pp. 76–77). However, see also Russell B. Goodman, *Pragmatism: A Contemporary Reader* (New York and London: Routledge, 1995).

6. Though the new alignment I am proposing knits American thinkers such as Emerson and Dewey more closely together, at the same time it reveals connections between the Americans and such European thinkers as Rousseau, Nietzsche, and Heidegger. For connections with Wordsworth, Rousseau, and others, see sect. 3 and my *American Philosophy and the Romantic Tradition* (Cambridge: Cambridge University Press, 1990). On Emerson and Nietzsche see Van Leer, *Emerson's Epistemology,* p. 217, note

52; and Rucker, "Philosophy and Constitution," p. 100. On Emerson and Heidegger see Cavell, "Thinking of Emerson."

7. John Dewey, *The Middle Works of John Dewey,* vol. 3, ed. Jo Ann Boydston (Carbondale and Edwardsville: Southern Illinois University Press, 1977), pp. 188–89.

8. Emerson, *The Collected Works of Ralph Waldo Emerson,* vol. 2, p. 203.

9. Dewey, *The Middle Works of John Dewey,* vol. 3, p. 188.

10. John Dewey, *The Later Works of John Dewey,* vol. 4, ed. Jo Ann Boydston (Carbondale and Edwardsville: Southern Illinois University Press, 1984), pp. 240–41.

11. Emerson, *The Collected Works of Ralph Waldo Emerson,* vol. 2, p. 159.

12. Emerson, *The Collected Works of Ralph Waldo Emerson,* vol. 1, p. 10. The last sentence of this quotation is from the familiar 1849 edition of Emerson's works. The original reads, "Almost I fear to think how glad I am."

13. Dewey, *The Middle Works of John Dewey,* vol. 3, p. 189.

14. Emerson, *The Collected Works of Ralph Waldo Emerson,* vol. 2, p. 198.

15. Ibid., p. 199.

16. Dewey, *The Later Works of John Dewey,* vol. 4, pp. 164–65.

17. Emerson, *The Collected Works of Ralph Waldo Emerson,* vol. 1, pp. 150, 159.

18. Emerson, *The Collected Works of Ralph Waldo Emerson,* vol. 2, p. 28.

19. Emerson, *The Collected Works of Ralph Waldo Emerson,* vol. 1, p. 57.

20. Ibid., p. 67.

21. Ibid., pp. 36, 39.

22. Ibid., p. 31.

23. Emerson, *The Collected Works of Ralph Waldo Emerson,* vol. 2, p. 198.

24. Dewey, *The Later Works of John Dewey,* vol. 4, pp. 241, 237, 248.

25. Ibid., pp. 4, 90.

26. Emerson, *The Collected Works of Ralph Waldo Emerson,* vol. 2, p. 188.

27. Emerson, *The Collected Works of Ralph Waldo Emerson,* vol. 3, p. 47.

28. Emerson, *The Collected Works of Ralph Waldo Emerson,* vol. 2, p. 202.

29. Emerson, *The Collected Works of Ralph Waldo Emerson,* vol. 3, p. 20.

30. Dewey, *The Later Works of John Dewey,* vol. 4, p. 92.

31. R. W. Sleeper, *The Necessity of Pragmatism* (New Haven: Yale University Press, 1986), p. 69.

32. Emerson, *The Collected Works of Ralph Waldo Emerson,* vol. 2, pp. 28–29.

33. Ibid., p. 23.

34. Ibid., p. 16.

35. Emerson, *The Collected Works of Ralph Waldo Emerson,* vol. 1, p. 61.

36. Emerson, *The Collected Works of Ralph Waldo Emerson,* vol. 2, p. 15.

37. John Dewey, *The Early Works of John Dewey,* vol. 5, ed. Jo Ann Boydston (Carbondale and Edwardsville: Southern Illinois University Press, 1972), p. 87.

38. John Dewey, *The Middle Works of John Dewey,* vol. 8, ed. Jo Ann Boydston (Carbondale and Edwardsville: Southern Illinois University Press, 1979), p. 211.

39. John Dewey, *The Middle Works of John Dewey,* vol. 9, ed. Jo Ann Boydston (Carbondale and Edwardsville: Southern Illinois University Press, 1980), p. 99.

40. Ibid., p. 57. Emerson's statement appears in his essay "Education," in Ralph Waldo Emerson, *Lectures and Biographical Sketches* (Boston and New York: Houghton Mifflin, 1904), p. 144.

41. Dewey, *The Middle Works of John Dewey,* vol. 9, p. 82.

42. Emerson, *The Collected Works of Ralph Waldo Emerson,* vol. 1, p. 41.

COMMUNITY AND CULTURE

The Search for Commonality in a Diverse World

PATRICK J. HILL

To be a Christian feminist is to be deluded. For a woman to remain in the Catholic Church is akin to a black person being in the Ku-Klux-Klan.

Mary Daly

Despite all our differences in political and philosophical views, in ideals and values, we must remember one thing: we are all keepers of the flame of life handed down to us by earlier generations.

Mikhail Gorbachev

Section I

I was in London last year during the elections. At that time, the English government was in the process of denying a petition of the Irish people in England to be classified officially as a minority and thus to be given the same access to the several privileges accorded persons more acknowledgedly different from the British majority as the peoples from Jamaica and India. A few days later, I met with theologians in Belfast who were struggling to rid their understanding of Christianity from any essential connection to the partisan histories and cultures of the warring factions of that troubled land.[1] Subsequently, I visited with cousins in the south of Ireland who had never questioned their identification with either a narrow strip of earth in the midlands of Ireland or with just one of the partisan versions of the Christian message fueling the war to their north. Back in the United States, the value of the seemingly provincial outlook of my cousins was echoed by Native American philosopher Vine Deloria, who attacked the quest for universal meaning and defended tribal meanings ultimately rooted in land and history as the sole source of vitality in religions and philosophies.

The issues underlying the dynamics of Celtic and Native American societies are echoed in many quarters. The concern of the Irish theologians to evolve a more civilizing religion is paralleled in Gorbachev's reconciliatory speech in 1985 to the French parliament, quoted above, in which capitalist and socialist societies were urged "to rise above our differences,"[2] as it is in Jesse Jackson's efforts to build coalitions among hitherto distant subcultures. In the other direction, the separatist or decentralizing resistance to "false universalism" of the Irish in Britain or of Native Americans is echoed in the feminist critique of patriarchal Christianity, the extent of which is sampled in the above quotation from Mary Daly,[3] and in the countless attempts within our institutions, our nations, and our world to gain the space and liberty to articulate the dignity of a new and different version of the human story. The issues were eloquently stated in John McDermott's ground-clearing essay "The Community of Experience and Religious Metaphors."

> [W]e come to the most crucial question in the problems of belief and modern [men and women], namely: are we able to believe together as a community without suppressing our differences? And can this belief have truly religious significance for us, that is open us to the endowed and sacred quality of all that is, while not yet offering a hierarchy of meanings, fixed or holy things which divide us from our (brothers and sisters)? Can we actually celebrate this belief? Celebrate it in the way of historical religion, that is liturgically, or in the way of contemporary protest movements, with song and ritual born of adversity? Or is it to remain an abstract goal, a containment keeping us from destroying each other but without building new symbols of human solidarity and affection?[4]

The present essay is a reflection in a Deweyan vein on the search for commonality in an increasingly diverse world. I seek to clarify the nature of that search, to distinguish it from both sentimental and illiberal quests for a less complex and more manageable world, and to reflect within the framework of democratic values on what it makes sense to do and not to do in that search.

Section II

I begin with three preliminary observations of a general sort. The first observation, the most abstract of the paper, concerns the nature of commonality and diversity, or sameness and difference. Commonality or its opposite is not an objective property of two or more objects or groups or beliefs or belief-systems. Instead, it is a judgment that we make in assimilating two or more things for some particular purpose and in some particular context. Further, sets of belief that appear dissimilar in one context may appear virtually identical in another.

Baptists and Catholics could be said to have extremely dissimilar spiritualities but seem in comparison with Judaism to share the most fundamental and animating beliefs. All three religions in comparison with secular humanism seem more similar than different in crucial respects; and yet Marxists and Christians in Nicaragua find much in common and appear to the established order as part of a single conspiracy.[5]

This sort of contextual analysis, secondly, needs to be extended from the nature of assimilating and differentiating judgments to the value we attribute to commonality and diversity. In those parts of the world where our lives are characterizable as isolated and alienated, and in those global regions where nothing seems as pressing as agreement on nuclear disarmament or environmental endangerment or the senseless starvation of children, it is hard to resist believing that a commitment to community is unqualifiedly valuable and that only the selfish withhold such a commitment. It is easy, further, to believe that what is common is inherently more valuable and even more self-defining than what is diverse and unshared.

We will, in my judgment, make no progress in forging a concept of community appropriate to the contemporary world unless we abandon the notion that what is common is inherently more valuable than what is diverse. It is that assumption that has led many people to characterize the notion of community as essentially illiberal if not totalitarian. The messy truth is this: sometimes what is common is more important for some purposes than what is diverse, and sometimes the opposite is true. Moreover, even when the case seems strongest for the greater importance of what is held in common, it will often seem otherwise to other groups. The comparative noninvolvement of the minority populations of this country in the nuclear disarmament issue is a case in point.

The third observation, an implication of the previous two, might be described as the rationalist assumption about the importance of an articulated set of beliefs or doctrines in the generation and sustaining of community. Philosophers and theologians are understandably preoccupied with this dimension of communal life, but it is indeed only one dimension. In some contexts, e.g., the Husserl Society, a shared set of beliefs is necessary and perhaps nearly a sufficient condition for sustaining a viable community. In other contexts, shared beliefs may be at most a necessary condition for sustaining community. More complicatedly still, communities can be sustained with remarkable diversity of belief, and pressures toward unanimity of belief are not welcomed. Lastly, as an important instance of the two previous observations and of the overall role of ideas in history, one and the same articulation of what unites can be ignored for decades or centuries only to become in another period a revitalization of an ancient community or the generating insight of a new one. The rationalist assumption might be regarded as benign did it not detract attention from those actions that might indeed be helpful in generating perceptions of significant commonality in appropriate times and places.[6]

These observations suggest a clarification of what it is we are seeking—or ought to be seeking—as we pursue the emergence of greater commonality. First, under what conditions do commonalities come to be perceived by hitherto distant or dissimilar groups and judged by them to be more important than (or attractively compatible with) the always present diversities? Secondly, and as importantly, what if anything can or ought to be done in this or that circumstance to hasten the emergence of shared perceptions of significant commonality?[7]

Section III

How did the Germans and the French come to see themselves as Europeans, or (almost as amazingly) how did Virginians and West Virginians come to see themselves as Americans? Even a rudimentary understanding of the conditions under which commonalities come to be perceived and judged to be more important than differences would require a full-length interdisciplinary study. Here, more for the sake of clarifying the nature of the inquiry than for answering the question, I mention but a few of the often neglected factors that are relevant in the formation and sustenance of the perception of significant commonality.

(1) *A common enemy*. Few things make our differences seem as insignificant as a threat from the outside. The unifying impact of war upon hitherto diverse societies has attracted the sustained attention of sociologists of community.[8] In a more recent example, Jesse Jackson's division of the world into the barracudas and the little fish enabled many white farmers to identify with other exploited people whom they had hitherto scorned.

(2) *The challenge of a cooperative adventure*. Given the opportunity to participate in a gripping adventure that requires our cooperation, our energies focus on the goal and only incidentally upon our differences. This insight underlaid the team-building efforts of Willi Unsoeld's "Outward Bound" program. Eric Hoffer, among others, called our attention to the extraordinary drop-off in energy and cooperation when the task turned from that of building an institution to that of maintaining it.

(3) *The intolerability of continuing the enmity*. All negotiators understand that the perception of differences will change over time as the consequences of rigidity mount. Peacemakers in Belfast elicit their greatest response following incidents that make it obvious that the violence will not end. Gorbachev hopes that capitalist and socialist societies have reached the point of intolerability.

(4) *The passage of time*. What Kuhn said about changes in the thinking of scientists applies to the thought patterns of many groups. If the source of continuing

enmity has been removed, the children will feel less strongly about the differences for which their fathers fought.

This incomplete list of conditions under which perceptions of significant commonality emerge might provide a useful framework for a research agenda. More interestingly, perhaps, is the extent to which the list provides any guidance for action. The unifying impact of a common enemy has been used to manipulate whole populations into concerted action. Less destructively, the adventure of artificially created danger has been used to build at least temporary communities based upon the need under those circumstances to trust one's companions. Two ethical constraints come immediately to mind when we begin to think about employing any of these insights. The first constraint is that we are committed to respecting the value of diversity. Secondly and relatedly, we are operating within the context of democratic values. Together the constraints amount to a prohibition—more or less absolute—of manipulative techniques or solutions imposed without the consent of the diverse other.

Where does that leave us? In the hands of the gods, some will answer. Although acknowledging in the end some important extent to which the emergence of community depends on factors other than our efforts, there is yet much that creative intelligence can contribute to the emergence of the perception of significant commonality. I list below three such contributions.

(1) *Intellectual, artistic, and political vision.* Despite the rationalist assumption described above, intellectuals, artists, and politicians frequently contribute to the perception of significant commonality in forging visions that challenge us to see ourselves as more like than unlike other groups. In the context of Northern Ireland, Daniel Martin and Ian Adamson have articulated broader, reconciling identities for the warring factions: the former through Celtic spirituality that predates any version of Christianity,[9] the latter through the shared history and geographical uniqueness of the land of Ulster.[10] In the context of sectarian religion, Thomas Berry has bypassed sterile ecumenism in proposing in a Teilhardian vein that we view the universe itself as "the primary religious reality" and the diversity of religious experience not as a hindrance to religious goals but as an enrichment and a resource for sustaining the asymmetry and unbalance characteristic of life and creativity.[11] "The power of these visions, important as they are philosophically, theologically and even politically, are but one dimension, perhaps not even a necessary much less a sufficient dimension for many people, in effecting the emergence of widespread perceptions of significant commonality among hitherto distant or conflicting peoples."

(2) *Shared purposes.* We need not sit upon our hands waiting for some environmental catastrophe to engulf distant or warring parties. We can seek to identify interests that are shared: not what ought to be shared, but which are de

facto shared by the separate parties. In Northern Ireland, Catholics and Protestants have cooperated in caring for the children of victims of the war. In many states of this country, majority and minority populations are cooperating in addressing a problem that threatens the survival of business, the university, and the minority populations: namely, the alarming nonretention rate of our students of color in secondary schools. For these purposes, we are in the same boat. Out of such cooperation may emerge fewer hard-edged conceptions of the separateness of our identities.

(3) *Creating conditions of reciprocity.* The problem of effecting a perception of significant commonality was addressed explicitly by Dewey for one specific context: namely, education. What he said is of course limited by that context, but it is nonetheless instructive. In a passage that I regard as the single most important insight about our quest for commonality, Dewey wrote: "Setting up conditions which stimulate certain visible and tangible ways of acting is the first step. Making the individual a sharer or partner in the associated activity so that he feels its success as his success, its failure as his failure, is the completing step. As soon as he is possessed by the emotional attitude of a group, he will be alert to recognize the special ends at which it aims and the means employed to secure success. His beliefs and ideas, in other words, will take a form similar to those of others in the group."[12]

Two important suggestions of this passage deserve our attention.

(1) Obviously, it has to be adapted to be relevant to nonclassroom situations. In trying to effect a common political agenda regarding nuclear disarmament, those who are already committed to the importance of that issue are not in the relationship of teacher to child with respect to those who regard the unemployment of Catholics in Northern Ireland or apartheid in South Africa as the most important issue. But in this situation and in the educational context, there is a disparate set of evaluations that, according to Dewey, can be made similar (though not necessarily preserving the preexisting valuations of either party) to the extent that conditions are established that effect what Dewey refers to as "reciprocity of interests."[13] The claim, of course, is not that a reciprocity of interests preexists but that if conditions are established that confer the status of partner on the diverse other, then in time there will emerge a framework of shared beliefs and valuations (within which even greater diversity might still flourish). What it means to confer the status of partner will vary greatly from the context of the classroom to international relations to male-female relations in churches and temples. What is important in any of these efforts to secure a perception of significant commonality is a movement away from a monological or hierarchical transmission of information and away as well from mere dialogue toward the actual creation of the material conditions of genuine partnership. This will allow the participants in the associated

activity to perceive themselves as having a significant voice and stake in defining a common future.[14]

(2) For this transformation of the search for a common faith, of the quest for shared perceptions of significant commonality, to be accepted, at least two additional issues of a profound sort would have to be faced. The most obvious would be the willingness of those in positions of power and authority to create, with appropriate haste, conditions of genuine partnership for those currently in excluded or subordinate positions. The second, a function of the nature of one's vision of the future, would be the question of whom to include in the associated activities. The interplay of power and vision is exemplified in Denis Goulet's perhaps generalizable reflections on First World-Third World relations. "Wisdom for our times can only emerge from creative dialogue—conducted in the mode of reciprocity—between 'old' and 'new' societies. Such reciprocity can only be achieved if all patterns of domination, cultural no less than economic, are abolished."[15]

Section IV

In the rephrasing of the search for commonality, we asked above, what if anything can or ought to be done in this or that circumstance to hasten the emergence of shared perceptions of significant commonality? We have addressed the question of what could be done. Were we to ignore the question of what ought to be done, we would be contributing to the perpetuation of the tendency to regard what is common as more important than what is diverse or separate.

Those who have participated in any attempt to define a new identity or a new movement or a new society recognize the need for isolation from at least the dominating other and perhaps from all but those of an extreme like-mindedness. In that isolation, one defines a different agenda and gains support and time and opportunities to create without the distraction of the other's incomprehension, impatience, curiosity, and judgment. The isolation is, at least temporarily, a source of creativity and vitality. Despite the importance in many contexts of what we all share as human beings, or as believers in one or another form of divine presence, there is a more pressing and equally religious imperative. "Women in contemporary churches are suffering from linguistic deprivation and eucharistic famine. They can no longer nurture their souls in alienating words that ignore or systematically deny their existence. They are starved for the words of life, for symbolic forms that fully and wholeheartedly affirm their personhood and speak truth about the evils of sexism and the possibilities of a future beyond patriarchy. They desperately need primary communities that nurture their journey into wholeness, rather than constantly negating and thwarting it."[16]

In a democratic society, the search for commonality must celebrate—not just tolerate—separate or newly separating "primary communities." They are to be encouraged, not only as a political right but, more importantly, in the sense that our commonality will eventually be enriched by their exploration. There are excesses to be avoided, as Dewey noted, particularly those that threaten the existence of other communities—in that sense, the recognition of our abstract commonality remains important—and those that might yield a systematic or long-term isolation from other communities.[17]

In the end, no matter how burning the thirst for commonality or reconciliation, no matter how great the need for concerted action, once those who are searching within the context of democratic values for commonality have exhausted creative options such as those listed above, it ought to be accepted and even celebrated that the time is not yet ripe. And in that limited sense, the matter is not entirely in our hands.

Notes

1. Inter-Church Group on Faith and Politics, *Choose Life: Christian Responses to the Northern Ireland Conflict* (Belfast: Privately published, 1986).

2. William F. Brazier and Joel S. Hellman, "Gorbachev's New World View," *Social Policy* 18 (no. 1, summer, 1987).

3. Paul Surlis, "Third International Congress on Women," Report on the Third International Interdisciplinary Congress on Women, Dublin, July 6–10, 1987, *The Ecumenist* (vol. 26, no. 3, March–April, 1988): 39.

4. John McDermott, "The Community of Experience and Religious Metaphors," *The Culture of Experience* (New York: New York University Press, 1976), pp. 70–71.

5. This analysis of judgments of commonality and diversity was, of course, generalized by Wittgenstein. The most thorough exploration of its consequences is in a much-neglected book, Rupert Crawshay-Williams's *Methods and Criteria of Reasoning* (London: Routledge and Kegan Paul, 1957). In his chapter "Empirical Criteria," he concludes on p. 23, "If two qualities are correctly called the same, this in itself is not sufficient ground for concluding that they cannot be correctly called different (and vice versa)."

6. An understanding of a more limited role of shared faith seems to be emerging in recent literature on the history of Christianity and on contemporary ecumenism. Though the New Testament characterized Jesus Christ as "the same yesterday and today and forever" (*Epistle to the Hebrews* 13:8), Jaroslav Pelikan's intellectual and cultural history of Christianity concludes that "it is not sameness but kaleidoscopic variety that is its most conspicuous feature" (Jaroslav Pelikan, *Jesus through the Centuries* [New York: Harper and Row, 1985], p. 2). Even within a limited historical period, that diversity of belief is obvious: it was obvious to Abelard in the twelfth century and it is obvious today, even within a single sect of Christianity. That diversity of belief has led some theologians to abandon a belief in anything approaching the essence of Christianity and to reconceive the basis of Christian community in terms of allegedly shared ethical goals (Ronald F. Marshall, "Exploring Christian Unity," *The Ecumenist* [vol. 26, no. 3, March–April, 1988]: 33–34). Others locate the origins of community in a wider socio-historical and psychological web in which faith plays a surprisingly nonmajor role.

Faith bonds with the senses. As philosopher Ernest Gellner says, "Traditional cultures smell." They may smell of incense or garlic, the must of sweeping compound in churches or the coffee pot perking during an overlong sermon before social hour. Faith, no matter what the purists say, comes as a package deal. It is part of a life fired point-blank at believers. I, for one, admit that a visit to a nearly empty sanctuary where an organist is practicing on a Saturday afternoon does more for building my faith than does reading systematic theology. If so, I am recognizing that faith comes along with connotations and supports. I will not nurture these elements if I am blurred and blended into a nondescript communion.

(Martin E. Marty, *The Public Church* [New York: Crossroad Pub. Co., 1981], p. 78.)

7. This descriptive or historical rephrasing of the question ought not to be interpreted as an elimination of the normative dimension of a philosophy of community. It is merely a first step. The normative dimension, obvious even in Dewey, with whom this rephrasing is most compatible, reenters as we attempt to shape responses in a certain value-direction.

The rephrasing recalls historian David Russo's critique of nondescriptive and noninterdisciplinary approaches to the study of community. With a touch of self-indulgence, he wrote:

What makes all these efforts at definition by sociologists like Konig and theologian-philosophers like Buber ultimately unsatisfactory is the failure of these individuals to be good historians as well. Their attempts to grasp the essential nature of community are excessively schematic. Just as the meaning of the term *community* has changed, over the centuries of western history, so too have the actual shape and substance of the communities themselves changed. Sociologists, in their attempt to understand contemporary society, are not sufficiently aware of the long, varied life of humanity in villages, cities, and nations to make definitions that stand the test of time. Philosophers are too concerned with the ultimate meaning of community to be sufficiently aware of the complicated and variegated shape of their subject when it is examined in the matrix of actual human experience.

This means that historians are—theoretically at least—in the best position to comment on the meanings of community through human history. As to definition, one is tempted to urge that students of community allow the people whom they study to say what a community is. The people who live in them have always had some perception of what communities are. This suggestion is contrary to much of twentieth-century philosophy, as well as social and physical scientific theorizing which has placed a great deal of emphasis in linguistic precision. But it is by no means obvious whether the lack of consensus—and precision—that frequently follows such efforts leaves us in a better position than we were in when we relied upon the vague, imprecise terms evolved in common parlance.

(David J. Russo, *Families and Communities* [Nashville: The American Association for State and Local History, 1974], pp. 11–12.)

8. Robert Nisbet, *The Social Philosophers* (New York: Thomas Y. Crowell Co., 1973).

9. Daniel Martin, "Celtic Spirituality: Towards a United-Separate Ireland" (unpublished manuscript, 1987).

10. Ian Adamson, *The Identity of Ulster: The Land, the Language, and the People* (Belfast: Pretani Press, 1982), p. 108.

Adamson advanced a concept of community akin to the land-based tribalism of Native Americans. Quoting the nineteenth-century Ulster poet Samuel Ferguson, he urged the writing of a history so that "men may feel that we are not come into the world strangers, but members of a family long planted in the land before them, giving reverence to the place and institutions of their forefathers and by that common sentiment strengthening the social bond among one another."

11. Anne Lonergan and Caroline Richards, eds., *Thomas Berry and the New Cosmology* (Connecticut: Twenty-third Pub., 1987), pp. 35–37.

12. John Dewey, *Democracy and Education* (New York: The Free Press, 1976), p. 14.

13. Ibid., p. 85.

14. One possible application of Dewey's insight to the political realm is given in Michael Ignatieff's recent book, *The Needs of Strangers*. The author argues forcefully for the importance of our recognizing and basing action upon a common human nature. He judges, however, that modernity has ushered in an insatiability of desires and with it a predisposition to identify ourselves with our differences instead of our commonality. He concludes with a suggestion in the spirit of Rousseau, quoted here solely to illustrate the perceived interaction in a noneducational context between changed conditions and perceptions of commonality.

> Millions of people have perished since 1945 in the wars, revolutions and civil strife safely conducted under the umbrella of a nuclear peace. . . . Most of this dying has been in the name of freedom, in the name of liberation from a colonial, tribal, religious or racial oppressor. It is a waste of breath to press the claims of common human identity on men and women prepared to die in defense of their claims of difference. There will be no end to the dying and no time for the claim of our common species being, until each people is safe within its borders, with a sovereignty which makes them masters of their needs. Only when difference has its home, when the need for belonging in all its murderous intensity has been assuaged, can our common identity begin to find its voice.

(Michael Ignatieff, *The Needs of Strangers* [New York: Viking-Penguin Books, 1985], p. 131.)

15. Denis Goulet, "A Summary Statement," *Review of Social Economy* (September, 1968): v–120.

16. Rosemary Radford Reuther, *Women-Church* (New York: Harper and Row, 1985), p. 38.

17. Although Dewey did not specifically address the phenomenon of a separating community, he did indeed address the phenomenon of long-term separateness. He employed two criteria for evaluating communities, both functions of his primary concern with growth. The first criterion was the number and variety of the interests consciously shared by the group. The second, more relevant to the concerns of this paper, was the fullness and freedom of the interplay with other communities. "An undesirable society . . . is one which internally and externally sets up barriers to free intercourse and communication of experience" (Dewey, *Democracy and Education*, p. 99). When full and free interplay with other communities is absent, according to Dewey, an inward orientation develops that turns the prevailing purpose of the community toward "the protection of what it has got instead of reorganizations and progress toward wider relationships" (Dewey, *Democracy and Education*, p. 86).

Community and the Cultural Frontier

JOHN J. STUHR

The essay that follows, like life, has no introduction. We find ourselves always in process, unsure but surely underway. Any explanation, criticism, change of course, or reconstruction must be made on the move, piecemeal, and imperfectly.

And so these observations, like all experience, will yield no certainty, complete or lasting generality, guarantee, final conclusion, or proof. With Emerson I say, "I hope it is somewhat better than whim at last, but we cannot spend the day in explanation."[1] This fact, of course, marks a parameter instead of an incapacity for our thought, as Peirce made clear.[2] Accordingly, it is not cause for regret. Wallace Stevens captures this in "The Poems of Our Climate": "The imperfect is our paradise. / Note that, in this bitterness, delight, / Since the imperfect is so hot in us, / Lies in flawed words and stubborn sounds."[3]

Although undeniably situated and socially conditioned, these words and sounds are also irreducibly personal in origin, form, and aim. Thus Whitman announces: "Behold, I do not give lectures or a little charity./ When I give I give myself."[4] As James showed, thought is owned,[5] and philosophy, even professional philosophy, is inescapably biographical, and so, at its best, personal vision. "Vision is the great fact. . . . A philosophy is the expression of a man's intimate character, and all the definitions of the universe are but the deliberately adopted reactions of human characters upon it."[6] The upshot of James's work, Santayana tells us in his critical discussion of the "genteel tradition," is that we now "need not be afraid of being less profound, for being direct and sincere"[7] and that the intellectual world, perhaps in spite of some scholarly work in the humanities today, must be and legitimately may be traversed in many ways and in many directions.

My direction here is this: I intend a series of forays or border raids on, through, and toward an American philosophical and cultural frontier. To do this, I suspect, is to transgress present boundaries and take up residence in marginal territories. In attempting this, here at least form may follow function. My exploratory purpose may require an unfamiliar, even camouflaged, form, a frontier outfitting and strategy that may be risky, nonconformist, and, as William Carlos Williams put it, unsanctioned. "This is plainly not scholarship, neither is it a man. It is writing about knowledge which must seize a sanction before it can seriously proceed, valid in the eyes of scholarship itself."[8]

To think at the frontier: this is a difficult requirement for American philosophers (and perhaps an ironic theme for an academic conference and scholarly book—hardly frontier formats for thought). The difficulty results not simply from the fact that we have become habituated to philosophical inquiry done in the safety of established intellectual settlements guarded by professional garrisons of scholars. The difficulty of "thinking at the frontier" of and in American philosophy stems mainly from the fact that "thinking at the frontier" is itself a settled and long-established form of thought and goal for characteristically American philosophers.

Of course, we too may set out for the philosophical frontier. We pack with us Emerson, James, and Dewey, for instance, gaining inspiration from them, using their categories and methods, quoting their brilliant passages, and citing their work. These activities do seem familiar, I trust! But in proceeding this way, we often fail to embody knowledge,[9] fail to reach new frontiers. We thus often resemble not genuine explorers but heavily laden campers in shiny, plush motor homes, rising for another day of dependence and long apprenticeship.[10]

We do this despite the clear warnings of the American tradition itself. What the philosophers of earlier periods did, Dewey tells us, is no longer called for,[11] and so we now must apply the logic of experience to our own needs. "Emphasis must vary with the stress and special impact of the troubles which perplex men. Each age knows its own ills, and seeks it own remedies."[12] If philosophy avoids this, everything it touches is shopworn, James observes. He adds, as a consequence, "The overtechnicality and consequent dreariness of the younger disciples at our American universities is appalling."[13] Emerson is more direct, even blunt. "I hate quotations," he writes, and I quote uneasily; instead, "tell me what you know."[14]

There are, I too now believe, only few footnotes on the American philosophical frontier. And so in large part I will travel lightly here, relying confidently on your long study and collective understanding—not simply of Emerson, Thoreau, Peirce, James, Royce, Santayana, Dewey, Mead, Lewis, and Whitehead, but also earlier and later American philosophical writers. And when, perhaps bound by academic habits, I do not journey without citing these thinkers, I will recall them in the spirit of Whitman. "Do I contradict myself? / Very well then I contradict myself / (I am large, I contain multitudes)."[15]

In any case, any thought at this frontier cannot and will not be so much brand new as remade, reconstructed, reappropriated. Emerson, the hater of quotes, understood this too, of course. "In fact, it is as difficult to appropriate the thoughts of others as it is to invent."[16]

The American philosophical frontier, then, lies not simply in valuable scholarly recalling, repeating, rehearsing, fine-tuning, or defending characteristically

American thought, but also and especially in using, widening, extending, and reappropriating it so as to transform intelligently our lives in response to changing cultural frontiers. That is, the frontier of and for American philosophy is supplied by changing global conditions, by the frontiers of our culture.

However, it is not enough now simply to say all this, particularly in the abstract, perhaps with a devotional tone, and to sympathetic, well-meaning philosophers and other humanists. It may make for good conversation, but this conversational strategy, favored and employed by what I call right-wing pragmatists like Richard Rorty[17]—if there can be left-wing Hegelians then surely there can be right-wing pragmatists—evades the demand for critical cultural reconstruction at the frontier. In the work of right-wing pragmatists, Dewey's radical social criticism is missing, having been transformed and allowed to deteriorate into escapist postcard messages mailed from motor homes broken down near intellectual and cultural wilderness areas.

What else, then, does thinking at the frontier, appropriating the thought of others, entail? In his account of Daniel Boone, William Carlos Williams articulates both this task and its moral and aesthetic difficulties. He writes: "Boone had run past the difficulties encountered by his fellows in making the New World their own. . . . To Boone, the Indian was his greatest master. Not for himself surely to be an Indian, though they eagerly sought to adopt him into their tribes, but the reverse: to be himself in a new world, *Indianlike*."[18] Forty years later, Gary Snyder raised this issue in similar terms. "I would like, / with a sense of helpful order, / with respect for laws / of nature, / to help my land / with a burn, a hot clean / burn. / And then / it would be more / like, / when it belonged to the Indians. / Before."[19]

Is this simply nostalgia, a different kind of tame, romantic postcard message like that sent from Alaska by Richard Brautigan's character, Trout Fishing in America?[20] It has been a long time since America belonged to the Indians. Then, of course, America often (though not always) was described and understood by European explorers as a frontier paradise. In 1492, Columbus described the beauty, diversity, and richness of the New World. "There are mountains of very great size and beauty, vast plains, groves, and very fruitful fields, admirably adapted for tillage, pasture, and habitation. The convenience and excellence of the harbours in this island, and the abundance of the rivers, so indispensable to the health of man, surpass anything that would be believed by one who had not seen it."[21] Eleven years later, Amerigo Vespucci offered a similar account of this "terrestrial paradise." "The land is very fertile, abounding in many hills and valleys, and in large rivers, and is irrigated by very refreshing springs. It is covered with extensive and dense forests . . . and full of every kind of wild beast . . . and there are innumerable different kinds of fruits and herbs." He concluded, "If they were our property, I do not doubt but that they would be useful to man."[22] (At the 1968 Democratic Presidential Convention in Chicago 365 years later, poet Allen Ginsberg questioned this line of thinking, asking: who wants to own paradise, "Who wants to be President of the / Garden of Eden?")[23]

Vespucci was right that America would be useful—to some people, at least. We must remember that the historical physical American frontier was experienced quite differently by enslaved Africans transported to America, by women journeying west,[24] and by Indians viewing a new kind of wilderness with an advancing instead of receding frontier. Recall the words of Chief Seattle, necessarily but reluctantly signing a treaty in the Northwest in 1854. "It matters little where we pass the remnant of our days. They will not be many. A few more moons; a few more winters.... But why should I mourn at the untimely fate of my people? Tribe follows tribe, and nation follows nation, like the waves of the sea. It is the order of nature, and regret is useless. Your time of decay may be distant, but it will surely come, for even the White Man whose God walked and talked with him as friend with friend, cannot be exempt from the common destiny. We may be brothers after all."[25] (Similar and equally striking points about the flourishing and decay of schools or cultures of thought are made by Williams in "The Pluralism of Experience"[26] and by Sigurd Olson in "Frontiers."[27]

Surely *this* is not nostalgia. But still, the fact is that the much celebrated and analyzed American frontier[28]—the physical frontier and its particular kinds of opportunities for action, the open land and life to the west—is now long gone. Toxic chemicals routinely spill, flow, and seep into the great rivers, lakes, and groundwater of the Middle West. Black clouds of pollution hang over Denver, capital city of the plains. The greater Los Angeles area is expected to add more than six million people to its population by the year 2000. The Colorado, Snake, and Columbia rivers are dammed. The Oregon Trail is an interstate freeway, and the once pristine eastern Oregon deserts are covered with litter and torn up by off-road vehicles. Even Alaska is crisscrossed more and more by people, pipelines, and planes. In short, the city on the hill, the United States of America, has sprawled from coast to coast, and there is no physical frontier and precious little nature left in "nature's nation." The Eagles wrote and sang the clear, sad truth in "The Last Resort": "You call some place paradise / Kiss it goodbye / They call it paradise / I don't know why."[29]

Is there a new American frontier? Was Alaska, as some claim, the last American frontier? Or is Jacques Cousteau right—is the new frontier undersea? Or was Star Trek on target—is space the final frontier? Or, finally, is some inner (instead of outer) space the last frontier, beckoning "Inward Bound" enthusiasts and "New Age" pioneers to new drugs, new religions, and new genetic and cybernetic understandings, lifestyles, and lives?

Surely remaining pockets of wilderness—the sea, space, and the human mind itself—all are ripe for inquiry and exploration. In this sense, they unquestionably are new frontiers.

However, there is, in addition, another American frontier, another zone that continues to mark the limit of our expansion, development, and civilization.

Pervasive, pressing, significant, and experienced with overwhelming immediacy, it is a cultural, not a physical, frontier. Again, the Eagles summarized this succinctly. "There is no more new frontier / We have got to make it here."[30] Said differently, collectively "making it here" is the new frontier. In short, this cultural frontier constitutes the boundary or gap between the actually existing American *society*, on the one hand, and realization of a genuine American (and global) *community*, on the other.

This notion of community (and the contrast of community with mere society) is brilliantly articulated and deeply developed in classical American philosophy. In "The Body and the Members," Josiah Royce defines a community as selves who seek meaning and ideally enlarge their own lives so as to share an ideal common past and future. Such a community, Royce explains, requires selves capable of ideally and imaginatively extending themselves into the past and future, self-directing and cooperating selves capable of and engaged consciously in communication and appreciative coordination with one another, and selves who share goals and at least some common ideal experience. Concluding that a highly organized society is by no means identical to a community in this more precise sense, Royce adds, "There is a strong mutual opposition between the social tendencies which secure cooperation on a vast scale, and the very conditions which so interest the individual in the common life of his community that it forms part of his own ideally extended life."[31]

This has fundamental personal as well as social significance. As Mead (with Royce and Dewey, among others) makes clear, the self, unlike the organic body, is intrinsically a social structure. He writes: the individual becomes a self through communication, "not directly or immediately, not by becoming a subject to himself, but only in so far as he first becomes an object to himself just as other individuals are objects to him or in his experience; and he becomes an object to himself only by taking the attitudes of other individuals toward himself within a social environment or context of experience and behavior in which both he and they are involved."[32]

This is what Mead calls the "generalized other." But although the attitude or behavior of an organized social group is fundamental in the process of self-formation, I would claim that when the generalized other is an organized society that fails to be a genuine community, then the selves it helps form fail to be genuine individuals. Mead, writing with purposes different from mine here, may obscure this point by failing to distinguish, as Royce and Dewey do, the notion of society from that of community. For instance, he writes, "The organized community or social group . . . gives to the individual his unity of self."[33] But, in the absence of community, these selves are incomplete and undeveloped, deprived and unfulfilled, isolated and, as Dewey describes so well, lost.[34] The self, that is, arises in society, but individuals—selves with individuality—require (and in turn sustain) communities. For individuality to flourish, societies must become communities.

This need was thoroughly grasped, of course, by John Dewey in his writings on freedom, individualism, liberalism, and the public. He noted and analyzed this frontier for culture. "The beginning of a culture stripped of egoistic illusions is the perception that we have as yet no culture; that our culture is something to achieve, to create.... To transmute a society built on an industry which is not yet humanized into a society which wields its knowledge and its industrial power in behalf of a democratic culture requires the courage of an inspired imagination."[35]

Despite this beginning, sadly, we have not yet substantially developed a culture—what Royce terms "a humanized society" or what Dewey labels "the great community." In fact, in many respects it seems that we have made little if any recent progress. Perhaps since Dewey's time we have even lost ground to a spreading cultural wilderness. We are, after all, a society: of growing pollution, illiteracy, crime, drug abuse, and institutional, personal, physical, and psychic violence; of increasing polarization of wealth, cultural disenfranchisement, personal isolation, and often merely formal democracy; of leaders who govern more with image and power than with imagination and principle. In this context, Dewey's meliorism—not infrequently mistaken for simple optimism—feels out of tune to many. Paul Simon's "American Tune" of the shattered dreams of battered souls who have "lived so well so long" conveys a mood both more like that of Chief Seattle but also more contemporary. "We come on a ship they call the Mayflower / We come on the ship that sailed the moon / We come in the age's most uncertain hour / and sing an American tune / But it's all right, it's all right / You can't be forever blessed / Still, tomorrow's going to be another working day / And I'm trying to get some rest / That's all I'm trying to get some rest."[36]

Classical American philosophy has provided us with a rich vision of fuller lives. Now, how can we appropriate and act to realize this vision? How, in Dewey's words, can we today convert the Great Society into the Great Community?[37]

There is no easy answer or strategy, of course, but for Royce and Dewey (and for many other great American philosophers), communication is a crucial prerequisite for community. Imagination, interpretation, and inquiry are important, even necessary (though not sufficient), conditions for the creation of community.

This view, insightfully set forth and compellingly developed, is, I think, deeply instructive and valuable for practice. Still, this position must be seen against the background of Emerson's and Dewey's calls for each generation or age to address its own problems with its own stress and slant. I agree, and so seek to reappropriate this view. In doing this, I wholeheartedly accept and recommend Williams's advice to those seeking education in America. "Let scholarship learn me—Knowledge must be proven to us, not we to it."[38]

Royce's first requirement or condition for the possibility of community is "the power of an individual self to extend his life, in ideal fashion, so as to regard it as including past and future events which lie far away in time, and which he does not now personally remember."[39] Royce's selves thus say of distant past and distant future events "I view that event as a part of my own life."[40] Is this possible? Royce tells us that "we all know" that this power exists, even if apparently it is not always exercised. This power of ideal extension of the self rests, Royce claims, on the principle that the self is "no mere datum, but is in its essence a life which is interpreted, and which interprets itself, and which, apart from some sort of ideal interpretation, is a mere flight of ideas, or a meaningless flow of feelings, or a vision that sees nothing, or else a barren abstract conception."[41]

Is Royce correct? Although I agree, as I've said above, that the self is not a "mere datum" and that a self may search for meaning that extends beyond his or her own life, I must admit that I find nothing in my experience to support a belief in a self's power of ideal extension. In interpreting past and future, and in narrations of my own life, in myriad ways I am linked, bound, connected, and related—and constituted—in, through, and to the lives of other selves. But I do not and cannot *identify* these lives with myself, *identify* these events as events of my own life. Instead, it is precisely because these related events and related selves and lives are *other* events and *other* selves and lives that I may develop as my self, this particular self. Despite his claims that his view does not slight the actual variety and differences among selves or preclude their individuality, much of Royce's discussion of ideal extension of the self does involve loss in practice of the self through its submergence.

As a result, Royce's requirement for community—that selves possess the power to ideally extend their lives in the past and future—is problematic. But does my objection perhaps simply mark a limit or deficiency of my own imagination, or some bias against the big, the general, or the whole? I doubt it, of course, but even if I could ideally extend myself in this way, I would not want to, and, more importantly, I would not see it as a prerequisite for the possibility of community. In fact, in many cases I think the possibility of community may depend on inability or refusal to ideally extend one's self or "identify" with other selves and affirm their actions. The possible creation of community, I think, does not require that I identify as *my* actions the actions of P. T. Barnum, Stan Laurel, or Ronald Reagan, for instance. It does not require that I ideally incorporate into *my* life past treatment in America of Indians, Afro-Americans, or women. I see a reason and a need to say that "they are connected to me" but no need to say, in order to condemn them and strive for something better, that "they are me." Similarly, I see no reason why American Indians today, for instance, must say that past campaigns of extermination, land grabs, broken treaties, and systematic mistreatment and injustice are parts of their own lives (instead of parts of the conditions that gave rise to and shaped their own lives).

Communities of memory and hope do not require this. What now is needed to transform society into genuine community is not so much the *ideal* extension of selves but the *actual* extension of social practices and institutions so as to create and sustain participation by and benefit of all members of the society. Royce, I think is too worried, mistakenly worried, about exclusionary *conceptions* of self—conceptions of the self that prevent one's ideal identification with others. He is not sufficiently worried about exclusionary *practices* of society: practices of a society that prevent some from actually living in harmony (but not identity) with others.

By concentrating on the establishment of an ideal self instead of the transformation of actual social conditions as fundamental for the possibility of community, Royce offers us a political as well as a philosophical idealism. He writes that it is not "the fleeting individual of to-day" but "the ideally extended self that is worthy to belong to a significant community."[42] In contrast, I think that "the fleeting individual" *is* worthy of significant community and that any idealized unity or harmony of selves is actually possible only if and when real, fleeting social conditions allow and sustain harmonious, inclusive interests and ways of life. Without this, those who have been denied full membership in a society will not likely identify with those who exclude them but instead, at best, with social change in the service of more fully communal values. Langston Hughes made this clear: "I swear to the Lord / I still can't see / Why Democracy means / Everybody but me."[43] And so did Chief Joseph: "I have heard talk and talk, but nothing is done. Good words do not last long unless they amount to something.... There need be no trouble. Treat all men alike. Give them all the same law. Give them an even chance to live and grow. All men were made by the same Great Spirit Chief. They are all brothers"[44] and sisters.

As long as actual social conditions produce and reproduce selves with economic, political, religious, familial, environmental, technological, and sexual interests and powers that are in radical conflict with one another, neither actual community nor ideal self-extension is possible (except perhaps for small groups). It is now the task—the frontier—of education in the broadest sense to identify, radically resist, and begin to alter these continuing conditions of domination. Philosophers, if they are to be philosophers of community, must accept this task. Their inquiry must be counter-memory and criticism and must issue in public communication that itself effectively resists containment.

Dewey, it is well known, understands philosophy as criticism. Like Royce, he sees a life of communion and communication—selves engaged in communication, as Royce puts it—as a necessary condition of community. Unlike Royce, who simply briefly mentions actual communication as a condition for the possibility of community and seems to take for granted that it is satisfied, Dewey discusses the practical need to create and develop the "highest and most difficult kind of inquiry and a subtle, delicate, vivid and responsive art of communication."[45]

In "The Search for the Great Community," Dewey discusses the need to overcome deeply rooted emotional and intellectual habits that now limit free communication so as to apply an experimental method of inquiry to and in human concerns. In turn, he argues, the results of this inquiry must be disseminated so as to produce genuinely public judgment and opinion. Furthermore, both the inquiry and the dissemination of its results must be freed from manipulation and distortion by pecuniary interests and must be presented so as to reach men's and women's *lives*. This process of effective presentation, Dewey says, is art. "Artists have always been the real purveyors of news," and thus Walt Whitman is the seer of democracy that achieves community.[46] (Here key parallels between Dewey and William Carlos Williams are most evident. However, apparently they were not evident to Williams, who complained: "John Dewey and others appear to look for a solution to the problem of education in psychology and sociology—in philosophy then. They might do worse than to seek it in poetry. . . . Philosophy could not be better occupied than in translating [the poetic forms of an age] to its idioms.")[47]

Goethe said that in the presence of genius, the only available response is a smile. So, smiling at Dewey's analysis of inquiry and communication, I want to develop two of its strands by a narrowing of focus. Instead of asking, with Royce and Dewey, what conditions must be fulfilled for a society to become a community, I now ask what philosophers must do to assist in the creation of these conditions necessary for community.

Dewey makes two brief and perhaps obvious but nonetheless remarkable suggestions. The first concerns philosophers' subject matter. He asserts that the division of social knowledge into isolated and insulated branches of learning is a measure of the backwardness of this knowledge and its aloofness from and opposition to physical knowledge.[48] I will not argue that this is so. I take this as a given at present, assuming that you all are intimately familiar with the intellectual division (and subdivision) of knowledge and with the departmentalized administration of divided knowledges in the academy. Neither will I argue that this creates highly undesirable consequences, assuming that you all are painfully aware of the intellectual narrowness that this tends to impose on one's own work and the even greater intellectual quarantine and incoherence this inflicts on all but the brightest and most persistent of students.

I see no reason to explain or argue the obvious: life is cross-disciplinary, and inquiry, accordingly, also should be. This, however, raises a more difficult issue. In light of philosophers' widespread recognition of the artificiality and drawbacks of the separation and insulation of branches of human and social learning from one another, why then do they continue so thoroughly to act so as to sustain and reinforce this separation and insulation? In part, this question is historical: it asks how several mutually isolated branches of teaching, research, and professional institutions and practices arose. In part, the question is moral and political: it asks what interests are served, who is excluded, what is produced, and who and what are legitimized. And, in part, it is psychological: it asks about individual motives in the face of this apparent weakness of will.

These questions render most discussions of community ironic and impotent today. Until philosophers (with other humanists) at least begin to change their own institutions and practices of inquiry, it seems unlikely that their inquiry can consistently produce results that contribute to the creation of community. I see no preferable goal for the inquiry of philosophers. Such changes, were they to happen, would be subversive. Though many, they must include undermining existing *departmental* divisions of instruction, research, budgets, and faculty appointments within colleges and universities; unsettling existing *disciplinary* divisions and structures of knowledge (through, e.g., learned organizations, conferences, journals, and other forums) within both colleges and universities as well as scholarly organizations; and unsettling existing *professional* systems of sanctions, recognitions, rewards, incentives, and exclusions (and their notion of individual accomplishment and preference for the production of scholarly texts).

Dewey makes a second suggestion concerning the presentation or form of philosophy. After suggesting that social science might "manifest its reality" better in the daily press (as long as the press is not "technically high-brow") than in scholarly books and articles alone, Dewey asserts that the "freeing of the artist in literary presentation, in other words, is as much a precondition of the desirable creation of adequate opinion on public matters as is the freeing of social inquiry."[49] Again, I will not argue for this position or even develop it in detail, assuming instead that experience has thoroughly convinced you that communication requires dissemination and that the mode of presentation is decisive for successful dissemination and hence successful communication. We all know learned, informed, even ground-breaking thinkers who cannot communicate to others—or, at least, to certain others—and, on the other side, we all know "great communicators" with nothing to say.

Granted this point, again a different, more difficult issue arises. In light of this recognition of the importance of presentation for communication, then why is it that philosophers (even popular teachers) most of the time continue to present the results of their inquiry almost exclusively in ways that address a very small and specialized audience: receiving little attention, much less understanding, and virtually no social action? As above, this issue raises important questions that are historical, political, and psychological.

No matter how these questions are answered, they point to a need for change now. Without such change, philosophers in effect, in practice, have only inadequate ways to communicate publicly what they have to say. This is a requirement for any philosophy that seeks to be a public philosophy, and here I admit that I see no preferable role for philosophers than that of public educators in the broadest sense. This does not mean that philosophy must simply translate poetic forms into its own idioms. Instead, I urge philosophy to translate its own forms into effective, moving artistic idioms—in Dewey's sense, in which the presentation of results of inquiry is an art. Again, this does not mean that philosophers must imitate artists. Williams got this right: at the frontier, in the New World, Daniel Boone did not become an Indian—he became *Indianlike*[50]—and philosophers, similarly, must become *artistlike* in creatively reaching human lives. This too would be subversive. It would require that philosophers address different, broader *audiences*; invent and utilize different *media* to do so; and seek to dislodge and empower instead of merely to disprove.

Travelers at the philosophical and cultural frontier really have no other acceptable choice. In this new world, they must act so as to participate in and forge a community of humanistic inquirers and to imaginatively transfer and share the products of this critical inquiry with society. They must make possible, increasingly, a community of individuals. In short, they—myself included—now must more fully do in their own lives what they have long recommended to others. The landscape has changed, of course, but this is a familiar frontier.

Notes

1. Ralph Waldo Emerson, *The Complete Works of Ralph Waldo Emerson*, vol. 2, ed. Edward Waldo Emerson (Boston and New York: Charles Scribner's Sons, 1903), p. 52.

2. Charles S. Peirce, "Some Consequences of Four Incapacities," *The Journal of Speculative Philosophy* 2 (1868): 140.

3. Wallace Stevens, *Parts of a World* (New York: Alfred A. Knopf, 1942), p. 18.

4. Walt Whitman, *Leaves of Grass*, 10th ed. (New York: 1855), p. 40.

5. William James, *The Principles of Psychology*, 2 vols. (Cambridge: Harvard University Press, 1981), p. 220.

6. William James, *A Pluralistic Universe* (Cambridge: Harvard University Press, 1977), p. 14.

7. George Santayana, *Winds of Doctrine and Platonism and the Spiritual Life* (Gloucester, Mass.: Peter Smith, 1971), p. 211.

8. William Carlos Williams, *The Embodiment of Knowledge* (New York: New Directions, 1974), p. 60.

9. Ibid., p. xi.

10. Ralph Waldo Emerson, "The American Scholar," in *Selected Writings of Ralph Waldo Emerson*, ed. William H. Gilman (New York: New American Library, 1965), p. 224.

11. John Dewey, MS p. 102/58/10, in *Classical American Philosophy*, ed. John J. Stuhr (New York: Oxford University Press, 1987), p. 324.

12. John Dewey, "The Need for a Recovery of Philosophy," in *John Dewey: The Middle Works, 1899–1924*, vol. 10, ed. Jo Ann Boydston (Carbondale: Southern Illinois University Press, 1980), p. 46.

13. James, *A Pluralistic Universe*, p. 13.

14. Emerson, "The American Scholar," p. 227.

15. Whitman, *Leaves of Grass*, p. 51.

16. Ralph Waldo Emerson, *Letters and Social Aims* (New York: 1876), p. 28.

17. Richard Rorty, *Philosophy and the Mirror of Nature* (Princeton: Princeton University Press, 1979).

18. William Carlos Williams, *In the American Grain* (New York: New Directions, 1956), p. 137.
19. Gary Snyder, *Turtle Island* (New York: New Directions, 1974), p. 19.
20. Richard Brautigan, *Trout Fishing in America* (New York: Dell, 1967), p. 77.
21. Christopher Columbus, "Letter of Lord Raphael Sanchez, Treasurer, to Ferdinand and Isabella, King and Queen of Spain, on his First Voyage," in *New World Metaphysics*, ed. Giles Gunn (New York: Oxford University Press, 1981), p. 7.
22. Amerigo Vespucci, "Mundus Novus," in *New World Metaphysics*, ed. Giles Gunn (New York: Oxford University Press, 1981), pp. 11–12.
23. Allen Ginsberg, *The Fall of America: Poems of These States, 1965–1971* (New York: New Directions, 1972), p. 101.
24. Lillian Schlissel, *Women's Diaries of the Westward Journey* (New York: Schocken Books, 1982), p. 19.
25. Chief Seattle, in *New World Metaphysics*, ed. Giles Gunn (New York: Oxford University Press, 1981), p. 284.
26. Williams, *The Embodiment of Knowledge*, pp. 149–50.
27. Sigurd F. Olson, *Reflections from the North Country* (New York: Alfred A. Knopf, 1976), p. 3.
28. See, for instance, the following: Arthur A. Ekirch, Jr., *The Idea of Progress in America, 1815–1860* (New York: Columbia University Press, 1944); Henry Nash Smith, *Virgin Land: The American West as Symbol and Myth* (Cambridge: Harvard University Press, 1950); George R. Taylor, ed., *The Turner Thesis* (Boston: Heath, 1956); and Frederick Jackson Turner, *The Frontier in American History* (New York: Holt, Rinehart & Winston, 1962).
29. The Eagles, *Hotel California*, Asylum Records, 1976, band 8.
30. Ibid., band 8.
31. Josiah Royce, *The Problem of Christianity* (Chicago: University of Chicago Press, 1968), pp. 251–71.
32. George Herbert Mead, *Mind, Self, and Society: From the Standpoint of a Social Behaviorist* (Chicago: University of Chicago Press, 1934), pp. 136–41.
33. Ibid., p. 154.
34. John Dewey, "The Lost Individual," in *John Dewey: The Later Works, 1925–1953*, vol. 5, ed. Jo Ann Boydston (Carbondale: Southern Illinois University Press, 1984), pp. 66–76.
35. John Dewey, "American Education and Culture," in *John Dewey: The Middle Works, 1899–1924*, vol. 10, ed. Jo Ann Boydston (Carbondale: Southern Illinois University Press, 1980), p. 198.
36. Paul Simon, *There Goes Rhymin' Simon*, New York, Columbia Records, 1973, band 6.
37. Dewey, "The Lost Individual," pp. 327–50.
38. Williams, *The Embodiment of Knowledge*, pp. 44, 60.
39. Royce, *The Problem of Christianity*, p. 252.
40. Ibid., p. 251.
41. Ibid., p. 253.
42. Ibid., p. 256.
43. Langston Hughes, *The Black Man Speaks* (Boston: Heath, 1952), p. 23.
44. Chief Joseph, in *New World Metaphysics*, ed. Giles Gunn (New York: Oxford University Press, 1981), p. 286.
45. Dewey, "The Lost Individual," p. 350.

46. Ibid.
47. Williams, *The Embodiment of Knowledge*, p. 7.
48. Dewey, "The Lost Individual."
49. Ibid., p. 350.
50. Williams, *In the American Grain*, p. 137.

Spatial and Temporal Ethics

PETER A. FRENCH

It is commonplace in textbooks for ethical theories to be classed as either (predominantly) deontological or consequentialistic. Such a classification, I would argue, despite the volume of ink expended on it, actually identifies nothing more than an intramural distinction from within a shared basic perspective, a shared network of metaphysical and meta-ethical concepts. If I am right, both of these traditional classifications of moral theory, of providing grounds for judgments as to what is right (and wrong) and what one ought to do, depend upon the same basic conception of the identity and individuation of persons. That perspective, which I shall characterize as "temporal," can be contrasted with another that offers altogether different grounds on which to raise the standard questions of ethics. In most books on ethics, this second perspective (which, for reasons that will become clear, I propose to call "spatial") is overlooked or relegated to a short paragraph and a brief footnote. In practice, however, it is a perspective adopted by many of us when we evaluate each other's behavior and justify or excuse our own. Furthermore, it is (and has been) the characteristic moral outlook of a significant percentage of the world's population.

I do not claim to be developing a new way to do ethics. My goal is much more modest. I hope only to propose a different way of conceptualizing differences in ethical perspectives. I cannot claim to have invented the distinction, but I hope to reexpose it and, perhaps, reveal some of the virtues of seeing moral thinking in these terms.

A reading of Charles Dickens's *Bleak House*[1] provides a helpful introduction to the two perspectives. It certainly opened my eyes to them. Dickens develops the plot of that novel by alternating two narrators, each using a different tense. Roughly half of the book is written in the present tense, the narration of an unnamed observer. The other half is written in the past tense, ostensibly the work of one of the major characters. This dual narrative technique reveals two very different metaphysical perspectives that in turn produce two radically different moral analyses of society and the actions of people.

The present tense, as has been noted by a host of literary critics,[2] freezes the action of the scenes being described. A string of present-tense descriptions is more like a slide show than a moving picture. The present is an inventorial tense, giving us structures, arrangements, associations, and objects but not flowing, connected movements. The social world Dickens describes in the present tense narration is static, patterned. The reader is captured in a poetic "thereness" in which clusters of objects are mapped in relation to each other, suspended in time. There is no time for human intentions, extended actions, and associated motivations. Indeed, human identities for this narrator are station identities. In effect, personal identity is exhaustively given through location and association, thereby forming and defining a social grid. Who one is is a matter of where one is. This sort of narrative and its metaphysic lends itself to a moral focus on social institutions seen as ultimate bearers of responsibility, credit, and blame.

In a memorable passage, Dickens writes: "The system . . . its the system. I mustn't look to individuals. It's the system. I mustn't go into court and say, "My Lord, I beg to know this from you—is this right or wrong? My Lord knows nothing of it. He sits there to administer the system. . . . He is not responsible. It's the system."[3]

The theme of Dickens's spatialist narrator is the disgrace of a house (not, by the way, Bleak House, but the House of Dedlock) that is brought on by the to-be-uncovered fact that people are out of their proper social places, like an incorrectly set chessboard. Although Dickens's intent probably was to show the destructive force over individuals of institutions—at least the entrenched ones—he provides marvelous insights into the social interdependency of all levels, to which F. H. Bradley would, a few years later, give a positive spin in *Ethical Studies*.[4]

Where the present-tense narrator of *Bleak House* shows us society as an interlocked grid of stations and associations and the identities of people all but exclusively derived from the places they occupy in that grid, Dickens's past-tense narrator offers quite the opposite perspective. The past tense has duration; hence, events are describable. Actions occur, have prior causes, and a history, and they move on to effects. Actors, more or less Cartesian egos, endure through time and reveal plans, goals, and hopes: the elements of action that are the foci of the Kantians and the utilitarians. The moral perspective is act- or agent-centered. Human relations are shaped by events and, therefore, in and over time.

Temporalists tend to be defenders of some or all of the following: individual liberty, rights, self-determination, and (even) romance. They see human life in terms of intentional actions and the isolatable, independent action as the central—the ultimate—moral subject. Collectivities are characteristically defined by them as aggregates that are exhaustively reducible for moral purposes to their individual members. Bentham, for example, makes a cornerstone of utilitarianism the view that "the community is a fictitious body composed of the individual persons who are considered as constituting as it were its members. The interest of the community then is . . . the sum of the interests of the several members who compose it."[5]

The utilitarian calculus surely depends on totally redistributable community interests. The spatialists, on the other hand, focus on role, station, status, and social unity. The temporalist's individual actors, when stripped of their social relations, for them, are revealed to be not an isolatable ego, the naked emperor, but a mere abstraction of no particular moral significance.

It is not uncommon for spatialists to shift the object of ultimate moral evaluation entirely away from individual humans to different types of collectivities. Marx might be described as doing so, and Bradley (though he does not turn his back completely on the individual) writes: "That objective institutions exist is of course an obvious fact; and it is a fact, which every day is becoming plainer, that these institutions are organic, and further, that they are moral. . . . Let us take the point of view which regards the community as the real moral organism."[6]

Bradley goes on to argue that understanding the community as the basic moral unit has the virtue of destroying the antithesis of despotism and individualism (traditionally conjured up by the temporalist) by (1) denying both and (2) taking something of value from each. "The truth of individualism is saved, because, unless we have intense life and self-consciousness in the members of the state, the whole state is ossified. The truth of despotism is saved, because, unless the member realizes the whole by and in himself, he fails to reach his own individuality."[7]

Individuality for spatialists like Bradley, of course, is a far cry from the (romantic) individualism of the Humean, the Kantian, and the act-utilitarian. Individuals, as Bradley defines them, are "organs of the whole," only real because they are social, pulse-beats in the system. Bradley explains that an individual human being insofar as he is "the object of his self-consciousness" is characterized and penetrated "by the existence of others." In short, the content of a self is a pattern of relations within a community. "I am myself by sharing with others, by including in my essence relations to them, the relations of the social state."[8]

The primary moral obligation for Bradley and most other spatialist theorists comes to a version of the Socratic injunction to know oneself, combined with the stoic command to realize oneself in one's proper place in the natural-social order of things. Self-realization is finding one's position and acting accordingly. To find one's place, of course, requires identifying the places of others: not all others, but a significant element of the whole grid. "To know what a man is must not take him in isolation. . . . What he has to do depends on what his place is, what his function is, and that all comes from his station."[9]

Moral duty is neither a subjective matter nor discovered by working a calculus or algorithm. It is objective in two senses: (1) that whatever one's duty is, it would be the duty of anyone else occupying the place in society one occupies; and (2) it is one's duty regardless of one's motives, thoughts, or appreciation of the circumstances.

The moral imperative for Bradley is to realize oneself in the moral world.

But what is the moral world? Unsurprisingly, it is the system of institutions—"from the family to the nation"—that Bradley calls "the body of the moral world," and it is the spirit that vitalizes those institutions. (In terms I have used in a related context, it is the structural/procedural and policy recognitors of institutions such as corporations.[10]) In effect, Bradley is committed to a moral person theory of certain kinds of corporate collectivities that flies in the face of temporalistic methodology individualism. The first half of his famous essay, "My Station and Its Duties," is devoted to a sarcastic attack on the MI reductionistic program. "An individual man is what he is because of and by virtue of community, and . . . communities are thus not mere names but something real, and can be regarded . . . only as the one in the many."[11]

The basic moral injunction, for Bradley, is to live in accordance with the requirements placed on one by the role one plays in the community. (This type of view is also found in Confucian ethics and surfaces as well in the writings of the Roman stoics.) Role, station, place for Bradley serve to make an individual a concrete entity and not the abstract subject of Kantian and utilitarian ethics that Bernard Williams exposed in his well-known paper, "Persons, Character, and Morality."[12] A rather odd outcome of the temporalist focus on the act or the agent is that those who take that perspective in modern times have tended to produce a conception of the moral subject that is impersonal, impoverished, and indistinct. The separateness of persons, as Williams notes, is utterly ignored by the utilitarian, and the Kantian, while arguably making less of an abstraction of the agent, still ends up with a moral world composed of interchangeable rational decision-makers lacking the peculiar characteristics that individuate persons in ordinary social collectivities.

Bradley's theory, which is representative of the spatialists, provides a general outline of the perspective but seems to provide little content as to its moral epistemology. Bradley does have something interesting to say about the method by which we are to learn what we should do, but it is buried in his anglicized Hegelian rhetoric and may resist excavation. Typically, Bradley is classed as an intuitionist, and there is no denying that he talks of instincts being stronger than principles and of knowing what is right in particular cases by immediate judgment or "an intuitive subsumption."[13] But what he intends, as he goes on to say, is not any sort of subjective intuitionist theory but a denial of the view that moral judgments are discursive. In this he sounds remarkably like Hilary Putnam, who has vigorously defended the role of imagination in moral reasoning.[14]

Bradley argues that crucial to providing content to the duties of stations is reference to archetypical occupiers for each station. He writes, "The ideal self appealed to by the moral man is an ideally presented will in his position and circumstances which rightly particularizes the general laws which answer to the general functions and systems of spheres of the moral organism (the society)."[15]

What Bradley might mean, and what many spatialists would readily endorse, is that for each position in the social grid there is (or can be developed) an exemplar that provides content to the moral duties associated with that station. Each actual occupant is bound to fall a bit short of the ideal, for duty is "an infinite process, an unending 'not-yet.' "[16] But duty is not a threshold notion for the spatialist. It is scaled, so the ordinary moral person, though far from perfect, will probably be good enough and need suffer none of the pangs of "emptiness and guilt" associated with Kantian moral failure. Furthermore, a person's reasons for acting, Bradley assures, are irrelevant to moral worth as long as the job gets done. "The heart is an idle abstraction."[17]

Even if Bradley's is not a full-scale exemplar theory, he is certainly committed to the view that for a person to know what is right, what duty requires with respect to his position or station, he needs to be imbibed by example. "Precept is good, but example is better; for by a series of particulars . . . we identify ourselves on the sides both of will and judgement."[18]

In a note, Bradley tells us that the custom of many ordinary people of thinking about what a known person, real or fictional, of high character associated with their stations would do in their (presumably) trying circumstances is the best sort of moral reasoning. It is important to understand that Bradley is not championing role reversal: putting oneself in another's shoes or imagining him in yours. Entertaining as that might be for Golden Rule theorists, it entails a commitment to an interchangeability of individuals that divorces them as moral subjects from their stations. Changing places for the spatialist is a profound identity shift, and it is difficult to see how, except in jest, one could use it as the foundation of moral decision-making. Hence, the appeal is made internal to the station, to a model identity or exemplar. When one thinks of what someone one admires would do and acts in imitation, it must be a member of one's type to which one refers. Even so, spatialists do have a problem with similarity over stations because, as each position is defined by a particular set of relations, each station is, strictly speaking, unique. Nonetheless, similarities of stations, classes, or types of jobs exist in society, and more general exemplars can get a foothold. Still, Bradley often talks as if each of us has a peculiar exemplar.

The spatialist also has a problem with the changing of stations, moving up or down in the social world, rags to riches. Every such change must be an identity shift—some clearly are crises. Many stations are invariably linked within institutions and must be passed through in the process of social advancement. If such stations were indexed to a time in a life, then the problem might seem to be solved. But not really. The temporal dimension would be introduced with all of its metaphysical commitments flying in the face of spatial personal identity theory. Minimization of the temporal could be accomplished were one to deny, as Bradley does not, a continuous self through time. (Bradley needs that notion for his responsibility doctrine in the first essay of *Ethical Studies*.) A closet continuer theory of the self, however, could nicely serve the spatialist's interests. Identity over time can be denied, and full dependency on the spatial dimensions of station can be maintained. The appeal to exemplars peculiar to stations (or station-types) then remains a viable moral methodology. In fact, it is the appeal to exemplars in setting the conditions of moral action that seems a distinguishing feature of spatial ethics.

Spatialists will point out that ingrained in our conception of the classes of stations across the social grid are model identities or archetypes: pictures or, better, portraits of the ideal role player. We think of them as the good doctor, the ideal engineer, the lawyer's lawyer, the good soldier, and so on. Certainly these exemplars are not derived or drawn from sets of rules or codes of behavior. The good doctor, for example, is not the embodiment of the AMA's code of ethics. Role model identities evidence a holistic quality, a dimensionality. They are, purely and not so simply, works of fiction. Importantly, they tend to be visual in their most accessible form, and they are commonly conveyed to and recalled by station-dwellers, as Bradley does mention, via stories.

These model identities define the acceptable limits of the roles of which they are exemplars. They are the controlling devices of the permissible and set the outer boundaries on the required. They are the products of many decades of grooming, arising and thriving in the public domain, creations of popular (as well as role-restricted) culture. The good soldier, for example, is not a purely military invention. John Wayne, George C. Scott, Gary Cooper, and Alex Guinness have had as much, if not more, to do with molding his features as have Omar Bradley and Douglas MacArthur. The good doctor owes a great deal to Alan Alda, the lawyer's lawyer to Perry Mason and Atticus Finch.

The spatialists see the process of internalization of the exemplar by the role player as a matter of identity assimilation. The basic moral project is, as much as is possible, to act like the model identity of one's station in the social institutions to which one belongs. Admittedly, the ideals are always beyond realization, but approaching them, even still at some distance, accounts for the satisfaction, so Bradley believes, of the ordinary moral person.

There are, as might be imagined, major problems with the grid-based conception of roles. Most obvious are those created by overlapping institutional commitments. The same person may be vice president of a corporation, alderman of a city, and father of two children. What is his station? To what exemplar does he relate? The answer, I think, must recall the import of the literary or fictive element in spatial ethics. Model identities are multidimensional. They are not cardboard paste-ups that reflect only on fatherhood, for example. A significant part of what it is to be a good father is to do well at whatever other roles one plays in society.

The spatialist's ethics are dominated by concerns for place that are defined in terms of sets of duties. The criteria of evaluation for station-occupiers need not be collections of rules or formuli for action. Instead, exemplars provide both motivation and grounds of evaluation. Though rules and formuli might be devised, they are not usually used in practice. All of these features conspire to produce another typical characteristic of spatial ethics: that they are predominately shame-based.

For the spatialist, the primary moral motivation is to measure up, to not be seen as inadequate to the tasks that define one's identity. In short, shame avoidance propels spatial ethics. The exemplar associated with each station sets the highest standard of behavior for it. Falling significantly below the standard is much more than the moral lapse of not living up to rules. It is failure on a far grander scale, an intimate matter, an identity crisis. The way the spatialist arranges the moral world, such failures must constitute severe threats both of not being the very person one thought one was and of putting oneself forth as being to others. Though this would take much more consideration, if Bradley's metaphysical position with respect to individual identity is adopted, should one fail to perform the essential tasks of one's station(s), one would be in danger of losing one's identity altogether. The primary moral motivation is maintenance of identity. The problem is that the spatialist does not seem to allow for anything like a person without such a station identity—a man without a country. There is a place for everyone, and everyone is in a place.

In any event, shame plays a key role, and none other than another great spatialist clearly noted it. Plato, in *The Laws*,[19] identifies shame as the foundation of law. The fear of shame he cites as saving "us from many great evils, playing a greater role than anything else in procuring for us victory and safety."[20] The sense of shame is the wellspring of moderation, courage, and especially justice. At least in *The Laws*, Plato seems to see shame as the unifier of the virtues. In that, of course, he is opposed by Aristotle, a confirmed temporalist, who argues that "it is incorrect to speak of a sense of shame as being a virtue or excellence for it resembles an emotion more than a characteristic. . . . It is defined as a kind of fear of disrepute, and the effect it produces is very much like that produced by fear of danger."[21] Aristotle goes on to say that shame does not befit every stage of life. He seems to think that only the young are likely to be affected by it. But that seems just wrong, at least with the youth of our day. The inhibitions engendered by shame are seldom in evidence in their lives. At any rate, the effects that Aristotle notes for shame are exactly those the spatialist wants to achieve. The fear of being uncovered as inadequate to one's station, as noted above, dominates the spatialist's moral arsenal. Of course, such a fear can lead in two distinct directions. First, the shameful person may cover up too well, stonewalling his or her moral shortcomings, and so a general social failure may be precipitated. Second, as Plato seemed to imagine would more likely happen, the shameful person may be driven by shame to those greater achievements in the position that are necessary to restore social status.

It is of some interest that shame-based morality, insofar as it stresses the measure of the station-occupier against an objective ideal model, has both a private and a public aspect. There is the private sense of inadequacy and the public ostracization, the holding in contempt, the derogation of the shameful for the failure to measure up. In effect, the spatial, shame-based ethicist integrates the private person of the Kantian with the Bradleyian pulse-beat of the system. Time does not, however, allow investigation of the multiple aspects of this conception. I promise to do so in a book on spatial ethics: the aesthetics of morality, of which this paper is something of an outline.

Notes

1. Charles Dickens, *Bleak House* (New York, 1964), originally published in 1853.
2. For an excellent example, see Geoffrey Thurley, *The Dickens Myth* (London, 1976).
3. Dickens, *Bleak House*, p. 228.
4. F. H. Bradley, *Ethical Studies* (Oxford, 1876).
5. Jeremy Bentham, *An Introduction to the Principles of Morals and Legislation* (1789), ch. 1.
6. Bradley, *Ethical Studies*, pp. 174, 187.
7. Ibid., p. 187.
8. Ibid., p. 187.
9. Ibid., p. 173.
10. Peter A. French, *Collective and Corporate Responsibility* (New York, 1984).
11. Bradley, *Ethical Studies*, p. 166.
12. Bernard Williams, *Persons, Character, and Morality* (Berkeley, 1976), pp. 197–216.
13. Bradley, *Ethical Studies*, p. 194.
14. Hilary Putnam, *Meaning and the Moral Sciences* (London, 1978), esp. pt. 2.
15. Bradley, *Ethical Studies*, p. 179.
16. Ibid., p. 181.
17. Ibid.
18. Ibid., p. 197.
19. Plato, *The Laws*, trans. Thomas Prangle (New York, 1980).
20. Ibid., p. 27.
21. Aristotle, *Nicomachean Ethics*, 1128 b 10–35.

APPLIED PHILOSOPHY

A Roycean Pragmatic:
Insights for Applied Ethics

MARY B. MAHOWALD

During the past fifteen years, well-respected philosophers have published articles and books in various areas of applied ethics, and courses in applied ethics have proliferated on college campuses.[1] Although the trend is far from universal, it represents a considerable change from previous decades, when philosophers were mainly preoccupied with logic and meta-ethics and applications to actual situations were generally viewed as beyond the pale of genuine philosophical inquiry. For example, when Bertrand Russell wrote about pacifism or sexual morality, his views were not construed (even by himself) as philosophical. Possibly he saw himself as thus fulfilling Hume's advice: "Be a philosopher; but, amidst all your philosophy, be still a man."[2]

Of course, not all philosophers of the past have eschewed participation in "real-life" issues, even from a professional perspective. Socrates and Marx are obvious examples of those who in fact construed the essential task of philosophy as practical. The history of casuistry and traditional moral theology reflects an interest in ethical issues persisting through hundreds of years. At the turn of the century, however, American pragmatism provided a philosophical framework especially congenial to applied ethics. Although Josiah Royce is not typically considered a pragmatist, several of his views provide insights in this regard. In this paper I wish to discuss two of his insights and their application. First, however, I need to review the meaning of pragmatism on which my version of a Roycean pragmatic is based.

What Is Meant by Pragmatism?

Among the various definitions of pragmatism proposed by the pragmatists themselves, as well as by critics and historians of pragmatism, consider the meaning provided by H. S. Thayer in his *Meaning and Action: A Critical History of Pragmatism*.[3] After carefully analyzing the pragmatisms of Peirce, James, Dewey, Lewis, and Mead, Thayer proposes a definition that "emphasizes the practical character of thought and reality."[4] Admitting that this definition requires further clarification, Thayer continues, "What pragmatism argues as 'the practical nature of thought and reality' is that since existence is transitional, knowledge is one of the ways of effecting transitions of events, and the only reliable way of guiding them."[5]

Implied in this understanding of "the practical" are its process-context ("existence is transitional") and its insistence on the future-directedness of knowledge (knowledge effects the transitions and guides events). The empirical orientation of pragmatism necessarily involves reference to the future. As Dewey noted in *Philosophy and Civilization*, "Pragmatism, thus, presents itself as an extension of historical empiricism, but with this fundamental difference, that it does not insist upon antecedent phenomena but upon consequent phenomena; not upon the precedents but upon the possibility of action."[6]

In other words, pragmatism as such is concerned with experience: not as the origin but as the end of our ideas.

Thayer also contends that pragmatism, through all its differing expressions, involves three related claims, each of which can be interpreted as implying relatedness to future experience.[7] The first claim is that "possibility is in some sense a trait of reality." Somewhat like the Aristotelian notion of potency, a positive note attaches to pragmatic "possibilities." Their presently positive reality stems from their functioning as anticipations of future experience. Without that future foreseen, possibilities are unreal and void of meaning.

The second claim is that thinking, as a way of behavior, inevitably has practical effects. The pragmatic approach to knowing and reality insists on the inseparableness of theory and practice, of ideas from conduct. As Thayer puts it, "The world will be different from what it would have been if thought had not intervened." Thus construed, thought is a present guide for future behavior. Although the knowing activity is itself an expression of the whole person (for example, *I* philosophize, not just my mind), action, as one's way of plunging into future experience, is the link between being and becoming.

Thirdly, pragmatism involves the claim that conceptualization is always purposive or teleological. We abstract essential meanings from experience with the motivation of applying these meanings to subsequent experience. Hence, what constitutes the end of our ideas or concepts is their directedness toward future results. Apart from such purposiveness, no one thinks at all.

As with the original pragmatists, therefore, Thayer's conception of pragmatism as a doctrine that stresses the practical nature of reason, and reality can be identified with a definition of pragmatism as a doctrine that essentially accents future experience.

Possibilities for a Roycean Pragmatic

Thayer does not impute the essential traits of pragmatism to Josiah Royce. In what follows, however, I shall draw on Roycean texts to show that he could have done so. Although Royce never diverged from the absolute idealism that characterizes the entirety of his philosophy, pragmatic elements are present from the beginning and are increasingly evident in the development of his thought.[8] The views of Peirce and James, both of whom were greatly respected by Royce, contributed to this trend, which Royce himself characterized in *The Problem of Christianity* as an "absolute pragmatism."[9]

Royce was well aware that pragmatism is generally construed as antithetical to an absolutism that maintains "that the world in its wholeness has an absolute constitution in the light of which all finite truth must be interpreted."[10] He insisted, however, that idealists need not so view the world, and he himself disclaimed "any peculiar revelation as to what the content of absolute truth may be."[11] Royce, like Peirce, posited an absolute truth as grounds for rejecting relativism, and he emphasized the crucial role of experience in understanding the world as it unfolds. Whether we be absolutists or relativists, he wrote, "in acknowledging truth we are indeed meeting, or endeavoring to meet, a need which always expresses itself in finite form. But this need can never be satisfied by the acknowledgment of anything finite as the whole truth."[12]

There are thus two futures about which Royce is concerned: one is the near or temporal future, which constitutes our presently projected field of action; the other is the future fulfillment of experience in the Absolute. The absolute future is an indispensable dimension of a Roycean pragmatic because it grounds the value and meaning of temporal future experience.

Royce's notion of "possible reality" is more complicated than the concept of possibility (as a trait of reality) with which Thayer associates pragmatism. To Royce there are different kinds of possible beings. Some are empty possibilities or pure imaginations (for example, as in "I could possibly have wings and a long tail, a hundred eyes, and a mountain of gold"), and some are real possibilities (for example, as in "the pages of that closed book, the bones inside the body of that cat, my own brain").[13] The whole of postulated reality, he claims, "can only be known as possible, not as actual, experience."[14] Its possibility is thus a trait of its reality.

Just as James compares the method of pragmatism to Papini's corridor, where one straddles opposing philosophical temperaments such as empiricism and rationalism, materialism and idealism,[15] Royce affirms an inextricable tie between reason and experience as means of understanding reality and ascertaining truth. "For we all not only gather but interpret experience," he writes, "[a]nd to interpret experience is to regard facts as the fulfillment of rational ideals."[16] In the context of Royce's idealism, then, truth must always be related "to action, to practice, to the will."[17] Nothing is true except insofar as its purpose or meaning is expressed or carried out. Truth is "a construction, a process, an activity, a creation, an attainment."[18]

Thayer's account of "the essential ideas" of pragmatism is obviously reflected in the Roycean views described above. But perhaps the most important clue to a Roycean pragmatic is the starting point of his idealism, viz., Royce's definition of "idea" as a "conscious embodiment of purpose."[19] The term *purpose* is construed as an active orientation of one's consciousness. Without such practical directedness Royce believes there is no idea, and thus no idealism. Throughout his writing, he continually stresses this practical or pragmatic aspect. To the extent that he succeeds in maintaining a tie between thought and action, his philosophy is not only incidentally or partially pragmatic but essentially so. It should not be surprising, therefore, to discover that key Roycean insights are applicable to current ethical issues.

Roycean Insights for Applied Ethics

As applied ethics has gained in respectability during the past decade, pragmatism has renewed its appeal to those frustrated by the practical sterility of empty theorizing. In fact, pragmatism suggests a way of resolving the apparently irresolvable conflict between deontological and consequentialist theories of normative ethics. By insisting on the essential interplay between a priori and a posteriori reasoning, a pragmatic method rejects the rigid dichotomy that the traditional theories presuppose. Jonsen's recent work on casuistry, a case-based method of resolving ethical dilemmas, illustrates the usefulness of this approach.[20]

Simply put, applied ethics means moving explicitly from the general to the particular, from ethical theory or theories to particular moral problems that must be resolved. For the pragmatist or casuist, specific issues may trigger the theoretical considerations. Royce practiced applied ethics when he dealt with specific problems of war and racism. Like other issues, these represent personal or social dilemmas requiring individual or policy decisions. Some dilemmas arise from the fact that the individual occupies a certain role: for example, that of a family member or member of some profession. Professional ethics is concerned with the latter type of question. More specific areas of applied ethics have been defined by their focus on distinct professions or roles: for example, medical ethics, business ethics, legal ethics. In what follows I shall discuss two significant insights of Royce regarding social or professional roles. The first is applicable to any profession; the second applies mainly to the health care context.

Loyalty and the Commitment of the Professional

Royce's concept of loyalty captures the unique trait of a profession as distinct from a business; that is, its human service orientation. Loyalty to a cause, he claims, entails an altruistic practical commitment to a good beyond oneself. The professional embraces this good freely as his or her own; it thus becomes the professional's own cause as well. Ultimately, this cause is identified with the Absolute. As loyalty to loyalty, the commitment to another goes beyond one's client, patient, or student to other persons, and beyond them to the Absolute Cause toward which all partial or transient loyalties are finally directed.

This concept of loyalty to a cause is an apt description of the dedication of a professional to the specific goal of the profession—for example, in medicine, the health of one's patients; in law, the just interests of one's clients; in teaching, the knowledge of one's students. Roycean loyalty also implies allegiance to the profession itself, and thereby to one's professional colleagues, as embodying the collective pursuit of the good that distinguishes one's own profession from others. "Fidelity" is a term that Royce uses in this context, suggesting Marcel's (later) distinction between fidelity and constancy.[21] Constancy means only the observance of one's literal obligations; fidelity entails an ongoing, open-ended commitment to the person. Because persons are dynamic, commitment to the person's welfare (for example, health, just interests, or knowledge) requires continual reinterpretation of what at any point in time is most conducive to that welfare. This entails fidelity (as absolute loyalty to the person) instead of constancy (as mere fulfillment of predefined duties or obligations).

Royce's concept of loyalty is particularly relevant to the professional's assessment of situations involving conflicts of interest: for example, between the professional's own interests and others' interests, or where patients' or clients' or students' needs cannot all be immediately or adequately met. It enjoins the professional to look to the wider community's interests instead of confine himself or herself to the client's, student's, or patient's interests. This view is different from the traditional view of the professional as singularly and exclusively focused on the client or patient. It is a particularly useful perspective for dealing with situations of limited professional resources, whether these be ordinary resources such as time, space, and energy, or extraordinary resources such as scarce, expensive equipment or lifesaving organs. On Royce's view, loyal professionals are "in truth, not loyal *merely* to their own private cause. *They are loyal to the cause of all loyal people.*"[22] He would thus advise the professional: "[O]ne cannot finally approve or accept any cause or any mode of living that, while seeming in itself to be a cause or a mode of living such as embodies the spirit of loyalty, still depends upon or involves contempt for the loyalty of other men, or a disposition to prey upon their loyalty and to deprive them of any cause to which they can be loyal. No loyalty that lives by destroying the loyalty of your neighbor is just to its own true intent. And that is why charity and justice are fruits of the loyal spirit."[23]

For Royce, then, loyalty that goes beyond one's commitment to individuals represents a challenge greater than "mere morality." He regards such loyalty as "in essence a religion."[24] We might instead (or also) associate it with an ethics of virtue instead of one of obligation. In viewing loyalty to loyalty as an invitation to virtue, consider the commitment of the professional as one of empowering others. If professional power or expertise is exercised in order to promote one's own interests (for example, personal gratification, prestige, or income), it is hardly an exercise of virtue. But if the professional's loyalty entails a will to empower others so that they in turn can act loyally toward others, such loyalty, as loyalty to loyalty, is surely virtuous. Lest it be thought that the spirit of loyalty that Royce thus advocates is impractical, it should be construed as an ideal worth approximating, even if not completely achievable. Such, I believe, is the pragmatic import of Royce's idealistic account.

Health Care Decisions and the Community of Interpretation

The second Roycean insight relevant to applied ethics has to do with his notion of a community of interpretation. Taking the health care context as an illustrative situation, we may construe this concept both descriptively and prescriptively. A minimal account of interpretation describes the manner in which clinical decisions are often made and ethical decisions are sometimes made. A full account of Royce's community of interpretation prescribes a model for optimizing the process of decision-making. Before considering the applications, however, we need first to become clear on what Royce means by interpretation and community.

Interpretation for Royce is essentially a method of mediation. On a cognitive level, it mediates between perception and conception; on a practical level, it mediates between individual selves and communities. Following Peirce, Royce explicates his theory of interpretation as triadic. The three members of the triad are the interpreter, the mind to which she addresses her interpretation, and the mind that she undertakes to interpret. The interpretive process can only occur through an exchange of signs; that is, communication. An essential factor in the process is a principle of unity (for example, a common goal) that motivates and facilitates communication. Using signs as media, the members of the triad may reciprocally interchange the roles of interpreter, interpretant, and interpreted through the ongoing process of interpretation. Because every "interpretation of a sign is, in its turn, the expression of the interpreter's mind, it constitutes a new sign, which again calls for interpretation; and so on without end."[25] The term *sign* is used by Royce as it was by Peirce, in a very general sense. It may take the form of words, gestures, or physical facts—in brief, whatever is subject to interpretation by a mind or minds for the sake of another (or other) mind(s). "A sign, then, is an object whose being consists in the fact that the sign calls for an interpretation."[26] The sign serves its interpretive purpose by associating an already-received meaning with the future fulfillment toward which it points.

The professional person is essentially a mediator who interprets the effective symbols or signs of one's profession to individuals who are prepared to receive them. In health care, interpretation appropriately describes the healing process, through which the signs of language and various (other?) modes of treatment are expressed. The process is, of course, interactive, because patients are interpreters to their caregivers of the signs of their own illnesses, and family members and different caregivers all have different signs to interpret to one another. A complex set of mediating, ongoing interpretations thus takes place among all the participants. In order to achieve the best possible practical outcome, the interchange must be conducted in a truly collaborative fashion; that is, in a context consistent with Royce's notion of a community.

In *The Problem of Christianity,* Royce describes three conditions as essential to the existence of a genuine community. The first requisite is an integrated individuality or, rather, two or more such integrated individualities. Community is founded upon "the power of an individual self to extend his life, in ideal fashion, so as to regard it as including past and future events which lie far away in time, and which he does not now personally remember."[27] Each self is the present reality of a particular past and a particular future, the interpreter of what has been and will be for him or her. It is precisely from one's own unrepeatable individuality that each person contributes to the greater reality that is community.

The second condition for true community is communication among the various selves. This goal is not something that happens automatically, for "a community does not become one . . . by virtue of any reduction or melting of these various selves into a single merely present self, or into a mass of passing experience."[28] Instead, the existence of community depends upon the fact that there are in the social world a number of distinct selves who are not only capable of social communication but are also generally engaged in such communication.

The last requisite is a principle of unity through which the individuals involved share a common past or a common future. In regard to their past, the group constitutes a community of memory; in regard to their future, a community of hope. Insofar as they are conscious of their unity, the members are empowered to act as a community as well as individuals. In so acting they achieve a personal reality over and above their isolated individualities. Thus, community is always greater than the mere summation of its parts.

This notion of community is applicable both to the professionals who work together toward the common goal of restoring health or maintaining life and to cooperative interactions among patients, family members, and caregivers who work toward that end in specific cases. Modern medicine is so complex that it is hardly possible, let alone desirable, for an individual practitioner to "go it alone" in professional life. Because the complexity is not only clinical but legal and moral as well, the community of those needed to optimize decision-making is greater (both qualitatively and quantitatively) than ever before.

Structurally, the practice of medicine is clearly more collaborative than most professions. Not only is it necessary for different health care professions (for example, medicine, nursing, and social work) to cooperate in providing services to patients, it is also essential that those within one field of specialization consult others: the intensive care specialist consulting the neurologist or psychiatrist and the cardiologist consulting the cardiac surgeon, for example. Health care team meetings are common occurrences, and ethics review committees have proliferated in recent years. Health care providers also maintain a faithful schedule of teaching rounds and conferences through which their ongoing education is pursued in a collaborative mode.

Admittedly, competition instead of community can be the motivation that underlies collaboration. Royce's account clearly critiques that motivation. If his account is taken prescriptively, it calls for replacement of the traditional paternalistic model of the physician's role as well as replacement of newer models that construe the physician as provider of paid-for services or an instrument of the patient's will. What is stressed through Royce's view of a community is the mutuality of response-abilities among all those involved. Patients and caregivers alike interpret each other in the context of a shared goal or cause. They are a community of hope comprising distinct selves engaged in ongoing communication.

As with the Roycean insight on loyalty, Royce's insights about community suggest a useful strategy for assessing whether communities of professionals, or communities of health care recipients as caretakers, are genuine. The assessment must be tied to Royce's ideal of a Beloved Community that unites all separate individuals or separate groups through a spirit of loyalty. No one, and no group, belongs to any one community exclusively. The Beloved Community is the ideal end, whose attainment is rendered possible by the existence of communities that approximate the ideal and facilitate its ultimate achievement. The key question to ask in evaluating the lesser communities is whether they are in fact conducive to the ideal or are merely self-serving.[29] For Royce, self-service is a futile goal, because individuals can only find fulfillment through the relatedness to one another that is community. A Roycean pragmatic emphasizes community not only as a means of measuring practical progress toward the ideal but also as a necessary practical means of overcoming the limitations of individuals. Communities in health care, as elsewhere, exist for the sake of a wider community.[30]

Concluding Remarks

The two insights described above clearly conform to Royce's own definition of insight: "knowledge that makes us aware of the unity of many facts in one whole and that at the same time brings us into intimate personal contact with these facts and with the whole wherein they are united."[31] Both concepts function as practical guides linking present decisions to an ultimate (absolute) ideal. Both concepts emphasize future experience, reflecting the pragmatist's view that theoretical and practical considerations are inseparable and that conceptualization is practically purposive.[32] To be sure, the Roycean pragmatic remains idealistic, but its idealistic context in no way impedes the relevance of these concepts to contemporary ethics. His concept of loyalty suggests a useful strategy for addressing ethical conflicts that increasingly confront today's professional. And his concept of a community of interpretation outlines a model for decision-making that is particularly applicable to the health care setting. Other Roycean themes would be instructive for applied ethics: I doubt, however, that they could be more crucial.

Notes

1. Joseph DeMarco and Richard Fox, *New Directions in Ethics* (New York: New Directions in Ethics, 1986).
2. David Hume, in James Collins, *A History of Modern European Philosophy* (Milwaukee: Bruce Pub. Co., 1961), p. 406.
3. H. S. Thayer, *Meaning and Action: A Critical History of Pragmatism* (New York: Bobbs-Merrill Co., 1968).
4. Ibid., p. 425.
5. Ibid.
6. John Dewey, *Philosophy and Civilization* (New York: G. P. Putnam's Sons, 1931), p. 27.
7. Thayer, *Meaning and Action*, pp. 426–29.
8. Mary B. Mahowald, *An Idealistic Pragmatism* (The Hague: Nijhoff, 1972).
9. Josiah Royce, *The Problem of Christianity*, ed. John E. Smith (Chicago: University of Chicago Press, 1968), p. 279.
10. Josiah Royce, *Lectures on Modern Idealism*, ed. J. Loewenberg (New Haven: Yale University Press, 1919), p. 257.
11. Royce, *Lectures on Modern Idealism*, p. 256.
12. Ibid., pp. 257–58.
13. Josiah Royce, *The Religious Aspect of Philosophy* (New York: Houghton Mifflin Co., 1885), pp. 364–65.
14. Ibid., p. 365.
15. Royce, *The Problem of Christianity*, pp. 365, 380.
16. Royce, *Lectures on Modern Idealism*, p. 259.
17. Ibid.

18. Ibid., p. 86.
19. Josiah Royce, *The World and the Individual,* 1st ser. (New York: Dover Pub. Co., 1959), p. 24.
20. Albert R. Jonsen, "Casuistry and Clinical Ethics," *Theoretical Medicine* (February, 1986): 65–73.
21. Gabriel Marcel, *Creative Fidelity* (New York: Farrar, Strauss, 1964).
22. Josiah Royce, in Max H. Fisch, ed. *Classic American Philosophers* (Englewood Cliffs, N.J.: Prentice-Hall, 1951), p. 254.
23. Ibid., pp. 254–55.
24. Ibid., p. 255.
25. Royce, *The Problem of Christianity,* p. 345.
26. Ibid.
27. Ibid., p. 253.
28. Ibid., pp. 255–56.
29. Mahowald, *An Idealistic Pragmatism,* pp. 153–63.
30. Mary L. Briody, "Community in Royce: An Interpretation," *Transactions of the Charles S. Peirce Society* 4 (1969): 224–42.
31. Josiah Royce, *Sources of Religious Insight* (New York: Charles Scribner's Sons, 1914), pp. 5–6.
32. Thayer, *Meaning and Action.*

Process-Relational Philosophy:
The Raw, Unabashed Cash Value of a Mere Metaphysical Speculation

PETE A. Y. GUNTER

The one sure philosophical contribution of American thought to world philosophy is pragmatism. This talk is intended as an exercise in "pragmatism," with no apologies offered. Its basic thesis (which will not be elaborated here) is that we are undoing the very fabric of which we are woven: the biosphere, the web of climate and water and living things in which our elaborate disquisitions are the merest, faintest ripples. We are wrecking the ozone layer,[1] the tropical rain forests,[2] even the rain.[3] That is, on top of all the other problems that could be mentioned, we are beginning to destabilize world climate—a rather larger problem, I think, than saving the snail darter. Our philosophy ought, on "pragmatic" grounds, to bring us to stop doing this. I leave it to you to decide whether contemporary philosophy will lead us to stop us from doing this.

We recall A. O. Lovejoy's essay "The Thirteen Pragmatisms."[4] I suspect that analytically inclined philosophers could find still more versions of the pragmatist doctrine than Lovejoy's baker's dozen. All that is asserted here is that a significant part of the meaning of a concept includes the uses to which it can be put, *use* being understood in a broad, polyglot sense. Obviously, there is an infinity of uses—some more significant than others. A philosophical doctrine that could help to forestall the diminution or even cessation of human life—and most other life forms—on the planet would, I take it, be so far forth a significant doctrine. It would also be—so far forth—true.

It would be tempting to pass in review the various philosophies that have dominated twentieth-century philosophy to see what significance they might have for the "environmental problem." Possibly the places in which philosophers philosophize will provide a suggestion. Clearly, judging from the literature, Anglo-American philosophers cerebrate among desks, chairs, and walls; French philosophers reflect in bistros and cafes; Marxists philosophize in factories or on tractors. I always wondered, as an undergraduate at Cambridge University in the late 1950s, how the dons could content themselves with living in castles of words, however intricately constructed. Whether those words were part of the syntax of *Principia Mathematica* or fragments of mere "ordinary" language, they were decreed to be the center of the universe. Across the channel on the continent, things were little better. There you could choose between a peppy, alienated Sartrean existentialism or various phenomenologies whose bias toward the subjective was as obvious as their claims to be at one with linguistic analysis were loud. Why were the philosophers, as if moved by an Invisible Hand, drifting toward the voluptuous mists of narcissism? Well, if one asked the question, one was not answered, either at Paris or at Oxbridge; one was simply treated as a fool. Doubtless one would still be so treated.

The fact is that in the first half of the twentieth century, out of the thousands of academic philosophers, *only two* have had a word to say about "ecology"—*only two*. I state this as a challenge. If anyone can come up with another entry, I will cheerfully add it to the list. The dates are 1900–50; only professional philosophers are admitted to the contest. Void where prohibited.

I add, as an afterthought, how curious all this is. In the period under consideration, almost everyone in English and American philosophy—even theists—wanted to be known as "naturalists." I suppose by this they meant that desks are real.

By now I'm sure the tension over just who these two philosophers are has risen to a fever pitch, and so I will, as it were, let them out of the bag. They are Henri Bergson and Alfred North Whitehead.

Bergson's remarks were made in the postscript to *The Two Sources of Morality and Religion* (1932). The fundamental practical concern of this study was, we will perhaps remember, the elimination of war—an elimination that he seems to have felt was not only imposed by war's increasing cost but by the imminent use of atomic weapons. A great moral and religious leader could, he felt, lead humanity away from the Armageddon it was preparing for itself. Barring such an extraordinary phenomenon, however, there are plainer measures that must be taken. The two most important of these are birth control and an improved agriculture. That there is a close connection between Mars and Venus was known by the ancients; in modern industrial nations the problems are more complex, but the underlying relations are the same. Overpopulation without compensating agricultural production leads toward war. We have, essentially, the means to deal with both. But to have the means is not necessarily to use them.[5]

Whitehead's environmental attitude is outlined in the concluding section of *Science and the Modern World* (1925), "Requisites for Social Progress," though fragments of this attitude are found elsewhere in this work. I quote a representative passage.

> The trees in a Brazilian forest depend upon the association of various species of organisms, each of which is mutually dependent on the other species. A single

tree by itself is dependent upon the adverse chances of shifting circumstances. The wind stunts it: variations in temperature check its foliage: the rains denude its soil: its leaves are blown away and are lost for the purpose of fertilization. You may obtain individual specimens of fine trees either in exceptional circumstances, or where human cultivation has intervened. But in nature the normal way trees flourish is by their association in a forest. Each tree may lose something of its individual perfection of growth, but they mutually assist each other in preserving the conditions for survival. The soil is preserved and shaded: and the microbes necessary for its fertility are neither scorched, nor frozen, nor washed away. A forest is the triumph of the organization of mutually dependent species. Further a species of microbes which kills the forest, also exterminates itself.[6]

The moral of this passage, and of many others in Whitehead's writings, is clear. Unless we respect the delicate internal relatedness in nature, we will disbalance and diminish nature. Not only, on Whitehead's terms, does this entail a loss of value: in the end, if the process goes too far, it will entail a diminution, perhaps a loss, of us.

These two documents may be considered a slender harvest out of the first half of twentieth-century philosophy. I will forgo examining the question as to why this harvest is slender, however, in order to ask why it occurred at all. Why did it occur in *these* philosophers in particular?

Whitehead and Bergson are certainly not the only process-relational philosophers. There are many others: William James, Charles Sanders Pierce, Lloyd Morgan, Samuel Alexander, Pierre Teilhard de Chardin, Pierre Le Comte du Noüy, John Dewey, George Herbert Mead, and Charles Hartshorne, to name only the best known. None of them, not even Whitehead, is "canonical," in my opinion.[7] Any one taken singly and certainly the group taken as a whole suggest a variety of approaches.

By process-relational philosophy, I mean no more than did Nicholas Rescher in referring, earlier in this conference, to "The Promise of Process Philosophy." The adjective *relational* is added to bring out a characteristic of this philosophy that otherwise might be overlooked; namely, its depiction of the world and its creatures as profoundly and inherently *relational* in character. Which brings us to the point.

Process-relational philosophers were the only ones in the first half of our century to take broadly environmental issues seriously because they believed: (1) that the world exists, (2) that the world is significantly relational in character, (3) that relations are fundamentally dynamic, and (4) that we, including our perceptions, our affections, and our actions, are "parts of" the world.

It does not follow from this that for these philosophers relations are all that exist. There are also terms of relations, i.e. individuals. Another way of putting this is to say that although process-relational philosophers have insisted that there are internal relations in nature, they have never insisted that internal relations are the only real relations or that the two sorts of relations (internal and external) are never a matter of degree. I am aware of no process-relational philosopher who has gone as far in the direction of internal relations as F. H. Bradley to constitute a monism. Equally, it is the basic content of process thinkers that process is a *dynamic, internal, and asymmetrical relation.* The most important sorts of internal relations are therefore dynamic, a conclusion Bradley would have resisted.

If one holds this viewpoint, then one is *already prepared to understand* environmental problems even if one has never encountered them. For one will inevitably understand things (whatever the things) through their mutually sustaining relationships: the child in its family, the nation in its history, the species in its evolutionary environment, the chemical in its milieu, the mass in (and part of) its gravitational field, the pause in the song. And one will have overcome the all-too-human tendency to conceive or to frame relations in static terms. The child grows, the nation changes, the chemical combines, the field transforms, the pause—long continued—transforms the song. Process-relational thinking, even if it is limited initially to Edwardian poetry or to chemical kinetics, quickly broadens to take in the problems of habitat preservation and species extinction, pollution and ecosystem simplification, land resources and land-use planning. They—all of these—turn out to be similar phenomena, posing similar problems.

The second and third of these assumptions (that we concede fundamental sustaining relations and assert that these are dynamic) lead together to the first and fourth assumptions (that there is a world and that we are part of it). Decades of careful desk-peering have led us to believe that the mind is somehow outside of nature (hence innumerable doomed attempts to "prove" the existence of the external world as a kind of absolute substantial). A walk through a forest—or for that matter through a clear-cut—should persuade us otherwise. The most immediate *given* of experience is the causal efficacy of the world, pressing against and swarming through us like the heat of the sun or the smell of crushed leaves (or in a clear-cut, perhaps, of rotting animals). Perception is just another interaction in the world: an apprehension, raw and powerful, of presences other than us: a dynamic relationship, partly internal. And in the clear-cut or the forest around us, other things, myriads of them, perceive, and are influenced (doubtless infinitesimally), by us.

Failure to see this has led to some very strange theories of perception indeed: that is, the ones most commonly held today.

Acceptance of this view of experience—I would say, in a fundamental sense, the acceptance of experience—leaves us where common sense ought to leave us: woven into a real world of dynamic relationships, relationships that support their *relata*. It will doubtless be objected that all this is far too subjective to form the basis for an acceptable philosophy, much less for a philosophy that can hope to bear the banner of environmentalism. But this objection entirely misses the point. The model of experience suggested here can be applied—and most fruitfully—as a model of reality (perhaps we should say realities) more generally. On the grounds suggested here, neither our experience nor our knowledge is ever merely subjective.

I therefore urge—by now to no one's surprise—that process-relational philosophy ought to be the bedrock of environmental thinking and of the environmental movement; that it ought to be taught not merely by professional philosophers to philosophy students but to business, art, forestry, political science, prelaw, pretheological, and premedical students; and that so far as possible, it should emerge from the ivory tower and into the parlance of writers, filmmakers, political and legal practitioners, media hacks, journalists: in short, into the living fiber of our civilization.

Perhaps there is one name that some will consider this paper to have neglected: that of Martin Heidegger. In "The Question concerning Technology"[8] and elsewhere, Heidegger elaborates a theory of technology as a way of revealing the world as "standing reserve," for human purposes. I do not doubt that one can learn a great deal from Heidegger's notion of "enframing," as from his philosophy of technology generally—or for that matter, from his later reflections on the "fourfold." Indeed, for those interested in philosophy/ecology, Heidegger should be made required reading. But there is a fundamental flaw—or limitation—in Heidegger's approach. That is, *all* significant realities in Heidegger's writings are systematically viewed from the vantage-point of man, and man alone. From a purely phenomenological standpoint this is inescapable, but I am all the more convinced that such a methodological limitation must be escaped. We need to know not only how man relates to the woods but how the trees relate to each other, and to the birds, squirrels, fungi, parasites, and saprophytes that in turn relate to them and constitute a forest. From a process-relational viewpoint, aspects of our own experience-in-the-world can be imputed to other dynamic relations than those we are directly involved in. Nature is not merely "standing reserve" for phenomenologically inclined philosophers, either.[9]

I would make a similar criticism of the philosophy of John Dewey, with its methodological limitation to the first-person plural, paralleling phenomenology's analogous limitation to the first-person singular. In both cases, human perceiving-knowing relationships, singular or collective, are taken to be the only relationship philosophy can examine and reflect upon in any profound way. In such *Lebenswelts*, strangely, only man can be said to live.

I would like to end this brief talk where it began:[10] with the insistent notion that there are very real, very serious environmental problems, involving the future not only of rare species but of the global climate and of the biosphere generally. I will not accept the view that the discussion of such facts has no place in a philosophical conference. Nor will I accept the response that philosophy has nothing to say about them.

Notes

1. For example, "Decline of the CFC Empire," *Science News* 133, no. 15 (April 9, 1988): 234–36.
2. For example, J. Raloff, "New Acid Rain Threat Identified," *Science News* 133, no. 18 (April 30, 1988): 276; and L. Roberts, "Fresh Look at Acid Rain," *Science* 240, no. 4853 (May 6, 1988): 715.
3. For example, Peter H. Raven, *The Global Ecosystem in Crisis* (Chicago: John D. and Catherine MacArthur Foundation, 1987), esp. pp. 7–10.
4. In A. O. Lovejoy, *The Thirteen Pragmatisms and Other Essays* (Baltimore: Johns Hopkins Press, 1963), pp. 1–29.
5. Henri Bergson, *The Two Sources of Morality and Religion,* trans. A. Audra and C. Brereton with the assistance of W. H. Carter (Notre Dame, Ind.: University of Notre Dame Press, 1977), pp. 287–306.
6. Alfred North Whitehead, *Science and the Modern World* (New York: The Free Press, 1953), p. 206.
7. As a recent, highly successful attempt to present a coherent, consistent, and canonical Whitehead, I would recommend Jorge Nobo, *Whitehead's Metaphysics of Extension and Solidarity* (Albany: State University of New York Press, 1986).
8. Martin Heidegger, *Martin Heidegger: Basic Writings*, ed. D. F. Krell (New York: Harper and Row, 1976), pp. 284–317.
9. However, cf. Professor Sandra B. Rosenthal, "Pragmatism and Heidegger: A Common World," delivered earlier in this conference. Professor Rosenthal informs me that she may be able to find, in the later Heidegger, a philosophical basis whereby nonhuman organisms may be understood in their relations to each other.
10. There has not been space here to deal with some of the problems involved in relating process-relational philosophy with ecology. Cf. Pete A. Y. Gunter, "Creativity and Ecology," *Creativity in Art, Religion, and Culture*, ed. Michael H. Mitias (Amsterdam: Rodopi, 1985), pp. 107–16.

Of Algorithms and Apple Pie:
A Pragmatist Critique of AI

PETER LIMPER

Criticisms of current work in Artificial Intelligence (AI) have been made by analytic philosophers such as John Searle;[1] phenomenologists, notably Hubert Dreyfus;[2] and some computer scientists, especially Joseph Weizenbaum.[3] In the following discussion, an alternative, though related, critique will be developed making use of concepts of mind and intelligence taken from classical American pragmatism, particularly the thought of Charles Peirce.

The critique will be directed against what Searle calls "strong AI," which he defines as the view that "the appropriately programmed computer really *is* a mind, in the sense that computers given the right programs can be literally said to *understand* and have other cognitive states,"[4] and that conversely "the brain is just a digital computer and the [human] mind is just a computer program."[5] The digital computer is assumed to be operating as a "universal Turing machine" and its program to be an algorithm or "effective procedure," a set of completely unambiguous, step-by-step instructions. The claim made by those who advocate the strong AI thesis is that such a computer, executing such a program, can be "intelligent" in a humanlike way and, conversely, that human "intelligence" must entail the following of implicit or explicit algorithms.

In beginning to criticize this view, let us consider an example that Peirce introduces in discussing the idea of generality.[6] Suppose, he says, a cook wishes to make an apple pie. The cook has her[7] recipe book, "a collection of rules," to guide her. Peirce notes that she has only a *general* idea of the pie she aims to make: "It is not [yet] any particular apple pie; for it is to be made for the occasion." She goes to the cellar to select some apples; again, not with a predetermined idea of the *particular* apples she will take. Yet "from the nature of things, she ... must take the particular thing"; her doing so is "an example of following a general rule." And so it goes through the process of following the recipe, a set of general rules, until the outcome, which is the transformation of the indeterminate aim into a concrete, particular pie.

The example, although a simple one, is highly significant, for it can be taken as paradigmatic of Peirce's concept of intelligence: the governing of behavior by appropriate general rules (or "habits") in order to attain a desired end. As seems evident, and as the subsequent discussion will show in more detail, there is a sharp difference between Peirce's account of the cook's intelligence in following a general rule and the AI researchers' concept of the "intelligence" of a computer (or a human mind) in executing a step-by-step program.

Let us consider several aspects of this difference. To begin with, the example is intended to show that a rule such as the cook's recipe really is *general*. For Peirce, of course, this is to say that a rule is an example of his category of Thirdness, real generality. Its generality is irreducible; its very being consists in the fact that it can apply to or govern an indefinite number of specific instances and yet that its meaning is not exhaustively captured by enumerating those instances. The cook may bake apple pies for a lifetime, and no two pies, or bakings, will be exactly alike. Plainly, the rule or recipe for making pies does not consist of a detailed description of all possible pies or all possible variations in the process of baking them.

Yet it seems that this is precisely what a computer program or "recipe" for pie-making must be. As anyone who has ever tried to program a computer will recognize, the computer must be given *exact* instructions covering every possible contingency. Much recent work in AI has been concerned with the need to provide the computer with "knowledge structures" within a particular domain so that it may function like a human "expert."[8] But as critics point out, insofar as this requires a program that specifies responses for all possible variations of a situation, it seems impossibly difficult even within quite restrictive domains.[9] The AI researchers' reply is that intelligent human behavior *must* in fact be governed by such detailed algorithms, that the apparent generality of rules is simply a result of the fact that we are somehow not aware of the details of the "instructions" with which our brains are programmed. Peirce, however, would respond that this is to miss the very point of the nature of a general rule.[10]

This concept of the generality of rules is intimately associated with the idea that rules are "final causes" in Peirce's sense of this term.[11] "[W]e must understand by final causation that mode of bringing facts about according to which a general description of result is made to come about, quite irrespective of any compulsion for it to come about in this or that particular way."[12]

The cook *aims at* or *desires* a result that is not yet determinate. The recipe gives her general rules for the attaining of that result but does not "compel" her to choose particular apples or to mix and bake the pie in an exactly specified way. Only when the aim is attained is the nature of the particular pie fully specified.

If the conduct of a person following a rule can be said to be governed by "final causes," then surely the actions of a computer executing a program are determined by "efficient causes." These actions are predetermined by the program itself, and despite the fact that AI researchers may speak of the "goal" or "aim" of the program (as the "goal" of a chess-playing program is to win the game), there is always something Pickwickian about such terminology.[13] The chess-playing program does not "desire" to win a not-yet-completed game in the sense in which Peirce thinks that the cook "desires" to serve a not-yet-baked apple pie. Instead, the computer has a repertory of determinate (though perhaps highly diverse) responses to particular chess moves or board configurations, responses that might be said to be part of the *programmer's* aim that the computer should win the game.[14]

For Peirce, the idea of final causality is essential for an understanding of human rationality. "The essence of rationality lies in the fact that the rational being will act so as to attain certain ends. Prevent his doing so in one way and he will act in some utterly different way which will produce the same result. Rationality is being governed by final causes."[15]

This linking of rationality with purposive behavior is of course at the core of the concept of pragmatism; as Peirce notes, the very name of his new theory was determined by "its recognition of an inseparable connection between rational cognition and rational purpose."[16] Furthermore, it must be remembered that pragmatism is a theory of *meaning* and that for Peirce, meaning is also related to purpose and "final causality." "The rational meaning of every proposition lies in the future. . . . [The meaning] is, according to the pragmaticist, that form in which the proposition becomes applicable to human conduct, not in these or those special circumstances, nor when one entertains this or that special design, but that form which is most directly applicable to self-control under every situation, and to every purpose. This is why he locates the meaning in future time; for future conduct is the only conduct that is subject to self-control."[17]

Given what has already been said, this implies that such meaning is irreducibly *general*.

The problem of meaning has been a particularly difficult one for AI. As many critics have pointed out, the symbols that are used by the computer (ultimately strings of ones and zeros) do not seem to have "meaning" except as they are interpreted by the programmer or computer user. Even the most "intelligent" program simply manipulates these arbitrary symbols in complex ways. Put another way, the computer deals with the *syntax* of the symbolic structures but not the *semantics*.[18]

To say that the symbols with which the computer operates are completely arbitrary is, as David Bolter notes, to say that "computer thought is a triumph of nominalism," in contrast to "the long Western tradition of realism, of the conviction that the human mind does not construct its ideas purely at will but that instead those ideas have some force, necessity, or reality of their own."[19] Although Bolter intends this primarily as a description of "computer thought," for Peirce it would be another indication that the computer cannot properly be said to "think" at all and certainly does not model human thinking. "Nominalism" is of course for Peirce a term of the strongest philosophical reproach: it entails the denial not only that ideas have "force, necessity, or reality of their own" but that they have real *generality*. As we have seen, it is precisely the generality of ideas that allows them to function as guides for purposive behavior in Peirce's view and thus to have "meaning" in his sense. Once again, from a pragmatist standpoint the symbols manipulated by the computer, though they may *stand for* ideas when interpreted by the programmer or computer user, do not function as "ideas" within the computer. Contrary to the language of some AI researchers, it cannot be said that the computer has "knowledge" or "understanding" because of its operations on these arbitrary symbols.

Finally, we should note the importance of Peirce's (and other pragmatists') emphasis on the evaluative aspect of intelligence. To say that pragmatism recognizes an intimate connection between "rational cognition and rational purpose" is to say that for the pragmatist, thinking always concerns *ends* as well as *means*. We have already considered the relation between the generality of rules and their role in shaping future conduct. It should also be emphasized that the rules themselves are subject to constant review and reevaluation. It is this that Peirce has in mind when he says that future conduct is "subject to self-control." He further asserts that such self-control is ultimately guided by an appeal to fundamental values.

> There are . . . modes of self-control which seem quite instinctive. Next, there is a kind of self-control which results from training. Next, a man can be his own training-master and thus control his self-control. . . . When a man trains himself, thus controlling control, he must have some moral rule in view, however special and irrational it may be. But next he may undertake to improve this rule; that is, to exercise a control over his control of control. To do this he must have in view something higher than an irrational rule. He must have some sort of moral principle. This, in turn, may be controlled by reference to an aesthetic ideal of what is fine.[20]

Although Peirce never completely developed his idea of logic, ethics, and aesthetics as the three "normative sciences" of which aesthetics is the most fundamental,[21] it is clear that he thought that all human reasoning involves a normative element and that the higher modes of thought (including science) are characterized by an increasing reflection upon and criticism of norms.

It has already been remarked that the computer cannot be said in any meaningful sense to have purposes or goals, much less the ability to assess those goals in terms of broader principles or norms. AI researchers may speak of programs that "understand" different human goals and their relative importance,[22] but as has been argued above, such "understanding" is really that of the programmer. The computer can be programmed to *act* in ways that reflect certain human norms, but they are not *its* norms. Computers do not have *self*-control in Peirce's sense because they do not have *selves*; to have a self is to be concerned with one's future conduct and with the ideals that should govern it.

I have now enumerated a number of ways in which the pragmatist conception of intelligence, as exemplified by the activity of the cook in making an apple pie, differs from current notions of machine "intelligence" and from models of human thinking based on the operation of digital computers. No attempt has been made to claim that the criticisms made of strong AI from the standpoint of Peirce's pragmatism are unique to that perspective. Many of them have been made in different ways by other critics. For example, the idea that human thinking (unlike the operation of a computer) is always an activity with some aim or purpose is echoed in both Searle's and Dreyfus's accounts of intentionality: Dreyfus's discussion of "the situation [of thinking] as a function of human needs"[23] has a particularly "pragmatic" ring to it.

What, then, is the point of a specifically pragmatist critique of AI? First of all, I would argue that given the often exaggerated claims for the future of machine intelligence and the increasing dominance of the machine model of human intelligence, it is important to examine AI critically from as many perspectives as possible. It is also interesting to note once again how classical American pragmatism has affinities with, and indeed anticipates, a number of the important ideas of phenomenology and analytic philosophy.[24] Finally, and most significantly, by raising criticisms of strong AI from the standpoint of pragmatism, those criticisms are placed in a particularly rich context. Pragmatism not only provides useful insights into what is wrong with the strong AI thesis but gives an alternative account of intelligence that still has great power and relevance to contemporary discussions. Let me briefly indicate a few respects in which I think that this pragmatist alternative may be especially valuable.

First, while critics from a number of perspectives have argued convincingly that machine "intelligence" falls short of human intelligence in important ways, they are often less successful in their positive characterization of human mental processes as these differ from the operation of machines. Dreyfus contrasts "the power of human intuition" with the operation of computerized expert systems;[25] Weizenbaum compares human "intuition, hunch, and other such informal means [of thinking]" with the more "systematic" reasoning processes of the computer.[26] There is a danger here, I think, in conceding to the computer the power to "reason" in an abstract, "logical" fashion while reserving to the human mind some special and perhaps mysterious and even nonrational intellectual ability. By contrast, the pragmatist account makes particularly plain how true intelligence involves being guided by nonalgorithmic general rules, purposes, and concerns and how this is not "nonrational" but is the very essence of true rationality.

I believe that the particular way in which pragmatism deals with the *normative* character of all reasoning is especially significant. The proponents of strong AI of course believe that "intelligence" is simply a matter of calculation, not of evaluation. But even some of their critics, such as Weizenbaum when he contrasts "wisdom" or "judgment" with calculative intelligence,[27] seem to assume that some sorts of thinking are value-free and, conversely, that normative thinking is restricted to some special (and again perhaps nonrational) domain of human reflection. The pragmatists, however (perhaps James and Dewey even more than Peirce) give powerful accounts of the way in which intelligence always involves valuation. They thus avoid the trap of dichotomizing the rational and the normative, a trap that sometimes catches the critics of AI as well as its advocates.[28]

One other point can be only briefly noted. For Peirce and the other pragmatists, human thinking is always "situated," not only in terms of the needs and goals of the individual but in a wider human context. The role played by the concept of *community* in Peirce's thought, the way in which it is connected with such previously discussed ideas as generality, "rational purpose," and self-control, is worthy of much more discussion than can be given here. I can only suggest that the fact that pragmatism provides a *social* theory of intelligence may be one of its most important contributions to the AI debate.

I would like to close on a somewhat speculative note. It is sometimes thought that critics of strong AI must be mind-body dualists of some sort; that in denying that computers have "minds," they are tacitly assuming that "minds" are not physical at all. Searle sharply rejects this; in fact, he argues that it is strong AI that makes a "dualistic assumption"; namely, that "programs are independent of their realization in machines."[29] By contrast, his view is that *only* human brains, and conceivably "machines that had the same causal powers as brains," could think, because thinking depends on the special *intentional* causal powers of the (material) brain.[30] He concedes that there *might* be some machine simulation of thinking that did not depend on the idea that "mental processes are computational processes over formally defined elements" but regards this claim as trivial because it has nothing to do with current work in AI.[31]

Recently, however, there has been increasing discussion of an alternative approach to AI by means of what are variously called "connectionist," "parallel distributed processing," or "neural network" systems.[32] Such systems, although they do not model the details of the human (or animal) brain, are intended to simulate certain of its important characteristics. They consist of a number of units that can be "activated" at different levels, interconnected so that the activation level of one unit affects various other units. Introducing changes in some activation levels may result in various changes in the overall configuration until the system reaches a new stable state. Such systems can seemingly "learn" to recognize patterns (letters of the alphabet, faces, and so on) without having been explicitly programmed to do so. They can be interpreted as providing a nonalgorithmic machine "model" of the functioning of the brain (albeit on a very simplified level at present).

Now Peirce, like all the pragmatists, certainly thought that there is a physical (organic) basis for human intelligence, and there are some interesting parallels between his speculations, in the 1890s, on what this physical basis might be [33] and the model provided by connectionist systems. Peirce argued that protoplasm is characterized by its instability and its tendency when disturbed to acquire and retain a new state or "habit." This is especially true of nervous tissue. "The nerves are particularly ready to take and change their habits."[34] Peirce's account is tentative, and many of the details are of course outdated, but what is striking is the idea that the physical properties of the nervous system are consonant with the formation and *re*-formation of "habits" that in humans become the *general* rules of conduct that we have been discussing. Peirce even says that his account shows that "a tendency to act intelligently, that is, so as to bring about a certain result, might arise in a mere mechanical system."[35] If it really is the case that connectionist systems "take and change habits" in something like Peirce's sense, then perhaps they are a first small step toward what he would regard as a more genuine "artificial intelligence."[36] In any case, this example once again suggests the continuing relevance of his ideas to subjects of contemporary interest.

Notes

1. John Searle, "Minds, Brains, and Programs," *The Behavioral and Brain Sciences* 3 (1980): 417–24, reprinted in *The Mind's I*, ed. Douglas Hofstadter and Daniel Dennett (New York: Basic Books, 1981), pp. 353–73, and in John Searle, *Minds, Brains, and Science* (Cambridge: Harvard University Press, 1984).

2. Hubert Dreyfus, *What Computers Can't Do*, 2nd rev. ed. (New York: Harper and Row, 1979); Hubert Dreyfus and Stuart Dreyfus, *Mind over Machine* (New York: The Free Press, 1986).

3. Joseph Weizenbaum, *Computer Power and Human Reason* (San Francisco: W. H. Freeman and Co., 1976).

4. Searle, "Minds, Brains, and Programs," p. 353.

5. Searle, *Minds, Brains, and Science*, p. 28.

6. Charles Sanders Peirce, 1.341. All references to Peirce are to the volume and paragraph number in *The Collected Papers of Charles Sanders Peirce*, vols. 1–6, ed. Charles Hartshorne and Paul Weiss (Cambridge: Harvard University Press, 1931–35).

7. I will follow Peirce's usage here, but this should not be taken as endorsing any claim that cooks in general are or should be female.

8. See, for example, Roger Schank, *The Cognitive Computer* (Reading, Mass.: Addison-Wesley Pub. Co., 1984), pp. 110–33.

9. See, for example, Dreyfus, *What Computers Can't Do*, pp. 55–66.

10. See D. B. Burrell, "Obeying Rules and Following Instructions," *Philosophy and Cybernetics*, ed. Frederick Crosson and Kenneth Sayer (New York: Simon and Schuster, 1968), pp. 203–32, for an early discussion of this distinction and its significance for AI. Burrell appears to have been influenced by the ideas of both Wittgenstein and Peirce on this point.

11. For Peirce, final causality, like generality, is a concept that applies to the entire natural world and not just to the operations of the human mind. For the purposes of the

present discussion, it does not seem necessary to enter into the question of whether there are "real generals" or "real final causes" in nature, or of Peirce's metaphysical interpretation of these concepts.

12. Peirce, *Collected Papers*, 1.211.
13. See, for example, Schank, *The Cognitive Computer*, pp. 123–33.
14. Dreyfus, *What Computers Can't Do*, pp. 272–80.
15. Peirce, *Collected Papers*, 2.66.
16. Ibid., 5.412.
17. Ibid., 5.427.
18. See, for example, Weizenbaum, *Computer Power and Human Reason*, pp. 67–68; and Searle, "Minds, Brains, and Programs," p. 370.
19. J. David Bolter, *Turing's Man* (Chapel Hill: University of North Carolina Press, 1984), p. 77.
20. Peirce, *Collected Papers*, 5.533.
21. See, for example, Peirce, *Collected Papers*, 1.191, 5.120–50.
22. See, for example, Schank, *The Cognitive Computer*, pp. 126, 132.
23. Dreyfus, *What Computers Can't Do*, pp. 272–80.
24. Richard Bernstein has often emphasized similarities between pragmatism and analytic and recent continental philosophy. See especially Richard J. Bernstein, *Praxis and Action* (Philadelphia: University of Pennsylvania Press, 1971).
25. Dreyfus and Dreyfus, *Mind over Machine*, pp. 101–21, and passim.
26. Weizenbaum, *Computer Power and Human Reason*, p. 214.
27. Ibid., pp. 202–27.
28. Dreyfus, however, clearly sees the need to avoid this "trap." See, e.g., Dreyfus, *What Computers Can't Do*, p. 280.
29. Searle, "Minds, Brains, and Programs," p. 371.
30. Ibid., p. 372.
31. Ibid., p. 366.
32. See, for example, William Bechtel, "Connectionism and the Philosophy of Mind: An Overview," *Southern Journal of Philosophy* 26 (1987 supplement): 17–38.
33. See, for example, Peirce, *Collected Papers*, 6.246–69, 6.278–86.
34. Ibid., 6.281.
35. Ibid., 6.285.
36. If the pragmatist account of intelligence is correct, a genuinely "intelligent" connectionist system would have to have something like purposes, concerns, and values. There are obviously enormous difficulties in the way of developing any such system, and if it ever could be developed, this would also raise serious moral questions for its builders.

PEIRCE AND BUCHLER

Peirce on Evolution by Revolution

H. WILLIAM DAVENPORT

Introduction

In his later writings, Peirce advocated a broader recognition of the possibility and actuality of a kind of evolution that may be aptly described as evolution by revolution.[1] At various times he identified actual and apparent examples of this mode of evolution in a number of different domains, including the sciences, biological evolution, and human culture. Peirce's ideas about evolution by revolution appear to have considerable relevance to certain contemporary debates about these subjects.

Continuity and Evolution by Revolution

Peirce was a contender for continuity, as is well known. He advocated "synechism," the regulative version of which is that continuity ought to be hypothesized until discontinuity has been proved. One way to hypothesize continuity is to suppose that things are a matter of degree along a continuum. Apply this idea to continuity itself, and the result is that continuity and discontinuity are themselves matters of degree and that absolute continuity and absolute discontinuity are the extreme limits of a continuum. A consequence of this is that we may suppose a process to be continuous in a sense and to a degree, and also assume that the process is episodic or even subject to disruptions so severe that they amount to revolutions. We have then the possibility of evolution by revolution—a drastic change that does not necessarily involve a complete or absolute breach of continuity.

It should thus be clear that the recognition of evolution by revolution as one possible mode of evolution is quite consistent with Peirce's synechism and, by the reasoning sketched above, is in fact a logical consequence of it.[2] It will become evident in what follows that Peirce's notion of revolutionary evolution involves a certain sort of causal mechanism, which brings about an episode of very rapid change.

Let us now turn to the different domains in which Peirce found or hypothesized evolution by revolution.

Evolution by Revolution in the Sciences

Peirce recognized the occurrence of a number of revolutions in the history of the sciences, including several during his own lifetime. Early in his career he experienced the Darwinian revolution, and late in life he believed that he was witnessing yet another revolution at least as great: "[T]he new conception of matter which has resulted from the study of various finds of radiation is now taking on the aspect of a greater revolution in science than did the advent of the doctrine of energy or that of natural selection, and therefore of the greatest since Newton, if not since Copernicus."[3]

Such revolutions provide the major source of progress in science, according to Peirce. He acknowledged the worth of the slow, steady, gradual accumulation of results that Thomas Kuhn has called "normal science." This latter was the sort of scientific work that Peirce himself did, for the most part, so he would not have wished to underestimate its role in the advancement of science. "Science, however, mainly progresses by great leaps, by decisive conquests, by mutations in theories," as Professor Edward Madden has summarized Peirce's judgment.[4]

Madden quite accurately and appropriately points up the contrast between Peirce's view that scientific revolutions really do bring progress toward truth and Kuhn's view that successive paradigm-theories are incommensurable and no measure of progress is possible, apart from success in predicting. Because of this crucial difference, Madden even refrains from using the term *revolution* to describe Peirce's views and applies it only to the Kuhnian succession of (supposedly) incommensurable paradigms. But Peirce himself uses the term *revolution* in this context, without implying incommensurability, and it is often such a natural and useful term for the "extraordinary leaps" and "cataclysmic epochs" envisioned by Peirce that it would be unwise to allow Kuhn to usurp it. Peirce's idea or hypothesis is "that while it may be true that all evolution, be it physiological or physical, intellectual or spiritual, individual or social, proceeds without any *strict* breach of continuity, yet it is universally found that in every development there are at least two extraordinary leaps. . . . There is a natural presumption in favor of something like the doctrine of universal continuity, but upon uniformitarianism, which goes further, there lies a heavy burden of proof."[5]

What Peirce has in mind, then, is a period of change so rapid and profound that it is rightly considered an extraordinary leap, or a cataclysm, or a revolution. Yet the change does not necessarily involve any *strict* breach of continuity, any *absolute* discontinuity.[6] This is a revolution in which some kind and degree of continuity is preserved. This continuity will presumably allow for some degree of commensurability in cases of scientific revolutions, even those in which a new paradigm-theory has displaced its predecessor. What the continuity and the commensurability will consist of will of course need to be worked out for each particular revolution. But in the general idea of a kind and degree of continuity that persists through a revolution, we have a first step toward a non-Kuhnian, nonrelativist interpretation of scientific revolutions. According to this interpretation, revolutions in the sciences will form one set of cases of "evolution by revolution." They will be cases of evolution because they are part of a course of development that is continuous in a sense and to a degree. They will be cases of evolution by revolution because of the rapidity and profundity of the change involved.

One reason that the problem of incommensurability arises for skeptics such as Kuhn and Richard Rorty is that they can attach no meaning to the notion of an absolute, transcendent world-view, one relative to which objective measures of absolute progress (toward truth or whatever) might be made. As they see it, any world-view relative to which measures are made is simply one more world-view, itself destined to be replaced by another, in what is potentially an indefinitely long succession of world-views. They see no basis on which any one of these world-views might claim the absoluteness or superiority needed to justify judgments about progress toward truth. But it seems that Peirce's notion of the long-run consensus of the (ideal) community of inquirers does provide a meaning to the idea of an absolute or objective world-view, relative to which judgments about progress toward truth would be valid. On Peirce's hypothesis, there is an ultimate world-view, namely the one that would be accepted by the ideal community of inquirers in its long-run consensus. This is the world-view that will never be replaced or superseded by another, no matter how long inquiry may be pursued.

This is the pragmatic meaning of an ultimate world-view, the meaning that the scientific community attaches to it. There may be problems with it, and the dialogue with the skeptical relativists ought to be pursued, but no Peirceian is compelled to accept the claim that the notion of an ultimate world-view is meaningless. Peirceians will not of course claim to know infallibly that there is such an ultimate world-view, but they do hold that all truth-seekers fervently *hope* that there is such an ultimate truth. To the extent that we act as though we are ourselves members of this ideal community of truth-seekers, our hope becomes a habit of action, a genuine belief for us. Only in that way can our hope—our hypothesis—that there are such things as truth and reality be brought to the test. But the test is one of the long run, and no individual member of the community will live long enough to learn its outcome.

Evolution by Revolution in Biology

In the 1890s, Darwin's theory of evolution by chance variation and natural selection had not yet carried the day against two main competing theories. One of these was Lamarck's theory that the efforts of individual organisms produce imperceptible changes that are then transmitted to their offspring. Thus, like Darwinism, Lamarck's theory is gradualistic; that is, change from one generation to the next is very slight, so that an organism can be transformed quickly only if generations succeed one another rapidly. Peirce, writing as a historian of science in 1898, described a very different third theory,

> the theory of cataclysmal evolution, according to which the changes have not been small and have not been fortuitous; but they have taken place chiefly in reproduction. According to this view, sudden changes of environment have taken place from time to time. These changes have put certain organs at a disadvantage, and there has been effort to use them in new ways. Such organs are particularly apt to sport in reproduction and to change in the way which adapts them better to their recent mode of exercise.
>
> Notwithstanding the teachings of Weismann, it seems altogether probable that all three of these modes of evolution have acted. It is probable that the last has been the most efficient.[7]

Most efficient, that is, in the generation of new species. Peirce and others at that time attributed superior efficiency to cataclysmal evolution in part because the geological and fossil records show episodes of rapid, drastic changes in the environment, in conjunction with changes in plant and animal life of corresponding tempo and magnitude. Another factor that particularly swayed Peirce and other physicists of the day toward cataclysmal evolution was the great physicist Kelvin's conclusion that the age of the solar system was on the order of hundreds of thousands of years. On that time scale there has not been time enough for life to have developed to its present condition solely through a series of imperceptibly slight steps. Some sort of cataclysmal or revolutionary or episodic evolution is called for.[8]

But here a distinction must be noted between the tempo or rate or pattern of evolution, on the one hand, and the causal mechanism that is hypothesized to produce that tempo on the other. Given that the tempo or rate or pattern of development is episodic and "jerky" as opposed to smooth and gradual, what is the cause of that tempo? The causal mechanism associated by Peirce with cataclysmic evolution appears from a contemporary perspective to be highly implausible as a cause of biological evolution. It involves not the Lamarckian inheritance of acquired characteristics, exactly, but instead the assumption that the response by an organism to a drastic environmental change can cause in its offspring a tendency to "sport," or mutate, and, moreover, in a direction better adapting them to the changed environment. But even if we reject this hypothesis as a possible cause of organic, biological evolution, it may still be a possible cause of cultural or intellectual development, as we shall see in the next section.

Furthermore, Peirce's advocacy of an episodic tempo of the development of life is one of some interest, quite apart from the causal mechanism, in light of the challenge to Darwinian gradualism and even to natural selection by contemporary biologists Stephen Gould and Niles Eldredge.[9] They call the episodic tempo "punctuated equilibria," and they have postulated a causal mechanism called "allopatric speciation" that downplays the role of natural selection in the evolution of new species as well as new families and orders of organisms (macroevolution). This view apparently remains a minority viewpoint among contemporary biologists, and its fate is still in doubt. But its power and vitality as a hypothesis suggest that Peirce may not have been far off the track, after all, in accepting a pattern of revolutionary organic evolution.

Moreover, if we follow Peirce's advice that we transfer successful theories from one field to another, we should take the hypothesis of punctuated equilibria caused by allopatric speciation and try it out in the domains of cultural and intellectual evolution. Because some proponents of punctuated equilibria have already begun to do this, we would do well to study their work and assist them as best we can in developing and evaluating it.[10]

Evolution by Revolution in Culture

Peirce asserted that evolution by revolution is probably the most potent source of change in human culture as well.

> According to the Lamarckian theory, it is exercise and the consequent growth which by imperceptible steps has transformed the Moner into Man. But according to Darwin's hypothesis exercise had nothing to do with it. The whole gulf has been bridged by imperceptible variations at birth. But if we can trust to the lessons of the history of the human mind [and] the history of habits of life, development does not take place chiefly by imperceptible changes but by revolutions. For some cause or other trade which had been taking one route suddenly begins to take another. In consequence merchants bring new goods; and new goods make new habits. Or some invention like that of writing, or printing, or gunpowder, or the mariners' compass, or the steam engine, in a comparatively short time changes men very profoundly. It seems strange that we who have seen such tremendous revolutions in all the habits of men during this century should put our faith in the influence of imperceptible variations to an extent that no other age ever did. Is it because we have so little of Asiatic immovability before our eyes that we do not realize now what the conservatism of old habit really is?

> That habit alone can produce development I do not believe.
>
> It is catastrophe, accident, reaction which brings habit into an active condition and creates a habit of changing habits.
>
> To learn is to acquire a habit. What makes men learn? Not merely the sight of what they are accustomed to, but perpetual new experiences which throws them into a habit of tossing aside old ideas and forming new ones.
>
> The most striking difference between the state of society today and that of Dr. Johnson's and Horace Walpole's time is the readiness of people nowadays to adopt new ways of life and new ways of thinking. And think what it was before the invention of printing! This plastic habit which we have acquired has not been brought about by imperceptible degrees but by a succession of revolutions, printing, the reformation, Newton, the French Revolution, steam, and so on.
>
> Consider the changes which take place in men's inmost habits, in their character and purposes. Are they brought about by imperceptible changes? Only in the way of decay. Conversions and reformations—which after all are not unknown phenomena—are always consequent upon impressive experiences.[11]

Here in the realms of culture and of individual psychology, the causal explanation involved in the theory of cataclysmal evolution assumes much greater plausibility. Rapid, drastic environmental changes generate novel experiences that stimulate learning, the casting aside of old habits, and the taking on of new ones. This in turn creates "a habit of changing habits." We see in such processes the cultural and psychological analogues of the scientific revolutions discussed above.

Conclusion

We have seen that the notion of evolution by revolution, so long as it does not involve *absolute* discontinuity, does not violate Peirce's synechism. Peirce wrote about a number of different domains in which evolution by revolution has occurred and continues to occur, including the sciences, biological evolution, and human culture. He recognized that revolutions in the sciences are the most important sources of scientific progress, but his synechism stayed him from drawing the conclusion of Kuhn and Rorty that successive paradigms are absolutely incommensurable. With respect to biological evolution, Peirce's expectation of revolutionary phases was one factor behind his strong criticisms of the gradualism of Darwin and the neo-Darwinists. There are some fascinating parallels between Peirce's views and the contemporary theory of punctuated equilibria advocated by Eldredge and Gould. Those who extend the punctuational theory to the evolution of human culture are in effect following Peirce's proposal that biological theories of evolution be tried as hypotheses about the development of human culture. In all these respects, Peirce's ideas about evolution by revolution clearly provide bridges from classic American philosophy to contemporary debates.

Peirce also developed mathematical models and logical analyses of continuity and discontinuity, which have not been utilized in this paper. These may provide a basis for further elucidation of the notion of evolution by revolution, thereby opening new frontiers of research and understanding.

Notes

1. In 1891 Peirce first published a triadic classification of kinds of evolution, derived by an application of his categories, in "The Architecture of Theories" (*Collected Papers of Charles S. Peirce* [ed. in 8 vols. by C. Hartshorne, P. Weiss, and A. Burks, Cambridge: Harvard University Press, 1931–58], vol. 6, paragraphs 15–17; hereafter cited as CP). Ten years before, Peirce had referred to chance variations, catastrophes, and habit-taking as three causes of evolution in his 1881 advanced logic course at Johns Hopkins University, according to his student Ellery W. Davis's valuable account of it: "He [Peirce] held, further, that without catastrophes from time to time the accumulation of minute chance variations by the survival of the fittest was insufficient for the development of a new species. His reason was that chance variations, in accordance with Bernoulli's law, would always preserve the dominance of the original type. He admitted that, assuming (in accordance with his philosophy) the habit-acquiring property in the universe, the development of a new species by minute variations is possible; but he insisted that the biologists had never called attention to this fact" ("Charles Peirce at Johns Hopkins," *Mid-West Quarterly* 2 [1914]: 48–56, p. 55).

The kind of evolution I here call "evolution by revolution" is the sort associated by Peirce with his category of Secondness, which in 1893 he called "evolution by mechanical necessity" or "anancastic evolution" or "anancasm," from the "necessity" of Secondness or Actuality breaking in to disrupt current habits and provoke new ones ("Evolutionary Love" [1893]: CP 6.298, 302, 307, 312–14). Although I have not found the phrase *evolution by revolution* in Peirce's writings, he comes close to it in the passage quoted in the next to last section: "Development [in this context a synonym for 'evolution'] does not take place chiefly by imperceptible changes but by revolutions" (1897; see note 11). This passage and others seem to justify the phrase as an apt designation, at least for one major species under the genus of anancastic evolution. As a synonym for that genus it is somewhat misleading, because Peirce apparently recognizes "leaps" that are not "revolutions"—e.g., the discoveries of Pasteur (CP 1.109, 1898). In any case, the tempo of this kind of evolution is episodic: "Anancastic evolution advances by successive strides with pauses between" (CP 6.312).

A few of the issues touched on in this paper are treated in more detail in my doctoral thesis, "Peirce's Evolutionary Explanation of Laws of Nature: 1880–1893" (University of Illinois at Urbana-Champaign, 1977).

2. About 1894, Peirce wrote that "to say that anything is continuous is to leave possibilities open which are closed by asserting that it is discontinuous. Accordingly a regulative principle of logic requires us to hold anything as continuous until it is proved discontinuous. But absolute discontinuity cannot be proved to be real, nor can any good reason for believing it real be alleged. We thus reach the conclusion that as a regulative principle, at least, ultimate continuity ought to be presumed everywhere" (CP 8.278).

Noteworthy here is that it is not discontinuity of any sort or degree that is being ruled out, but only *absolute* discontinuity. About eight years later, in his definition of *synechism* for Baldwin's *Dictionary of Philosophy and Psychology* (1902), Peirce insisted that "synechism is not an ultimate and absolute metaphysical doctrine; it is a regulative principle of logic, prescribing what sort of hypothesis is fit to be entertained and examined" (CP 6.173). It is an excellent question, raised by Charles Hartshorne, whether Peirce's synechism is compatible with the discrete quanta of quantum theory ("Charles Peirce and Quantum Mechanics," *Transactions of the Charles S. Peirce Society* 9 [1973]: 191–201). Peirce objects to hypothesizing any absoluteness or ultimacy that makes a thing absolutely inexplicable. But obviously he faces a serious problem in establishing a nonarbitrary means of distinguishing between objectionable and nonobjectionable ultimacy or absoluteness. Still, it seems clear that Peirce intends his synechism to allow for and even to require the hypothesizing of nonabsolute discontinuities in phenomena. And even in disallowing absolute discontinuity, he is doing so, not on the basis of a metaphysical dictum but on the basis of a regulative principle of the logic of explanation, which says that one should avoid trying to explain anything by means of something that is itself absolutely inexplicable. In that light, it may be that the theories of quantum mechanics can pass synechistic muster, after all. Jamila Jauhari has found "profound semantical similarities between Peircean and quantum generals," on the ground that the "objective correlatives of at least some quantum predicates are to be construed as potentialities, rather than as a set of actual events" ("Peircean and Quantum Generals," *Transactions of the Charles S. Peirce Society* 21 [1985]: 511–34).

3. Charles S. Peirce, *Contributions to the Nation*, ed. K. L. Ketner and J. E. Cook (Lubbock: Texas Tech Univ. Press, 1979), vol. 3, p. 243; November 23, 1905.

4. Edward Madden, "Max H. Fisch: Rigorous Humanist," *Transactions of the Charles S. Peirce Society* 22 (1986): 375–96, p. 391. Peirce wrote in 1898, "But this [Lamarckian evolution] is not the way in which science mainly progresses. It advances by leaps; and the impulse for each leap is either some new observational resource, or some novel way of reasoning about the observations" (CP 1.109). Robert Sharpe has suggested that Peirce's emphasis on scientific progress by leaps derives from his views on abduction ("Induction, Abduction, and the Evolution of Science," *Transactions of the Charles S. Peirce Society* 6 [1970]: 17–33).

5. Peirce, *Contributions to the Nation*, vol. 3, p. 270; June 7, 1906; my emphasis.

6. Peirce used the phrase *no absolute breach of continuity* in 1894 (Peirce, *Contributions to the Nation*, vol. 2, p. 57; April 26, 1894). That Peirce's insistence on the reality of scientific revolutions does not amount to countenancing an absolute discontinuity is clear from his strong skepticism about "an opinion which has of late years attained some vogue among men of science, that we cannot expect any physical hypothesis to maintain its ground indefinitely even with modifications, but must expect that from time to time there will be a complete cataclysm that shall utterly sweep away old theories and replace them by new ones" (CP 2.150, from *Minute Logic*, 1902).

7. CP 1.104–105 (from Robin MS 1288, dated 1898 on the basis of the correspondence with Putnam's, published in Peirce, *Historical Perspectives on Peirce's Philosophy of Science*, ed. C. Eisele [Mouton, 1985], pp. 299–306).

8. There was a dramatic change in Peirce's views on the age of the earth between October and November, 1905, apparently as a direct result of his attendance of the November meeting of the National Academy of Sciences, where he heard papers on atomic radioactivity and the radiometric dating of geological samples. Compare Peirce's reference of Oct. 5, placed in the mouth of William Clifford in a hypothetical dialogue about the origin of life, to "the thousands of centuries of time that are in question," with his report of the NAS meeting held on Nov. 14 and 15. "The newly discovered source of

energy by radio-active decomposition of elements of high atomic weight is so tremendous that the age of the sun, and consequently the length of geological eras, must probably be far greater than those [such as Peirce himself] who have listened to Kelvin and the physicists have been accustomed to think" (Peirce, *Contributions to the Nation*, vol. 3, pp. 238f. [Oct. 5, 1905], pp. 243f. [Nov. 23, 1905]). See J. D. Burchfield, *Lord Kelvin and the Age of the Earth* (Science History Pub., 1975).

9. See Niles Eldredge, *Time Frames* (New York: Simon & Schuster, 1985), esp. the appendix, "Punctuated Equilibria: An Alternative to Phyletic Gradualism," pp. 193–223, a reprint of the original 1972 paper by Eldredge and Stephen Jay Gould. For references to other writings, see Eldredge's bibliography. For trenchant criticisms of the theory of punctuated equilibria, see Richard Dawkins, *The Blind Watchmaker* (New York: Norton, 1985), chap. 9; Michael Ruse, *Darwinism Defended* (Addison-Wesley, 1982), chap. 9; and Ruse, *Taking Darwin Seriously* (Blackwell, 1986), chap. 1.

10. The value of transferring theories from one field to another is an underlying theme in "The Architecture of Theories" (CP 6.7–34) and was an explicit lesson in Peirce's logic courses at Johns Hopkins (CP 7.66–67). Peirce applied the three modes of organic evolution to the history of human thought in "Evolutionary Love" (CP 6.306–317).

11. Peirce, *New Elements of Mathematics*, ed. C. Eisele (Mouton, 1976), vol. 4, pp. 141–43. This is from Robin MS 942, pp. 25–26, datable to December, 1897, on the basis of correspondence between Peirce and William James, parts of which have been published in Kenneth Ketner and Hilary Putnam's introduction to Peirce, *Reasoning and the Logic of Things*, ed. K. L. Ketner (Cambridge: Harvard University Press, 1992); see the references to the proposed lecture 8, p. 24. This MS is not one of the eight lectures eventually delivered by Peirce in Cambridge in 1898 and so is not included in Ketner's invaluable edition of those remarkable lectures. (The final *s* of the last word in the quoted passage, "experiences," is in the MS (p. 26), even though it is omitted in *New Elements*.) In his first published description of this mode of evolution, "by external forces and the breaking up of habits," Peirce asserted that "it certainly has been the chief factor in the historical evolution of institutions as in that of ideas" (CP 6.17, 1891). Peirce added that it "cannot possibly be refused a very prominent place in the process of evolution of the universe in general." On Peirce's evolutionary cosmology, see my thesis, cited in note 1, and lectures 6–8 in Peirce, *Reasoning and the Logic of Things*, as well as the introduction and comments on the lectures.

Buchler's Poetic Theory:
Questions of Meaning and Interpretation

RICHARD E. HART

The generic burden in a poetic work is not: this is what has here been found to be; but rather: this is what has here been found indomitably and unaccountably to be; or: here is a relation of traits sovereign unto itself and irreducible.[1]

Justus Buchler

Readers of Justus Buchler's *The Main of Light: On the Concept of Poetry* will recall his generic characterization of poetry as a form of query (or exploration) embodied in exhibitive judgment and wrought in language. Additionally, says Buchler, "What poetry judges to prevail it communicates as prevailing, as sovereign and ineluctable. This is what is implied by saying that poetry conveys the sense of prevalence."[1]

Critics of Buchler's account of poetry, notably Richard Kuhns, have found difficulty in understanding and accepting Buchler's most basic concepts. In a significant, albeit flawed, *Southern Journal* article Kuhns contends that the Buchlerian concept of "prevalence" does not, when applied to poetry, help with two aspects of poetry that he finds dominant in his "perception and understanding of it [poetry] as a kind of event: the structure of the language and the meaning of the thought."[2] In terms of the formal side of poetic language, Kuhns fears that the "concept of prevalence cannot stand up to the formalist analyses of poetry current today."[3] He views the structure of "poetic language" as related to the notion of poetic prevalence, but he wishes "to know more intimately and in greater detail how poetry works as query."[4] Kuhns proposes that one way (perhaps, on his account, the most usual way) of determining the details of "meaning" in poetry is through the use of a variety of different interpretive theories, depending upon the particular poem(s) under study. Hence, psychoanalytic theory, Marxist theory, a formalist theory of meaning (such as that of Jakobson), or several taken together might be useful—even essential—in articulating the "language structure" and "meaning" of a given poem. In other words, one typically employs various specific literary or interpretive theories in attempting to get at "a poem's fullest prevalence."[5] But Kuhns is not convinced that the Buchlerian notion of "prevalence" is fully capable of rendering these specific meanings. Although he agrees with Buchler "that the presence of poetry as a real as real as any real must be defended" (language that Buchler would not condone), for Kuhns "the concept of prevalence does not help me to prepare myself for the varied responses I am called upon to give."[6] What is Kuhns really getting at?

Essential to Kuhns's criticism is the untested assumption that a theory of literature (or, more specifically, of poetry) is by necessity involved with explicating the "structure of language" and "meaning"[7] of the literary work. That is, the assumption is that the real purpose of literary theory is to provide the groundwork for specific interpretation and criticism of texts. On this view, various questions are regarded as central to literary theory: how are the details of meaning in poetry determined or achieved? How does the language structure of a particular poem contribute to its meaning? How is the poem to be interpreted or criticized in specific terms? To put the matter in Kuhns's own words, "As philosophers, when we talk about poetry we have an interest in discovering how it is that poetry achieves the depth and complexity of meaning which separates it from other language uses."[8] While language structure and meaning are considered by Buchler in *The Main of Light* (as we shall see later), Kuhns does appear to pose a rather substantial challenge. As Kuhns argues, although *The Main of Light* admirably defends poetry as a major human activity, the theory it advances leaves one wondering how it works—how meaning in poetry is ever achieved. How does one arrive at the "deep" or "found" meaning of poetry, and how do the internal forces of language, understood as linguistic structures,[9] generate "poetic meaning"? From this query it is apparent that Kuhns and Buchler have markedly different views as to what poetic theory should be about.

If one accepts Kuhns's assumptions about poetic theory, certain initial assessments of Buchler's theory inevitably follow. Hence, it could be charged that Buchler's concepts are too general and too vague; that, although his generic conceptions apply to every instance of poetry (indeed, every instance of literary art) and are capable of explaining all literary works as exhibitive utterances, the theory does not and cannot explain or interpret any particular work with sufficient detail. In other words, the theory does not provide the resources, the groundwork, or the machinery necessary for specific descriptions and interpretations of particular works. Nor does it put one in a position to evaluate literary works as good or bad, as works of genius or of shoddiness. In essence, the theory has no normative component. Thus, critics or literary interpreters cannot readily use the Buchlerian concepts and terminology in their attempts to better understand and evaluate any particular literary text.

From this critical view, to say, as Buchler does, that any poem is a product of methodic query of the exhibitive sort, to say that a poem "conveys a sense of prevalence" in this or that respect or that a poem is an "exhibitive judgment wrought in language," is to provide a generic definition or theoretic conception of literature, within the broad outlines of a metaphysical system. It offers little, however, in the way of specific interpretive machinery. A comparison of Buchler's outlook with, for example, Sartre's theory (in *What Is Literature?*)—that literature must be an "engagement" of social problems in order to advance freedom—or Wordsworth's contention (in the preface to *Lyrical Ballads*)—that poetry imaginatively recreates the simple but profound passions of the heart—is revealing. These literary theories, it could be argued, do provide a detailed framework by which any literary work can be evaluated as good or bad, humanly worthy or frivolous, while also providing an interpretive mechanism through which the precise "meaning" or "significance" of the work can be readily exposed. As an illustration, consider Sartre's reading of Richard Wright's *Black Boy*. In essence, Buchler's theory is said to "explain" all instances of poetry on a generic level but, in explaining so generally, to provide no substantial way of distinguishing any given poem from any other instance of exhibitive query wrought in language, except to say that each poem conveys a specific "sense of prevalence."

In response, Buchler would argue in part that, with theoretical pronouncements such as those of Sartre or Wordsworth, the actual motive (though it may not be consciously realized) is to "prescribe" what good or worthy literature must be. This function is arbitrarily preferred over a "descriptive" account of the nature and function of literature as a unique human product, an account involving an understanding and explanation on the metaphysical level.[10] In both cases, and in many other literary theories to which Buchler refers, judgments of value or literary preference, even ideological conflicts, are confused with generic explanations.[11] Even though both Sartre and Wordsworth claim to be explaining what literature (or poetry) is, they instead promote a view as to what literature should be and what it should accomplish. In accordance with their sense of literature's mission or their holding of certain presuppositions about the nature of language and the passions, they establish a regulative standard by which good or appropriate literature can be distinguished from that which is bad or inappropriate. In the most extreme sense, they put themselves in the position of determining even what is entitled to fall under the label of "literature."

Buchler is, of course, not preoccupied in *The Main of Light* with developing a theory of literary value *per se*. Nor does he explicitly address the problem of interpreting or criticizing specific poems. In the introduction he admits the importance of other types of interests or emphases in literature—for example, "the diversity of values, forms of meaning, or social and psychological conditions of utterance,"[12] but contends that in pursuing the "theory of poetry" one must be occupied with the discrimination of generic complexes appropriate to the explanation of what poetry is and how it functions.[13] In essence, *The Main of Light*, in terms of its professed objectives, does not have as its primary purpose the offering of conceptual resources necessary for the interpretation of any specific poem or for the general evaluation of poems as good or bad. It does not occupy itself directly with the "formal" or structural dimensions of "poetic language" or other technical aspects of poetic construction. Nor does it exclusively confront the question of "poetic meaning," for, on the Buchlerian view, both "meaning" and "language structure" are secondary or derivative topics within the more general theory of poetry. As opposed to Kuhns, Buchler regards the "formal structure of language" as but one (and not the most important) constituent or aspect of the poetry-making process. It is one among many traits of the poetic product. Although poetry undeniably constitutes a distinctive structure and usage of language, this fact says nothing more than what could be claimed about any other usage of language, such as a rhetorical appeal, a novel, or a deductive argument. To what extent, then, could Kuhns's theoretical focus on "language structure" account for the complete poetic process and offer up the meaning of the poem? In effect, Kuhns's exclusive focus on language or "the meaning of the thought" does not allow for other, equally important considerations such as what poetry is "about," what sort of analysis or query it is, or how poetry goes about presenting its various subject matters. In Buchler's words, if Kuhns's assumption is that "the presence or absence of a poetic character depends on the structure of the language involved, . . . we are off on the wrong foot."[14] For "it is not the kind of structure the language has that makes it poetic but the kind of stance the poet takes in relation to what he is dealing with that makes his language poetic"[15] instead of assertive, propositional, or rhetorical.

Likewise, poetic meaning is but one phase or constituent of the entire poetic process and itself rests upon the larger question of communication and dialogic encounter vis-à-vis a poem. Buchler's work addresses each of these topics insofar as each fits within his overall theoretical structure. Hence, the "structure of language" is taken up within Buchler's discussion of the distinguishing traits of a poem: its formality, cadence, rhythm, and solemnity, among others. Further, "poetic meaning" is a topic necessarily integrated within Buchler's notion of "articulation"; that is, the manner in which a poem engenders additional queries within its readers-hearers, prompting articulation and rearticulation of the poetic meaning in other orders or other forms of query. This articulation and rearticulation is what Buchler means by the phrase *the growth of meaning*. In this connection, he contends "that the aim of query is further query, and that the meaning of poetry, like all meaning, lies only in the articulative process—the transportation of the judgments of query into ever newer perspectives."[16] But Buchler does not pretend to be able definitively to answer the difficult question of how meaning in poetry is achieved. "With the 'how' as indeterminate as it is, I do not know how meaning in poetry is achieved, just as I do not know how meaning in philosophy, architecture, science, or religion is achieved."[17] Although the phrase *how meaning in poetry is achieved* stands in need of clarification, Buchler is convinced that "meaning in a poem" is "a relational trait effected in communication"; thus, that meaning is achieved through an ongoing process, through articulating in any mode the functions that "actualize the poem's meaning possibilities."[18]

Though *The Main of Light* is not concerned directly with questions of value judgment, interpretation, or literary criticism, Buchler does believe that "the concepts framed in [the book] are relevant to investigations stemming from such interests."[19] If it can be demonstrated that Buchler's theoretical work does have an impact on the practices of interpretation and criticism, even though it does not put forward a specific theory of interpretation, then Kuhnsian-type criticisms of his theoretical approach to literature can be, at least in part, answered. Perhaps a reconception of the precise nature of this impact on interpretation and criticism is required.

I contend that Buchler's theory of poetry can be conceived to have, though somewhat indirectly, an effect upon the assumptions and practice of literary interpretation and criticism. This effect I characterize as a "democratization" or "liberalization" of the critical, interpretive process in that his approach is not tied to a specific ideology or limited metaphysical dogma (recall, for example, Sartre or Wordsworth). From Buchler's point of view, every critical or interpretive prescription rests upon metaphysical conceptions of the nature and function of literature, no matter how unrecognized the relationship may be or how unanalyzed the concepts involved. Furthermore, the more adequate the leading metaphysical conceptions that ground a literary theory, the more likely that theory will avoid reckless or biased evaluations and interpretations. Accordingly, Buchler's explanation of the poetic process in the most generic and expansive terms—particularly the application of his principles of ontological parity, poetic query, and prevalence and the focus on a manifold of possible subject matters—causes the interpreter or critic to reconsider and reevaluate the assumed primacy of certain underlying concepts operative in many literary theories. Theories, like those discussed earlier in this paper, can each be shown to rest upon limited metaphysical and aesthetic conceptions or narrow ideological commitments. The most obvious sign of such theoretical narrowness (and the defensiveness it engenders) is the inclination of each theorist to discredit, or even eliminate from the realm of literary art, works of literature or literary theories that presuppose different foundational structures.[20] Examples include Sartre's attack on the literature and theory of "Pure Poetry" (Valèry), calling it, in effect, nonliterature, while assuming, of course, that literature, properly understood, must engage a social problematic and contribute to humanity's quest for freedom. Similarly, Aristotle disqualifies "epic stories" as the highest literature, for they are too lengthy and thus nonconformable to the structural needs of organic unity, the whole-ness model of nature. In the same spirit, Coleridge attacks some of Wordsworth's poetry for the baseness and crudity of its thematic concerns and the lack of imaginative genius and formal unity. Even in the context of critical reviews of contemporary books and plays, appropriate instances are as numerous as they are revealing. As one example, the late John Gardner, novelist and theorist of fiction, condemned Walker Percy's novel *Lancelot* for not being sufficiently sophisticated in a philosophical sense. From Gardner's point of view, the book fools around with philosophy but is never serious and never really goes for any answers.[21] Gardner, as revealed in his own essay, *On Moral Fiction*, unhesitatingly presupposes a theoretical conception of how the greatest literature performs a decidedly philosophic function.[22]

From Buchler's perspective, such critical admonitions, though offered by astute artists and philosophers, reflect basic theoretical limitations in the way literature is conceived. Such statements as Gardner's, for example, reflect confusion about the proper role and function of literature, on the one hand, and philosophy, on the other. Such judgments lack the theoretical diplomacy and open-endedness that is prerequisite to a healthy and constructive understanding of literary art, whether from a theoretical or interpretational perspective. For Buchler, the preceding cases would be similar in kind to Santayana's censure (in *Three Philosophical Poets*) of Dante for not having a true, reasoned philosophical view of nature or the path to happiness. In effect, Dante is criticized by Santayana for not being Aristotle, but such criticism rests upon a misguided conflation of philosophy and poetry. Santayana, like Gardner, slips into the unfortunate pattern of judging poetry by philosophical goals and methods. Though each domain can and does penetrate the other—for example, there are numerous instances of what can genuinely be called "philosophical poetry"—the two areas of inquiry have different structures, objectives, and methods of operation. In understanding the nature of each and in making critical assessments within each domain, one must not confuse them. Likewise, in the aforementioned examples, Aristotle, Sartre, and Coleridge render critical judgments of literary works in terms of criteria appropriate to their particular and limited literary theories, metaphysics, or ideological presuppositions. Thus, all instances of literary art are forced into conformity with the criteria of judgment presupposed by a particular theory. For instance, if literature is defined as essentially an imaginative, highly formalized construct arising from poetic genius, then literary works that concern everyday lives and social concerns, or works that are not constructed in terms of formal stylistics, must inevitably be regarded as lesser art or even nonart, in the extreme case. The strict delimiting of theoretical possibilities makes it impossible to say anything expository or constructive about instances of literature that do not fall into the preordained mold. Among the most significant contributions of Buchler's generic approach to the explanation of poetry is that it deliberately attempts to counteract metaphysical limitations inherent in more narrowly drawn and tightly focused literary theories. The positing of the generic traits of all poetry, as a distinct kind of human query, functions to liberate critical and interpretational judgments from narrow and biased criteria. Using his theory, no subject matters (feelings, objects, hypotheses) are a priori eliminated from the domain of literature, no way of treating themes or issues narrowly circumscribed, and no particular formal constructions required. In this context, the primary burden of the interpreter or critic is to recognize and understand the complexes discriminated by the poetry under consideration and to articulate, in whatever mode, the "sense of prevalence" conveyed by the literary work.

Although Buchler's theory of poetry seeks conceptual expansiveness and, in effect, democratizes the critical-interpretive process, one may still wonder whether this marks a true gain. In effect, one may wonder whether the Buchlerian approach is worthwhile if it appears to involve a sacrifice of the more detailed interpretational and critical machinery operative in alternative theories of literature. Importantly, in the literary domain, as in science or philosophy, every theoretical proposal involves certain gains and losses. In Buchler's case, as with comparisons that can be drawn between any other literary theories, the question is whether the gains outweigh the losses. In an important respect, this question raises a basic concern as to the role of literary theory in interpretational theories and criticism. Of what importance is theory? To what extent should the desired metaphysical adequacy (that is, exhaustiveness or application to varied examples) of a literary theory take priority over the practical need to render very particularized interpretations or criticisms of specific literary works? To what extent, if at all, should literary concerns be addressed through the imposition of philosophical criteria and assessments of adequacy based on metaphysical grounds? What basically is, or should be, the relationship between literary theory and interpretation-criticism? In the final analysis, I would propose that Buchler's response to Kuhns on the limited issues of meaning and interpretation indicates that his literary theory is far from devoid of interpretive resourcefulness, though it assuredly does not offer the immediate specificity of interpretation of other theories.[23]

The present discussion reflects a genuine and serious issue, for, in a certain respect, the history of literary theory does seem to illustrate that theoretical movement (not to be confused with progress) is achieved through the substitution of one set of partial, underlying concepts for another in an open-ended sequence (for instance, nature, organicism, mind, freedom, economic foundations, language structure). But are there alternative ways of comprehending a progressive movement of literary theory? Can literary theory be fruitfully reconceived on generic, metaphysical grounds? At the least, Buchler's work on poetry constitutes a challenge to find answers to these questions.

To date, a relatively small amount of critical exposition and commentary has been undertaken in relation to Buchler's theory of literature. *The Main of Light* represents an application and extension of Buchlerian metaphysics. To the student of literary theory and interpretation, the importance and applicability of this theory will ultimately be a function of continuing critical examinations of Buchler's concepts and repeated attempts to render constructive, enlightening interpretations based upon such notions. For now, the extent of its gains and liabilities remains to be fully articulated.

Notes

1. Justus Buchler, *The Main of Light: On the Concept of Poetry* (New York: Oxford University Press, 1974), p. 144.

2. Richard Kuhns, "Some Observations on Justus Buchler's Theory of Poetry," *The Southern Journal of Philosophy* 14:1 (Spring, 1976): 116.

3. Ibid.

4. Ibid., p. 117.

5. The problem here, according to Buchler, is that the particular interpretive theory adopted provides the meaning instead of allowing the poem to speak for itself; that is, reveal its own orders of relatedness. Here Buchler seems close to Heidegger in spirit, though Heidegger ties the poem to an elusive notion of Being (disclosure of Being) and persists in assuming that poetic *language* is the key to opening up meaning.

6. Kuhns, "Some Observations," p. 116.

7. More precisely, in Kuhn's language, "The meaning of the thought." Buchler would regard this formulation as simply too mentalistic. Does poetry convey only thoughts? Is its meaning a function of interpreting the thoughts conveyed? For Buchler, the meaning of any poem must be seen as exceeding any particular thought or possibly as distinct from thought altogether. Compare the Buchlerian reading of Baudelaire's "A Carrion" in Buchler, *The Main of Light,* p. 140.

8. Kuhns, "Some Observations," p. 118.

9. A certain type of linguistic structure and style, or what Buchler calls "traits of the linguistic complex," is, of course, pertinent, even essential, to poetry qua poetry. In other words, for poetry to have the sort of integrity it has as a natural complex, a "poetic structure of language" is required (including the possibilities of rhyme, rhythm, cadence, and intensity of expression). But Kuhns, according to Buchler, is wrong in assuming that this linguistic structure *alone* provides the key to unlocking the "meaning" ("deep" or "found") of a poem. The "meaning" of any literary work of art extends well beyond the particular linguistic contrivance constitutive of the text, as illustrated by the examples of Baudelaire's "A Carrion" or Marianne Moore's "A Fish."

10. Indeed, the "prescriptive" impulse, according to Buchler, overrides the objective of rendering the meaning of the poem vis-à-vis the expressiveness of the poem itself and its capacity for establishing relations outside itself and promoting action.

11. In Buchler's words, those who theorize about literature often become involved in a "confusion between the nature of a discipline or the conditions of its productivity, and the merit of its products" (Buchler, *The Main of Light,* p. 10).

12. Ibid., p. 6.

13. The discrimination of generic complexes does, however, allow for the rendering of a poem's meaning, if not its evaluation as a good or bad instance of poetry.

14. Justus Buchler, "Reply to Kuhns: Poetry, Assertiveness, and Prevalence," *The Southern Journal of Philosophy* 14:1 (Spring, 1976): 124.

15. Ibid.

16. Ibid., p. 126.

17. Ibid.
18. Ibid., p. 127.
19. Buchler, *The Main of Light,* p. 16.
20. Buchler does not seek to eliminate certain instances of literary art from consideration as literature on the grounds that they are of the wrong organization or style, deal with inappropriate subject matters, or render a flawed view of humanity. Indeed, quite the opposite is the case. His approach seeks to identify the underlying concepts that ground various literary theories and to examine such concepts in terms of their contribution to or detraction from the generic understanding of what literature is and, moreover, to reject those notions (interior-exterior, the eulogistic bias, poetic genius) that clearly inhibit a fresh and open view of literature as a human product, including the interpretation and evaluation of any given work.
21. John Gardner, *The New York Times Book Review* (Feb. 20, 1977).
22. John Gardner, *On Moral Fiction* (New York: Basic Books, 1978).
23. In Buchler, *The Main of Light,* he gives examples of what a Buchlerian reading of a given poem would be like. In illustrating the theoretical notion of prevalence (prevalence of a complex or complexes) within a specific poem, he selects and examines four pieces of poetry, each describable as an instance of exhibitive judgment in which ruthlessness is a dominating feature. Moreover, each happens "to be marked by a strain of bitterness, and by a perception of the incommensurables that prevail in the human situation" (p. 138). The works are from such notable poets as William Carlos Williams, Marianne Moore, and Baudelaire. Those who question the richness, incisiveness, indeed the applicability of Buchler's theoretical categories in connection with matters of interpretation and meaning should consult pp. 132–40 of this work and perhaps compare, for instance, Buchler's reading of Baudelaire with the existential psychoanalysis of Baudelaire offered by Sartre.

The Subject as Index and as Icon:
A Critique of Kaja Silverman's Reading of C. S. Peirce on the Human Subject

LENORE LANGSDORF

Kaja Silverman's work on "the dominant symbolic order within which the Western subject emerges" begins with a consideration of Peirce's and others' work as a historical progression "within which the subject assumes priority, both as the concrete support for discourse and a critical discursive category."[1] She seeks to "alter our own relationship to [the] texts" that manifest this "Western subject," as a means for carrying out her project of "re-speaking both our own subjectivity and the symbolic order."[2]

In this paper, I propose that Silverman's project implicitly presumes that subjectivity can be pried loose (so to speak) from its symbolic manifestation. I go on to suggest that she could use Peirce's theory to support that articulation of subject and symbol instead of presuming it. Otherwise stated: I agree with Silverman's recognition of an "irreducible distance which separates being from signification."[3] But I claim that her reading of Peirce fails to see that his semiotic enables us to understand that "distance" as a condition of the possibility of the radical change—the "re-speaking"—that she seeks. Because my claim has developed from reflection on three pairs of remarks by Peirce and Silverman, I shall quote the relevant passages and then go on to give an alternate reading.

Charles Sanders Peirce provides us with a semiotic that resists any attempt to collapse subject, sign, and object (referent) into one another. That tripartite scheme enables us to understand experience and knowledge as interdependent but distinct. This understanding, in turn, accounts for the possibility of one aspect of the scheme—the subject—having access to both extrasymbolic experience and symbolically ordered knowledge. Peirce writes: "We have direct experience of things in themselves. Nothing can be more completely false than that we can experience only our own ideas. . . . Our knowledge of things in themselves is entirely relative, it is true; but all experience and all knowledge of that which is, is independently of being represented"[hereafter referred to as CSP 1].[4]

In her comment on this passage, Silverman states that it establishes a dichotomy.

> The crucial distinction which is here maintained is that between experience and thought. Peirce argues that we have *direct experience*, but *indirect knowledge* of reality. The former teaches us that there is a world of things, but gives us no intellectual access to them, while the latter supplies the only means of knowing those things, but no way of verifying our knowledge. Reality bumps up against us, impinges upon us, yet until we have found a way of representing that reality, it remains impervious to thought. At times, Peirce pushes the argument even further, insisting that only those portions of reality which are capable of being represented can affect us [hereafter, KS 1].[5]

The quotation she gives in apparent support of this claim is a puzzling one, for which I offer an interpretation a bit later in this paper. In the text, Silverman's comment follows immediately after the following quotation from Peirce: "If those earthquakes, droughts, and pestilences are subject to laws, those laws being of the nature of signs, then, no doubt being signs of those laws they are thereby made worthy of human attention, but if they be mere arbitrary brute interruptions of our course of life, let us . . . endure them as we may; for they cannot injure us, though they may strike us down"[hereafter, CSP 2].[6] Silverman comments: "If representations provide us with our only access to reality, then the authenticity of those representations becomes an issue of pressing importance. Peirce never abandons his belief that reality can be truly represented. However, he does admit that the means for determining the truth of a representation lie beyond the reach of the individual"[hereafter, KS 2].[7]

Three features of this comment are problematic. First, Silverman glosses "signs" (in the Peirce quotation) as "representations." Also, she understands Peirce's "they cannot injure us" as "they allow of no access." These two readings, then, encourage an understanding of Peirce as maintaining that we only have access to signs/representations, although we do experience a "world of things."

Given this limitation, the dichotomy she states (in KS 1) between experience and thought (or knowledge) is inevitable: our experience is direct, but our knowledge is indirect. Because our pragmatic needs and goals depend on knowing as well as experiencing, we must contend with the question of whether indirect knowledge is accurate. Or, in Silverman's words, we must deal with the problem of whether "reality" is "truly represented" by our representations. This consequence becomes evident in the third set of quotations. Thus Peirce: "The real . . . is that which, sooner or later, information and reasoning would finally result in. . . . Thus, the very origin of the conception essentially involves the notion of a community, without definite limits, and capable of an indefinite increase of knowledge"[hereafter, CSP 3].[8] And Silverman: "In view of the provisional nature of this reality, and the fact that it can be known only via signs, it seems evident that the object or referent is as fully excluded from Peirce's semiotic scheme as it is from Saussure's. It is present within signification only as a concept which may or may not be representative of it"[hereafter, KS 3].[9]

The first two comments by Silverman develop a reading of Peirce's tripartite semiotic (subject, sign, and referent) that culminates in the third comment's identification of the "object or referent" as a "concept," which is, in turn, associated with the sign.

When Silverman turns to Peirce's doctrine that man is a sign, then, she finds in his semiotic no support for her assumption that subjectivity is not inevitably bound to the symbolic manifestation. In what follows, I propose an alternative reading of Peirce's remarks that retains the three aspects. Also, I argue that Peirce's remarks support an understanding of the human sign as dual: that is, as both icon and index. I go on to suggest the importance of this tripartite semiotic and dual nature of the human sign for the possibility of "re-speaking both our own subjectivity and the symbolic order."

The significance of Silverman's reading of "signs" as "representation" and "they cannot injure us" as "they allow of no access" emerges in relation to what she identifies as one of his most radical assertions: "Peirce tells us that reality is accessible to man himself as a sign. . . . [He] insists . . . that our access to and knowledge of ourselves is subject to the same semiotic restrictions as our access to and knowledge of the eternal world"[hereafter, KS 4].[10]

My own understanding of just what these "semiotic restrictions" might be develops from an interpretation of some of the puzzling aspects of CSP 2. In any usual way of speaking, we would consider that anything that can "strike us down" does, thereby, "injure us." One way to understand Peirce's denial of that association would be to take the phrase *worthy of human attention* very seriously. We could than construe his meaning as relying upon a differentiation between what "bumps up against us, impinges upon us" (quoting from KS 1) and thus can "strike us down" as spatiotemporal, physical beings—as contrasted with what can "injure us" as spiritual and mental beings; that is, as *human* beings. In order to avoid the honorific connotations of that stress on human, I shall refer to the former as "the physical subject" and to the latter as "the cultural subject."[11]

If this distinction is accepted as an implicit assumption in Pierce's consideration of the "semiotic restrictions" operative in our "access to and knowledge of ourselves" (KS 4), we can begin to understand his remarks on experience and knowledge quite differently than Silverman does (in KS 1). On the basis of the dichotomy that she finds in those remarks, she understands the "semiotic restrictions" as very restrictive indeed: we have no "intellectual access," and perhaps no access at all (as suggested in her KS 1 and KS 2, respectively) to reality, other than what is cognitively available to us through signs/representations. Thus, for Silverman, we have only "indirect" knowledge (KS 1) of a "provisional" reality (KS 3). Otherwise stated: Silverman understands Peirce as holding that we know ourselves only indirectly, and only as signs, instead of as subjects who institute signs or as objects/referents who are represented by signs.

In the section entitled "Man, A Sign," however, Peirce points out that our knowledge is affected by our status as the sort of being who both institutes signs and is instituted by them.

> Man makes the word, and the word means nothing which the man has not made it mean, and that only to some man. But since man can think only by means of words or other external symbols, these might turn round and say: you mean nothing which we have not taught you, and then only so far as you can address some word as the interpretant of your thought. In fact, therefore, men and words reciprocally educate each other; each increase of a man's information involves and is involved by, a corresponding increase of a word's information [hereafter CSP 4].[12]

Here again we have Peirce insisting that the human subject has a dual nature. We are physical beings, who institute signs (that is, make words); and we are cultural beings, who are instituted by signs (that is, are meaningful by virtue of the signs we have made). As signs, then, we are both "icons" of the historicity that institutes us and "indices" of the agency (human activity) that institutes history.[13] We are "icons" insofar as we can be understood as "images" of the community mentioned in CSP 3. But we are also "indices" insofar as we can be understood as "symptoms" of the agency—ourselves—that is doing the understanding.

There may well be a variety of objections to this reading of Peirce on the nature of that peculiar sign that is the human subject, but I shall respond to only one all-too-obvious objection here. At our current postmodern pause in the "conversation of mankind," any mention of a "dual nature" carries connotations of "Cartesian dualism." Silverman's chapter on "The Subject" is an example of contemporary attitudes toward that dualism. It opens with a critique of Descartes's "classic demonstration of private consciousness, of a cognitive operation which believes itself to be both independent and authentic for all time."[14] A response to the question of how this reading of Peirce differs from Cartesian dualism, then, seems almost obligatory.

The primary difference is that the line of delineation between the two aspects of the dual subject that I find in Peirce is not drawn between mental (or spiritual) and physical entities. Instead, it is drawn between the instituting and instituted senses of subjectivity. In other words, the crucial distinction is between the subject as agency, as index of the activity that institutes signs, and the subject as product or result, as icon of the historical community that institutes it. The subject as agency is both physical and cultural: natural events can "strike us down" but not "injure us." Correlatively, the subject as product is both physical and cultural: we are partially, but not completely, formed by natural events (for example, food supply and disease).

A second difference is that neither of these senses of the subject pretends to be a "private consciousness . . . independent and authentic for all time"[15]—or, as Silverman characterizes it elsewhere, a "transcendental signified" that is "capable of thinking worlds into existence."[16] Instead, the subject as sign exists at the very public and dynamic intersection between words and men, as they "reciprocally educate each other (CSP 4)."

A third difference is more complex and leads us to the issue of how Peirce's theory of the human subject provides support for the possibility of Silverman's characterization of Descartes's theory and values.[17] Here, Peirce's distinction between experience and knowledge, in contrast to the things that are the *focus of* experience and knowledge, is relevant. He holds, as indicated in CSP 1, that the intrinsically relative (to the subject) character of experience and knowledge means that they are mediated activities. However, the "real objects and values" that are the focus of interest for those mediated activities are themselves "unmediated."[18] This sharp differentiation between acts of the human subject and the objects of those acts rests upon a metaphysics that specifies existence, reality, and being in a relationship of increasing inclusion: "Existence, then, is a special mode of reality, which, whatever other characteristics it possesses, has that of being absolutely determinate. Reality, in its turn, is a special mode of being, the characteristic of which is that things that are real are whatever they really are, independently of any assertion about them. If Man is the measure of all things, as Protagoras said, then there is no complete reality, but being there certainly is, even then" [hereafter, CSP 5].[19]

This tripartite metaphysics allows Peirce to say that *real*, existing things are known by us as relative to mind, although they display independent *being* in our experience of them: "There is no thing which is in-itself in the sense of not being relative to the mind, though things which are relative to the mind doubtless are, apart from that relation"[hereafter, CSP 6].[20]

Peirce's theory, then, recognizes a distinction between experience of things (which display their independence as *reality*, "independent of any assertion about them," and which "impinge upon us") and knowledge of things (which, as objects or foci of our knowing, *exist*—are "absolutely determinate"—as relative-to-mind).

In KS 1, Silverman construes this distinction as a disjunction between direct experience, to which we have no access, and indirect knowledge, for which we have no means of verification. Subsequently, she does not find, in Peirce's remarks on the subject as sign, any basis for seeing the reality of that particular sign's referent as independent of the symbolic order in which it exists. This is to say that she cannot recognize the human subject who has both experience and knowledge (or, even, is both known and knower) as both an index of an independent reality and an icon of an existing symbolic order. Accordingly, in KS 3, she concludes that the "object or referent" is "excluded from Peirce's semiotic" or, more exactly, is "present within signification only as a concept" that may not be an accurate "representation."

In contrast, the reading of Peirce that I offer here agrees with Silverman's reading in regard to our knowing the human subject as existing in a symbolic manifestation, as an icon of its historicity. But it diverges from Silverman's reading in stressing that our access to the human subject is not limited to that iconic presence within signification. As I understand Peirce's theory, we also experience the human subject as index of a real object/referent, independent of assertions about itself—indeed, prone to instituting assertions that disagree with its existing signification.[21]

The value of my reading of Peirce for accomplishing Silverman's goal of "respeaking" both our own subjectivity and the symbolic order rests precisely here, on the subject-as-index's ability to institute discourse in opposition to the subject-as-icon's symbolic manifestation. An observation she makes on the basis of her study of Freudian and Lacanian models of subjectivity locates the crucial point of contact between my reading and Silverman's goal: there is, she notes, "an irreducible distance which separates being from signification."[22]

Peirce's semiotic, based as it is on a tripartite metaphysics of existence, reality, and being, provides us with a map of that distance. Furthermore, my reading of his theory of human being as sign suggests that the subject as agency can use this distance as a condition of the possibility of the radical change—the "respeaking"—that is Silverman's goal. In order to develop that thesis, we shall have to consider the model of subjectivity that Silverman opposes. It is one, she tells us, that has been instituted by "the dominant symbolic order within which the Western subject emerges,"[23] and it has a literary counterpart in the "classic" or "readerly" text as described by Roland Barthes.

In what follows, I use Silverman's presentation of Barthes's critique in order to state the model of subject/text that she would "respeak" and then conclude by specifying how Peirce's conception offers a more adequate theoretical basis for that endeavor. Silverman presents the model and her alternative in terms of two conceptions of text:

> The readerly or classic text strives above all for homogeneity.... [It] purports to be a transcript of a reality which pre-exists and exceeds it, and it tightly controls the play of signification by subordinating everything to this transcendental meaning. It encourages the reader or viewer to move away from its signifiers ... toward a privileged and originating signified.... [It] thus attempts to conceal all traces of itself as a factory within which a particular social reality is produced through standard representations and dominant signifying practices. Reflexivity provides one of the most successful means of effecting this concealment. [By]

foreground[ing] its own stylistic operations as a means of deflecting attention away from the more broadly cultural pressures at work upon it . . . the text seems to refer primarily to the reality of a "private consciousness." Reflexive texts feature the author as transcendental signified [hereafter, KS 5].[24]

Silverman's alternative to this model is the "writerly text." In her portrayal, she follows Barthes's "concentration on coding operations," which function as "a kind of 'jamming' of the interpretive machine so as to prevent transcendental meaning from emerging."[25]

The writerly text promotes an infinite play of signification; in it there can be no transcendental signified, only provisional ones which function in turn as signifiers. . . . [It] replaces the concepts of "product" and "structure" with those of "process" and "segmentation." . . . [The] process suggests . . . a reader or viewer who participates in an on-going manufacture of meaning. . . . Segmentation . . . fragments the structure of the classic text in order to reveal the cultural voices which speak it, the codes which constitute its "reality" [hereafter, KS 6].[26]

Silverman goes on to say that segmentation "provides more than an agency of *de*construction; it also offers the possibility of a radical *re*construction."[27] I find, nevertheless, that her reconstruction of the subject is insufficiently radical precisely insofar as it relies upon "codes" as constitutive of reality.

The problem with this conception is that codes are *products* of historicity, which function here as transcendental signifiers. Thus, instead of preventing "transcendental meaning from emerging," codes specify an alternative transcendental meaning. Within this alternative conception, "segmentation" replaces "reflexivity" as the means to "conceal all traces of itself [now, the 'writerly text'] as a factory for producing the dominant model of the subject." In other words, instead of a situation in which "reflexivity . . . feature[s] the author as transcendental signified,"[28] we have one in which fragmentation features the code as transcendental signified. (Indeed, reading the whole of KS 5 with the substitution of "writerly text" and "code" for "readerly text" and "author" reveals the lack of radicality in Silverman's reconstruction.) The result is a reversed domination, which retains the structure of the old in opposite form. The product is now heterogeneous instead of homogeneous. But the human subject is no more able to "participate" in the "manufacture of meaning" than before, because the move from "product" to "process" has not been accomplished by replacing "structure" with "segmentation."

Peirce's tripartite metaphysics and his conception of the human subject as sign suggest a way to expand this rather limited "respeaking." The crucial *process* is a reciprocal one: as Peirce notes (in CSP 4), "Men and words reciprocally educate each other." Reciprocity occurs because we are indices of that agency that institutes history, as well as icons of that historicity that institutes us. With respect to the tripartite metaphysics, this means that we constitute what exists as we "make words."[29] But this existence need not be simply reconstituted from the pieces available to us when segmentation deconstructs structure. For the relations Peirce identifies among existence, reality, and being suggest that we have access to the multiplicity of possibilities summarized by the category of "being," as we ("men") engage in constituting existing "words" (that is, the symbolic order).

Although Silverman notes that Peirce's definition of "reality" necessitates its "provisional nature (KS 3)," she does not recognize the metaphysical impetus that status provides for affirming the process character of the symbolic order that we constitute: if reality is provisional, it is a process instead of a product. This impetus is only applicable, of course, insofar as our constitution of existence is oriented toward reality—"that which, sooner or later, information and reasoning would finally result in" (CSP 3)—instead of toward preservation of any existing product of the "dominant symbolic order" or toward justification of either product or process on the basis of being.

As human subjects, we do exist within a symbolic order. When we draw upon our experience of indeterminate being in order to actualize alternative models of subjectivity—instead of repeating known, determinate existence in yet another signification—we are prying our subjectivity loose from the dominant symbolic order in a creative, not mimetic, way.[30] We are then using the distance between being and signification as a condition of the possibility of "respeaking both our subjectivity and the symbolic order."

Notes

1. Kaja Silverman, *The Subject of Semiotics* (New York: Oxford University Press, 1983), p. 282.
2. Ibid., p. 283.
3. Ibid., p. 282.
4. Charles S. Peirce, *Collected Papers*, ed. Charles Hartshorne, Paul Weiss, and Arthur Burks, 8 vols. (Cambridge, Mass.: Harvard University Press, 1931–58), vol. 6, p. 73. Hereafter cited as CP.
5. Silverman, *Subject of Semiotics*, p. 16.
6. CP, vol. 6, p. 235.
7. Silverman, *Subject of Semiotics*, p. 17.
8. CP, vol. 5, pp. 186–87.
9. Silverman, *Subject of Semiotics*, p. 17.
10. Ibid., pp. 17–18.
11. This distinction is proposed by many philosophers. My own way of drawing it is dependent upon the works of Edmund Husserl and Ernst Cassirer. The most relevant texts would be Edmund Husserl, *Cartesian Meditations*, trans. D. Cairns (The Hague: Nijhoff, 1960), esp. sections 10, 11, and 64; Edmund Husserl, *Ideas Pertaining to a Pure Phenomenology and to a Phenomenological Philosophy*, first book, trans. F. Kersten (The Hague: Nijhoff, 1983), esp. sections 28, 29, 33, 55, and 56; and Ernst Cassirer, *The*

Logic of the Humanities, trans. C. S. Howe (New Haven: Yale University Press, 1960), esp. chapters 2 and 3. Peirce's text does refer to this sort of distinction in more direct ways in other places. For example, in the section entitled "Man, A Sign" (from which CSP 3 is taken), he speaks of a "consciousness . . . which is the more lively the better *animal* a man is, but which is not so, the better *man* he is" (CP 6.188; emphasis added).

12. CP, vol. 5, pp. 188–89.

13. Silverman discusses these terms in Silverman, *Subject of Semiotics*, pp. 19–20. For brief definitions by Peirce, see CP, vol. 6, p. 233.

14. Silverman, *Subject of Semiotics*, p. 127.

15. Ibid., p. 127.

16. Ibid., p. 244. More precisely, Peirce's distinction between reality and existence (in the section bearing that title, CP, vol. 6, pp. 237–39) does require us to say that "existence" depends upon agency, human or otherwise, whereas "reality" and "being" are independent. This point is discussed in the remarks on these three categories that follow in the main text. Consideration of the "independent and authentic" characteristics of the Cartesian subject would take us too far afield. Briefly, though, Peirce's remarks on the "relative" nature of things usurp the possibility of any independently authentic status for *existing* things while retaining the notion of authentic truth in relation to independent *being*. Cf. CSP 1, CP, vol. 5, p. 186, and CP, vol. 6, p. 238.

17. Silverman, *Subject of Semiotics*, p. 128.

18. Husserl's explication of this same point is made in his analysis of intentional acts as distinguishable (although not separable) into noetic and noematic aspects. There is a "core" of the latter aspect that presents the focus of interest (intentional object) "as such."

19. CP, vol. 6, p. 238.

20. CP, vol. 5, p. 186.

21. This duality is validated in a phenomenological description. In phenomenological terms, what I am discussing here is the contrast between transcendental and mundane subjectivity. Just as talk of a "dual nature" requires a discussion of how that notion differs from "Cartesian dualism," mention of "transcendental subjectivity" requires a discussion of how Husserl's notion differs from the semi-Cartesian one of a "transcendental signified" (cf. Silverman, *Subject of Semiotics*, p. 244). To some extent, I discuss this matter in connection with my comments in this paper on the "readerly text." But this point involves the large issue of postmodernism's rejection of Husserlian phenomenology's understanding of the human subject.

22. Silverman, *Subject of Semiotics*, p. 282.

23. Ibid., p. 282.

24. Ibid., pp. 243–44.

25. Ibid., p. 250.

26. Ibid., pp. 246–47.

27. Ibid., p. 249.

28. Ibid., p. 244.

29. CP, vol. 5, p. 188.

30. In phenomenological terms, this activity is called eidetic variation. In my reading of Peirce, I understand "being" as a domain of possibility, while "existence" signifies actualization of that domain. The phenomenological semiotic scheme I propose here thus depends upon considering any signification as an actualization among many possibilities and seeks to explicate both the actual and possible domains.

AESTHETICS

Through the Beautiful to the Human
(The Aesthetic and the Ethical in
the Experiencing of Landscape)

NIKITA E. POKROVSKY

Moral collisions and controversies of the twentieth century and the spread of ethical relativism and political pragmatism in all strata of contemporary society raise the question of how and where the spiritual *terra firma* can be found in the ocean of dissociation, apocalyptic horrors of nuclear war, and the destruction of human nature from within. Needless to say, the search for this desired *terra firma* reveals the true destination of modern philosophy of education and, more broadly, education as such. One can try to find the whole continent of moral and aesthetic values in the world of wild nature that gives us, perhaps, the last chance to construct some new moral structures. But every spiritual trend that has now appeared has its deep roots in the intellectual history of humanity, and "moral ecology" or "ecology of morality" is no exception.

Virtually every doctrine known to the history of philosophy has posed and offered its own solution to the problem of nature. What is nature? What are its structural principles? What is the source of its existence? How does it relate to humanity and human efforts to grasp it, to experience its aesthetic harmony? Each cultural epoch has developed its own distinctive and historically conditioned picture of nature, its own "philosophical landscape."

Romanticizing Nature

The influence of landscape on man's spiritual inner world is, to a degree, one of the "eternal" problems of philosophy, art, and education. However, this problem assumed particular importance in the works of the Romanticists in the late eighteenth and early nineteenth centuries. A product of rejecting the mechanistic trend of the Enlightenment, the European Romantic Movement, no longer having faith in the ability of reason to establish a just social order, was from the very beginning poisoned by the awareness of humanity's alienation from the political system. Having turned to nature, the romantic philosopher began to search it for what society refused him. And he found a new, heretofore unsuspected image of nature: the image of an almighty, mysterious, and divinely inspired partner in a dialogue, a friend—but an inconstant friend, easily turned into a cold and implacable enemy. The world of nature displayed a previously unknown meaning: it contained something that was unusual, exalted, and at the same time representative of salvation for the one who contemplated it, the one rejected by all and by himself.

The romantic vision of virgin nature was particularly pronounced in the philosophical works of the greatest American thinkers of the first half of the nineteenth century: Ralph Waldo Emerson (1803–1882) and Henry David Thoreau (1817–1862), the two major representatives of the so-called New England Transcendentalism. Both Emerson and Thoreau maintained that by exercising profound influence on humanity, virgin nature ennobled humanity ethically, raised it above the humdrum life of the industrial city, and made human beings feel more a product of nature than of society. And, while Emerson expounded this theme in *Nature,* his major work of 1836, Thoreau tried to translate doctrine into practice in his famous experiment of voluntary working solitude described in his 1854 work *Walden, or Life in the Woods.* Although they proceeded from an essentially correct precept, American Transcendentalists obscured the aesthetic connection between the individual and the landscape with romantic speculation, presenting this link as a special kind of mysterious "correspondence" between humanity and the Absolute.

In addition to the Transcendentalists, these problems were of profound concern to the outstanding German naturalist Alexander von Humboldt (1769–1859), author of numerous scientific works—many of which formed the theoretical basis of various natural sciences.

Humboldt's philosophical views have been studied by many researchers. In the context of the topic in question, of particular interest is a small book of his entitled *Pictures of Nature* (1828). Significantly, in this work on physical geography the author touched upon ethical and philosophical questions: to Humboldt, a great authority on natural science, ethical aspects of studying and artistically experiencing nature were inseparable from purely physical ones. Independently of each other, Humboldt and Thoreau arrived at similar conclusions about the link between landscape and the ethics of the individual contemplating it. The German scientist called this link "mysterious mutual penetration"; Emerson introduced the term *correspondence,* a special term with a Transcendentalist connotation. Meanwhile, Thoreau was, as it were, halfway between the two: he rejected Emerson's obvious spiritualism but did not go as far as Humboldt in recognizing a general natural science. In this case, however, the important point is not the correlation of the philosophical systems to which the three naturalists adhered but the common conclusion they reached. This conclusion was not so much a positive statement as a profound question: *does aesthetic contemplation and experiencing of landscape make humanity better ethically?*

Education by Nature

It would be logical to assume that the idea of nature's influence on ethics is a purely romantic invention, rooted solely in the transcendentalist-idealist doctrines of the late eighteenth and early nineteenth centuries. While dealing with this assumption, which concerns the history of philosophy, one should turn to the present. It will be easy to see that the idea of nature's aesthetic impact on ethics has not died along with the classic Romantic Movement but has lived on and evolved (naturally, in a substantially modified form) in the ideas of philosophers, educators, and artists.

Vasily Sukhomlinsky (1918–1970), an outstanding Soviet expert in the theory and practice of education, advanced the problem of "education by nature" to the forefront of his system of aesthetic and ethical education. Sukhomlinsky saw nature not as an independent, self-sufficient factor in the shaping of the personality of a child but as one of the more substantive components of the overall aesthetic environment surrounding the young person in the person's creative efforts.

The aesthetic environment—above all, nature—creates and awakens joy and an upsurge of emotions. The emergence of the personality, in terms of both phylogeny and ontogeny, is shaped both by conscious work and by the realization of the harmony of life made by human beings and natural life. The shaping of aesthetic taste and the aesthetic ideal, Sukhomlinsky maintains, is inseparable from aesthetic education. In his view, the ethical and the aesthetic are mutually dependent phenomena of the same order. The credo of Sukhomlinsky's theory of aesthetic education is *through the beautiful to the human.*

Unlike the romantic naturalists, Sukhomlinsky fills the beauty of nature with social value and considers the aesthetic understanding of landscape as a harmonious unity of contemplation, evaluation, and practical action. The Soviet educator sees the ethical significance of nature not only in the fact that the young person realizes the beauty of nature but also in what motivates this person in it, what goals the person sets for himself or herself, and finally what practical steps he or she takes to preserve and add to the beauty of nature. To Sukhomlinsky, all these aspects make up an integral whole: to take it apart into isolated fragments means to destroy it.

For the Romanticists, individual contemplation of nature was the only way of grasping its beauty. Sukhomlinsky's theory of education does not belittle such contemplation but makes it dependent on a range of other, social factors.

Still, Sukhomlinsky too recognizes and stresses the importance of the *individual* contemplative and emotional experiencing of nature: the latter influences ethics both through practical action to preserve and add to nature's wealth and through the individual's emotional and aesthetic experiencing of its beauty. Naturally, as a strictly social phenomenon, ethics cannot "stem" from nature the way the Romanticists and Thoreau claimed. No doubt, however, there is a certain, far-from-negligible *direct* influence of nature on human beings.

Breaking sharply with the Romanticists, Sukhomlinsky refuses to recognize the *leading* role of *individual* contemplation of nature compared to *collective* experience of knowing and practically using the world of nature. The way to the beautiful and lofty in nature is unthinkable without humanistic collectivism, without the sharing of emotional experience and social practice.

Intimate and Common Vision of Nature

Even in cases of extreme confrontation between nature and the individual, the human being does not face nature as an isolated spiritual monad. The personality always reflects the "totality of all social relations." Therefore, even extremely individualized, "intimate" communion with nature is a social phenomenon, which has, consequently, an ethical meaning. In any situation, a person acts on behalf of society and is therefore its full-fledged representative. But a person, with a legitimately autonomous individual aesthetic and ethical contemplation, sometimes strives to present this communion as his or her own personal affair independent of outside factors. This attempt creates the illusion of "direct" relations between a person and nature in the aesthetic and ethical experiencing of landscape.

Here, however, "personal" communion with nature has its own objective distinctive features and rules. Above all, as seen by the individual observer, nature is the object of aesthetic pleasure and of an aesthetic need.

Aesthetic need directs nature-oriented individual aesthetic contemplation. Because of this need, the individual enters into aesthetic interaction with the environment. As a rule, an aesthetic need does not presuppose the kind of practical use or transformation of the object that could destroy it or change its substance. This need dictates spiritual understanding of landscape, its "purely spiritual consumption" in the shape in which it is given by the very objectivity of landscape.

This profoundly human need is satisfied through live, contemplative communion of humanity with nature. This process orients the individual surrounded by virgin nature toward active aesthetic experience. However, the aesthetic aspect of nature can be expressed fully only in aesthetic activity.

Transcending the limits of direct interpersonal communication, aesthetic activity expresses the subject's orientation not toward other subjects but toward an object, including nature. What occurs is aesthetic experience, as it were, of activity aimed at natural objects. In this kind of activity (subject—natural object), aesthetic values have essentially the same origin as the values generated by interpersonal communication. However, ethical theory sees an important difference between these two types of values, one the Romanticists could not or would not discern. They equated the aesthetic values of the human's relation to nature with the aesthetic values of the human's relation to other humans. This equation enabled idealistic philosophers to endow nature with an ethical meaning, with ethics *per se*.

In actual fact, however, the subject's activity is oriented toward nature and not toward communication with other people, and it does not have an independent ethical significance. Nature's aesthetic value, revealed in an individual's aesthetic experience, does not transform itself directly into an ethical value but is inevitably mediated by social practice.

The aesthetic value of nature acquires ethical value only inasmuch as the object of activity displays its social significance. In other words, social values are inevitably superimposed on aesthetic—even strictly individual—contemplation of nature. Then nature (and the human being may not clearly be aware of this) begins to be perceived in its actual social function; that is, in the light of its significance for the life of society. Then and only then do the human attitude toward nature and the human aesthetic experience of its beauty, perfection, infinity, and eternity acquire an ethical coloration.

Community and Creativity:
Toward a Deweyan Aesthetic of Human Existence

THOMAS M. ALEXANDER

The last decade has been a portentous one for philosophy. There is an unmistakable sense of a subtle but nonetheless profound transformation going on, one that affects the paradigms that have governed philosophical reflection throughout most of the century. If one were to attempt to summarize this change, it could be called the end of objectivism and the commencement of coming to grips with the "postmodern condition," as Jean-Francois Lyotard has called it. The effort to make philosophy either a handmaid to the sciences or its own specialized science, whether of the logical or phenomenological variety, has certainly faltered and, some would say, played itself out at last. In the analytic tradition, the work of Quine, Sellars, Popper, and Kuhn has led to Feyerabend, Putnam, Rorty, and Cavell. In the continental tradition, Husserl's ideal of a pure methodology of phenomenology led to Heidegger's and Gadamer's antimethodological hermeneutics. Marxism is confronted by the negative dialectics of Adorno, structuralism by Foucault and Derrida, Freudianism by Lacan and Kristeva. Classical liberalism, monumentalized as late as Rawls's *A Theory of Justice*, is criticized from the radical left by people like Roberto Unger, while MacIntyre has subjected it to critique from the standpoint of a contextual traditionalism. Aside from the special critiques offered by postmodernism, perhaps the most important concerns what philosophy itself is and whether it has either a future or, if it successfully overcomes its tradition, even a past.

In this paper, I would like to examine the current crisis of "the postmodern condition." Philosophy is, I believe, moving away from seeing itself as a formal, autonomous discipline analogous to the pure or applied sciences to that of a multimethodological, pluralistic discipline whose central questions have more to do with the arts and humanities. Briefly put: the philosopher is seeing herself less as a scientist and more as an artist; epistemology is being displaced by aesthetics, or at least by criticism. There is, however, something of an air of fin de sieclism about the postmoderns; if not outright despair, then at least the substitutes for genuine hope: an almost Alexandrine fetishism of language and textualism; a love of playful intellectualism, conundrum, and paradox; and an academic introversion of the discipline as a whole.

After delineating some of the features of this side of postmodernism, using primarily Lyotard and Rorty, I will raise a question concerning the constructive value of their positions, or antipositions. Although I welcome the transformation of philosophy from an overly narrow, formalistic objectivism toward a humanistic search for cultural understanding and criticism, there is, I will argue, too much of an unreconstructed reliance either on the Enlightenment's aesthetics of taste or on the alter-ego of the Enlightenment's modernist project, the romantic view of creativity. (The romantic theory of artistic creativity, after all, was merely the active version of the Enlightenment's passive aesthetics of taste.) If we are to reconstruct the modernism of the Enlightenment, it is not enough to eliminate its epistemology in favor of its aesthetics. Instead of losing the philosophical project in a pure play of negation and contingency, perhaps an imaginative, intelligent, educated and socially committed mode of philosophizing is not only possible but needed.

Here is where I believe the thought of John Dewey is particularly valuable. Dewey saw understanding and imagination as integral aspects of that dynamic, social process of establishing meaning that he called "intelligence." By looking in particular at imagination, Dewey maintained that a fundamental dimension of human existence was revealed. Human experience seeks to encounter and embody meaning and value as concretely as possible. This can only be done in a social and cultural context. It is vital to this process that ideals be imaginatively generated and used to guide and interpret human activity. By these intelligence seeks to construct meaningful narratives of human existence. Its imagination is social, and its creativity is complemented by the preservation and establishment of meaningful traditions, for an educated imagination provides the context of all thought. It is part of the creative task of philosophy to articulate such ideals. Philosophy, then, can ultimately be understood as an aesthetics of human existence. By thinking through the implication of this project, I believe a richer and more progressive program for philosophical thinking is opened up than by those currently offered.

The term *modernism* is admittedly ambiguous and, like any "ism," of limited value. In fact, it expresses more of an attitude or a mood than a consistent doctrine, a sense of confidence and optimism in the progressive, self-critical power of reason, scientific methodology, and liberal society to enhance and liberate mankind. It is, in short, the project bequeathed by the Enlightenment. Its goal aims at a fixed, determinate body of truths attained by a rigorous, impersonal method, truths that could ultimately be described only in a precisely literal, strictly denotative language (ideally capable of a formalization akin to mathematics). The search for truth was also part of the emancipation of man: by establishing the formal principles of ethics, autonomous, free, and self-interested individuals could contract to form a political order best suited to the liberty and also progress of mankind. While science manifested human objectivity and politics human freedom, art celebrated our subjectivity, our capacity for play and pleasure, legitimately enjoyed when we were not seeking truth or acting morally. The outstanding example clearly is found in Kant.[1]

Of course, "modernism" revealed its paradoxes even in the very process of its genesis to articulate critics like Rousseau, Schopenhauer, and Marx. But the quintessential postmodern is Nietzsche. For Nietzsche, truth is just one expression of the Will to Power. Because the Will to Power achieves itself only through opposing itself—not dialectically, but Dionysically—any effort to realize a unified point of view, an objective description of reality, is not a moment in the progressive emancipation of man but a victory of power masked as truth, a lie strong enough to suppress other lies.

This is where Lyotard comes in. The brief but powerful essay appended to The Postmodern Condition, although a polemic addressed to Habermas, offers a good insight into the dynamics and commitments of the position, at least in one of its continental manifestations. Habermas, perhaps thinking of the curiously apolitical Nietzsche and the even more curious politics of Heidegger, accuses postmodernism of playing into the hands of conservatism. Where there is no faith in reason, how can there be progress, how can there be a community realized through rational, self-critical communication? Habermas extends this to aesthetics, desiring to overcome the fragmentation of our times by "changing the status of the aesthetic experience when it is no longer primarily expressed in judgments of taste" but instead is "used to explore a living historical situation." This is done by being "put into relation with the problems of existence."[2] Lyotard interprets this as a call for the return to realism in art and states, "What Habermas requires from the arts and the experiences they provide is, in short, to bridge the gap between cognitive, ethical, and political discourses, thus opening the way to a unity of experience."[3]

Lyotard's response here is: whose unity? The demand for realism is just a mask for totality achieved through power, through the suppression of divergence and diversity. Reality is stabilized only by smothering novelty and experimentation. Lyotard sees this desire for totality as a "failure of nerve" whose effect will be to "liquidate the heritage of the avant-garde."[4] The artist must resist this, for a stabilized view of the world will force him or her to conform to rules and preestablished canons when, for the artist at least, rules are only a "means to deceive, to seduce, to reassure, which makes it impossible for them to be 'true.'"[5] Because the artist makes and breaks rules in a Nietzschian process of self-overcoming, any effort to make him conform is a victory for a system of class power.

Postmodern art differs profoundly from modern art. The one is antirealist as much as the other offers reassuring images of reality (culminating in the photograph and cinema). Modern art relies on an aesthetics of the beautiful; it seeks to give well-defined, limited, and comprehensible objects. Postmodern art offers an aesthetics of the sublime. It is born in the conviction that "the unpresentable exists" and seeks to "make visible that there is something which can be conceived which can neither be seen nor made visible: this is what is at stake in modern painting."[6] Not only must this be an art of contradiction, of abstraction, of self-negation, it will be at once an assault on reality—which is to say, the community. Creativity is born in this basic act of violence. Postmodern art must be an art in which the conceptual is in conflict with the sensible and imagination is in conflict with reality.

Postmodern art is also directed against art (again, in good Nietzschian, Dionysic fashion). To be born, a work must annihilate its predecessors—its fathers, so to speak. "All that has been received, if only yesterday . . . must be suspected. What space does Cezanne challenge? The impressionists'. What object do Picasso and Braque attack? Cezanne's." "A work can become modern only if it is first postmodern," he adds. "Postmodernism thus understood is not modernism at its end but in the nascent state, and this state is constant."[7] Art is rooted, it seems, not in history but in perpetual revolution and primordial Oedipal vengeance. Even the modernist agenda began as criticism, overthrow of the old: properly speaking, Copernicus is postmodern, Newton modern. Lyotard's point here is that the postmodern is a movement of pure creation and thereby also destruction. This is the only alternative to a totalitarian desire for "totality," for stabilized reality, even if it masks itself as a desire for a common language, for an art rooted in life that offers the hope of an integrated community of experience. Postmodern art must be an anti-art, one opposed to the community, to the past, even to itself, for its genesis only provides the condition for its eventual destruction. To lose this is to lose experimentalism. "A postmodern artist or writer," says Lyotard, "is in the position of the philosopher: the text he writes, the work he produces are not in principle governed by preestablished rules. . . . Those rules and categories are what the work of art itself is looking for."[8]

It isn't difficult to discern the familiar themes of romanticism in Lyotard's position, indebted as it is from the start to Kant's theory of the beautiful and the sublime: the ideal of the artist as the perpetual outsider, the poète maudit, who exists beyond the complacent illusions of bourgeois society; the ideal of pure creation as a spontaneous process free from any constraints; the ideal of change for the sake of change and difference for the sake of difference, the artist as maker and breaker of laws; and the ideal of the work being only a cryptic sign for the ineffably higher state of the artist's soul, a supreme achievement of individuality itself. Lyotard's language may be less eloquent than Schiller's or Shelley's, but his ideas are hardly novel. Romanticism was a reaction to the Enlightenment and, like most reactionary positions, was deeply indebted to the movement it opposed. If reason is a rule-bound activity, then creativity isn't rational; if reason is impersonal and unemotional, then art reflects the essence of the personal and the emotional, and so on. It is precisely these old dichotomies that Dewey's aesthetics calls into question and, in my view, successfully overcomes.

I want, however briefly, to indicate that the postmodernism of someone in the "Anglo-American" tradition, Richard Rorty, encounters the same problems, even though he has tried to school himself in the pragmatist line of thought. Rorty's commitments to Nietzsche, romanticism, and an aesthetics of taste come out strongly in his three recent essays, "Contingency in Language," "Contingency in Selfhood," and "Contingency in Community." Rorty sounds here as loudly as anywhere his trumpet call for the day of judgment on foundationalism; and, because there can be no foundations, no "grounds," "principles," or criteria that can legitimate themselves or any one view of the world over another as necessary, everywhere the philosopher looks he will find contingency at play. Rorty sees us as operating in the grip of the Enlightenment's modernist project in our efforts to frame an objectivist theory of meaning and reference, to see self-same identity as the foundation of selfhood, and to appeal to principles beyond those of the community in our political or moral reasoning.

Rorty quite explicitly sees himself siding with the Romanticists and poets against the scientists and foundational thinkers. Indeed, science is merely one kind of successful poetry. For him (as for Santayana), "great scientists invent descriptions of the world which are useful for purposes of predicting and controlling what happens, just as poets and political thinkers invent descriptions of it for other purposes."[9] The world may be "out there" (to use Rorty's phrase), but truth is not. Thinking otherwise tacitly conserves the idea that there is a God's-eye view that our language can approximate and that propositional sentences are the basic ways of referring to the natural "chunks" of reality. Against this, Rorty sees "vocabularies" as constituting the essence of language. It doesn't make sense, for him, to ask whether the political vocabulary of the Athenians or Elizabethans was "more or less correct." "The world does not speak. Only we do."[10] (Note here that we are in language and language is not in the world: Rorty, in short, epiphenomenalizes man by epiphenomenalizing language. This dualism anticipates others.)

The moral is not that our criteria are "subjective" but "that there are no criteria." The shift from one vocabulary to another is not an intellectual one so much as a change in habits of speech brought about by the power of certain new descriptions to displace the old. Once we realize this, Rorty says, "then we should have assimilated what was true in the romantic idea that truth is made rather than found." Instead of progress, we simply get change. "What the Romantics expressed as the claim that imagination, rather than reason, was the central human faculty was the realization that a talent for speaking differently, rather than for arguing well, was the chief instrument of cultural change." Rorty is "sympathetic to this suggestion" because he "thinks of himself as auxiliary to the poet rather than to the physicist."[11]

It is already evident that the themes of creativity and imagination are fundamental for Rorty. This comes out more explicitly in his discussion of metaphor, which is central to the idea of "redescription." Indeed, the history of human intelligence, of the arts, sciences, and moral beliefs, is the history of language, which is "the history of metaphor." For Rorty, we live in "a world of blind, contingent, mechanical forces" so that we must "think of novelty as the sort of thing which happens when a cosmic ray scrambles the atoms in a DNA molecule, thus sending things off in the direction of the orchids or the anthropoids." The equation of contingency with creativity occurs also in Rorty's Davidsonian analysis of metaphor. A metaphor has no cognitive status; it is a complete rupture with the established rules of the language. "To have a meaning is to have a place in a language-game. Metaphors, by definition, do not." For Rorty, as for Davidson, "to toss a metaphor into a conversation is like suddenly breaking off the conversation long enough to make a face, or pull a photograph out of your pocket and display it, or point at the features of the surroundings, or slap your interlocutor's face, or kiss him."[12] Metaphors have no meaning, no truth or falsity; they can only "be savored." Once we attempt to give them meaning, they become part of our habitual way of life and lose their novel, creative status. Rorty's analysis of "intellectual progress" is simply that of "the literalization of selected metaphors."[13] The history of language is thus a history of conflict between the meaningless rupture of metaphor and the overpowering of metaphor by the community.[14]

Thus, for Rorty, chance rules language, which rules us. Only the one who is "the strong poet" can change language. The strong poet for Rorty, quoting Harold Bloom, is the one who is driven by a "'horror of finding oneself to be only a copy or replica'"—[15] in short, the utterly self-created, unique individual. This touches Rorty's second theme, that the self is a pure creation, and so of course a pure contingency. The commitment to Nietzsche becomes explicit, for "to see one's life, or the life of one's community, as a dramatic narrative is to see it as a process of Nietzschean self-overcoming."[16] Rorty does add that it is impossible for one to create oneself entirely, for creation is metaphoric redescription, and this is only possible against the backdrop of the old language. "A language which was 'all metaphor' would be a language which had no use, hence not a language, but just a babble."[17] The liberal society is the one where the play of contingency is celebrated for its own sake. Thus, while liberalism has no ultimate justification, it sticks to its guns, taking "the strong poet and the utopian revolutionary" as its heroes.[18]

Here, then, is postmodernism analytic-style. Yet I think we can see the similarities between Rorty's and Lyotard's commitments. Creativity for Rorty is pure contingency. It is a complete break (as far as possible) with what has gone before, with the habits and rules that constitute the community; and to the extent that it succeeds, it is meaningless and irrational. Although Rorty's strong poet may be somewhat more sociable than Lyotard's avant-gardist, he is still involved in a contest of power to redescribe the accepted language in order to achieve a unique individuality. Rorty says nothing about why certain metaphors make sense while others do not: the only appeal can be to taste or convention. The strong metaphors are those that, in retrospect, the community agrees were good, the very ones it set out to tame. Nor does he offer any account of why radical individuality as such is desirable.

To summarize here, both Lyotard and Rorty have outlined some important themes in postmodern philosophy: the importance of art over science, of imagination over reason, of creativity over conventionalism. Behind both positions lies a Nietzschian view in which man inhabits a universe of playful difference and no purpose. Although I think the move away from the modernist or objectivist tendencies in philosophy is desirable, I don't believe either thinker has succeeded to the extent that his views of reason, individuality, creativity, or imagination are deeply indebted to the modernist distinctions. Spontaneity is not creativity in any meaningful sense. Sheer otherness and difference do not provide any intrinsic value to human existence. Aestheticism as such is mere intellectual anarchy and is no guide for overcoming the alienation of the community. Lyotard's and Rorty's problems are generated by a host of dichotomies: individuality versus community, reason versus imagination, order versus freedom, truth as made versus discovered, and so on. Both positions are riddled with dualistic, either-or habits of thought. (This is why Putnam, in my view, is a pragmatist while Rorty is not, for Putnam's endeavor is to get beyond such habits.)

If anyone has been unusually successful in overcoming the tendency toward dichotomous thinking, it has been John Dewey. I would now like to turn briefly to an examination of the relation of intelligence, imagination, and the community in Dewey's thought as indicating a profitable direction for genuine postmodern thought to take. Dewey explicitly relied on the term *intelligence* instead of *reason* because he sought to emphasize that it included imagination and that it was social, not merely individual. In particular, intelligence meant the capacity to create significant ideals that would reveal the potentialities of a present situation so that it could be successfully transformed into a meaningful experience. When experience was thus liberated, it gained an aesthetic luster, marking it as "an experience," in Dewey's terms. Although such an experience achieved genuine individuality, it offered itself also as a means for further reconstruction of experience, becoming a way of continuing the social process.

Imagination for Dewey is not sheer novelty, it is the capacity to combine the old and the new so that continuity—growth of meaning—is the result. It requires on the one hand a rich background for its sense of context. To be effective, imagination must be educated. If we lack the resources to interpret the meaning of a present situation, our options for developing that situation significantly are hampered. Imagination begins, in short, with the capacity to be meaningfully surprised. When we attempt to interpret or appreciate the meaning of a situation, a rich, vibrant capacity to see the themes and threads at play is vital.

Only to the degree that our education has given us an integrated, pluralistic sense of tradition and symbol do we have that necessary initial aesthetic sense that opens up the situation for any critical or intellectual analysis. But an educated imagination is not passive aestheticism. It also is the capacity to work with a medium actively, to explore as yet undetected possibilities. To understand is not to behold but to engage. Intelligence thus connotes both the sensitivity to respond to the complexity of a situation, the aesthetic capacity of "undergoing," as well as the active engagement that transforms the possibilities of the situation into a significant whole: the artistic capacity of "doing."

Two other aspects of intelligence are noteworthy: its relation with the community and with emotion. First, it is intrinsically creative. It actively brings forth new meaning. But it does this not by simply rupturing with its heritage, the traditions and values of the community. As Aristotle said, to live outside the community, one must be a beast or a god. (Nietzsche's famous retort to this— "To be a philosopher, one must be both!"—exemplifies the contrast I am drawing.) Dewey's solution is to see the community as a process of renewal and growth. A meaningful life is possible only within the context of a culture and a tradition, as MacIntyre has recently shown so well. But it is the growth of a tradition, its creative development through a dynamic interplay, that marks the establishment of meaning and value, not its endless repetition. The creativity of intelligence is thus an active process that engages a social and cultural milieu.

The second point is that intelligence is not bloodless reason but resonant with emotion and articulate feeling. As Dewey says in *A Common Faith*, "Intelligence, as distinct from the older conception of reason, is inherently involved in action. Moreover, there is no opposition between it and emotion. There is such a thing as passionate intelligence, as ardor in behalf of light shining into the murky places of social existence."[19] Martha Nussbaum, without any awareness of Dewey's views, has added her own eloquent argument to this point in her book, *The Fragility of Goodness*, arguing that part of the moral nature of a situation is the feelings we have as well as the principles we adopt. I also think the recent work of Hilary Putnam has approached the same ideal. Intelligence, then, is the human desire, or eros, for living a life that concretely embodies meaning and value, consciously pursued—guided by ideals that hold forth the promise of establishing a community. In Hilary Putnam's terms, providing a "moral image of the world" (what I have called an "aesthetic of human existence") is a vital part of our effort to think responsibly and coherently in philosophy.[20]

This cannot be achieved without imagination. In *Art as Experience*, Dewey says that when we try to understand another person, especially a friend, mere information is not enough. It is only when information "becomes an integral part of sympathy through imagination," when "the desires and aims, the interests and modes of response of another become an expansion of our own being that we understand him. We learn to see with his eyes, hear with his ears, and their results give true instruction, for they are built into our own structure."[21]

Civilization, he adds, is nothing less than instruction in the arts of life, which is "a matter of communication and participation in values of life by means of the imagination, and works of art are the most intimate and energetic means of aiding individuals to share in the arts of living." Imaginative intelligence civilizes because it is both creative and social; it is what makes it possible for human beings to live significant lives together—for we do not live significant lives any other way, whatever Nietzsche may think.

A vital philosophy of the twenty-first century will be one that integrates, not disintegrates, humanity. Dewey's thought is thus even more "postmodern" than Nietzsche's. What is needed is first of all a more concrete integration of imagination and reason. In *Reason, Truth and History*, Hilary Putnam said, "It is significant that the ability to criticize one's own goals (and those of others) may depend just as much on one's imagination as on one's ability to accept true statements and disbelieve false ones."[22] But a far more radical as well as extensive analysis of the imaginative roots of reason has recently been outlined by Mark Johnson in his book, *The Body in the Mind*. Johnson explores the play of "image schematic structures" derived from our lived bodily experience and how they are elaborated into the very organizational fabric of our conscious rationality, although he ignores the social dimensions of imagination.[23]

From a Deweyan perspective, the search for the dynamics of imaginative intelligence must be pursued across the field of human cultural achievements. Such a project would see philosophy as the disciplined, educated exploration of human meaning as embodied in our cultural experience. Instead of a pure discipline wedded to mathematical logic or reductionistic physics or neurology, philosophy can be a multilingual, methodologically pluralistic, humanistic pursuit that seeks to discern the ways human beings create meaning and value in their lives. Nor is this merely a passive, speculative ideal, for philosophy itself is part of that creative process: it, perhaps more than any other art, seeks to generate ideals that can liberate us from our present blindness and frustrating dilemmas, constructively guiding us to a richer and more humane community. The ultimate project of an aesthetics of human existence is an art of life. Unless we are to remain with the romantic individualism of the postmoderns, such a project must turn toward tough-minded cultural and political idealism. At least, if philosophy can educate our society with an understanding of and imaginative sympathy for the variety of ways human beings pursue the quest for meaning and value, it may have helped remove the finger from the nuclear trigger.

Notes

1. See Jürgen Habermas, "Modernity versus Postmodernity," *New German Critique* 22 (1981): 3–14. See also Jürgen Habermas, *The Philosophical Discourse of Modernity*, trans. Frederick Lawrence (Cambridge, Mass.: MIT Press, 1987).

2. Jean-Francois Lyotard, *The Postmodern Condition*, trans. Geoff Bennington and Brian Massumi (Minneapolis: University of Minnesota Press, 1984), p. 72. See also Habermas, "Modernity versus Postmodernity," p. 11ff.

3. Lyotard, p. 72.

4. Ibid., p. 73.

5. Ibid., pp. 74–75.

6. Ibid., p. 78.

7. Ibid., p. 79.

8. Ibid., p. 81.

9. Richard Rorty, "The Contingency of Language," *London Review of Books* (April 17, 1986): 4.

10. Ibid., p. 6.

11. Ibid., p. 8.

12. Ibid., pp. 16–18.

13. Richard Rorty, "The Contingency of Community," *London Review of Books* (July 24, 1986): 44.

14. Rorty's view of language and metaphor has been recently critiqued by Mark Johnson, "Good Rorty; Bad Rorty," unpub. MS, 1988.

15. Richard Rorty, "The Contingency of Selfhood," *London Review of Books* (May 8, 1986): 24.

16. Ibid., p. 29.

17. Ibid., p. 41.

18. Rorty, "The Contingency of Community," p. 60.

19. John Dewey, *A Common Faith* (New Haven: Yale University Press, 1934), p. 79. See also John Dewey, *Human Nature and Conduct* (New York: Henry Holt and Co., 1922).

20. Hilary Putnam, *The Many Faces of Realism* (La Salle, Ill.: Open Court, 1987), p. 51.

21. John Dewey, *Art as Experience* (New York: G. P. Putnam's Sons, 1934), p. 336.

22. Hilary Putnam, *Reason, Truth, and History* (New York: Cambridge University Press, 1981), p. 170.

23. See also Vincent Colapietro, "Toward a More Comprehensive Conception of Human Reason," *International Philosophical Quarterly* 27 (no. 107, 1987): 281–98.

Meaning in the Arts:
Considerations for a General Theory

ARMEN T. MARSOOBIAN

In this essay I propose to develop a preliminary outline for a general theory of aesthetic meaning, one that is both adequate and sensitive to the multifarious forms of the fine arts. I will begin by first exploring two approaches to meaning common in contemporary discussions of art. These I call the "referential" and the "interpretational" approaches. I will then suggest an alternative generic approach that does not entail the rejection of either reference or interpretation but will seek to demonstrate their limited purview. My approach is in large part indebted to the philosophical work of Justus Buchler. By examining the nature of aesthetic meaning, I hope to extend his systematic insights into the human process.

Although most contemporary approaches to aesthetic meaning recognize the role of both reference and interpretation, one or the other of these plays the dominant role. These alternatives are typified by the works of Nelson Goodman and Arthur C. Danto. Though it is not my intention to examine the complexities of their respective philosophies of art, I must sketch some important features of their positions as they pertain to our issue.

Let me begin by making the somewhat bald assertion that one way of reading Danto's philosophy of art is to see it as a search for alternatives to Goodman's referential theory. Danto's dissatisfaction with Goodman's approach focuses primarily upon the latter's inability to answer identity questions for artworks; that is, to provide the defining difference between "works of art" and "mere real things." Denotation or the lack thereof is not enough to mark this distinction. According to Danto, the source of this difficulty rests ultimately in Goodman's desire to rescue some form of "representationalism" in the arts, albeit not in its traditional form of "resemblance."

For Goodman the notion of reference, which lies at the heart of representation, is a more complex affair than simple denotation. Denotation is only one of a number of species of reference and has itself a variety of subspecies. Reference is Goodman's most generic term for what he calls "all sorts of symbolizations, all cases of *standing for*." Denotation is reserved "for the application of a word or picture or other label to one or many things."[1] Among the many subspecies of denotation that pertain to art, Goodman has identified (1) verbal denotation (e.g., words, phrases, or predicates); (2) notation (e.g., musical scores, dance notation); and (3) pictorial denotation (e.g., depiction or representation by drawing, painting, sculpture, photograph, film, etc.).

Much of the initial criticism directed against Goodman's *Languages of Art* focused upon the third mentioned subspecies, pictorial denotation. Goodman had argued that for a symbol (i.e., a painting, drawing, sculpture) to represent or depict an object, it must participate in a conventional symbol system similar to that of verbal language. The possible resemblance of the symbol to its object has nothing to do with it being a representation of that object. What determines the referential relationship becomes a matter of the conventions in the symbol system. Symbol systems themselves vary, often greatly. They are characterized by what Goodman calls degrees of syntactical and semantic density. Further, he introduces a notion of "repleteness" (i.e., a form of relevant interconnectedness) to distinguish artistic representation from other forms of representation.

The details of the above analysis are not our primary concern. What does concern us is the elaborate extent to which Goodman expands and qualifies his theory in order to retain the primacy of reference. This can readily be seen in Goodman's handling of the traditionally nonrepresentational arts such as absolute music or abstract painting. Goodman introduces the concept of exemplification (i.e., the other key species of reference) to encompass these forms. Exemplification "runs in the opposite direction" from denotation. "[E]xemplification is selective, obtaining only between the symbol and some but not others of the labels denoting it or properties possessed by it. Exemplification is not mere possession of a feature but requires also reference to that feature.... Exemplification is thus a certain subrelation of the converse of denotation, distinguished through a return reference *to* denoter by denoted."[2]

The properties (or labels) that a symbol possesses may not all be among the so-called "literal properties" of that symbol. A symbol may have "metaphorical properties," for example, a symphony may be tragic, a painting powerful. When such metaphorical properties are exemplified, we have yet another subvariety of reference called "expression." The traditional nonrepresentational art forms are often expressive in this sense. Such artworks express their metaphorical properties. Goodman can thus have expression while still retaining reference.

In arguing against traditional theories of "pure" or nonrepresentational art, Goodman writes, "[P]lainly not all the countless features of the work matter (not, for example, the painting's weighing four pounds...) but only those qualities and relationships of color or sound, those spatial and temporal patterns, and so on that the work exemplifies and thus selectively refers to."[3] The important point to note is that all exemplification is *selective*. Not all the properties of the symbol are of equal relevance. Often the features that are selected in this self-referential process vary for any given symbol. Just as we may have ambiguity of reference in a language system, so may we have ambiguity of exemplification in the arts. Yet what, if anything, controls the selection of the properties of the symbol that are exemplified? Symbols, in Goodman's scheme, require reference to be the symbols that they are, but what requires the reference to be the kind of reference that it is? Though there may be multiple and often complex chains of reference, a crucial feature of symbolization is missing. Symbols are dyadic for Goodman. "A symbol system consists of a symbol scheme correlated with a field of reference."[4] What Goodman assiduously avoids is the Peircean insight into the triadicity of all signs.[5] For C. S. Peirce, a sign has meaning only if it is translatable by another sign (i.e., its interpretant). Reference is thus ultimately determined by interpretation.

Turning to Danto's analysis of artistic meaning and expression, we can see an extension of this Peircean insight into the centrality of the interpretant. Initially taking up what he calls Goodman's suggestion that metaphorical exemplification lies at the heart of expression, Danto soon finds it straining under a burden it is unable to handle. On Goodman's model, an artwork has both literal and metaphorical properties. In Goodman's words, "A symphony that expresses feelings of tragic loss does not literally have those feelings; nor are the feelings expressed those of the composer or spectator; they are feelings that the work has metaphorically and refers to by exemplification."[6] Thus a symphony may express a variety of emotions but does not express its literal predicates. Literal properties are exemplified by what Goodman calls "instantiation." This latter species of reference is illustrated by the example of a tailor's swatch instantiating certain physical properties of the cloth.

Danto takes exception to any such strict distinction between the literal and the metaphorical by citing examples of supposedly literal predicates that are both literally and metaphorically exemplified. Properties are not so easily classifiable. Even though artistic expression has traditionally been identified with emotion, expressive predicates may fall under the conventional extension of an artwork's alleged literal properties. The Beauvais Cathedral expresses "verticality," it does not merely instantiate it. According to Danto, we have to know *how* a predicate is employed by a work before we can grasp what its reference may be. It is not enough to know that certain properties are "ordinarily" or "conventionally" associated with specific symbol systems while others are not. The mere lack of conventional literalness is not an adequate basis upon which to identify metaphorical properties. More is needed to distinguish the *how* from the *what* than is provided for by denotation, inverse or otherwise. Danto concludes, "The philosophical point is that the concept of expression can be reduced to the concept of metaphor, when the *way* in which something is represented is taken in connection with the subject represented."[7] The notion of "standing for" at the heart of most referential theories of meaning is simply inadequate for this task.

Danto's philosophy of art does take another direction. He has argued quite persuasively that interpretation is constitutive of art. "[A]n object is an artwork *at all* only in relation to an interpretation."[8] Interpretation is the agency by which quite commonplace objects can be raised or "transfigured" to the level of art.[9] Even primarily referential works (e.g., portraits) are "never merely referential." They have what Danto calls a "semi-opacity," i.e., they present a content. An object is meaningful as an artwork only when we see the interrelation between the "what" (the content) and the "how" (the mode of presentation) of the work.

In his emphasis upon interpretation, Danto is striving to chart a middle course between two extremes in the theory of art. One extreme, deriving from semantical approaches to meaning, is labeled by Danto the "Transparency Theory." On such a view artworks themselves begin to "disappear" as they more adequately "mirror" what they are "about," what they "mean." On the other extreme, we find current literary theory's obsession with "intertextuality." A text, be it in language or some other medium, is meaningful solely in terms of other texts. While dismissing the semantical approach as committing what it calls the "Referential Fallacy," this latter approach errs by narrowly identifying meaning with the "literary culture" of the artist (e.g., the conscious or unconscious influence of other texts upon the artist).

Danto contends that both of these approaches distance artworks from their audiences. He writes that if art has "something important to do with our lives ... this is utterly unexplained if its meaning is a matter of its reference, and its candidate referenda are as bizarre a menagerie of imaginabilia as the fancy of man has framed."[10] Semantical theory falls short because the only kinds of connections it understands between symbols and the world are "reference, truth, instantiation, exemplification, satisfaction, and the like." This approach distorts the world "in order that it can *receive* literary representations. . . ."[11]

On the other hand, if artworks are simply Derridean "networks of reciprocal relationships," this puts them at an "intraversable" distance from their audience. As a consequence, literary works "become simply artifacts made of words, with no references save internal ones or incidental external ones. And reading them becomes external, as though they had nothing to do with us, were merely there, intricately wrought composites of logical lacework, puzzling and pretty and pointless."[12]

The middle course that Danto proposes ties together three of the points we have already stressed: (1) the importance of interpretation for reference, (2) the emphasis upon the way in which something is represented, and (3) the semi-opacity of artworks. In a number of recent essays, Danto brings these to bear upon an analysis of the differences and similarities between literature and philosophy. Though tentative in his claims, the implications of his approach are suggestive.

Danto claims that a literary work is a metaphor for the reader. Reference is still operating but in a very unusual fashion. "The universality of literary reference is only that it is about each individual that reads the text at the moment that individual reads it, . . . identifying himself not with the implied reader for whom the implied narrator writes, but with the actual subject of the text in such a way that each work becomes a metaphor for each reader: perhaps the same metaphor for each."[13] Although "metaphoric identification" of the reader with the work is at first blush a rather startling notion, it does hint at an important aspect of the alternative theory of meaning I wish to propose. In anticipation, let me say that this approach emphasizes the fact that meaning is an achievement of human communication. For something to "have" meaning it must *function* communicatively within some perspective. Meaning is a form of communicative efficacy. To understand meaning, we must look toward the "effect" of the work and not merely at what it "stands for."

For Danto the effect in artistic communication is achieved in a manner different from that in philosophy or other nonliterary forms. In art, the idea is "embodied" or "incarnate" in the work; in nonartistic works there is a weaker sense of embodiment, a greater transparency, a lesser opacity. "What makes [Warhol's] *Brillo Box* a work of art is that it incarnates, expresses, whatever idea it does express, hence is idea and mere thing at once, a box transfigured if only into the idea of a box."[14]

Embodiment is an admittedly vague notion. Citing Platonic dialogues as primary examples, Danto does recognize that certain philosophical texts do "embody" philosophical ideas. But the need to draw a stricter line between art and nonart forces him to set certain qualifications on the notion of embodiment. For the philosopher the character of the communication is essentially different from that of the artist. The assertive nature of language is paramount—or, to put it in Danto's terms, the ideas are more directly conveyed or "mainlined." He further qualifies the difference with a self-consciously banal remark concerning subject matter. "[L]iterature cannot stray very far from the structures that define the life of those who read novels: love, jealousy, friendship, adventure, conflict and crisis. . . ."[15] But in the end, Danto himself even admits that a restriction of subject matter is perhaps too arbitrary, yet he offers no alternatives.

Though having rightly focused the discussion of artistic meaning on artistic communication, Danto's analysis is stymied by an inability to generalize the notion of communication. For in the end, he relies upon a semantically based conception of expression: artworks express ideas, albeit in unique and unusual ways.

Justus Buchler's general theory of human judgment or utterance overcomes the difficulties of semantically based theories of meaning by broadening our understanding of communication. If we treat all human utterance broadly conceived as falling under three general functional types (that is, as assertions, contrivances, and actions), we avoid the need to rely upon either of Danto's criteria of "directness" of communication or "appropriateness" of subject matter to distinguish art from nonart. The focus must shift to the issue of *how* humans produce; that is, to the character of human production.

Buchler contends that "every product is a judgment." What he means is that every product is at bottom a stance adopted toward the world. Man naturally and continuously discriminates and selects from the complexes that make up his world.[16] Judgment, in this sense, is inevitable, ubiquitous, and never fully isolatable into discrete events. And most importantly, judgment is never exclusively identified with mental activity or consciousness. "[Man] judges continuously, through what he includes and excludes, preserves and destroys, is inclined to and averse to; through what he makes and fails to make, through the ways he acts and refrains from acting, through what he believes and disavows. His attitudes, and hence his commitments, are his whether he is aware of them or not."[17]

To fully appreciate this insight into the judicative nature of human production, it must be emphasized that judging is not primarily a discrete mental act preceding or subsequent to other forms of behavior. We do not necessarily judge first, in the sense of formulating a course of action, and then act. The action, the doing itself, is a form of judgment. Thus, as the artist in the act of making is judging, so too, albeit in a different sense, is the spectator in the act of appreciation. The emphasis and ultimately the basis for distinguishing the three modes of judgment (active, assertive, and exhibitive) rest upon the way in which the judging occurs. "To say that a man judges, for example, through what he makes, does not mean that he makes after he has discriminated and selected and become committed. It means that his making what he makes *is the way* he has discriminated and selected and become committed."[18]

Active, exhibitive, and assertive judgment do not mark structural but functional differences. A given product may function in more than one mode. This is an important consideration for resolving some of the difficulties raised in Danto's analysis, in particular his inability to adequately distinguish borderline cases between literature and philosophy. Summarizing the important functional differences between these modes, Buchler writes:

(1) When we can be said to predicate, state, or affirm, by the use of words or by any other means; when the underlying direction is to achieve or support belief; when it is relevant to cite evidence in behalf of our product, we produce in the mode of assertive judgment, we judge assertively. (2) When we can be said to do or to act; when the underlying direction is toward effecting a result; when "bringing about" is the central trait attributable to our product, we produce in the mode of active judgment, we judge actively. (3) When we contrive or make, in so far as the contrivance rather than its role in action is what dominates and is of underlying concern; when the process of shaping and the product as shaped is central, we

produce in the mode of exhibitive judgment, we judge exhibitively. On the methodic level, where (minimally) purposiveness and intention belong to judgments, assertive judgment is exemplified by science, or more generally, inquiry . . .; active judgment, by deliberate conduct morally assessable; exhibitive judgment, by art.[19]

This functional approach to judgment can clarify the difficulties we encountered earlier with literary and nonliterary exemplification. No product is intrinsically active, assertive, or exhibitive. The judicative function is determined by the communicative context. For a literary work, the communicative context typically does not call for interpretation through truth and falsity. The artwork does not primarily aim to compel or support belief, although this does not rule out its possible role in the articulation of beliefs. (For example, Harriet Beecher Stowe's *Uncle Tom's Cabin* may in this sense support certain beliefs about abolition.) A literary work offers itself to interpretation and appraisal in respect to the arrangement or the constellation of its materials; in literature, for example, these may be through the use of conventional or devised linguistic signs.[20] As an exhibitive judgment, its communicative effect is neither more nor less direct than we find with the assertive use of language.

On the other hand, the exhibitive dimension of philosophic writing, or for that matter even mathematics, subserves and even extends the role of assertion. In its aim to communicate univocally and compel greater unanimity of belief, a philosophical work may array its assertions in an exhibitive manner. Yet in this case, the showing ultimately subserves the saying.

The modes of judgment do not privilege one form of communication over another. Semantically based theories of meaning, while recognizing the role of the active and exhibitive dimensions of communication, tend to subordinate their judicative and cognitive value to that of the assertive. This leads, as Buchler says, to "the false implication . . . that the work of art always conforms to the model of a dumb-show pointing to one-knows-not-what [representational theories], or to the model of total-sensory-affective involvement [expression theories]—both wholly noncommittal."[21]

If we turn directly to the issue of meaning, we may say that in its most generic sense a product functions meaningfully *if it initiates the articulation of some perspective* within which it is located. The phrase *"articulation of perspective"* is more generic than interpretation. Articulation may take place in any of the three modes of judgment. The perspective that is articulated is the communicative context. This context varies in scope for each particular instance of communication. There are an indeterminate number of perspectives in which an artwork may function articulatively. This permits us to claim that an artwork has meaning in nonartistic orders of judgment. A Freudian interpretation, or any "deep interpretation," to use Danto's phrase, would thus be meaningful, but not in the same manner as that found in the exhibitive order of artworks.[22] In the latter order, articulation takes the form of either the *production* or the *discovery* of other elements within the perspective. Judgments are thus ramified and ramifiable.

The ramification of judgment is synonymous with the increased availability of its order for assimilation and manipulation. Within the order of artworks, ramified judgment may take the form of the artistic influence of one artwork upon another, or one school or style of artistic invention upon other schools, styles, or individual artists. Alternatively, the communicative effect might take the form of the ramified judgments of the spectator or audience. Thus, Danto's remark that the text is a metaphor for the reader can make sense if we interpret it in terms of the ramification of meaning in and for a viewer, reader, or audience.

The insight that articulation of perspective may be in any of the three modes of judgment, either singly or in combination, generalizes the notion of interpretation. The meaning of an artwork is not primarily or solely a function of reference. Meaning in the arts is no longer limited to a model of "messages" or "themes," whether in the form of a predicate or a property, to be conveyed or denoted by the artwork. Meaning is not fixed—either by the artist or the critic. Yet this does not mean that any meaning at all is possible. The artwork has determinate traits that enter into (or communicate with) viewers, other artworks, and even whole artistic movements. These communicative contexts become the *meanings* of an artwork. The need to encompass the multitude of articulations that an artwork engenders challenges us to fundamentally reformulate our standard conceptions of meaning. My remarks have been intended to serve as a prolegomenon to such a reformulation.

Notes

1. Nelson Goodman, *Of Mind and Other Matters* (Cambridge, Mass.: Harvard University Press, 1984), p. 55.
2. Ibid., p. 59.
3. Ibid., pp. 59–60.
4. Nelson Goodman, *Languages of Art: An Approach to a Theory of Symbols* (Indianapolis: Bobbs-Merrill Co., 1968), p. 143.
5. Unlike Goodman, for Charles Sanders Peirce "sign" is the generic term and "symbol" is a type of sign. Peirce maintained that every sign involves a triadic relation between a physical object or quality (the material thing taken as a sign), something that it denotes or refers to (its object), and another sign that it is said to "mean" or "connote" (its interpretant). Though many of the details of Peirce's general theory of signs are open to interpretation, it is clear that "sign" is a relational and functional notion. The sign relation requires not a particular class of things but an object functioning significatively. To function significatively (that is, to have meaning), a sign must be translatable—be interpretable by another sign, its interpretant. The sign-object relation (reference) is con-

ditioned upon the sign-interpretant relation (interpretation). The sign-interpretant relation, to use Peirce's language, provides the "ground of representation." This determining relation is a rule of interpretation. Rules needn't be formal or presented in propositional form. They are sign-conventions that take the form of habits, varying in strength and alterability. They provide the standpoint, the perspective for interpretation. All interpretation is thus selective or abstractive. Features of the sign (or to use Goodman's terms, labels of the symbol) are necessarily included or excluded in relation to this standpoint. All representation involves the selection and discrimination of specific properties by means of an interpretation. The object (referent) is thus related to a sign by the interpretant.

6. Goodman, *Of Mind and Other Matters*, p. 61.

7. Arthur C. Danto, *The Transfiguration of the Commonplace: A Philosophy of Art* (Cambridge, Mass.: Harvard University Press, 1981), p. 197.

8. Arthur C. Danto, *The Philosophical Disenfranchisement of Art* (New York: Columbia University Press, 1986), p. 44.

9. Ibid., pp. 44, 78.

10. Ibid., p. 144.

11. Ibid., p. 145.

12. Ibid., p. 160.

13. Ibid., p. 155.

14. Ibid., p. 178.

15. Ibid., p. 184.

16. "Complex" or "natural complex" is the most generic form of identification for Buchler. "Whatever is, in whatever way, is a natural complex" (Justus Buchler, *Metaphysics of Natural Complexes* [New York: Columbia University Press, 1966], pp. 1ff).

17. Justus Buchler, *The Main of Light: On the Concept of Poetry* (New York: Oxford University Press, 1974), p. 93.

18. Ibid., pp. 93–94.

19. Ibid., pp. 97–98.

20. See in particular Buchler's interpretations of the poems of Browning, Donne, Blake, and Pope (Justus Buchler, *The Main of Light*, pp. 101–16).

21. Ibid., p. 100.

22. Marking out such differences is a task beyond the scope of this essay, but clearly there is a growing recognition in current literary theory of the importance of non-reductionistic approaches to interpretation. Buchler's theory provides the philosophical basis to support such insights.

WILLIAM JAMES

James, Putnam, and Metaphysical Materialism

GERALD E. MYERS

For a tour of the "frontiers" in American philosophy, can anything equal Hilary Putnam's *Philosophical Papers*, especially his third volume, *Realism and Reason*?[1] I doubt there is a better scout than Putnam in tracking the whereabouts of influential contemporary philosophers. When the guide is also a major homesteader, showing you where and why he stakes his own claims, giving you a kind of at-home-on-the-range feeling, you have to be unusually grateful. If, like myself, you are assigned to locate the maverick William James yonder, you thank Putnam several times over.

Reading Putnam encourages me to call James a frontiersman insofar as his view of the theoretical landscape resembles Putnam's and Nelson Goodman's as espoused by Putnam. That the resemblance is coincidental instead of influential does not kill its interest. Thinkers-on-the-frontier are alert to coincidence, because where there's smoke there's likely flame out there; where there's coincidence there's likely serendipity somewhere. (Because this was written before *U.S. News and World Report*'s article on Putnam in its April 25, 1988, issue, in which he mentions his new interest in James, I was naturally pleased to learn that I was trailing the intended footprints.) Coincidentally, Putnam is aroused by the same danger that kept James awake: metaphysical materialism. Their reactions to materialism display intriguing similarities.

Metaphysical materialism, Putnam asserts, is today's "scientism," and because this is "one of the most dangerous contemporary intellectual tendencies, a critique of its most influential contemporary form is a duty a for a philosopher who views his enterprise as more than a purely technical discipline."[2] Like James, Putnam accuses materialism, in its seeking to reduce normative and intentional language to descriptive and naturalistic locutions, of threatening the autonomy of reason and philosophy itself. The idea that physics might replace philosophy violates our humanity as thoughtful beings, so Putnam closes *Realism and Reason* with E. Gilson's line, "Philosophy always buries its undertakers."

Materialism (physicalism) assumes the existence of a ready-made world with an intrinsic structure that but one system truly formulates. James had to fight this assumption on two fronts, because it marked absolute idealism as well. His celebrated pluralism attacked both idealism and materialism for claiming monistic access to a laid-out reality, and, like Putnam's, his pluralism abandoned essentialism.

Thinking there is a ready-made world with a built-in structure, consisting of essential properties that only physics can describe, encounters James's objection: "All ways of conceiving a concrete fact, if they are true ways at all, are equally true ways. There is no property *absolutely* essential to any one thing. The same property which figures as the essence of a thing on one occasion becomes a very inessential feature upon another."[3] Putnam concurs: Saul Kripke's essentialism, for instance, requires modal properties that are outlawed by materialism, leaving the materialist without essences and thus without the intrinsic structure of a ready-made world. Although there is no possible world in which water is not H_2O, this fact simply reflects how we intend to use "water" referringly. "But the 'essence' of water in this sense is the product of our use of the word, the kinds of referential intentions we have." This sort of essence is not 'built into the world' in the way required by an essentialist theory of reference "to get itself off the ground."[4]

How can materialism treat the concept of reference that is now before us? On Putnam's interpretation of contemporary physicalism, the brain becomes a computer, its computations are "representation" or "sentence-analogs," and we refer to (think about) A if the term "A" in our particular sentence-analog is in a physical relation R (reference-relation) to A. Citing Quine, Hartry Field, David Lewis, and Charles Tanner, Putnam finds this analysis a failure because R cannot be defined physically. Trying to define it, for example, by listing all possible reference situations won't work because the list must be infinite; consequently, it won't tell us what the reference situations share in common.[5] Another move, once made by Putnam himself, is to define reference taken as a functional property, as simply a higher-order physical property. But this move presupposes that causality, through which functional properties are defined, is itself definable physically. Putnam convincingly argues that causality can't be so defined, largely because the physicalists' use of "cause-and-effect" involves the intuitive idea of explanation.[6]

The preceding has Jamesian parallels. James stressed the opaqueness of causality: "The fact is that the whole question of interaction and influence between things is a metaphysical question. . . . It is truly hard enough to imagine the 'idea of a beef-steak binding two molecules together'; but since Hume's time it has been equally hard to imagine anything binding them together."[7] He stressed it when objecting to materialism's use of the concept for denying mental causation. "But one has no right to pull the pall over the psychic half of the subject only, as the automatists do, and to say that that causation is unintelligible, whilst in the same breath one dogmatizes about material causation as if Hume, Kant, and Lotze had never been born."[8] Later, in his *Essays in Radical Empiricism*, he tried to resolve causality's opaqueness by defining it experientially, as a special feeling of activity; but this was done very sketchily and, of course, from an antimaterialist perspective.

To an extent, what James said about "reference" accords with Putnam's view. Intentionality or objective reference, he agreed, certainly defies physical definition. Instead, the problem was that it seemed to defy analysis altogether: the relation between one's thought and its object appeared impenetrable. In 1895, however, he took the pragmatic route (a behavioristic one, some believe) of eliminating the mysterious self-transcendency of reference or intentionality. When I think, for example, about tigers in India, what is meant by saying that my thought refers to or "points" to tigers there is that, culminating a sequence of appropriate further thoughts and behaviors, I would be "satisfied" if I found tigers in India, "frustrated" if I did not. In what I deem a slip, at one point he called reference a physical relation, but typically he described it as both mental and physical. Thought's reference, then, "is no special inner mystery, but only an outer chain of physical or mental intermediaries connecting thought and thing."[9] How much this accords with Putnam's way of combining forces with Goodman's *Ways of Worldmaking*.[10] Pluralism, not pragmatism, unites Putnam and Goodman; the former is wary of the term,[11] and the latter can't accept equating truth with utility,[12] so the Jamesian shadow falls from another angle. Moreover, that we have coincidence instead of influence is reemphasized by the contemporary duo's stated respect for Kant, whereas James (put off by the architectonic and the notion of noumena) advised philosophers to go around, not through, Kant. There is no mention of James in Putnam's book, and in Goodman's, with its acknowledgment of Kant and C. I. Lewis (and Woody Allen) as influences, there is but one.

Goodman's single reference to James is to *A Pluralistic Universe*'s "equivocal" title.[13] It is equivocal in suggesting either one universe containing pluralistic features or a plurality of universes taken as a single collection. Generally, for Goodman, one can have it either way, although, when two or more versions of a universe conflict, the latter suggestion has the advantage.[14] Goodman's pluralism, inimical to metaphysical materialism and its commitment to one world-one version, continues to develop along the lines of his *Languages of Art*.[15] There, in company with E. H. Gombrich and others, he undermined the idea that an unconceptualized reality can be revealed to sense-perception.

Coincidentally, Jamesian motifs occur in Goodman's thought. Goodman's "multiplicity of worlds" evokes James's "many worlds,"[16] and his concept of ourselves as world-makers associates with James's declaration that the *fons et origo* of all reality is ourselves.[17] Jamesian parallels are easily found[18] for Goodman's remark that "some of the felt stubbornness of fact is the grip of habit."[19] Those familiar with such Jamesian contentions as that reality is in flux and thus not ready-made, that truth is accordingly in-the-making, and that we, through our interests and volitions and through our choice of concepts and categories, help to establish what is real and what is true will discern a Jamesian note in Goodman's exposition. "Truth, far from being a solemn and severe matter, is a docile and obedient servant. The scientist who supposes that he is single-mindedly dedicated to the search for truth deceives himself.... He seeks system, simplicity, scope; and when satisfied on those scores he tailors truth to fit.... He as much decrees as discovers the laws he sets forth, as much designs as discerns the patterns he delineates."[20] This quote also expresses a big chunk of what James meant by pragmatism.

My response to Putnam's views, including his assessment of Goodman's pluralism vis-à-vis materialism, is necessarily very selective, for in the time left I want to question them beyond simply uncovering further Jamesian connections. If I have it right, Putnam thinks there is a fairly direct run from Goodman's claim that equally valid descriptions or versions apply to sensations, to the conclusion that we can never compare theory or versions with a transcendental, unconceptualized reality: the most we can do is to compare versions. On the one hand, Putnam is virtually "sold" on this, but, on the other, "almost everyone regards the statement that there is no mind-independent reality, that there are just the 'versions,' or there is just the 'discourse,' or whatever, as itself intensely paradoxical. Because one cannot talk about the transcendent or even deny its existence without paradox, one's attitude to it must, perhaps, be the concern of religion rather than of rational philosophy."[21]

My first question is this: does Putnam believe that talk about a transcendent, mind-independent reality and talk about an absolute version of reality are one and the same?[22] If he does not, then the incoherence that the latter allegedly generates need not infect the former; a plurality of worlds or worldly versions, thus preserved, would block the incoherent effort to establish a unique form of reduction under the guise of an ontological identification.[23] I do not think that incoherence is guaranteed simply because we cannot match versions with an unconceptualized reality about which we continue to talk.

The versions, you recall, are not merely versions or just versions of versions: they are version of reality, of conceptualized but mind-independent realities. Putnam's and Goodman's pluralism is explicitly not subjectivism (but also see below). Putnam, although uncertain about Goodman's ways of subsuming truth under a concept of "rightness," agrees that some kind of realism must be retained that appreciates how "p" and "I think that p" differ. So I don't think Putnam would suppose that talk, uncommitted to "absolute" versions, about transcendent realities is doomed to incoherence.

I ask next: does Putnam believe that the notion of an unconceptualized reality is itself incoherent? Are there arguments, including Gombrich's against "the innocent eye," certifying its absurdity? James thought not, as his doctrine of "pure" (that is, unconceptualized) experience testifies: although pure instances of such elude us, they are conceptually approachable.[24] Mohan Matthen urges a similar view: perhaps perceptual content (mind-independent reality) can't be obtained by removing judgmental overlay, but, as laboratory work by Bela Julesz and Edwin H. Land indicates, it may be approachable through experiments wherein judgment, by being excluded from the input of requisite information, can't contaminate with its usual overlay.[25] If so, then versions are coherently matchable for approximating mind-independent realities.

Following Putnam's trail through the cactus of psychophysical dualism, I stumble again. He seems so right, apropos of Davidson's theory, in holding that a "type-type" theory is required for identifying a particular brain event with a mental one; without some general criteria, token identity becomes hopeless.[26] Yet, and I wish Putnam were more explicit here, whatever the criteria, surely we can never identify a brain and a mental event as we identify the evening and the morning star. We can never in a continuous operation point to a brain event, then to a mental one, and discover their sameness. Given this, the materialist's theoretical jump of identification certainly incorporates an element of legislation or posit. But does Putnam believe that one's reluctance to jump with the materialist is equally legislative? If one doesn't exclude physicalism definitionally but insists merely on the experimental inability to replace psychophysical correlation with that of identity, is one not thereby an antimaterialist with impressive, though nonlegislative, credentials?

What we owe most to a frontiersman like Putnam, peering over the cliffs above us, is the signal that there is a frontier. By contrast, Davidson and David Wiggins manage to tame irruptions from the wild without leaving their dens. They domesticate dualism, Putnam intimates, by yoking it peacefully with physics: dualism's intentional locutions become consistent with the nonintentional ones of physics. "But saying this is not," Putnam responds, "saying quite enough. I wish I knew what would be saying enough."[27]

For what is Putnam looking? Philosophy, it has been said, leaves the world as it found it. Perhaps Putnam, like James, thinks otherwise. And maybe pluralism by itself can't do more than leave things "as is"; by itself it can't get beyond asserting that Quine's physicalism is "mere prejudice,"[28] that physics and psychology employ different yet consistent languages, or that complementarily is just a quirk of nature. Consider Putnam's remarks about the dangers of relativism and historicism (which consort comfortably with pluralism and the tendency to leave things "as is") and his comment that Goodman, in wanting to build worlds for the enrichment they give, ought "to recognize that the notions of truth and rightness subserve a vision of the good."[29]

Here, it seems, Putnam endorses something like James's pragmatic thesis that truth is a species of good.[30] Maybe some such thesis is needed for setting priorities among the pluralistic versions, especially when they border more conspicuously on moral and social matters. Metaphysical theories, as James, Wittgenstein, and Ayer have said, are "pictures" we make of the world(s), and who doubts that some pictures fit better than others with one's moral sense of what ought to be?

Presumably, the search for hierarchical values in a pluralistic universe involves a hunt for nonarbitrary, objective criteria by which one selects what best subserves a vision of the good. But does Putnam really believe in this? I think of his sympathy for Goodman's confession that, for purposes of world-making and understanding, "selling" instead of arguing is more efficacious.[31] And I think of Putnam's reputation for finding incoherence lurking throughout philosophical argumentation, wondering then whether, like James and Bergson, he suspects concepts as inadequate to reality; whether, like them, he inclines toward approaching reality, at some point, intuitively instead of discursively. Either way, whether the intuitive and subjective or the discursive and objective, I wonder if Jamesian subjectivity can be avoided. James thought you had ultimately to believe in the kind of world(s) that the whole you, emotional and durational, prefers to believe in. For one whose frontier-vision detects a "burn-out" in formal argumentation such that not only is metaphysical materialism actually or potentially incoherent but so is any argument mounted against it—is there any other (than a Jamesian) way?

Notes

1. Hilary Putnam, *Realism and Reason* (Cambridge, U.K.: Cambridge University Press, 1983).
2. Putnam, *Realism and Reason*, p. 211.
3. William James, *The Works of William James*, 9 vols., ed. Frederick Burkhardt (gen. ed.) and Fredson Bowers (text. ed.) (Cambridge, Mass.: Harvard University Press, 1975–87), (1981), *The Principles of Psychology*, p. 959. Hereafter cited as James, *Principles of Psychology*.
4. Putnam, *Realism and Reason*, p. 221.
5. Ibid., p. 222.
6. Ibid., p. 213.
7. James, *Principles of Psychology*, vol. 1, p. 140.
8. Ibid.
9. William James, *The Works of William James*, 9 vols., ed. Frederick Burkhardt (gen. ed.) and Fredson Bowers (text. ed.) (Cambridge, Mass.: Harvard University Press, 1975–87), vol. 2 (1976), *Essays in Radical Empiricism*, p. 74. Hereafter cited as James, *Essays*.
10. Nelson Goodman, *Ways of Worldmaking* (Indianapolis and Cambridge, Mass.: Hackett Pub. Co., 1978).
11. Putnam, *Realism and Reason*, p. 225.
12. Goodman, *Ways of Worldmaking*, pp. 122–23.
13. William James, *The Works of William James*, 9 vols., ed. Frederick Burkhardt (gen. ed.) and Fredson Bowers (text. ed.) (Cambridge, Mass.: Harvard University Press, 1975–87), vol. 3 (1977), *A Pluralistic Universe*. Hereafter cited as James, *Pluralistic Universe*.

14. Goodman, *Ways of Worldmaking*, pp. 115–16.
15. Nelson Goodman, *Languages of Art* (Indianapolis and Cambridge, Mass.: Hackett Pub. Co., 1968).
16. James, *Essays*, pp. 162 ff.
17. Ibid.
18. For example, James, *Principles of Psychology*, pp. 924, 1229.
19. Goodman, *Ways of Worldmaking*, p. 97.
20. Ibid., p. 18.
21. Putnam, *Realism and Reason*, p. 226.
22. Ibid., pp. 227–28.
23. Ibid., p. 161.
24. James, *Essays*, pp. 21–44; see also James, *Pluralistic Universe*, pp. 125–35.
25. Mohan Matthen, "Biological Function and Perceptual Content," *Journal of Philosophy* (January, 1988): 5–27, esp. p. 21.
26. Putnam, *Realism and Reason*, p. 160.
27. Ibid., p. 302.
28. Ibid., p. 166.
29. Ibid., p. 169.
30. William James, *The Works of William James*, ed. Frederick Burkhardt (gen. ed.) and Fredson Bowers (text. ed.) (Cambridge, Mass.: Harvard University Press, 1975–87), vol. 1 (1975), *Pragmatism*, p. 40.
31. Goodman, *Ways of Worldmaking*, p. 129.

James's Pragmatic Personalism

EUGENE FONTINELL

Why designate James's philosophy "pragmatic personalism," or why attempt to articulate a pragmatic personalism out of the resources of James's thought? The ultimate pragmatic justification for the employment of any category, concept, or metaphor, of course, must be in terms of the difference it makes or can make in the lives of individual human beings. The justification, then, for articulating a pragmatic personalism will, in a sense, be a personalistic justification. But why a "pragmatic personalism" instead of a "personalistic pragmatism"? For two reasons: first, as I read James, his pragmatism is in the service of his personalism instead of this personalism being in the service of his pragmatism. "The whole function of philosophy," according to James, "ought to be to find out what definite difference it will make to you and me, at definite instants of our life, if this world-formula or that world-formula be the true one."[1] The second and more important reason for my purpose is that I wish to claim that James's metaphysics is a distinctive mode of personalism.[2]

Few would be surprised to hear that James's pragmatism as well as his moral and religious philosophy are characterized by a personalistic dimension. Too often, however, such a characterization leads to interpreting or, as I would contend, misinterpreting James's philosophy as a mode of superficial subjectivism. The principal reason for this misinterpretation is that James's pragmatism and moral and religious philosophy are considered in isolation from his metaphysics. Hence, I wish to stress the less evident metaphysical character of James's personalism.

A brief word is in order as to how the terms *metaphysics* and *metaphysical* can and cannot be used with reference to James's philosophy. For James, there is no metaphysics or metaphysical knowledge that pretends to give us a snap-shot or mirror-image or conceptual representation of reality.[3] James is a metaphysical agnostic insofar as he denies that we can know any alleged "ultimate reality" or a reality-in-itself unrelated to human experience. Further, he is agnostic concerning any ultimate origin or end of the world process or processes. In his posthumously published *Some Problems of Philosophy*, he states: "The question of being is the darkest in all philosophy. All of us are beggars here, and no school can speak disdainfully of another or give itself superior airs. For all of us alike, fact forms a datum, gift, or *Vorgefundenes*, which we cannot burrow under, explain, or get behind. It makes itself somehow, and our business is far more with its what than with its whence or why."[4]

Metaphysical agnostic though he may be, James does not hesitate to offer what might be called some metaphysical myths or metaphysical metaphors. These take the form of extrapolations from concrete experience as to how we might fruitfully characterize reality or the world. On the basis of what is available to human experience, we can discover no underlying reality or absolute origin or end, but we can discern and speculate about human and cosmic possibilities and opt to work for some possibilities and against others. Hence, in referring to James's metaphysics, I will be referring to an "angle of vision" permeated by a cluster of principles, assumptions, and metaphors from which we view reality or the world and by means of which we transact with and constitute reality or the world. It is within this sense of "metaphysics" that I wish to argue that James's metaphysics can properly and most effectively be characterized as "personalistic."

In his famous chapter from *The Principles of Psychology*, "The Stream of Thought," James claims that the first character that we note concerning the process of thoughts is that "every thought tends to be part of a personal consciousness." Hence, "the personal self rather than the thought might be treated as the immediate datum in psychology."[5] Even though James later admitted that he could not completely keep metaphysical concerns out of his psychology, the *Principles* is intended to be a work of psychology. In spite, then, of the centrality of personal experience throughout this work, experience as there articulated is not adequate to bear the metaphysical weight that I wish to assign to James's notion of personal experience. One way of viewing the relation between James's *Principles* and his later "metaphysical" works is that in the former, immediate personal experience is viewed psychologically and from within a methodological, not a metaphysical, dualism; in the late metaphysical works, this experience becomes the paradigm for all reality as well as the pathway to reality in its depth and "thickness."

It is personal experience as it is described by James in his later works, then, that serves as the source for the metaphysical paradigm that I wish to stress and explicate. My thesis is that anything that James feels can with reasonable justification be said about reality or the world as a whole must in some way be derived from personal experience. It is the continuity and analogous similarity between personal experience and other modes of reality or experience that are the grounds for any metaphysical generalizations as well as the avoidance of any isolating subjectivism or solipsistic atomism.[6] Paradoxically, then, instead of enclosing us within hermetically sealed human chambers, whether individual or collective, reflection upon personal experience opens us to both narrower and wider dimensions of reality. Hence, as John McDermott has noted, "The impact of James's philosophy is that an analysis of human activity turns out to be an 'ultimate' metaphysics, for there is no reality to be discussed apart from our participation and formulation."[7] James himself maintained that the world as a whole is unknown and hence "no philosophy can ever do more than interpret the whole ... after the analogy of some particular part which we know."[8] Elsewhere he stated that "the only material we have at our disposal for making a picture of the whole world is supplied by the various portions of that world of which we have already had experience."[9]

One of the most persistent and insistent themes in James's philosophy, then, is that any model of the world that we construct or any generalization concerning the character of reality that we draw must find its ordinary analogues in some experiential given, and it is biography, he tells us, that "is the concrete form in which all that is immediately given." Because "the perceptual flux is the authentic stuff of each of our biographies," only in "immediate perceptual experience ... is reality intimately and concretely found."[10] If we desire to grasp reality in its richest manifestations and at its deepest levels, we must immerse ourselves in the perceptual flux. James is explicit and unequivocal on this. "The deeper features of reality are found only in perceptual experience. Here alone do we acquaint ourselves with continuity, or the immersion of one thing in another, here alone with self, with substance, with qualities, with activity in its various modes, with time, with cause, with change, with novelty, with tendency, with freedom."[11]

I would like to suggest that "personal experience" instead of "perceptual experience" is a more appropriate and less misleading phrase for designating what is at the center of James's philosophy, inasmuch as it better avoids reducing experience to a superficial sensationalism or a narrow immediatism. In a relatively early essay, James contended that "the only form of thing that we directly encounter, the only experience that we concretely have is our own personal life."[12] Later, in *Some Problems of Philosophy*, he asks "whether we are not here witnessing in our own personal experience what is really the essential process of creation. Isn't the world really growing in these activities of ours? And where we predicate activities elsewhere, have we a right to suppose aught different in kind from this?"[13] In that same work, James is also endeavoring to soften the sharp contrast, which often bordered on opposition, between percepts and concepts. Hence, he tells us that "the substitution of concepts and their connections ... for the immediate perceptual flow ... widens enormously our mental panorama. ... With concepts we go in quest of the absent, meet the remote, actively turn this way or that, bend our experience, and make it tell us whither it is bound. ... We harness perceptual reality in concepts in order to drive it better to our ends."[14]

Where James states that "concepts flow out of percepts and into them again,"[15] I think he might better have said "concepts flow out of persons and into them again." I say this because even percepts have a richness and complexity too often missed by the notion of perceptual experience as it is often understood. There are no impersonal perceptions in the sense of brute sensations untouched by the character and history of the perceiver. When we turn to the role of concepts in human life, the case for speaking of personal instead of perceptual experience is even stronger. Concepts are in the service of extending and deepening personal life. Even if we retain the Jamesian emphasis upon the "perceptual," we must note an ambiguity accompanying "perceptual experience" not unlike the ambiguity that accompanies James's use of the phrase *immediate experience*. Elsewhere I have discussed this latter ambiguity, suggesting that "we must distinguish immediate or concrete experience from 'pure immediacy.' The latter would refer only to what is in conscious focus, including the conscious margins; the former would include 'virtualities' and 'other' relations that may or may not be brought to consciousness at a later time."[16] Similarly, a perceptual experience that has been enriched by conceptualization is deeper and more extensive and intensive than one that remains at the level of superficial sense perception. By substituting the rubric *personal* for *perceptual*, we retain the characteristics of concreteness and immediacy that James was anxious to emphasize while avoiding a thinness and a superficial ephemerality that so often characterize unreflective sense perception. Further, "personal" incorporates the fruits of conceptualization such as extension, breadth, richness, and depth while avoiding that abstractionism that is tempted to reify concepts and isolate them from the experiential flow from which they are derived and to which they ought to return.

The central claim I am making here, of course, is that through reflection upon personal experience we not only learn about the nature of human persons, whether individual or communal, but we also learn whatever we are able to learn about the nature of the world or reality and any realities that constitute the world. Nowhere does James emphasize this more than in *The Varieties of Religious Experience*. The paradox there articulated is that it is in the most individual and personal mode of experience that we grasp what it is to be an existing reality. "So long as we deal with the cosmic and the general," he tells us, "we deal only with the symbols or reality, but as soon as we deal with private and personal phenomena as such, we deal with realities in the complete sense of the term." It is in this individuality, founded in feeling, that "we catch real fact in the making, and directly perceive how events happen and how work is actually done." James goes on to say that "the unsharable feeling which each one of us has of the pinch of his individual destiny as he privately feels it rolling out on fortune's wheel may be disparaged for its egotism, may be sneered at as unscientific, but it is the one thing that fills up the measure of our concrete actuality, and any would-be existent that should lack such a feeling, or its analogue, would be a piece of reality only half made-up."[17]

But how does James understand this personal experience that I am maintaining plays such a central and decisive role in all aspects of his philosophy and that is the paradigm for whatever can be said to possess existential reality? Let me briefly describe three ways in which that which characterizes human persons can in some sense be said to characterize all existential realities. Persons and all realities can be viewed as processive-relational complexes or "fields," as transactional activities, and as centers of activity.

If we want "to describe the process of experience in its simplest terms with the fewest assumptions," according to James, we must not postulate any reality "whose whatness is not of some nature given in fields." These "fields" must be viewed as developing "under the categories of continuity with each other," each field being incomplete and pointing to a complement beyond its own content. "The final content," James suggests, "is that of a plurality of fields, more or less ejective to each other, but still continuous in various ways."[18] The metaphor *fields*, derived from and turned back upon personal experience, extends beyond the individual and the human insofar as it designates realities of both a narrower and wider scope than what is ordinarily referred to as "human."[19] The individual person is itself a field encompassing a plurality of narrower fields— electronic, molecular, cellular, and the like—and is itself encompassed within a plurality of wider fields: environmental, cultural, solar, galactic, and possibly a widest field that might be called "divine." Both the individual person and the world, therefore, can be described as "fields within fields within fields."

A field can be described as a processive-relational complex. Again, both the person and all other realities manifest themselves at all times as processive and relational. In a Jamesian world, there are no realities that are not processes and no processes that are not relational. The person, then, is not superadded to some allegedly "objective" reality but is continuous with a plurality of other realities: overlapping and interpenetrating, constituting and being constituted by these realities in a variety of ever-changing modes. There are, then, no atomistically isolated fields, no "fields-in themselves," for to be a "field" is to be relationally constituted by a variety of other fields.

Another way of saying this is with respect to transactional activity. "Transaction," of course, is a term associated with the later Dewey, but it is, I believe, perfectly appropriate for describing James's fields-activity. Hence, two comments referring to Dewey are applicable to James. Richard Bernstein has noted that "a transaction does not occur with an aggregate or combination of elements that have independent existence. On the contrary, what counts as an 'element' is dependent on its function within a transaction."[20] Similarly, George Geiger has pointed out that "within the various transactional situations, the related aspects are indeed mutual and completely interdependent, as they are in any 'field.'"[21] This transactional activity that constitutes all existential realities, from electrons to God, is most immediately and richly evidenced in personal experience.

Also presented most vividly and convincingly within personal experience is the third way in which persons and all other existential realities can be said to share a common character; namely, as centers of activity. If metaphysical pluralism instead of metaphysical monism is the more apt characterization of reality, as it was for James, then the plurality of fields constituting reality, however continuous, overlapping, and interpenetrating they may be, must also possess a distinction that renders them individual. Hence, I would suggest that, for James, to be an existential reality is to be an initiating center of activity. "Be the universe as much a unit as you like," he tells us, "plurality has once for all broken out within it. *Effectively* there are centers of reference and action . . . and these centres dispense each other's rays."[22] It is in his important essay "The Experience of Activity" that James speaks of activity and its original experience in a fashion that supports my metaphysical extension of it to all existential realities. The "original type and model" of what "activity" means, according to James, "must lie in some concrete kind of experience that can be definitely pointed out." It is only from personal experience, then, that we can extrapolate the modes of activity shared by other realities, because "the word 'activity' has no imaginable content whatever save those experiences of process, obstruction, striving, strain, or release."[23]

Granted that James views every reality after the fashion of an activity, is it not an unwarranted and unnecessary extension of his position to posit the activities as centered, especially at a time when contemporary deconstructionists have called into question the notion of a center within any of the processes that we encounter? I would maintain that it is both warranted and necessary, particularly if James's thought embodies the kind of metaphysical personalism that I am attributing to it. James contends that even among Buddhists and Humeians, for whom "the soul is only a succession of fields of consciousness, . . . there is found in each field a part, or sub-field, which figures as focal and contains the excitement, and from which, as from a centre, the aim seems to be taken." These lines appear in James's discussion of religious conversion, and he goes on to stress the importance of the *"habitual centre of . . . personal energy"* and what a great difference it makes to a person whether one set of ideas or another is the center of this energy.[24]

In speaking of existential realities as "centers of activity," it is crucial that "center" not be understood as some static, atomistic point of reference or origination. Here the field metaphor that I am employing must be kept in mind. All fields have centers, but these centers have no reality apart from the processes and relations that constitute the field. Inasmuch as every field is continually changing and shifting in relation to other fields, the center of every field is also continually changing and shifting. Of course, the rates of change can and do vary widely, and this allows us to recognize a stability in many fields of experience, permitting us to posit a degree of identity, sameness, and centeredness belonging to these ever-changing fields.

One might ask whether the interpretation of James that I am proposing is not simply a variation on the interpretation of James as a panpsychist. In a sense, of course, it is. James, no more than Whitehead, admits the reality of any purely passive entities or "vacuous actualities." Further, I find Marcus Ford's ably argued claim that James's pure experience is best interpreted as a pluralist, processive panpsychism[25] eminently more congenial than those interpretations of radical empiricism as an impersonal, neutral monism. Nevertheless, as I have suggested elsewhere, "panactivism" instead of "panpsychism" is a more accurate and less misleading characterization of James's metaphysics. Inasmuch as the mark of all real beings is centered activity, all totally passive entities are excluded. But while all realities are active, they are not all active in the same way; hence, the terms *psychic* or *conscious* are quite properly restricted to designating a specific mode of centered activity.[26] Recognizing consciousness as a distinct mode of activity, however, does not land us in any ontological dualism. According to the interpretation here suggested, consciousness will not be some totally new or completely different kind of reality unrelated to and radically discontinuous with nonconscious entities or fields. The task of phenomenologically distinguishing and characterizing consciousness is, of course, a formidable task. But what is crucial is that, presupposing the metaphysics earlier described, there is no need to go outside the stream of personal experience to discover those traits of consciousness that distinguish it from those nonconscious fields with which it is continuous but to which it cannot be reduced.

Granted, then, that panactivism avoids the embarrassment that shadows panpsychism of having to attribute consciousness to all entities, does the metaphysical personalism I am suggesting not give rise to an even greater embarrassment—that of having to attribute personality to all entities? James made a claim for radical empiricism that is at once the strongest support in his writings for interpreting his metaphysics as a mode of personalism and at the same time might be viewed as giving rise to the aforementioned embarrassment.

> If empiricism is to be radical it must indeed admit the concrete data of experience in their full completeness. The only fully complete data are, however, the successive moments of our own several histories, taken with their subjective personal aspect, as well as with their 'objective' deliverance or 'content.' After the analogy of these moments of experiences must all complete reality be conceived. Radical empiricism thus leads to the assumption of a collectivism of personal lives (which may be of any grade of complication, and superhuman or infrahuman as well as human), . . . and by their interaction and cumulative achievements making up the world.[27]

In speaking of the world as a "collectivism of personal lives," James intends this to be understood analogously. Linguistically sensitive thinkers would quite properly point out that it is an abuse of language to predicate without qualification "personality" of such realities as electrons, molecules, and cells. The operative phrase here, of course, is "without qualification," and this is why the analogous character of personality must be underlined. Without claiming any identity between humans and other realities, I have attempted to describe those traits, preeminently manifested in human beings, which are in some sense possessed by all existential realities. Although the mode of reality characterizing humans is not identical with other modes of reality, there is sufficient continuity with and similarity to these other realities to justify designating the latter "personalistic," understood in an extended and analogous sense. The use of the term *personalistic* in this fashion is more than linguistic legerdemain. Instead, in recognizing the personalist characteristic of all realities, we acknowledge the overlapping, interpenetrating, and continuous character not only of our individual experiences but of our experiences with other realities or events without positing any metaphysical identity. We thereby guard against not only a materialistic reductionism but also any ontological dualism that attributes human personality to some mode of reality radically discontinuous with the world of experience. At the same time, the individual person is continuous with and constituted by wider fields and possibly by a widest field, which might be designated "divine," without being absorbed into or subsumed within these fields or field. Such a metaphysical personalism, I believe, significantly advances one of James's deepest desires. I refer, of course, to his desire to construct a philosophy that recognizes both science and religion as indispensable to the continuing and fullest development of human beings, individually and communally.

Notes

1. William James, *The Works of William James*, ed. Frederick Burkhardt (gen. ed.) and Fredson Bowers (text. ed.) (Cambridge, Mass.: Harvard University Press, 1975–87), vol. 1 (1975), *Pragmatism*, p. 30.

2. A fuller treatment of my claim would require, in order to establish the distinctiveness of pragmatic personalism, a comparison with the various modes of realistic and idealistic personalism. Fortunately, the assigned brevity of this paper allows me to avoid such a full-scale comparison and concentrate on those features in James's thought that lend support to a pragmatic personalism. Even here, however, I will hide behind such terms as *sketch, hint,* and *suggestion*.

3. My use of "reality" and "experience" interchangeably is not accidental, for in the final analysis these are the same for James, as I will indicate a bit more fully later. Richard Bernstein has noted this interchangeability. See his introduction to William James, *The Works of William James*, ed. Frederick Burkhardt (gen. ed.) and Fredson Bowers (text. ed.) (Cambridge, Mass.: Harvard University Press, 1975–87), vol. 3 (1977), *A Pluralistic Universe*, pp. xxvi–vii. "A casual reader may think James is careless in the way in which he shifts from 'experience' to 'reality.' But this is *not* a sign of loose terminology or confusion. It reflects James's doctrine of 'pure experience' where the traditional distinction between 'experience' and 'reality' are broken down. . . . There is only a continuous reality which we *take* in different ways."

4. William James, *The Works of William James*, ed. Frederick Burkhardt (gen. ed.) and Fredson Bowers (text. ed.) (Cambridge, Mass.: Harvard University Press, 1975–87), vol. 6 (1979), *Some Problems of Philosophy*, p. 30.

5. William James, *The Works of William James*, ed. Frederick Burkhardt (gen. ed.)

and Fredson Bowers (text. ed.) (Cambridge, Mass.: Harvard University Press, 1975–87), vol. 7 (1981), *The Principles of Psychology*, pp. 220–21.

6. Cf. James, *Pragmatism*, p. 33. "So many rival formulations are proposed in all branches of science that investigators have become accustomed to the notion that no theory is absolutely a transcript of reality. . . . They are only a man-made language, a conceptual shorthand . . . in which we write our reports of nature." See also John J. McDermott, "Introduction to William James," *The Works of William James*, ed. Frederick Burkhardt (gen. ed.) and Fredson Bowers (text. ed.) (Cambridge, Mass.: Harvard University Press, 1975–87), vol. 4 (1978), *Essays in Philosophy*, p. xv. "For James the knower is not a passive witness to a simply existing order. We are in the dark about the ultimate nature of reality and about the nature of our own activities. Both reality and our interests are coercive of each other, and the nature of thought is to be worked out within the framework of that tension."

7. John J. McDermott, *The Culture of Experience* (New York: New York University Press, 1976), p. 110.

8. James, *Essays in Philosophy*, p. 150.

9. James, *A Pluralistic Universe*, p. 9.

10. James, *Some Problems*, pp. 78, 53.

11. Ibid., p. 54.

12. Ibid., p. 241.

13. Ibid., p. 108.

14. Ibid., p. 39.

15. Ibid., p. 31.

16. Eugene Fontinell, *Self, God, and Immortality: A Jamesian Investigation* (Philadelphia: Temple University Press, 1986), p. 108.

17. William James, *The Works of William James*, ed. Frederick Burkhardt (gen. ed.) and Fredson Bowers (text. ed.) (Cambridge, Mass.: Harvard University Press, 1975–87), vol. 8 (1985), *The Varieties of Religious Experience*, pp. 393–95.

18. Ralph Barton Perry, *The Thought and Character of William James*, 2 vols. (Boston: Little, Brown, 1935), vol. 1, p. 365.

19. In Fontinell, *Self, God, and Immortality*, I have suggested that the metaphor *fields* points toward a way of expressing a fundamental continuity between James's "pure experience" doctrine and his "fields of consciousness" doctrine. See in particular the section "James's 'Pure Experience' as Primordial Field" (pp. 32–43) and chapter 5, entitled "James: Full Self and Wider Fields."

20. Richard Bernstein, *John Dewey* (New York: Washington Square Press, 1976), p. 83.

21. George Geiger, *John Dewey* (New York: Oxford University Press, 1958), p. 17.

22. Perry, *Thought and Character*, vol. 2, p. 764.

23. James, *Some Problems*, pp. 81, 84.

24. James, *Varieties*, pp. 161–62.

25. Marcus Peter Ford, *William James's Philosophy* (Amherst, Mass.: University of Massachusetts Press, 1982), pp. 75ff.

26. Fontinell, *Self, God, and Immortality*, pp. 30, 42, 96.

27. William James, *The Works of William James*, ed. Frederick Burkhardt (gen. ed.) and Fredson Bowers (text. ed.) (Cambridge, Mass.: Harvard University Press, 1975–87), vol. 9 (1987), *Essays, Comments, and Reviews*, pp. 544–45.

Jamesian Reflections on Will, Freedom, and Values

ROBERT KANE

> *The straight warp of necessity, not to be swerved from the ultimate course* ... ; *[but] free will still free to ply her shuttle between given threads; only chance, though restrained in its play, within the right lines of necessity and sideways in its motions directed by free will, ... chance by turn rules either, and has the last featuring blow at events.*
>
> Herman Melville
> Moby Dick, *chapter 47*

This passage from what many regard as *the* American novel provides the theme of this paper. When the passage occurs, Ishmael is working on the deck of the whaling ship in a moment of reflection. He is engaged with his shipmates making mats, and the three features of the task remind him of three factors in human decision making. First, the loom, which moves back and forth over the threads with mechanical motions, represents necessity. Second, his own manual efforts weaving some threads through others between thrusts of the loom represent free will. And finally, the harpoonist, Queequeg, standing above the process and striking downward with his harpoon at random intervals to upset the pattern, represents chance. It is not made clear how this worked for mat making, but Melville's analogy to human freedom seems clear enough. Necessity, free will, and chance are three elements intimately woven into the pattern of human decision making and human life itself. This is an important countertheme in *Moby Dick*, which can often seem to be describing the merely fated behavior of its protagonist, Captain Ahab.

If *Moby Dick* were a tragedy in the Greek mold, Ahab would be the tragic protagonist and Ishmael the chorus. Or better, perhaps the chorus would be the whole motley crew, trying to make sense of what is going on. (There were thirty of them, representing the thirty states of the Union at the time of the novel.)

And in this passage the chorus seems to be telling us that, despite the appearances of fate and predestination, the whalers and even their captain, like the rest of us, are partly responsible for their fate, although their freedom is circled round with, and limited by, necessity and chance—or what nowadays some of our philosophers would call "moral luck." This theme of destiny, chance, and freedom is very much a theme of American thought in general, beginning with Jonathan Edwards, who weighed in heavily on the side of necessity, and on down to the classical American pragmatists Peirce and James, where chance began to have its day and in whom it became clear that "freedom" with its correlative notion of an "open universe" was an idea central to the American spirit.

But Melville is a novelist, and when writing about philosophy novelists are not "under oath." Many contemporary thinkers of compatibilist leanings would say that Ishmael's loom image makes no sense at all of human freedom and responsibility. If chance has "the last featuring blow at events," or indeed if chance is essentially involved in human decision making at all, how can we ascribe responsibility and control to the free agent? The same charge is often made against William James's famous essay "The Dilemma of Determinism,"[1] which is thought by many to be the definitive defense of the idea that chance or indeterminism is an essential feature of human freedom. But James is not writing a novel, and against him the charge is more serious.

My purpose in this paper is to defend a Jamesian view of will and freedom against its critics and in the process to throw some small light on other features of James's view—of value, the moral life, and pragmatism in general. We will come back to Ishmael only at the end. The view of will and freedom I defend is "Jamesian," but not exactly James's. It is a view I have worked out myself and written into several papers and a recent book, in an attempt to answer contemporary (mostly analytic) critics of indeterminist or incompatibilist theories of freedom.[2] I did not realize just *how* close it was to James until recently, when I began to look at the matter more closely after reading a paper on James's theory of freedom by Donald Viney.[3] I now think, more than ever, that James pointed us in the right direction on free will, although he did not go the whole way. There are ambiguities, lacunae, and difficulties—in short, more work to be done. It is also true that "The Dilemma of Determinism" is not the only place to look if you want to understand James's view of free will. Many of James's best insights on the subject appear in *The Principles of Psychology*.[4] This is another one of my themes. Charles Hartshorne reports that his teacher at Harvard, C. I. Lewis, who was himself a student of James, once said that "James usually came to the right conclusions, but only God knows how he did it." This, I think, is especially in evidence in James's discussions of will and freedom.

Let us use a term James sometimes uses to designate his view. In the *Talks to Teachers*, he calls himself a "free willist."[5] What is that? Free willists hold, first, that human freedom is not compatible with determinism. They are "incompatibilists." We know what James thought of the opposing doctrine, the "compatibilist" view of free will, which is probably the dominant view in contemporary Anglo-American philosophy. He called it a "quagmire of evasion,"[6] somewhat restrained language by comparison with Kant's "wretched subterfuge." Second, free willists are also "indeterminists." That is to say, they also believe that free choices can and do occur and, hence, that determinism is false. But that is not enough. Nowadays, those who hold incompatibilism plus indeterminism on free will are usually called "libertarians," an unfortunate term because of its potentially misleading political connotations. Free willists, like James, are libertarians in this technical sense, but they are libertarians *plus*. The third feature of their view is that freedom resides primarily *in the will* and only derivatively in action. This third feature is important because in contemporary philosophy, until very recently, it was customary to downplay the notion of "will" in discussions of freedom. Instead of talking about "free will" and "acts of will," it had become more common to talk about "free action" and "reasons for action."[7] Free willists believe that something is lost in this transition, and they want to go back to the discussion of free will in more than name only. I think they are right.

That James is a free willist in this sense is not hard to demonstrate. It began with his famous conversion experience in 1870, when he saw that there was "no reason why [Renouvier's] definition of Free Will—'the sustaining of a thought *because I choose to* when I might have other thoughts'—need be the definition of an illusion."[8] What James got from Renouvier and never relinquished throughout his life was the idea that the primary locus of action for free will was upon our inner patterns of thought, belief, and intention. In the *Principles*, James says, "The immediate point of volitional effort lies exclusively in the mental world. . . . The drama is a mental drama," and "the terminus of a psychological process of volition . . . is always an idea." Moreover, he adds later that "if the amount of [this volitional] effort be not indeterminate . . . then our wills are not free." In these passages of the *Principles*, we have the essentials of the free willist position as I have described it: incompatibilism plus indeterminism plus the belief that the locus of freedom resides primarily *in the will*.[9]

To go farther, we have to know more about what the phrase "in the will" means for James. The voluntary effort that is the locus of freedom in the will for him issues in a "fiat," which he variously describes in the *Principles* as a "decision," "consent," or "volitional mandate."[10] About James's use of this term "fiat" there is a process-product ambiguity. The fiat is sometimes the process or event that is the decision or consent of the will and sometimes the product of that decision or consent—which, according to James's descriptions, amounts to what we would call an "intention,"[11] although he does not use that term. There are thus at least three things to be considered within the will of the agent, which James presupposes but does not always clearly distinguish: the voluntary effort, the decision or choice, and the intention that issues from both the effort and the decision. There are other things as well that come into play in James's full theory, like past character and motives that influence effort and decision as well as the ideas of deliberation, indecision, attention,[12] and feeling of effort. But this triad—effort of will, decision, and intention—is pivotal for understanding James's theory and free will in general.

Before going any more deeply into James's view, it is necessary to look at the criticisms of such a free willist theory. There is no scarcity of them. The main problem is the indeterminism or chance that plays so large a role in James's writings on freedom. If the decision or fiat that issues from the agent's effort of will is a matter of chance, how can it be within the control of the agent? And if the agent could go either way—decide one way or the other—given exactly the same past character and motives, how can the outcome be anything but arbitrary or capricious relative to the agent's psychological history? These problems arise because, on a free willist view like James's, more than one option must be possible *given exactly the same past and laws of nature*. If the agent might either make a choice or do otherwise, given the same past, and the past includes the psychological history of the agent prior to choice, it seems that no explanation in terms of that psychological history—including prior character, motives, and deliberation—could account for the occurrence of one outcome *instead of* the other . . . for the choosing rather than doing otherwise, or vice versa. I think it is useful to call this the problem of *dual rationality*, because it concerns how, in a choice situation, we can go in two or more different directions *rationally*—how we can rationally act or act otherwise—given *exactly* the same reasons or motives and prior deliberation. It is a very deep problem and one that lies behind the common charges that undetermined free actions would be "arbitrary," "capricious," "random," "irrational," or "inexplicable" in terms of the agent's past—charges that have led so many philosophers today to reject a Jamesian, indeterminist approach to human freedom. James never completely solves this problem, but the rudiments of a correct solution are present, I believe, in *The Principles of Psychology* and several of his other essays.[13]

The first step in approaching the problem is to see that not all of our voluntary efforts and voluntary acts can be exercises of free will in the free willist sense. In fact, only a small number of everyday efforts and acts will be free in this sense. The rest may well be determined. But the voluntary efforts that do qualify play a pivotal role in our mental and moral lives. James is quite explicit about all this. Many of our voluntary acts, he tells us, are automatic, in the sense that the act "follows *unhesitatingly and immediately* the notion of it in the mind," and no explicit fiat or consent of the will is necessary. What characterizes many ordinary efforts and acts in everyday life, he says, is *"the absence of any conflicting notion in the mind."*[14] Suppose I am expecting a guest and my doorbell rings. I have every reason to answer the door and no good reason not to. My only *rational* choice in the situation is to answer. To do otherwise would be a fluke or accident, something capricious or irrational, given my reasons or motives. And we are often in such situations in everyday life, where the weight of reasons is so preponderant on one side that only one option is rational. In some cases, these situations may be momentous. Daniel Dennett has mentioned the fact that most of us have an overwhelming aversion to torturing someone and in normal circumstances would never do it.[15] Here again the preponderant reasons are on one side. Now situations of these kinds—both the comparatively trivial and the momentous—cannot involve free choices in the free willist sense because they are not *dual rational*. It is rational to go one way but not the other: they are one-way rational but not two-ways rational.[16]

Dennett and others think it is a serious objection to incompatibilist and free willist theories of freedom that most of our everyday choices and actions that are done for clearly preponderant motives would not qualify as free in the free willist sense. But James had the proper answer to these objections a century before they were made. Free will, in the strong incompatibilist sense, is not manifest in most everyday choices and actions but only in those special cases in everyday life when *the will is deeply divided* against itself.[17] Contrary to the preponderant motive cases where there is an "absence of any conflicting notion in the mind," the genuine cases of free will are those where, as James says, "the mind is the seat of many ideas related to each other in antagonistic . . . ways."[18] "The result," he goes on, "is that peculiar feeling of inward unrest known as *indecision*."[19] In addition, it is in such cases that the notion of a fiat, or decision or consent of the will, comes into play. "When finally," James says, "the original suggestion either prevails . . . or gets definitely quenched by its antagonists, we are said to *decide*, or to *utter our voluntary fiat* in favor of one or the other course. The reinforcing or inhibiting ideas meanwhile are termed the *reasons* or *motives* by which the decision is brought about."[20] But there is more to it. Of the five kinds of decisions or fiats that James goes on to distinguish in the *Principles*, it is the fifth kind that is the locus of this kind of genuine free will. In such cases, the will is so deeply divided that additional elements—an "inward effort of will" and the "feeling of (that) effort"—come to the fore. James says, "The immense majority of human decisions are decisions without effort. In comparatively few of them, in most people, does effort accompany the final act.[21] (Compare this to my earlier remarks about the comparative rarity of genuine acts of free will.) He then goes on to make a pivotal point: "Effort complicates volition . . . whenever a rarer and more ideal impulse is called upon to neutralize others of a more instinctual and habitual kind."[22]

This, I believe, is important stuff, though its importance is not widely recognized. To spell it out, consider some ordinary situations where the will is deeply divided: for example, a moral conflict in which the agent is torn between a strong temptation to steal and a duty not to steal, or a prudential struggle in which the agent is trying to choose to resist the temptation to overeat in the interests of long-term health. What characterizes these cases of moral or prudential conflict is that there is an effort of will involved to choose in a certain way, to resist temptation, with other motives pulling in another way—self-interested motives or desires for present satisfaction—and the outcome uncertain in the agents' minds until they choose. Compare James's claim that "effort complicates volition . . . whenever a rare or ideal impulse is called upon to neutralize others of a more instinctive . . . kind." Now, many argue that in such situations the stronger motives or reasons will prevail. But as Thomas Reid pointed out, this *need* not be so. Past character and motives may influence the decision without determining it. And what is interesting about the cases we are describing is that the will being divided against itself, prior character and motives explain this inner conflict from both sides. For prior character and motives in these situations include (1) the reasons and dispositions that account for the agent's trying to resist temptation, on the one hand, and (2) the self-interested reasons and inclinations that explain why it is *difficult* for the agent to resist temptation, on the other. In other words, the past motives and character explain the inner *conflict* from both sides: they explain why the agent is making an effort and why it is an *effort*. Note also that the resistance to the will's effort in these cases is also coming from the agent's will. Prior character and motives in such conflict situations, therefore, provide reasons for going either way—resisting or succumbing—without necessarily providing *decisive* reasons determining which way the agent will inevitably go.

What would make up the difference in these situations between motives and choice (or fiat) is the voluntary effort (to resist temptation) that intervenes between them. Now I ask you to suppose, following James, that this effort of will is itself indeterminate. Consider an analogue that was not available to James but is appropriate. An isolated quantum particle is moving toward a thin atomic barrier. Whether it will penetrate the barrier is undetermined. There are probabilities about the outcome but not certainty, because the relevant properties that might determine the outcome, notably position and momentum, are not determinate. Whether it will penetrate is therefore *undetermined*, because the process preceding it is *indeterminate*. Let us be clear that for anything like this to be more than mere analogy, there would have to be processes of amplification of quantum uncertainties in the brain, probably along the lines of Popper's "clocks over clouds" or Prigogine's "order over chaos." But this is not the aspect of the issue I want to consider here,[23] however much it would have interested James, given his normal procedure in the *Principles* of relating the phenomenology of willing on the one hand to neural phenomena on the other. The point I want to make here can be grasped merely by focusing on the analogy. Imagine that the Jamesian fiat or decision (to overcome temptation) is like the particle's penetrating the barrier, and the effort of will leading up to the fiat is the analogue of the movement of the particle toward the barrier. Then, just as the particle penetration is *undetermined* because the process leading up to it and potentially terminating in it is *indeterminate*, so the decision or fiat would be *undetermined* because the process leading up to it and potentially terminating in it is *indeterminate*.

The result would be that past character and motives would influence the outcome but not determine it—because deeply embedded within the complex of past character and motives was a conflict that could have gone either way. Character and motives would explain why the effort was made, but they would not explain the exact amount of effort (there would, in fact, be no such thing as "the exact amount of effort") because the effort is indeterminate. Moreover, because the effort of will (indeterminate though it be) is the *agent's* effort of will, and because the resistance to it *is coming from the agent's own will*, the choice outcome would be willed by the agent, whichever way it went. Thus, what makes these conflict situations unique, as James saw, allows the agent to go in either of two or more opposing directions *willingly*, given exactly the same past.

I believe a theory of this kind can be worked out in detail and can answer a host of objections that might be raised against it: about dual rationality, control, responsibility, weakness of will, and many other issues. But I have done this elsewhere in a book and several essays, as indicated earlier. The main concern here is to show how close such a theory would be to James's intentions in *The Principles of Psychology* and related essays. Note first that this theory does not appeal to occult forms of agency or causation that characterize most traditional libertarian theories of freedom: it does not appeal to noumenal selves, or agent or nonoccurrent causes, transempirical power centers, and like stratagems. This fits James's intentions, because, as Gerald Myers has pointed out, "James had . . . always striven . . . to describe our experiences of activity and effort, which cause us to believe we possess free will, without appealing to occult energies or forces."[24]

A few further quotations will buttress the case for saying that the above theory is close to James's intentions in the *Principles*. About the special kinds of decisions under conflict I have just described, James says, "Subjectively and phenomenally, the *feeling of effort*, absent from [other] decisions, accompanies these. . . . Both alternatives are steadily held in view, and in the very act of murdering the vanquished possibility, the chooser realizes how much in that instant he is making himself lose."[25] This feeling of loss, I would say, occurs because the agent deeply wants both outcomes, but in different ways and for vastly different reasons. Later in the *Principles*, responding to an argument of the psychologist Lipps, James makes the following interesting point. "Really," he says, in decisions of these kinds, "both the effort and resistance are ours, and [Lipps's] identification of our *self* with one of these factors is an illusion and a trick of speech."[26] In short, we identify with *both* conflicting motives. If we did not, there would be no genuine struggle and conflict in our wills. By recognizing this, a Jamesian theory of free will can resolve problems that Kant clearly saw but never could resolve. Again, concerning the above notion of indeterminacy of the effort, James says, "The question of fact in the free will controversy," as opposed to the many conceptual and evaluative questions involved in it, "relates solely . . . to the amount of effort [of will] which we can at any time put forth."[27] He adds that "the existence of [this] effort as a phenomenal fact in our consciousness cannot of course be doubted. . . . Its significance, on the other hand, is a matter about which the gravest difference of opinion prevails. Questions as momentous as that of the very existence of spiritual causality, as vast as that of universal predestination or free will, depend on its interpretation."[28] "What wonder if . . . it be the one strictly underived and original contribution which we make to the world."[29]

I conclude with some remarks about the implications of all this for James's theory of value. Cases of the divided will, or the will in conflict, which, I have argued, are so important for understanding free will, have important implications for value theory as well. For they are cases in which it can be *rational* for agents to go in two or more contrary directions at any given time. This is exactly what the free willist needs. But it also means that there must be a plurality of alternative options open to the free agent, each good in some ways, but in different and incommensurable ways. And the choice between them must be something like an experiment in living. The agent says, in effect, "Let me try this pathway. I realize it is not the only one possible, or even the only one reasonable. But life is a risk, and all valuing is experimental. In practice, we all must choose to take the risk." I need not elaborate here upon how nicely these thoughts fit into James's value theory, as in, say, his brilliant essay "The Moral Philosopher and the Moral Life,"[30] which takes this approach to the choice of values and the moral life. Nor need I elaborate on how the notions of a pluralism of values and value experimentation are intimately related to distinctively pragmatist ways of thinking about value and the moral life such as we find, for example, in Dewey as well as James. If I am right, these distinctively pragmatist themes are even more intimately related to a free willist conception of freedom than James himself realized.

Let the last word be on Ishmael. His loom image has three parts. The loom represents necessity, his own manual weaving represents voluntary effort or free will, and the thrusts of the harpoonist represent chance, which has "the last featuring blow at events." The image dissatisfies because the three features are seen as separate. In the Jamesian view I have described, the three are interwoven. If we thought of voluntary effort and chance as separate items in the choice process, one followed by the other, the view would not work. For the effort would be determined and the chance undetermined, and neither would be in the control of the agent. The trick is to *fuse* the effort and the chance elements of Ishmael's image—the weaver's efforts and the harpoonist's thrusts—so that they are one and the same thing: the effort of will *is* indeterminate, and the indeterminacy is *of* the effort. That way we can ascribe control to the agent, but never complete control. The control of the free agent, I think, is necessarily limited. We should learn from James that we live in an open and *risky* universe and adjust our view of human nature accordingly. James, more than any other free will advocate in the Western tradition, was ready to take fully seriously the limitations and moral luck built into the free willist position, along with its advantages. The reluctance to do so on the part of others, including many in our own day, is understandable. For, as I have argued elsewhere, to take seriously these limitations on human freedom requires thoroughly novel ways of thinking about human nature and human life.[31]

Notes

1. William James, *The Will To Believe and Other Essays* (New York: Dover Publications, 1956), pp. 145–83.
2. Robert Kane, *Free Will and Values* (Albany: State University of New York Press, 1985).
3. Donald Viney, "William James on Free Will and Determinism," *The Journal of Mind and Behavior* 7 (1986): 555–66. I owe a further debt to Viney, who suggested that my theory of freedom was a lot closer to James's than I had previously realized and thereby prompted the research that led to this paper.
4. William James, *The Principles of Psychology*, 2 vols. (New York: Dover Publications, 1950).
5. William James, *Talks to Teachers* (New York, 1899), chapter 15; reprinted in Bruce Wilshire, ed., *William James: The Essential Writings* (New York: Harper and Row, 1971), pp. 39–43.
6. James, *The Will To Believe*, p. 149.
7. Talk of the "will" and "volitions" has come back into prominence in the past couple of decades after being out of fashion, and there are interesting connections between some recent writings and James's discussions of the will. See Brian O'Shaughnessy, *The Will* (Cambridge, U.K.: Cambridge University Press, 1980), 2 vols.; and Hugh McCann, "Volition and Basic Action," *The Philosophical Review* 83 (1974): 451–73. To discuss these, however, would be another paper.
8. Henry James, ed., *The Letters of William James* (Boston: Atlantic Monthly Press, 1920), vol. 1, pp. 147–48.
9. James, *Principles of Psychology*, vol. 2, pp. 564, 567.
10. Ibid., p. 522.
11. Ibid., pp. 519–20.
12. One important feature of James's theory that I will not make use of here is his oft-repeated identification of free voluntary efforts with "acts of attention." Although I think something can be made of this idea in a complete account of free will, I think that James's overemphasis on it is a mistake. Not all acts of attention are voluntary, as James well knew, nor are all voluntary efforts acts of attention. Moreover, later in chapter 26 of the *Principles*, James concedes that "the effort to *attend* is therefore only a part of what the word 'will' covers; it covers also the effort to *consent* to something to which our attention is not quite complete" (p. 568). James should have kept this distinction more clearly in mind throughout his discussion. Myers's comments on James's account of attending and willing are especially good in this connection. See Gerald Myers, *William*

James: His Life and Thought (New Haven: Yale University Press, 1986), pp. 208–209.

13. These essays include "The Feeling of Effort" (1880) and "What the Will Effects" (1888), both of which appear in *The Works of William James: Essays on Psychology*, ed. F. Burkhardt et al. (Cambridge: Harvard University Press, 1983), pp. 83–124, 216–38.

14. James, *Principles of Psychology*, vol. 2, pp. 522, 523.

15. Daniel Dennett, *Elbow Room* (Cambridge: MIT Press, 1984), chapter 6.

16. Note, by contrast, that non-free willist, compatibilist views of freedom can easily handle such cases. For compatibilists can say that the agent may have done otherwise, if his or her prior character and motives or other prior circumstances *had been different* than they in fact were at the time of choice. Jamesian indeterminists cannot avail themselves of any such saving clause.

17. I have emphasized this point in the essays cited in note 2. A similar point is also made by Peter Van Inwagen, "When Is the Will Free?" in *Philosophical Perspectives*, vol. 4 (Atascadero: Ridgeview Press-Van Inwagen, forthcoming).

18. James, *Principles of Psychology*, vol. 2, p. 528.

19. Ibid.

20. Ibid.

21. Ibid., p. 534.

22. Ibid., p. 535.

23. I have discussed this in chapter 9 of Kane, *Free Will and Values*.

24. Myers, *William James*, p. 364.

25. James, *Principles of Psychology*, vol. 2, p. 534.

26. Ibid., p. 576.

27. Ibid., p. 571.

28. Ibid., p. 535.

29. Ibid., p. 579.

30. James, *The Will to Believe*, pp. 184–215.

31. See also Robert Kane, *The Significance of Free Will* forthcoming from Oxford University Press; and Robert Kane, "Libertarianism and Rationality Revisited," *The Southern Journal of Philosophy*, 26 (1986): 441–60; and Robert Kane, "Two Kinds of Incompatibilism," *Philosophy and Phenomenological Research* 50 (1989): 219–54.

Contributors

Thomas M. Alexander
Southern Illinois University

Karl-Otto Apel
Johann Wolfgang Goethe-
Universitaet, Frankfurt

Jo Ann Boydston
Southern Illinois University

Robert W. Burch
Texas A&M University

John Clendenning
California State University, Northridge

H. William Davenport
Western Illinois University

Gerard Deledalle
University of Perpignan, France

David A. Dilworth
SUNY at Stony Brook

Carolyn Eisele
Hunter College, CUNY

Michael Eldridge
Spring Hill College

Eugene Fontinell
Queens College, CUNY

Peter A. French
Trinity University

Russell B. Goodman
University of New Mexico

James Gouinlock
Emory University

Morris Grossman
Fairfield University

Pete A. Y. Gunter
University of North Texas

Richard E. Hart
Bloomfield College

Patrick J. Hill
The Evergreen State College

Robert Kane
The University of Texas, Austin

Angus Kerr-Lawson
University of Waterloo, Canada

Kenneth L. Ketner
Texas Tech University

Christian J. W. Kloesel
Indiana University and Purdue University at Indianapolis

Lenore Langsdorf
University of Texas at Arlington

Thelma Z. Lavine
George Mason University

David G. Leahy
Unaffiliated Scholar

Henry Samuel Levinson
University of North Carolina, Greensboro

Peter Limper
Christian Brothers College

Mary B. Mahowald
Case Western Reserve University

Armen T. Marsoobian
Southern Connecticut State University

Gerald E. Myers
Queens College and Graduate Center, CUNY

Nikita E. Pokrovsky
Moscow State University, Moscow

Sandra B. Rosenthal
Loyola University, New Orleans

Herman J. Saatkamp, Jr.
Texas A&M University

Edward S. Shirley
Louisiana State University

John J. Stuhr
University of Oregon

Henny Wenkart
Stern College

Zhu Xinmin
Vanderbilt University

www.ingramcontent.com/pod-product-compliance
Lightning Source LLC
Chambersburg PA
CBHW030300080526
44584CB00012B/381